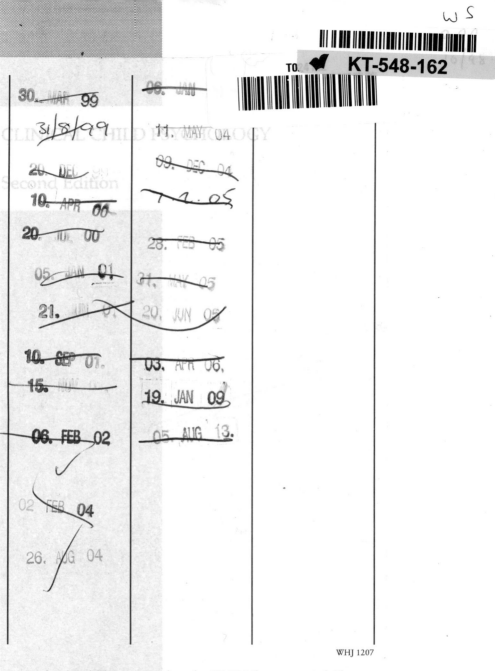

The Wiley Series in

CLINICAL PSYCHOLOGY

J. Mark G. Williams
(Series Editor)

School of Psychology, University of Wales, Bangor, UK

Martin Herbert	Clinical Child Psychology: Social Learning, Development and Behaviour (second edition)
Michael Bruch *Frank W. Bond*	Beyond Diagnosis: Case Formulation Approaches in CBT
Eric Emerson *Chris Hatton* *Jo Bromley* *Amanda Caine*	Clinical Psychology and People with Intellectual Disabilities
J. Mark G. Williams *Fraser N. Watts* *Colin MacLeod* *Andrew Mathews*	Cognitive Psychology and Emotional Disorders (second edition)
Phil Mollon	Multiple Selves, Multiple Voices: Working with Trauma, Violation and Dissociation
Paul Chadwick, *Max Birchwood* *and Peter Trower*	Cognitive Therapy for Delusions, Voices and Paranoia
Peter Sturmey	Functional Analysis in Clinical Psychology
Frank Tallis	Obsessive Compulsive Disorder: A Cognitive and Neuropsychological Perspective
David Fowler, *Philippa Garety* *and Elizabeth Kuipers*	Cognitive Behaviour Therapy for Psychosis: Theory and Practice
Robert S.P. Jones, *Peter G. Walsh and* *Peter Sturmey*	Stereotyped Movement Disorders
D. Colin Drummond, *Stephen T. Tiffany,* *Steven Glautier and* *Bob Remington (Editors)*	Addictive Behaviour: Cue Exposure Theory and Practice

Further titles in preparation. *A list of earlier titles in the series follows the index*

CLINICAL CHILD PSYCHOLOGY

Social Learning, Development and Behaviour

Second Edition

Martin Herbert
University of Exeter

JOHN WILEY & SONS
Chichester · New York · Weinheim · Brisbane · Singapore · Toronto

Other Wiley Editorial Offices

John Wiley & Sons, Inc., 605 Third Avenue,
New York NY 10158-0012, USA

WILEY-VCH Verlag GmbH,
Pappelallee 3, D-69469
Weinheim, Germany

Jacaranda Wiley Ltd, 33 Park Road, Milton,
Queensland 4064, Australia

John Wiley & Sons (Asia) Pte Ltd, 2 Clementi Loop #02-01,
Jin Xing Distripark, Singapore 129809

John Wiley & Sons (Canada) Ltd, 22 Worcester Road,
Rexdale, Ontario M9W 1L1, Canada

Library of Congress Cataloging-in-Publication Data

Herbert, Martin.
  Clinical child psychology: social learning, development, and behaviour/Martin Herbert.
    — 2nd ed.
  p.   cm. — (The Wiley series in clinical psychology)
Includes bibliographical references and index.
ISBN 0-471-96779-3 (cased: alk. paper)
1. Clinical child psychology. I. Title. II. Series.
[DNLM: 1. Child Psychology. 2. Psychology, Clinical — in infancy & childhood. WS 105 H537c 1998]
RJ503.3.H47 1998
618.92'89—dc21
DNLM/DLC
for Library of Congress   97-34228
                                                                            CIP

British Library Cataloguing in Publication Data

A catalogue record for this book is available from the British Library

ISBN 0-471-96779-3
ISBN 0-471-97663-6

Typeset in 10/12pt Palatino by Saxon Graphics Limited, Derby
Printed and bound in Great Britain by Bookcraft (Bath) Ltd, Midsomer Norton, Somerset
This book is printed on acid-free paper responsibly manufactured from sustainable forestry, in which at least two trees are planted for each one used for paper production.

For my mother, Kathleen Muriel Herbert (née Collier)
and my sister, Celia Sparks

CONTENTS

ABOUT THE AUTHOR

Martin Herbert is Professor of Clinical and Community Psychology at Exeter University and Consultant Psychologist at the Exeter Community National Health Service Healthcare Trust. Formerly he held teaching posts at the Universities of London and Leicester, and clinical posts at the Maudsley Hospital, Institute of Psychiatry; the Royal Infirmary, Leicester; and the Child and Family Consultation Centre, Plymouth. He has directed courses in Social Work as Professor of Social Work, and Clinical Psychology at the University of Leicester.

Professor Herbert, a Fellow of the British Psychological Society, was recently awarded the Monte Shapiro Prize by the Division of Clinical Psychology, for outstanding contribution to the profession. He is the author of many articles and books on clinical research, theory and practice.

SERIES PREFACE

The Wiley Series in Clinical Psychology consists of a set of volumes representing the entire spectrum of efficacy-based application of psychology to the problems of mental health and learning disability. Of all the changes that have taken place within clinical psychology in the years since the Series began, the need for more focus on the psychological problems of children has been predominant. This has been fuelled partly by increased public concern about a few high profile cases in which cruelty by some children towards others has occurred, but also by increased awareness that early difficulties can predict a range of later psychological problems. How may such risk be assessed? What genetic and environmental influences need to be taken into account, and how does a child's age affect how the assessment should be done? If we talk of 'early influences', how early are we to go (prenatally, for example?) and if we were to find problems at such an early stage, does this mean that little can be done to alter the later developmental pathway?

The first edition of Martin Herbert's book appeared in 1991. It quickly established itself as a classic text, a source of comprehensive and wise advice for clinical and educational psychologists, social workers and child psychiatrists, and an important textbook for undergraduates taking developmental courses who sought a bridge between the academic study of child development and its applications. This second edition, updated and with new material, promises to be an even greater success. No-one who has heard Martin Herbert speak, or read his many papers and books, has failed to be impressed by his immense knowledge and skill in dealing with these, often very complex, subjects. It is this combination of depth of intellect and warmth of personality which shines through in this edition, as it did in the first. I warmly commend it to you.

J. Mark G. Williams
Series Editor

PREFACE TO THE FIRST EDITION

It is a daunting task to attempt to convey the flavour, and something of the substance, of contemporary clinical child psychology theory and practice—such is the present-day range of the practitioner's activities and diversity of their approaches. With regard to the latter, I shall focus largely on a social learning theory and developmental perspective, although, heaven knows, this is a broad enough remit. In the case of the former (the range of problems to be found in the clinical child psychologist's caseload) I am forced to make some invidious choices. The awkward questions are: which subjects to leave out, which to mention in a somewhat cursory fashion (with some compensatory suggestions for further reading), and which to treat at some depth? Inevitably my choice will not be everyone else's, but the coverage is comprehensive enough to include most of the major disorders.

As this is a clinical psychology not a psychiatric text on childhood, the positioning of problem areas may differ somewhat from more conventional books. What has guided my organization of problems for discussion, broadly speaking, is a consideration of the life- or developmental-tasks that are salient at particular ages and stages in the child's progression toward maturity. Certain kinds of problems peak at these times and reflect the tensions associated with transition and change. Other problems, like severe learning disabilities, have their effect throughout the life-span, but are particularly to the forefront of parents' consciousness when they first learn about their child's handicap. At such a time a psychologist's knowledge and understanding could be invaluable. So handicap is placed early in the chronological time-span (from conception to early adolescence) around which the later chapters are organized. A framework of normal development and learning is, in my view, central to the understanding of a child's and his or her family's problems. The scope for this framework is life-span development, as parents and grandparents are also coping with significant developmental tasks, and their experiences have an influence on the child and other members of the family. Indeed, the family has a dynamic of its own, a life-history and life-tasks to perform. For these reasons the book is systemic, family-orientated in its approach.

Part One begins with the referral to a clinical child psychologist of a child with problems. This raises the question of the nature of psychological disorders in childhood, and leads on to the wider context of problems in parents and the family system. It poses the 'what' question: the complex issues of assessment, diagnosis and classification. The 'why' question—the matter of causation—introduces the theme of social learning theory and its applications. This is the particular but not exclusive emphasis of this book.

Part Two introduces the reader to the areas covered in a typical case history: biological/physical factors intrinsic to the child (e.g. genetic factors, physical anomalies, prematurity, resilience) and extrinsic (environmental influences) on the pre-, peri- and postnatal periods of the child's life.

Part Three is about preschool children and describes some of the crucial developments and associated problems—cognitive, emotional, linguistic, social and moral—one might expect, as the child moves from infancy to early childhood. It ends with a discussion of the emotional (internalizing) and conduct (externalizing) problems which beset parents, and which are likely to be a major concern of teachers as the child comes of school-going age.

Part Four deals with developmental tasks, events and associated difficulties of middle childhood and early adolescence. It examines a variety of school and classroom difficulties of the social, intellectual and behavioural kind. This means looking at specific learning difficulties, problems of attention, hyperactivity, motor-incoordination, perceptual problems and deficits in social skills. The section also addresses the question of what *special* skills the clinical psychologist brings to the area of health care. Among the subjects dealt with here are concepts of primary, secondary and tertiary prevention; psychophysiological disorders (e.g., bronchial asthma, diabetes mellitus, anorexia nervosa), and, of course, assessment and treatment.

Part Five provides a review of clinical psychology interventions ranging from psychological therapies (such as structural family therapy, behavioural family therapy and family-style residential treatment) to rehabilitation strategies for children with (say) head injuries. Special attention is paid to the consultation or triadic model of intervention. This includes a critical review of theories and methods of teaching social skills and problem-solving.

Part Six deals with five major clinical problems: my own on antisocial, disruptive disorders, and four invited contributions covering delinquency (Clive Hollin); fears and phobias (Tom Ollendick and Neville King); acute pain (Chrissi Ioannou) and post-traumatic stress (William Yule). The authors of the invited chapters provide stimulating and critical accounts of the present 'state of the art' in their chosen fields. The problems they eluci-date were chosen because they are among the most challenging difficulties dealt with by contemporary clinical child psychologists. They also illumi-nate in different ways the social learning and developmental perspective that has proved so fruitful in its theoretical and practical implications.

It is my hope that this book will provide a useful and thought-provoking introduction to the fascinating subject of clinical child psychology for undergraduate students of psychopathology, trainees on clinical psychol-ogy courses, and practitioners in the many and varied health services, social services and educational settings in which children and their fami-lies receive psychological help.

Martin Herbert
Clinical Psychology Department
University of Leicester 1990

PREFACE TO THE SECOND EDITION

The second (revised) edition of *Clinical Child Psychology* goes well beyond an update of the literature. I have broadened the scope of the book to integrate, as far as possible, practice as well as theoretical issues. The ASPIRE approach to clinical formulation and therapeutic programme planning is introduced. New topics are included (e.g. suicide and parasuicide, posttraumatic stress disorder, childhood bereavement, obsessions bulimia nervosa and special needs), others have been elaborated and extended (e.g. attention-deficit hyperactivity disorder, depression, the autistic continuum and elimination disorders). I have put a greater emphasis on school-related problems and health psychology. The new volume represents a comprehensive text for practitioners and students, but one which also tackle the 'nuts-and-bolts' practical decisions and strategies to which the theoretical issues give rise.

As this is a clinical psychology book, not a psychiatric text, on childhood, the positioning of problem areas may differ somewhat from more conventional books. What has guided my organization of problems for discussion, broadly speaking, is a consideration of the life- or developmental-tasks that are salient at particular ages and stages in the child's progression towards maturity. Certain kinds of problems peak at these times and reflect the tensions associated with transition and change. Other special-needs problems, like autistic disorder and severe learning disabilities, have their effect throughout the life-span, but are particularly to the forefront of parents' consciousness when they first learn about their child's handicap. At such a time a psychologist's knowledge and understanding could be invaluable. So handicap is placed in a section of its own.

A framework of normal development and learning is, in my view, central to the understanding of a child's and his or her family's problems. The scope for this framework is life-span development, as parents and grandparents are also coping with significant developmental tasks, and their experiences have an influence on the child and other members of the family. Indeed, the family has a dynamic of its own, a life-history and life-tasks to perform. For these reasons the book is systemic, family-orientated in its approach.

Part One begins with the referral to a clinical child psychologist of a child with problems. This raises the question of the nature of psychological disorders in childhood, and leads on to the wider context of problems in parents and the family system. The ASPIRE approach to assessment and intervention-planning is described, providing the practical steps generated by the theoretical framework. It poses the 'what' question: the complex issues of assessment, diagnosis and classification. The 'why' question—the matter of causation—introduces the theme of social learning theory and its applications. The 'How' question (How to help) is answered in terms of available, effective clinical psychology interventions.

Here I provide a review of clinical psychology interventions ranging from psychological therapies (such as structural family therapy and behavioural family therapy). Later in the book I deal with strategies for children with (say) long-term chronic problems. Special attention is paid to the consultation or triadic model of intervention.

Part Two introduces the reader to age-related difficulties in which relevant contemporary and historical causes, such as biological/physical factors intrinsic to the child (e.g., genetic factors, physical anomalies, prematurity, resilience) and extrinsic (environmental) influences on the pre-, peri- and post-natal periods of the child's life, are reviewed. It is about preschool children and describes some of the crucial developments and associated problems—cognitive, emotional, linguistic, social and moral—one might expect, as the child moves from infancy to early childhood. This section also deals with developmental tasks, events and associated difficulties of middle childhood and early adolescence. It examines a variety of school and classroom difficulties of the social, intellectual and behavioural kind.

Part Three is about special needs and developmental problems. This means looking at specific learning, communication and health difficulties. The section also addresses the question of what *special* skills the clinical psychologist brings to the area of health care and notably the seriously ill child. Among the subjects dealt with here are psychophysiological disorders (e.g. bronchial asthma, and anorexia/bulimia nervosa), and, of course, their assessment and treatment. Needs of dying children and their parents are considered.

Parts Four and Five deal with the major clinical problems faced by clinical child psychologists: antisocial, disruptive disorders, attention-deficit hyperactivity disorder and various anxiety conditions. It is thus concerned with discussion of the most common emotional (internalizing) and conduct (externalizing) problems which beset parents, and which are likely to be a major concern of teachers as the child comes of school-going-age. The problems were chosen because they are among the most challenging difficulties dealt with by contemporary clinical child psychologists. They also illuminate in different ways the social learning and developmental perspective that has proved so fruitful in its theoretical and practical implications.

It is my hope that this book will provide a useful and thought-provoking introduction to the fascinating subject of clinical child psychology for undergraduate students of psychopathology, trainees on clinical psychology courses, and practitioners in the many and varied health services, social services and educational settings in which children and their families receive psychological help.

Martin Herbert
May 1998

ACKNOWLEDGEMENTS

There are too many friends and colleagues who have influenced this book for me to name them all. However, I must mention three friends and colleagues for the inspiration they have provided:

> Tom Ollendick
> Carolyn Webster-Stratton
> Bill Yule

I am also indebted to Liz Mears for her support and help in preparing this work.

INTRODUCTION

It is a daunting task to attempt to convey the flavour, and something of the substance, of contemporary clinical child psychology theory and practice—such is the present-day range of the practitioners' activities and diversity of their approaches. With regard to the latter, I shall focus largely on a social learning theory and developmental perspective, although, heaven knows, this is a broad enough remit. In the case of the former (the range of problems to be found in the clinical child psychologist's caseload) I am forced to make some invidious choices. The awkward questions are: which subjects to leave out, which to mention in a somewhat cursory fashion (with some compensatory suggestions for further reading), and which to treat at some depth? Inevitably my choice will not be everyone else's, but the coverage is comprehensive enough to include most of the major disorders, ranging from common disorders such as bed-wetting, sleeping and eating difficulties to more serious emotional and behavioural disorders such as autism or anorexia nervosa. The referral might be for difficulties in peer or other social relationships; for developmental disorders of language and learning; or for profound impairments of mental and physical functioning. Other children will be referred because of problems relating to physical health. These could include (a) difficulties such as failure-to-thrive, persistent headache, abdominal pain, asthma, eczema, faecal incontinence or chronic constipation, (b) management problems such as non-compliance with medical prescriptions, fear of injections or (c) assistance in the management of head injuries, terminal illness or chronic pain, among many other primary physical conditions where there are important psychological components. Table 1 gives you an idea of the range and variety of the work of clinical child psychologists and the many settings in which it is conducted.

With the reduction of infectious diseases and other physical ailments, emotional and behavioural disorders have become the particular concern of parents. They constitute the new morbidity. For this reason they are also a major preoccupation of this book although I will naturally be paying attention to many of the other problems referred to above. The generic term

Table 1   Settings in which clinical child psychologists work and examples of their work. (Source: Fielding, 1987, reproduced by permission of Oxford University Press.)

Setting	Example
(a) *Health*	
(i) Community	
Child welfare clinics	Liaison/consultation with health visitors.
Health centres	
GP practices	Parents groups for behavioural, sleeping, feeding problems of under-fives.
(ii) Hospital	
Ante-natal clinics	Counselling of mothers with suspected handicapped child. Counselling of adolescents deciding about termination of pregnancy.
Intensive care neonatal units	Counselling for staff and parents.
Paediatric assessment clinics	Assessment and remediation of development delays.
Paediatric hospital wards	Preparation of parents/children for hospitalization. Counselling of parents/staff dealing with terminally ill children.
Casualty wards	Crisis counselling for adolescents who have taken overdoses.
Psychiatric in-patient and out-patient units	Assessment and treatment with families of children showing emotional and behavioural problems. Consultation/training of psychiatric child care staff (in psychological procedures).
(b) *Social services*	
(i) Local authority nurseries	Advice to nursery nurses concerning problems of child abuse. Assessment of development delays.
(ii) Community homes	Consultation with staff concerning management of difficult behaviour problems. Counselling foster parents.
(c) *Voluntary organizations*	Drop-in clinics for adolescents with drug taking or alcohol problems (e.g., Samaritans, Adoption Societies, Brook Advisory Centres, Grapevine, etc.).

'emotional and behavioural problems' refers to a large and heterogeneous collection of disorders ranging from depression, anxiety, inhibition and shyness to non-compliance, destructiveness, stealing and aggression. In essence, these problems represent exaggerations, deficits or disabling combinations of feelings, attitudes and behaviours common to all children.

Despite the absence of an agreed-upon set of criteria for defining childhood dysfunction there has been a remarkable consistency in the investigations of the prevalence of psychological problems in children. It has been estimated on the basis of epidemiological studies in the United Kingdom and United States, that some 12% of children manifest significant emotional or behavioural problems (Gould, Wunsch-Hitzig and Dohrenwend, 1980). Indeed, approximately 90% of all childhood psychiatric disorders fall into these categories; 45% of community child health referrals are concerned with behavioural disorders; casualty departments have to cope with accidents and poisonings, which are particularly frequent in children who manifest antisocial behaviour and conduct disorder (Bailey, Graham & Boniface, 1978; Bijun et al., 1988). Children with these problems (and their families) utilize multiple health, social and educational services. They are at particular risk of physical abuse. Social services departments devote most of their energies to child protection work, much of which arises from the harsh punishments meted out to children who are exceptionally difficult to manage. Residential care for children with disruptive behaviour disorders is extremely expensive (Knapp & Robertson, 1989) and, sadly, not always caring or curative. The same can be said with regard to the cost of the various forms of provision in the educational system which are required to cope with classroom disruption and violence (e.g. bullying) in and out of the school grounds (see DES, 1989).

Sadly, only 20–33% of children with clinically significant problems are thought to receive treatment (Knitzer, 1982); furthermore, the more seriously disturbed are less likely to obtain such help than those with milder dysfunctions (Sowder, 1975).

The knowledge base for understanding the wide range of childhood problems and the skills required for assessment and intervention have been extended to an extraordinary extent over a relatively short period of time. All of this has implications for training clinical child psychologists, a matter discussed by Long and Hollin (1997). It is worth noting that the training of psychologists, with its emphasis on empiricism and experimental method, has resonances with the present concentration in the health service on accountability and effectiveness of service delivery. The empiricism of psychologists, the methods of checking and evaluation built into many of their assessments (e.g., functional analysis, psychometrics) and clinical interventions (e.g., behaviour therapy) provides a model which other professions are increasingly interested in learning (Hollin, Wilkie and Herbert, 1987).

Although clinical child psychology builds upon a generic or core knowledge base of general psychology and psychopathology, it is a specialism with features that give the work of the child psychologist a distinctive flavour, one which is neatly captured in a quotation from Yule (1983):

> Children *are* different from adults. Working with children is more demanding in many ways. Not only are they developing rapidly, but they are also inextricably involved in a variety of social networks. Therein lies one of the challenges for an applied child psychologist.

A double-barrelled question which is often, and legitimately, put to psychologists is 'What is the role of clinical psychology in health care; what do clinical psychologists do that other health care personnel do not do?' The answer provided by the Manpower Advisory Service, following a study of psychologists' roles in the UK National Health service (MAS Review, 1989) is that clinical psychologists aim:

> to improve, either directly or indirectly, the standard and quality of life of people who are served by and provide health services, and to alleviate disability through the application of appropriate psychological theories. The *process* is unique to the profession: the *outcomes* are shared with other health care professions.

There are (they suggest) three levels of psychological skill and knowledge used in health care:

- *Level 1.* Basic psychology, such as establishing relationships with patients and relatives, maintaining and supporting a relationship, interviewing and using some simple, often intuitive techniques, such as counselling and stress management.
- *Level 2.* Undertaking circumscribed psychological activities, such as behaviour modification. These activities may be described by protocol. At this level there should be awareness of the criteria for referral to a psychologist.
- *Level 3.* A thorough understanding of varied and complex psychological theories and their application.

Almost all health care workers use Level 1 and 2 skills. In particular, medical, nursing, occupational therapy, speech therapy and social work staff make varying use of them. Some have well developed specialist training in Level 2 activities. Health care psychologists possess skills and knowledge at all three levels. Their particular contribution is in their rounded knowledge of psychological theories and their application.

One of the most interesting—perhaps significant—developments in the field of child treatment has involved psychologists in the altruistic task of 'giving away' or (as I prefer it) 'sharing', their skills with others who can then mobilize them to help others and/or themselves. The triadic model, as it is called, has built into it the objective of making the therapist redundant as soon as possible in the life of a particular case or client. Hopefully, such an approach is not subversive to the profession: far from making the psychologist's role surplus to requirements, it provides an additional and powerful focus for his or her expertise. Much of what I have referred to as shared psychology or the triadic approach has been written about—particularly in America—under the title 'consultation'.

The use of the triadic model of intervention for treatment, training or remedial work began from an assumption that parents, surrogate parents, teachers and other caregivers have a profound effect on children's development and mental health. Because they exert such a significant foundational influence during the impressionable years of childhood, they are usually in a strong position to facilitate prosocial learning, and moderate the genesis of behaviour disorder. Here then is a theme that will recur in this book. The approach, based as it often is, on social learning theory, has crucial implications not only for the way in which the psychologist works, but also for the location of that work. The child's natural environment (be it home, classroom or playground) becomes another setting to add to the consulting room or playroom for the therapeutic endeavour. The parents—it could also be teachers or care staff—are drawn into the therapeutic alliance, but on the basis of a very *active* partnership. Indeed, the partnership model of practice (be it with other professions or caregivers) will be another theme in the chapters that follow.

It may seem a paradox but clinical psychologists are increasingly at work in non-clinical settings—out in the community. Community psychology is a comparatively new discipline within applied psychology, but a community approach to childhood problems—with its overarching philosophy of person-in-context—is a growing trend.

Child psychologists working with a community psychology orientation help families (or it may be teachers, perhaps residential social workers) to identify needs, to come together in a group, and support them in the achievement of their goals. They seek to empower people who are significant in the child's world encouraging them to work on problems collectively rather than a one-to-one basis, enabling them to increase their understanding and confidence, mobilize resources, and gain positive influence.

Inevitably one has to face the fact that the problems of childhood and adolescence have to be understood within a wide framework that includes the family, the peer group, the school, the neighbourhood, attitudes and norms prevailing within the community, in addition to the biological and psychological attributes of individual youngsters.

One of the many advantages of an applied social learning theory approach is its breadth. It is the major perspective of this book because of its firm roots in systemic thinking, in empirical evidence, and its heuristic value for theory and practice in clinical child psychology.

The early chapters of this book set out the general approach taken to childhood problems, showing how they should be assessed and how a developmental history can be relevant to understanding the presenting problem. Next, the book turns to common childhood problems, beginning with preschool children, and continuing through the problems of school-age children and early adolescents. With this background, the range of available psychological interventions to help children is reviewed. The book concludes with more detailed reviews of several common or representative childhood problems.

Martin Herbert,
Professor of Clinical and Community Psychology
University of Exeter.

Consultant Clinical Psychologist
Exeter Community NHS Trust

May 1998

Part I　　THE NATURE OF THE PROBLEM

THE REFERRAL

Parents and teachers tend to become worried about the children in their care when their behaviour appears (a) to be out of control, (b) to be unpredictable, or (c) to lack sense or meaning. If these tendencies are extreme and/or persistent they are likely to be thought of as 'problematic' or 'abnormal' and the growing concern they engender may result in a referral (usually through a social worker or general practitioner) to a clinical child psychologist or child psychiatrist.

Another concern arises from an expectation (not always accurate) of *what* an infant should be doing, and *when*—the notion of a developmental timetable in the parent's mind. When some activity (e.g., talking, relating to people) seems to be delayed or 'odd' in some way, it is quite likely that the chain of referrals will lead, among others, to a clinical psychologist. He or she might carry out an assessment alone, or in partnership with other specialists. It all depends on the nature and location of the referral. Their findings could lead to a reassuring ('there is nothing untoward') sort of statement; perhaps some advice; or in the case of a serious problem, an intervention—a therapeutic or remedial programme.

Decisions are open to value judgements—a potential Pandora's box of personal and cultural (not to mention theoretical) bias and prejudice. After all, the word 'norm' from its Latin root means a standard, rule or pattern. Thus 'abnormal' applied to children's behaviour implies (with the prefix 'ab' meaning 'away from') a deviation from a standard. An analysis of these standards, in public and professional usage, makes it clear that they are *social standards* (rules, expectations, codes, conventions) and comparisons made with patterns of *normal child and adolescent development* (Herbert, 1987a). Psychological problems are seen as having unfavourable social and personal consequences for the child himself or herself, for the family, and, sometimes, for the wider community.

The reality is that childhood signs of psychological abnormality are, by and large, manifestations of behavioural, cognitive and emotional responses common to all children. Their quality of being dysfunctional lies in their inappropriate intensity, frequency and persistence; most childhood disorders differ in degree, rather than kind, from normal behaviour. The exceptions to this generalization are rare (see Herbert, 1994a). That generalization does, however, raise ethical problems for the practitioner.

If abnormal behaviour is considered learned, therapists are involved in making, or at least concerning themselves with, judgements that some other behaviour would be preferable—a social, subjective and, therefore, potentially prejudicial decision. This leads inexorably to the following questions, the answers to which have the status of ethical imperatives for the therapist as agent of change: 'To whom is the behaviour undesirable? Is it *really* in need of modification, and if so, to what must it reasonably change?' What are the cognitive and emotional aspects of behavioural choice in situations where the child's behaviour is likely to impinge adversely on self and other people? There will be no problem in designating self-injurious (self-mutilating) behaviours as abnormal: but where does one draw the line between assertive and aggressive actions? The context or (more accurately) contexts for such actions become critical in making judgements. And it is the dynamic, transactional and individualized process of assessment to which this requirement gives rise, that gives a *broadly based* functional analysis, in my view, an advantage over traditional classification.

THE ASSESSMENT

The assessment leads to a formulation (a set of hypotheses about the nature and causes of the difficulties) which, in turn, leads directly and logically to a plan of action, possibly discussed and debated by members of a multi-disciplinary team, and designed to help the child and family. The action could be a multi-level, broadly based programme involving several members of the team (e.g., the speech therapist, group worker, social worker). It might consist of a focused treatment for which the psychologist or psychiatrist takes responsibility. This, on the face of it, looks fairly straightforward; in reality it isn't so. I have put forward my preferred way of looking at assessment, but there could be, and are, disagreements about what the focus should be in asking the 'what' question (in other words, what information is relevant), about the causes of problems covered by the 'why' question, and the means of helping clients.

Given that there is no grand, general psychological theory of human activity on offer in academic psychology departments, but rather a number of poorly integrated middle range theories (e.g. learning theory, cognitive science, etc.) it should not be surprising that clinical psychologists find few convincing overarching theories or integrative models to make sense of psychopathology in childhood or adulthood. The Kendall and Lochman (1994) description of the cognitive–behavioural therapies is in terms that suggest there is a broader convergence of concepts in their rationale than most of the other approaches. They state that:

> ... they integrate cognitive, behavioral, affective, social and contextual strategies for change. The cognitive–behavioral model includes the relationships of cognition and behavior to the affective state of the organism and the functioning of the organism in the larger social context.

The reality for psychologists and psychiatrists is the complex, multivariate nature of most of the phenomena they study. In their clinical formulations, they have to take into account both intrinsic (organismic) factors and extrinsic (environmental) influences—both past and present (Figure 1).

A rationale for many practitioners is that all therapies contain an element of *learning*, something about which psychologists have considerable knowledge and experience of workable applications. Goldstein, Heller and Sechrest (1966) propose the following definition of psychotherapy:

> Whatever else it is, psychotherapy must be considered a learning enterprise. We need not specify too narrowly just what it is to be learned in psychotherapy; it may be specific behaviors or a whole new outlook on life; but it cannot be denied that the intended outcome of psychotherapy is a change in an individual that can only be termed a manifestation of learning.

Social and developmental psychologists with a cognitive orientation have a fruitful literature to share with clinical child psychologists (e.g. Durkin, 1995; Goodnow, 1988) much of it, these days, about parents' states of mind. It is certainly time to redress the balance, given the long-standing willingness of many theorists (e.g., Aronfreed, Bruner, Kohlberg and Piaget) to explain the behaviour of their offspring (in social situations) in terms of their interpretations of events, as well as their cognitive maturity and capacity to assimilate information.

Therapists assess, as primary data, children's problematic behaviour, but also the phenomenology of their problems: their verbal reports of internal representations of events, experiences and opinions, such as attitudes towards self, parents and school. These attitudes, like theories, have, *inter alia*, a knowledge function. They provide a frame of reference with which individuals make interpretations of their world, creating a model—a figurative set

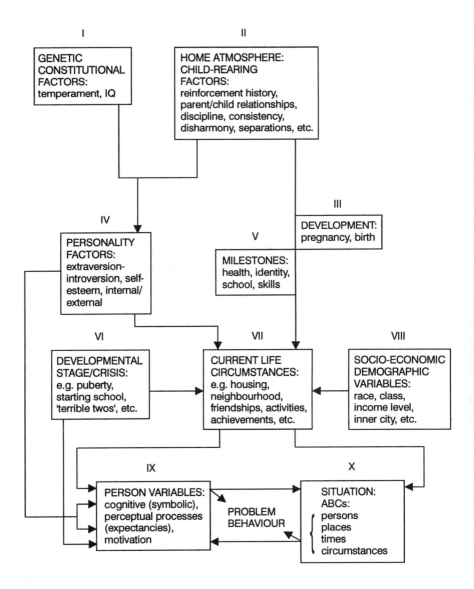

Figure 1.   The 10-factor clinical formation of causation (adapted from Clarke, 1977; reproduced by permission of the British Psychological Society)

of 'goggles'—through which they construe and make sense of people and life-events. This personal construct system (Kelly, 1955) is accessible to investigation by means of the Kelly Repertory Grid.

The constructs of parents, some developed in the bosom of their family of origin, others elaborated with more recent experiences of parenting, give meanings to their offspring's behaviour and can facilitate mutually satisfactory interactions. Sadly, some constructs, if distorted by ignorance, misunderstandings or paranoia, can mislead parents into self-defeating confrontations with their children.

The convergence of these cognitive perspectives directed towards adults *and* children makes sense as a way of integrating theories (e.g., cycles of disadvantage) linking the experiences and actions of succeeding generations. There are theories, for example, which interpret the effects of early experience on later personal actions and personality attributes in terms of the 'internal models' that people develop about the nature of relationships; and these models are based on their own childhood experiences, carried forward in time and functioning as 'filters' through which the behaviour of their own offspring is perceived (Belsky, 1984; Crowell and Feldman, 1988).

Chapter 1

CLINICAL ASSESSMENT: THEORETICAL CONSIDERATIONS

Assessment, and its conceptual partner, intervention, are major activities in the professional life of clinical child psychologists. How they go about them—the objectives and goals they set, the procedures they use, the information they focus on, the meaning they impose on it—will vary according to the 'model' of psychopathology that informs their practice. And in uttering (or writing) that word 'psycho*pathology*' we receive our first hint of the pervasiveness of medical conceptualizing in the area of childhood psychological problems. Table 2 shows a list of terms child psychiatrists (and many clinical psychologists) use, ones which other professionals (and, to be fair, some psychiatrists) studiously avoid.

Are these distinctions academic, indeed pedantic; or are they ideologically important, not merely reflecting significant theoretical but also metatheoretical perspectives, i.e. ways of thinking about the nature of human action and of valuing people? Whatever one's point of view, it is difficult—and in many instances inappropriate—to avoid (as you will see in this text) medical concepts.

Table 2 Terminology of child psychology

Medically orientated terminology	Alternative usage
Patient	Client/resident
Psychopathology ⎫	⎧ Psychological problems,
	⎨ surplus behaviour,
Illness/disease ⎬	⎩ deficits, difficulties
Symptom ⎭	Target behaviour/problem/ difficulty
Treatment/therapy	Intervention
Causation	Antecedents/determinants
Cure	Reduction in X or increase in Y behaviours/skills
Diagnosis	Assessment
Mental handicap	Learning difficulty/disability

In clinical child psychology research, matters of definition are inextricably enmeshed with issues of classification and measurement. Clinical judgements of whether a child is manifesting a psychological problem involve two important and distinguishable processes:

- *Assessment,* which aims to differentiate, operationalize and measure those behavioural, cognitive, and affective patterns that are considered to be problematic.
- *Classification,* which aims to group individuals according to their distinguishing problematic behavioural, cognitive, and affective patterns.

ASSESSMENT: THE CLINICAL FORMULATION:

The skills involved in specifying the problem, formulating explanatory hypotheses, determining and evaluating a test of the formulation, and translating it into a treatment plan have their roots in psychological science and art (Herbert, 1998a). The assertion that there is a place for art (imagination and lateral thinking) as well as science (empirical research) in the many complex activities that contribute to the final clinical formulation, might well be regarded as contentious. Indeed those who embrace a scientist–practitioner approach to clinical psychology practice may well see it as erroneous—a matter I return to later. Generally speaking, the formulation is a means to an end, an intervention of some kind. However, it may be an end in itself: an expert report for the courts, or an assessment for the social, health or, educational services.

THE ASPIRE PROCESS

The way in which clinical formulations are conceptualized and the consequent selection of data usually involves four kinds of activity, summarized by the mnemonic ASPIRE (Sutton and Herbert, 1992) which represents the stages in working up a case study and, more specifically, a clinical formulation.

- *Stage 1.*   *Assessment*
Focusing on the 'What' question,
i.e. *what is/are the problem(s)?*
and the 'Which?' question,
i.e. *which of the problems are to be addressed,*
and in what order?
Focusing on the 'Why?' question,
i.e. *why have the problems arisen?*

- *Stage 2.*   *Planning*
  Focusing on the 'How?' question,
  i.e. how are we (practitioner and clients) going to
  address the problems?

- *Stage 3.*   *Implementation of the intervention*

- *Stage 4.*   *Rigorous evaluation*

The process of formulating is, figuratively speaking, like the action of a funnel containing a series of filters which represent choice and decision points. They have the function of distilling a many-sided childhood problem into a relatively brief, formal statement about one's conclusions and recommendations. These filters play a critical role in determining what information is pertinent in the investigation of the client's problems, and which assessment methods will generate the clinical data necessary for an intervention. As the funnel narrows, so does the focus of the questions—What, Which, Why, and How?—that give direction to the assessment. The final 'how' query leads to the formulation of a precise treatment plan, and the *tactical* specification of methods/techniques for bringing about change.

THE 'WHICH' QUESTION

One of the clinician's earliest choices is where to concentrate attention in what may present itself as a welter of conflicting claims, complaints and accusations. Some of the problems will reside mainly within an individual (for example, fear) but even then they will have repercussions. The individual's parents (or partner) worry about his or her suffering. Or the problems put constraints on the activities of the family, as when holidays are not possible because (say) a mother is agoraphobic, feeling anxious about leaving the house and panicky in a crowded shopping centre.

Other problems arise from the relationships and interactions (such as the give-and-take transactions) between people. For example:

- *Mother–father.*   For example, disagreements about the children, quarrels over decisions, other *marital* difficulties.
- *Parent(s)–child.*   For example, management difficulties; disappointments over the child's achievements or lack of them.
- *Child–parent(s).*   For example, resentments about being 'babied'; complaints about unfairness, favouritism.
- *Child–child.*   For example, sibling rivalry, jealousy.

As the assessment proceeds the client(s) may by any of these persons. In answering the 'What' and 'Which' questions there arises an important issue of what constitutes a priority in any clinical investigation: description or categorization—a debate centring around the concepts of assessment and diagnosis.

At the broad end of the figurative funnel referred to earlier, is a filter influencing the clinical information that is edited in (and out) of the formulation. It involves the choice or rejection of a science-based philosophy of clinical work.

Long and Hollin (1997), point out that the history of the scientist–practitioner stance is marked by an enduring struggle between advocates and opponents of a research-based profession, which is to say, a practice that is based on an empirically based assessment of problems, and the application of validated treatment methods which are linked (through the formulation) to theoretically coherent causal hypotheses. The reliance of the 'scientist–practitioner' on empirical methods generates a model for service provision that is competency based. For Gambrill (1990) this requires:

- A focus on the present, which may be related to events in the past, and require clarification by an exploration of the past (e.g. the person's learning history, deeply rooted attributions and ideologies).
- A focus on describing problems (assessing them by a process of surveying, selecting and prioritizing difficulties) and operationalizing them by means of multi-dimensional measurable outcomes.
- A focus on multiple response systems of an individual nature (e.g. cognition affect and physiology) and of an interactional kind (e.g. family, school, workplace).
- A focus on positive behaviours and events.
- A focus on the relationship between behaviour and events in the external environment that elicit or maintain it.

THE 'WHAT' QUESTION: THEORETICAL MODELS

Nowhere is the influence of medical ideologies in clinical child psychology more pronounced than in the reliance on classification and diagnosis in answer to the question: 'What is the nature of the child's psychological problem? Underlying the creation of classificatory systems (e.g. the DSM-IV (American Psychiatric Association, 1994) and ICD-10 (World Health Organization, 1992) and taxonomies of 'symptoms', is the assumption that specific syndromes (disease patterns) with identifiable and specific causes (etiologies) can be diagnosed. It might be added that the only justification for applying diagnostic categories to children is that not only should they imply reliable descriptive criteria and clear causal theories, but also that treatment implications should flow from the choice of label (see Volkmar & Schwab-Stone, 1996).

For all its medical 'flavouring' DSM-IV is not essentially a categorical taxonomy, but a *multiaxial* system of classification. It provides more than a diagnostic label; it adds a set of independent dimensions (axes) which are coded or rated along with the psychiatric diagnosis: Axes I and II are used to describe the patient's current condition, i.e., clinical conditions.

Axis I includes (inter alia) the following:

● disruptive behaviour disorders;
● anxiety disorders of childhood or adolescence;
● eating disorders;
● gender identity disorders;
● tic disorders;
● elimination disorders;
● speech disorders.

Axis II lists personality or developmental disorders. Disorders usually first evident in infancy, childhood or adolescence are coded on this axis when they fall within the following categories:

● mental retardation;
● pervasive developmental disorders;
● specific developmental disorders.

Axis III. Here the clinician lists all physical disorders or conditions, e.g. hypothyroidism, epilepsy, bronchial asthma.

Axis IV contains a 'severity of psychological stressors scale' for children and adolescents (there is also one for adults).

Axis V. Here the clinician estimates the patient's level of function at the time of evaluation and the patient's highest level of function during the past year.

A good deal of discussion, positive and critical, and a mixture of both, has been generated by the publication of the DSM manuals. Achenbach and Edelbrock (1989) made the point that in order to be effective, formal diagnoses (and diagnostic formulations) require reliable taxonomic distinctions so that we can link cases that share useful similarities and distinguish between cases that differ in important ways. The DSM's criteria for childhood psychopathology consist mainly of lists of behavioural–emotional problems. Whether the child is deemed to have a particular problem depends on when and how the child is assessed. Because problems for which mental health services are sought occur outside the clinic setting, assessment typically requires information from people other than clinicians, such as parents and teachers. The different situations in which they see the child and the different roles they play with respect to the child are bound to affect what they report.

Achenbach, McConaughy and Howell (1987) carried out a meta-analysis of 269 samples (in studies published from 1960 to 1986) of correlations between different informants (parents, teachers, trained observers, mental health workers, peers, and the children themselves) reporting children's behavioural–emotional problems. The mean correlations between informants playing similar roles with respect to the children, including pairs of parents, teachers, mental health workers and trained observers ranged from 0.54 (mental health workers) to 0.64 (pairs of teachers) with an overall mean of 0.60. This substantial, although far from perfect, level of agreement dropped considerably when informants had different roles with the children. The mean correlations ranged from 0.24 (between parents and mental health workers) to 0.42 (between teachers and direct observers) with an overall mean of 0.28—statistically significant but low. With regard to the self-reports and others' reports of the same child, the mean correlation of 0.22 is statistically significant but even lower.

Whatever the reliability and validity of diagnostic schemes, there is an objection raised by many psychologists (and psychiatrists) to what they see as invidious 'labelling' and stigmatizing of individuals by reducing complex 'life–problems' to a restrictive medical category. There is concern about how parents, teachers and the child make sense of a diagnosis. Such reification may absolve parents from any sense that they can influence the difficulties. It may 'tell' the child that he or she is different from other children, and furthermore, not in control of his or her actions—a pessimistic message to instil in someone at an impressionable stage of life.

A pitfall of using diagnostic classification in clinical formulations is the tempting but illusory impression it can give the practitioner of having explained the problem, when all it may amount to is a renaming process (Herbert, 1964; see also Chapter 12).

The Statistical Model

Multivariate Analyses

Statistical (and particularly factor analytic) methods have proved popular in the search for clusters of problems which might lend support to the classifications built upon clinical observation and experience. What is advocated is an empirical approach which involves a minimum of assumptions and constructs regarding the causation of behaviour disorders. It endeavours to tease out, from masses of data culled from clinic records and epidemiological surveys, dimensions of disturbed behaviour which are explicit and operational.

The various researchers find, despite further diversity in subjects, nationalities, raters, and statistical analyses, that empirical investigations consistently elicit problems of an *undercontrolled* type (variously referred to as conduct disorder, aggressive, externalizing, acting out) and an *overcontrolled* type (emotional disturbance, personality disorder, inhibited, internalizing, anxious). There is a convergence between clinical and factor analytical studies with regard to these dimensions. Fischer *et al.* (1984) focused on the two kinds of psychological maladjustment: the 'internalizing' and 'externalizing' dimensions with a study of 541 children. They were first seen when they were between 2 and 6 years of age and then again seven years later. At both ages parents were asked to complete a behaviour checklist, comprising about 100 items dealing with the frequency with which specific kinds of behaviour occurred and indicating the presence and severity of problems, with particular reference to those falling into the internalizing and externalizing categories.

Of these two, the externalizing dimension appears to be the more stable. For both sexes externalizing symptoms found during the preschool period showed a significant continuity with externalizing symptoms seven years later. No such stability over age was found for internalizing behaviour. The same conclusion emerged when a clinically disturbed group was selected from the total sample on the basis of their deviant score on the various instruments, depending on the expected source of information (say, parents, teachers or peers), the context of assessment (for example, children in a general population study as opposed to children referred to a clinic), the choice of methodology made by the researcher (say, observational ratings as opposed to interview ratings), and the theoretical perspective of the research (e.g. 2-factor versus 3-factor models of behavioural dysfunction).

Quay's 1984 review of 55 factor analytic investigations (see Table 3) elicited seven behavioural dimensions (each with its cluster of associated characteristics) that had been replicated in as many as ten separate studies. Essentially they are (with the exception of number (7)) refinements of the two major categories mentioned above.

(1) conduct disorder;
(2) socialized aggression;
(3) motor overactivity;
(4) problems of attention;
(5) anxious–depressed;
(6) somatic complaints;
(7) psychotic disorder.

Table 3   Empirically derived dimensions of behaviour set against DSM-III-R categories.

Behavioural dimension	Co-varying characteristics	DSM-III category
CONDUCT DISORDER	Disobedient, defiant Fighting, hitting Destructive Uncooperative, resistant	CONDUCT DISORDER (Group type (Solitary aggressive type (Undifferentiated type
SOCIALIZED AGGRESSION	Has 'bad' companions Truants from school/home Loyal to delinquent friends Steals in the company of others	
MOTOR OVERACTIVITY	Restless, overactive Overtalkative Excitable, impulsive Squirmy, jittery	

ATTENTION PROBLEMS	Poor concentration,
	    short attention span
	
	Daydreaming
	Preoccupied, stares
	    into space
	Impulsive
		ATTENTION-DEFICIT
		    HYPERACTIVITY
		    DISORDER (ADHD)
		
		Without hyperactivity

ANXIOUS–DEPRESSED WITHDRAWAL	Anxious, fearful, tense Shy, timid, bashful Depressed, sad, disturbed Feels inferior, worthless	ANXIETY DISORDERS Overanxious disorder Separation anxiety disorder Avoidant disorder
SOMATIC COMPLAINTS	Stomach aches Vomiting, nausea Headaches	

PSYCHOTIC DISORDER	Bizarre, odd, peculiar
	
	Incoherent speech
	Visual hallucinations
	Strange ideas and
	    behaviour
		PERVASIVE
		    DEVELOPMENTAL
		    DISORDERS
		Autistic disorder
		Pervasive developmental
		    disorder not otherwise
		    specified

		OTHER DISORDERS
		    (*inter alia*)
		Reactive attachment disorder
		    of infancy
		Identity disorder
		Elective mutism
		Oppositional defiant
		    disorder
		Gender identity disorder

Each of these 'syndromes' will be considered later.

Reviews of the literature suggest that despite interesting correlations between 'problematic' childhood behaviours, the vast majority of 'disorders' (it is difficult to avoid medical usage) cannot be conceptualized—except figuratively—as disease entities (Graham, 1980; Yule, 1981). Unlike many of the acute physical illnesses the structure of a presenting psychological problem, the etiology of the problem, and the implied treatment do not closely map onto each other (Sturmey, 1996).

Personality Typology Models

The personality structure approach to assessment postulates personality dimensions, in part inherited, that influence what and how children learn as they grow up. It has been observed that every person is in certain respects like all other persons, like some other persons, like no other person. The nomothetic disciplines which favour the philosophy and methods of the exact sciences have been applied to the study of the highly generalized personality attributes (types and traits) while idiographic methods have been used to explore the aspect of uniqueness and individuality.

There are several limitations to the use of personality typing in the formulating process. The situations sampled are restricted in range, for example, behaviour at home or at school. Furthermore, assessment methods tend to emphasize verbal behaviour such as interviews, self-reports and questionnaires. In the applications of such methods of assessment, personality differences in behaviour across settings are seen as error variance in an imperfect measurement system. Greatest weight is placed on the initial assessment and diagnosis rather than on repeated, ongoing assessments. In personality-type assessments the person's behaviour is compared to statistical norms.

The practical implications of an assigned personality 'diagnosis' or profile for a treatment plan are limited (Herbert, 1965; Meehl, 1960; Moore, Bobblitt and Wildman, 1968). The issue of situation specificity makes it difficult to make predictions or arrive at precise conclusions of an individual kind, on the basis of generalized constructs. The idiographic disciplines, such as biography, literature and history, endeavour to understand and illuminate some particular event. The use of idiosyncratic and subjective projective techniques is an example of this tradition in clinical work.

Developmental Models

Developmental frameworks for assessing individuals and families emerged from research and theory relating to their progress through life-cycle stages, and the therapeutic strategies they generate (e.g. Carter and McGoldrick, 1988). Several theorists (e.g. Achenbach, 1974, 1982; Cicchetti, 1984a, b; Herbert, 1974; Sroufe and Rutter, 1984) have urged the necessity for underpinning the study of child psychopathology with principles and findings from developmental psychology—an approach which has been referred to as the 'developmental psychopathology movement' (Gelfand, Jenson and Drew, 1988).

The essence of this work, in the words of Susan Campbell (1989), is 'a transactional and ecological view that assumes the coherence and pre-dictability of development and adaptation, despite change and transfor-mation . . . and that emphasizes the importance of family and social environmental factors in understanding the nature and direction of that change'. It necessitates a comprehensive knowledge of children how they think and talk, their skills and limitations at various ages, their typical repertoires of behaviour and the life-tasks and crises that they confront.

The normal development of the infant is well documented (see Bremner, 1988; Kaye, 1982), and yet is still a closed book to many of the profession-als who would find this data base invaluable.

The most dramatic transformations take place in the first years of life, the child acquiring skills in many different ways: physical growth, the devel-opment of gross motor movements, the development of vision and fine motor movements, social relationships, cognition and the understanding and use of language. We shall be looking at some of these skills in later chapters. Undoubtedly, this developmental literature has enriched, of late, the clinical study of childhood problems. After all, some 'problematic behaviours' are *characteristic* of a particular developmental stage and often prove to be transient; others are developmental problems and reflect *exaggerations* of age-appropriate behaviours or awkward *transitions* from one stage of development to the next.

For Cicchetti and his colleagues (Cicchetti, Toth and Bush, 1988) abnormal patterns of behavioural adaptation—as represented by clinical problems such as hyperactivity and failure-to-thrive—are most fruitfully construed and formulated as a series of stage- and age-related 'tasks'. The issue of 'competence' is common to all of them and, as the child gets older, his or her self-esteem. If the child fails to develop skills and social competence he or she is likely to suffer a sense of inadequacy which has spiralling ramifi-cations. There is evidence, not only of the power of parents to facilitate the child's mastery of developmental tasks or hinder him or her, but to do this unwittingly (Cicchetti, Toth and Bush, 1988).

The difficulty for the clinician formulating an assessment within a devel-opmental context is that there is no agreed conceptually coherent theory of normal child development as a touchstone for understanding and assessing clinical abnormality, nor any single explanation of the processes of normal growth and development. Developmental theories range from the psychoanalytic (e.g. Freud's stages of psychosexual development), the ethological (e.g. Bowlby's attachment theory), behavioural (e.g. Bandura's social-learning theory) to the structural–developmental (e.g. Kohlberg's theory of moral development). Each of these theoretical perspectives provides a particular methodology and conceptual framework for viewing the specifics of developmental processes. Conceptions of individual characteristics also vary from those postulating stability to those assuming constant change. For example, trait theorists investigate relationships between characteristics (e.g. temperament, intelligence) across various ages, while those favouring an idiographic approach examine the individual's unique organization of personality attributes across various ages.

A contemporary assessment framework leading to a formulation and treatment plan for childhood psychological disorders requires measures of behavioural, cognitive, and physiological responding as well as, notably, a determination of the developmental, social and cultural context within which the problem occurs.

Systemic Models

An individual in a family system is affected by the activities of other members of the family. Whereas the traditional treatment model tended to identify the nominated client or patient as the unit of attention (for example, the child referred to the child guidance clinic) the focus of assessment in the light of this interactional frame of reference is far more broadly conceived. Thus the focus of help is not necessarily prejudged as only the child who was referred.

This perspective, influenced by a general systems or cybernetic paradigm, was originally conceived by Bertalanffy in the late 1920s in an attempt to understand living organisms in a holistic way, but it was many years later, in the 1950s (as we have seen), that practitioners such as Jackson (1957) applied it to work with families. There are many variants: the Milan Systemic Approach (Tomm, 1984); the McMaster Family Model (1983); de Shazer's Brief Family Therapy (de Shazer, 1985); Problem-solving therapy (Haley, 1976); Social Network Therapy (Speck and Attneave, 1974) to name but a few.

Not surprisingly, there are significant differences when it comes to defining the activity of treatment covered by the rubric 'family therapy' (Dare, 1985). The nearest to a consensus is probably that provided by Gurman and his colleagues:

Family therapy is: any psychotherapeutic endeavour that explicitly focuses on altering the interactions between or among family members and seeks to improve the functioning of the family as a unit, or its subsystems and/or the functioning of individual members of the family. This is the goal regardless of whether or not an individual is identified as 'the patient'. Family therapy typically involves face to face work with more than one family member . . . although it may involve only a single member for the entire course of treatment (Gurman, Kniskern and Pinsof, 1986).

It is impossible to do justice to the different theoretical and practical nuances of the family therapies in this chapter. A summary of their underlying assumptions which draws on comparisons and accounts from Goldenberg and Goldenberg (1985) and Walsh (1982) is provided in Table 4.

The family, as a small group, can be observed and assessed on a variety of dimensions: patterns of communication, cohesion, processes of decision making (see Vetere and Gale, 1987). The major concepts for an assessment and formulation in family therapy are listed by Dare (1985) as follows:

(1) seeing the family as having an overall structure;
(2) understanding the symptom as having a potential function;
(3) understanding the location of the family on the life cycle;
(4) understanding the intergenerational structure of this family;
(5) making an overall formulation linking the preceding four features;
(6) linking the formulation to appropriate interventions.

Typically, an assessment by a family therapist (see Lask, 1987) might concern itself with whether there is:

(1) Too great a distance between members of the family leading potentially to emotional isolation and physical deprivation.
(2) Excessive closeness between members of the family leading potentially to over-identification and loss of individuality.
(3) An inability to work through conflicts, solve problems or make decisions.
(4) An inability on the part of parents to form a coalition and to work together, with detrimental effects on the marriage and/or the children.
(5) An alliance across the generations disrupting family life, as when a grandparent interferes with the mother's child-rearing decisions.
(6) Poor communication between members.
(7) A failure to respond appropriately to each other's feelings.

Some of the ways in which a child may contribute (wittingly or unwittingly) to a family's inability to cope with conflict have been described by Lask (1987):

Table 4   Major models of family therapy

Model of family therapy	View of normal family functioning	View of dysfunction, symptoms	Goals of therapy

Structural
Minuchin, Montalvo, Aponte
	(1) Boundaries clear and firm
	(2) Hierarchy with strong parental subsystem.
	(3) Flexibility of system for
	  (a) autonomy and interdependence;
	  (b) individual growth and system maintenance;
	  (c) continuity and adaptive restructuring in response to changing internal (developmental) and external (environmental) demands.
		Symptoms result from current family structural imbalance:
		(a) malfunctioning hierarchical arrangement, boundaries;
		(b) maladaptive reaction to changing requirements (developmental, environmental).
			Reorganize family structure:
			(a) shift members' relative positions to disrupt malfunctioning pattern and strengthen parental hierarchy
			(b) create clear, flexible boundaries;
			(c) mobilize more adaptive alternative patterns.

Strategic
Haley, Milan Team, Palo Alto Group
	(1) Flexibility.
	(2) Large behavioural repertoire for
	  (a) Problem resolution;
	  (b) Life-cycle passage.
	(3) Clear rules governing hierarchy (Haley).
		(1) Multiple origins of problems: symptoms maintained by family's
		  (a) unsuccessful problem-solving attempts;
		  (b) inability to adjust to life-cycle transitions (Haley);
		  (c) malfunctioning hierarchy; triangle of coalition across hierarchy (Haley);
		(2) Symptom is a communicative act embedded in interaction pattern.
			(1) Resolve presenting problem only; specific behaviourally defined objectives. Interrupt rigid feedback cycle: change symptom-maintaining sequence to new outcomes.
			(2) Define clearer hierarchy (Haley).

Behavioural–social exchange
Liberman, Patterson, Alexander
	(1) Maladaptive behaviour is not reinforced.
	(2) Adaptive behaviour is rewarded.
	(3) Exchange of benefits outweighs costs.
	(4) Long-term reciprocity.
		(1) Maladaptive, symptomatic behaviour reinforced by
		  (a) family attention and reward;
		  (b) deficient reward exchanges (e.g. coercion);
		  (c) communication deficit.
			(1) Concrete, observable behavioural goals: change contingencies of social reinforcement (interpersonal consequences of behaviour):
			  (a) Rewards for adaptive behaviour.
			  (b) No rewards for maladaptive behaviour.

(continues)

Table 4 Major models of family therapy *(continued)*

Model of family therapy	View of normal family functioning	View of dysfunction, symptoms	Goals of therapy
Psychodynamic Ackerman, Boszormenyi-Nagy, Framo, Lidz, Meissner, Paul, Stierlin	(1) Parental personalities and relationships well differentiated. (2) Relationship perceptions based on current realities, not projections from past. (3) Relational equitability (Boszormenyi–Nagy). (4) Family task requisites (Lidz): (a) parental coalition; (b) generation boundaries; (c) sex-linked parental roles	Symptoms due to family projection process stemming from unresolved conflicts and losses in family origin.	(1) Insight and resolution of family of origin conflict and losses. (2) Family projection processes. (3) Relationship reconstruction and reunion. (4) Individual and family growth.
Family system therapy Bowen	(1) Differentiation of self. (2) Intellectual/emotional balance.	(1) Functioning impaired by relationship with family origin: (a) poor differentiation; (b) anxiety (reactivity); (c) family projection process; (d) triangulation.	(1) Differentiation. (2) Cognitive functioning. (3) Emotional reactivity. Modification of relationships in family system: (a) detriangulation; (b) repair of cut-offs.

Source: Adapted from Walsh (1982)

(1) *Parent–child coalition,* where one parent attacks the other, using one of the children as an ally.
(2) *Triangulation,* where both parents attempt to induce a child to take *their* side.
(3) *Go-between,* where a child is used to transmit messages and feelings.

There have been disagreements over the years about the appropriate unit of focus in family therapy, thus we have exhortations in the 1960s for therapists to win the battle for structure by convening all family members to the first, and often ongoing, sessions, and some twenty years later, Anderson and Goolishian (1988) challenging the idea of any standard unit of treatment. They question the presumption of 'individual' or 'couple' or 'family' as a natural focus for therapy. They choose to work with whichever system can be defined to be relevant to a problem at any one time; its composition may vary over time and should be decided collaboratively by negotiation between the therapist and patient(s).

There are other continuing controversies or gaps in our knowledge: how to assess family patterns that relate functionally to the day-to-day specificities (i.e. changes) and syndrome specificity, of the referred problem; how to bring about change most effectively and how to evaluate such change; how to make a sometimes daunting (to clients) therapy more 'user friendly' (Reimers and Treacher, 1995). What hinders assessment in non-behavioural family therapy is the paucity of adequate micro-theories about change processes, a criticism that does not apply to social learning theory based behavioural family therapy (see Alexander and Parsons, 1982; Bandura, 1977; Herbert, 1981a, 1991; Patterson and Chamberlain, 1988; Reiss, 1988). The majority of non-behavioural family therapy processes are formulated at a high level of abstraction. It becomes very difficult to define operationally the key independent treatment variables at this level of strategy generality as sources of influence. It is an article of faith that the outward and visible signs of the family's problems, as manifested to a group of observers/commentators behind a one-way screen, represent reliably what is going wrong. How representative of a family's repertoire the samples of interaction (sometimes distorted by observer effects) are in reality is a moot point.

Applied Social Learning Theory: Behaviour Therapy

Behavioural interventions play an important role in alleviating problems of childhood. Watts (1990) observes that several factors contributed to their impact: (a) they represent a distinct and novel addition to the range of treatment techniques available for clinical problems; (b) they were developed by the deliberate application of well-established psychological principles; and (c) they are accompanied by a sustained and rigorous attempt to evaluate their effectiveness. Behaviour therapy, or to use our preferred term (for its interdisciplinary and systemic connotations) 'behavioural family therapy', represents a philosophy of change rather than a technology or collection of *ad hoc* techniques. It is based upon a *broad* and empirically based theory of normal and abnormal behaviour.

The discipline of behavioural work is much more conceptually elaborate than it was in its behaviouristic beginnings, with its bias towards operant technology and an 'applied behaviour analysis' formulation of problems. Cognitive processes—heresy in the eyes of positivist behaviour modifiers—now complicate the learning question. Given that several varieties of learning are central to the applied social learning theory paradigm, it is worth reviewing some of them, albeit briefly.

Learning by Direct Reinforcement

This perspective begins from a focus on the stimulus which impinges on the person; the person then responds with behaviour. Learning may be said to have taken place when a given stimulus regularly elicits a given response. The stimulus–response association is generally established by reinforcement, which may be stimulus-contingent or response-contingent, providing two different learning paradigms:

- *Stimulus-contingent reinforcement* is referred to as classical conditioning. A previously neutral stimulus (say, a tone) is repeatedly paired with an 'unconditioned stimulus' (say a puff of air to the eye) and gradually acquires its response-eliciting properties (it brings about an eye blink). The response of the individual (the eye blink) has, in technical parlance, been 'conditioned' to the tone (the 'conditioned stimulus').
- *Response-contingent reinforcement* is referred to as instrumental or operant conditioning. A mother wishes to teach her young child a particular skill—for example, asking to go to the toilet. After explanations and prompts the child's behaviour is 'shaped' by positive reinforcement such as words of encouragement and praise whenever it approximates to the required skill sequence. When this skilled response has been mastered it may be elicited repeatedly by making reinforcement contingent on its correct performance.

All forms of learning which are generally functional (adaptive) in their effects—i.e. they help children to adapt to life's demands—can in certain circumstances contribute to maladjustment. In such circumstances learning is dysfunctional in its effects. Thus a youngster who learns usefully on the basis of classical and operant 'conditioning' processes to avoid dangerous situations, can also learn (maladaptively) to fear and avoid school or social gatherings. A parent may unwittingly reinforce temper tantrums by attending to them. The operant equations, which are commonly discussed with parents in training groups, are simple but powerful:

acceptable behaviour + reinforcement =
more acceptable behaviour
acceptable behaviour + no reinforcement =
less acceptable behaviour
unacceptable behaviour + reinforcement =
more unacceptable behaviour
unacceptable behaviour + no reinforcement =
less unacceptable behaviour

For all the usefulness of these theories of learning, it is obvious that, as children develop, the speed and complexity of their learning are difficult to explain in terms of direct reinforcement and punishment alone. It became apparent to psychologists in the 1950s that their behavioural/learning theories were inadequate to deal with the subtleties of normal and abnormal behaviour.

Learning by Induction

In mature beings, much instrumental behaviour and more especially a great part of verbal behaviour is organized into higher-order routines and is, in many instances, better understood in terms of the operation of rules, principles, strategies and the like. Proven (1990) makes the point that although conditioning principles are excellent when used to teach targeted learning in specific situations, in the real world they are of less value when the child needs to extrapolate from a general principle to particular instances. Consider for example (she suggests) the 3-year-old who, having been rebuked for throwing water over the floor out of a plastic bucket, and having within a few seconds emptied more water over the floor from a different receptacle, sobs with indignation at further chastisement: 'I didn't throw it out of my bucket, I threw it out of my tortoise'.

She adds that this is not to argue that specific skills training is without merit; quite the contrary, because the adult as well as the child needs to know specifically which behaviours are functional, say personally or socially desirable, and which are not. But it is not usually enough. Whether training parents or children, a more fundamental change in perception may be necessary to bring about the sort of change in behaviour which is self-monitoring and self-adjusting. The subject may possess firmly entrenched beliefs about his or her functioning which learning based on conditioning alone would not change.

Inductive methods, giving reasons and explanations to the child, have been demonstrated to facilitate the internalization of rules and principles.

Learning by Observation (Imitation)

Most complex and novel behaviour (be it adaptive or maladaptive) is acquired by watching the behaviour of exemplary models. These may be people children observe in their everyday life or they may be symbolic models that they read about or see on television. This is called 'observational learning'. It is considered by social learning theorists to be the cornerstone of learning for socialization, and a significant basis for therapeutic interventions. As with the forms of learning mentioned above, what are normally functional processes can sometimes be perverse in their consequences. Thus an immature child who learns by imitating an adult will not necessarily understand when it is undesirable (antisocial/dysfunctional) behaviour that is being modelled.

Bandura and Walters (1963) made the acquisition of novel responses through the process of 'observational learning' the foundational principle of their theory of social learning. Their concept of vicarious conditioning was of central importance. As Bandura (1969) puts it:

> Virtually all learning phenomena resulting from direct experience can occur on a vicarious basis, through observation of other persons' behaviour and its consequences for them. Thus, for example, one can acquire intricate response patterns merely by observing the performance of appropriate models; emotional responses can be conditioned observationally by witnessing the affective reactions of others undergoing painful or pleasurable experiences; fearful and avoidant behaviour can be extinguished.

The vicarious conditioning of those responses usually elicited by classical conditioning techniques—gross emotional and 'autonomic' responses—was established as a possibility in a number of experiments. Bandura describes what happens when the observer performs no overt imitative response at the time of observing the model. He or she can acquire the behaviour only in cognitive representational form.

> Observational learning involves two representational systems—an imaginal one and a verbal one. After modelling stimuli have been coded into images or words for memory representation, they function as mediators for subsequent response retrieval and reproduction. Imagery formation is assumed to occur through a process of sensory conditioning . . . modelling stimuli elicit in observers perceptual responses that become sequentially associated and centrally integrated on the basis of temporal contiguity of stimulation (Bandura, 1969).

Performance is thought to be influenced by the observed consequences of responses, or more generally operant conditioning. Bandura demonstrated the separability of these two processes in an experiment where children observed a film-mediated model perform aggressive acts, with rewarding, punishing or no consequences (Bandura, 1969). While response consequences for the model clearly affected subsequent imitative behaviour in the children, attractive incentives offered to them to reproduce the aggressive behaviour completely wiped out these performance differences, revealing an equivalent amount of learning or acquisition.

Social Learning

Learning occurs within a *social context:* rewards, punishments and other contingencies and events are mediated by human agents and within attachment systems, and are *not* simply the consequences of behaviour. Bandura (1977) underlines the reciprocal influence and relationship between behaviour and environment when he suggests that the dictum 'change behaviour and you change contingencies' should be added to the better-known 'change contingencies and you change behaviour'. By their *actions* (and humans are *active* agents, not simply passively reacting organisms) people play a positive role in producing the reinforcing contingencies that impinge upon them. It is often said that operant theorists pay insufficient attention to the element that comes in between antecedents (A) and consequences (C), namely the learner's own behaviour (B). This behaviour is not simply something *elicited* by a stimulus and strengthened or otherwise by the nature of the reinforcement that follows; it is in fact a highly complex activity which involves three major processes, namely (a) the acquisition of information, (b) the manipulation or transformation of this information into a form suitable for dealing with the task in hand, (c) testing and checking the adequacy of this transformation. Again we see an emphasis on the active role of the learner. One aspect of behaviour therapy in particular, the view that abnormal behaviour differs mainly in degree rather than kind from normal behaviour, and is acquired by similar processes of learning and influence, leads to misunderstandings about its boundaries. The confusion arises not only in the public mind but also in the minds of many in the therapeutic/helping professions. The term is sometimes applied inappropriately to methods of social control, for example the punitive use of seclusion in residential settings, which has nothing to do with therapeutic work in its technical or ethical sense.

The Scientific Status of Behaviour Therapy

A suitable textbook on this subject is Masters *et al.* (1987).

Traditional psychotherapy is not a natural science, even though the value of its methods may often have been empirically evaluated. But it is the proud claim of many behaviour therapists that *behavioural* psychotherapy (behaviour modification) enjoys a scientific status which stands in sharp contrast to alternative psychological therapies, such as psychoanalysis. This *is* a critical issue, since explanations dealing with complex aspects of human functioning have tended, in the past, to be intuitive, literary or semantic, rather than scientific (see Farrell, 1970; Rycroft, 1970). For the first time (Kazdin, 1978), viable, testable and *successful* theories of human behaviour (adaptive and maladaptive) have been developed and applied to a wide variety of child and adult psychopathological phenomena (see Erwin, 1979, for a critical view).

Kazdin (1978) observes, in his history of behaviour therapy, that the discipline has grown and diversified out of all recognition since its formal beginnings in the late 1950s and early 1960s. It is no longer the monolithic entity it once was, and certainly is not tied by an 'all-sustaining' behaviouristic umbilical cord. Indeed, as he acknowledges, behaviour therapy has become so variegated in its conceptualizations of behaviour, research methods, and techniques, that no unifying schema or set of assumptions can incorporate all extant techniques. He states that although behaviour therapy emphasizes the principles of classical and operant conditioning it is not restricted to them; it draws upon principles from other branches of experimental psychology such as social and developmental psychology. The importance of 'private events' or the cognitive mediation of behaviour is recognized; and a major role is attributed to vicarious and symbolic learning processes, for example modelling.

The behavioural treatment of children (specifically) can be traced back to some innovative (but strangely isolated) work carried out by Mary Cover Jones in the early 1920s. Whereas Little Hans with his fear of horses became the much quoted hero of the psychoanalytic paradigm, Little Peter (aged 2 years 10 months at the beginning of his treatment for a fear of rabbits) became the hero of the behavioural paradigm (see Jones, 1924). In this he was to join Little Albert, victim of a distasteful experiment—the deliberate attempt to 'engineer' an experimental neurosis in the hapless infant—by John Watson and Rosalie Rayner (Watson and Rayner, 1920). By the application of conditioning methods they claimed to convert his fondness for white rats into phobic anxiety; and by stimulus generalization, they engendered milder aversive reactions to a fur coat, a dog and a Santa Claus mask.

Little Peter was treated for his phobia by Mary Cover Jones by methods which foreshadowed contemporary methods (see Chapter 13). Apart from some isolated studies, this experimental work (based upon learning theory) seemed to be forgotten; its humane potential certainly did not catch on within mainstream child therapy—which was mainly psychodynamic and very often play therapy (Axline, 1947). It is worth mentioning the studies of Holmes who conducted a survey of children's fears and the most effective ways they were dealt with by parents and the sufferers themselves. She advocated encouraging the child to cope actively with the feared situation, following the attempt with a reward (Holmes, 1935). In effect, she was putting forward an operant conditioning paradigm combined with exposure training.

The 1960s saw a revival of interest in behavioural theory and it derived much of its impetus from operant work ('behaviour modification') with mentally handicapped and autistic children (e.g. Baer, Wolf and Risley (1968)), and respondent work ('behaviour therapy') with phobic children (e.g. Rachman, 1962).

A consistent theoretical framework is of vital importance to the clinical child psychologist trying to make sense of, predictions about, and intervention plans for, the dysfunctional behaviours and interactions of children and/or their parents. Social learning theory, with its emphasis on the active nature of learning, the social context in which it takes place, and the role of cognition and meaning, is well-suited to such a remit in clinical work. The view put forward here is that abnormal behaviour in children and adults (our particular concern is their caregivers) does not differ, by and large, from *normal* behaviour in its development, its persistence and the way it can be changed. It follows the same laws and principles from experimental psychology, notably the areas of learning theory, social and developmental psychology (Herbert, 1985a).

Functional Analysis

A formulation is directed towards the precise identification of the antecedent, outcome and symbolic conditions which control the problem behaviour. Behaviour theorists refer to their assessment as a *functional analysis*.

The formulation involving an ABC linear analysis is, of necessity (given the complexity of behaviour) elaborated into a recursive sequence such that Cs become As that generate new Cs, and so on. An assessment in the behavioural mode involves a recursive process both in repeatedly testing and in revising the model of the person's behaviour. It is also repeatedly used to monitor changes in the person's behaviour across time and settings. Repeated evaluation is also essential to evaluate and modify treatment. The assessment procedure is idiographic and tailored very carefully to the individual. A functional analysis is the identification of important, controllable, causal, functional relationships applicable to a specified set of target behaviours for an individual client.

A stands for antecedent events
↓
B stands for behaviour(s)—the *target behaviour(s)* or interactions.
↓
C stands for the consequences that flow from these behaviours/interactions.

Figure 3 illustrates the complexities of a clinical formulation. It shows in diagrammatic form the multilevel and multidimensional nature of causal influences on problem behaviour.

It is useful, in a clinical formulation—the putting forward of hypotheses to explain clinical problems—to draw a distinction between proximal and distal, direct and indirect causal influences. These are explained below.

1. ANTECEDENT EVENTS

Peter is asked to do something or to stop doing it. Or he is asked to answer a question about the work, or about his lateness.

2. BEHAVIOUR

(i) Non-compliance. He takes no notice; if Miss Smith insists, he resorts to

(ii) Verbal abuse. He makes rude comments, criticizes, occasionally swears and shouts.

3. CONSEQUENCES

Miss Smith shouts at him, scolds him or discusses with him what he has done.

Sends him out of the classroom.

All classroom work comes to a stop; all the pupils watch the confrontation.

The original cause of the confrontation is forgotten.

PERSONS: He is rude and disobedient mainly with Miss Smith; occasionally to other teachers; never with Mrs Simpson or Mr Jackson.

PLACES: Classroom only, never in the playground.

TIMES: Mondays in particular—usually at the beginning of teaching periods.

SITUATIONS: Mainly when asked to do something or when challenged over being late or without his equipment. Particularly when questioned about, or criticized for, his work.

Figure 2   Lay-out for a preliminary analysis of a problematic classroom situation. (Here we see a simple linear causal analysis. This fits into X in the 10-factor clinical formulation in Figure 1)

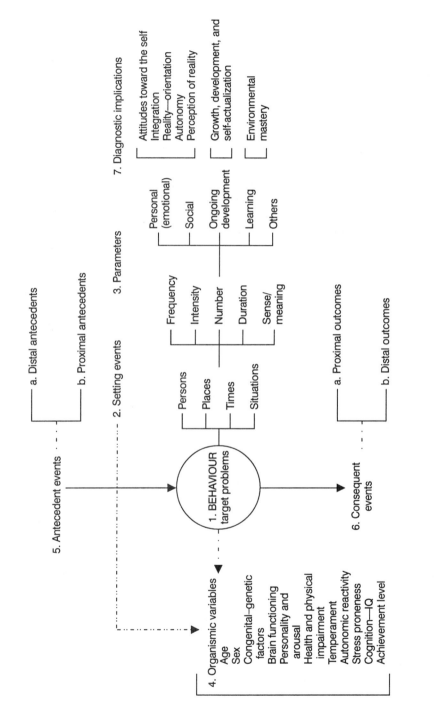

Figure 3   A conceptual framework for an assessment of behaviour problems.

(1) *Direct causal influences.* Proximal (current) influences are direct in their effects and close in time to the actions they influence. They are *functionally* related to behaviour and can thus—as hypotheses about causation—be tested in therapy using single-case experimental designs (Herbert, 1990; Morley, 1989). A formulation might indicate particular *antecedent conditions* which directly *elicit* or *signal the reinforcing potential* of problematic responses. Other conditions involve some lack of appropriate stimulus control over the person's behaviour.

    (a) *Inappropriate stimulus control of behaviour.* A situation in which a normally neutral stimulus configuration (e.g. boarding a bus) acquires the capability of eliciting a dysfunctional response like anxiety. This might arise—in part—from a history of classical conditioning (e.g. a fearful experience while taking a bus journey);

    (b) *Defective stimulus control over behaviour.* This means the inability of a stimulus, normally associated with a pattern of behaviour, to cue this pattern in a person. The fact that it is an essentially vulnerable infant, crying insistently from distress, for example, does not inhibit an enraged parent from administering a violent beating. Another example might be the child who reacts invariably to imagined 'provocation' from peers by acts of aggression. This pattern of defective control in children might stem from inconsistent discipline, *laissez faire* parenting, extreme permissiveness, or the lack of outcomes to actions—such as to make discriminating between socially desirable or undesirable behaviour irrelevant or unimportant.

There could be 'outcome conditions' which either reinforce problem behaviour, or punish desirable responses. Aversive behavioural repertoires, such as violent actions or extreme dependency behaviours, could well originate from learning conditions such as these.

Any of these inappropriate forms of antecedent or outcome control might be operating in the person's symbolic processes, rather than in his or her external environment or as a function of physiological changes. In the case of 'aversive self-reinforcing systems' the person sets high standards in evaluating himself or herself, thus leading to self-depreciation and criticism rather than self-approval. Such punitive conditions may have originated from an early history in which the individual was taught to rely on stern standards of self-appraisal. An example might be found in the depressed, suicidal individual, or the youngster who badly lacks self-confidence and self-esteem.

(2) *Contemporary indirect (contextual) influences.* These influences include the peer group, neighbourhood values and the school ethos. Differences in the performance of schools (according to the findings of Rutter *et al.*, 1979) are not a matter of buildings, available space or the size of the school. In other words, they are not due to physical factors, even when seemingly unpromising (see Chapter 6).

(3) *Indirect predisposing influences.* These include genetic factors, family upbringing, intellectual ability and health. These are dealt with in later chapters.

(4) *Historical (distal) influences.* These are factors distant in time from the current life-situation, but significant as predisposing causes, e.g. early learning, traumatic experiences and so on. These are the subject (*inter alia*) of Parts One and Two. Such influences obviously cannot be modified or manipulated directly.

An analysis of these factors is not necessarily a condition of successful interventions. It is not possible to change history. Nevertheless they are worth considering. Haynes (1978) lists four reasons for obtaining a history:

(a) It may suggest conditions under which the behaviour problem may reappear after successful modification.
(b) It may provide clues concerning controlling variables.
(c) Understanding of how behaviour problems begin is very instructive to clients.
(d) The historical information may be relevant to behaviour theory and to the development of preventative programmes.

It may not be possible to reverse history but people bring their past into the present through their attitudes and attributions: they *can* be 'liberated' (it is suggested), by cognitive restructuring and therapeutic conversations, from the hold their past has on their present. In that sense therapists set out to help clients to 'rewrite' history. Or, to change the metaphor, ghosts can be put to rest.

(5) *Proximal consequences.* Turning to the maintenance of problematic behaviour, this is postulated to be largely dependent on its consequences. Maladaptive actions that are rewarded tend to be repeated, whereas those that are unrewarded or punished are generally discarded. The reinforcement which strengthens an adolescent's disruptive behaviour—to take an increasingly typical example from the contemporary classroom—may be in terms of direct external reinforcement, vicarious or observed reinforcement or self-reinforcement.

(6) *Distal consequences and 'diagnostic implications'*. While it is true to say that clinicians delineate certain 'symptoms' as pathognomonic of particular psychiatric disorders the fact is that in our chosen area of disorders of childhood we are dealing mainly with social rather than medical criteria of what is abnormal. It is important to look, not only at the immediate consequences of a client's behaviour, but also at the longer-term implications (distal outcomes). What are the likely consequences of non-intervention in the problem for the person and his/her family? Problem behaviours are usually so called because they have a variety of unfavourable short-term and long-term outcomes. They are therefore referred to as maladaptive actions or dysfunctional thoughts and feelings: they are inappropriate in terms of several criteria which are assessed by the therapist. The 'diagnostic' criteria are listed as distal outcomes.

Ultimately the professional judgement of a client's behavioural/psychosocial/mental status is made in individual terms, taking into account his or her particular circumstances. It involves an estimate of the consequences that flow from the client's specific thoughts, feelings and behaviours and general approach to life, with particular reference to their personal and emotional well-being, their ability to form and maintain social relationships, their ongoing development toward (rather than away from) maturity and self-actualization, their ability to work effectively and (in the case of children) learn academically, and their accessibility to socialization. All are subject to disruption in emotional and behavioural disorders, and are gravely affected in the conduct disorders of childhood and adolescence. Other factors to be considered are youngsters' self-esteem and competence.

Cognitive–Behavioural Models

Bandura (1977) points to a therapeutic paradox, when he comments that

> . . . explanations are becoming more cognitive. On the other hand, it is performance based treatments that are proving most powerful in effecting psychological changes. Regardless of the method involved, the treatments implemented through actual performance achieve results consistently superior to those in which fears are eliminated by cognitive representations of threats.

Interestingly, behavioural procedures seem to be among the most powerful methods of activating cognitive processes. Not surprisingly they are recruited for the remediation of a wide range of intrapersonal and interpersonal problems. There is an irony in the burgeoning literature on the cognitive aspects of behaviour therapy. Nowadays the approach encompasses a plethora of techniques that depend upon those mediating processes and private events which were once so passionately repudiated as 'ghosts in the machine'. Thus self-verbalizations, illogical thoughts, misperceptions and misinterpretations, attributions and self-appraisals (in other words what the client thinks, imagines, and says to himself or herself prior to, accompanying, and following their overt behaviour, become a primary focus for a therapeutic intervention (See Hewstone, 1989, for a theoretical account of causal attribution.) What, essentially, is being claimed is that people can be taught to eliminate some of their maladaptive behaviours by challenging their irrational beliefs and faulty logic or by getting them to instruct themselves in certain ways, or to associate wanted behaviour with positive self-statements, and unwanted ones with negative self-statements.

There is another aspect to the issue of cognitive processes which is a matter of concern in the psychologist's assessment. It has to do with what are called 'mutual cognitions'. Maccoby and Martin (1983) observe that if we are to study the effect of ideas on parenting and on parent–child interactions, we shall need to come to terms with the ideas held by both parents and children. If we are to do so, we shall certainly need to ask about the causes and consequences of a lack of match in their ideas and expectations which may arise from differences in conceptual level. With regard to the consequences of a lack of congruence in ideas about the way a relationship should proceed, the consensus is that smooth interactions require that both parent and child must act from the same 'script' (Hinde, 1979; Maccoby, 1984). Mismatches are thought to promote conflict (e.g., Damon, 1989; Selman, 1980). Further information comes from a study by MacKinnon and Arbuckle (1989). Mothers and their 7–9-year-old sons were observed while working together on an Etch-a-Sketch task. Each person controls one of the two knobs. Interactions were rated for their overall coerciveness. Mothers and sons were also asked, when given stories where the intent of one party was ambiguous, to describe how the situation may have come about. These descriptions, and other comments, were then coded for the extent to which the situation was seen as brought about by the other's negative intentions, as opposed to a prosocial intention or an accidental outcome. The highest incidence of coercive interactions occurred within dyads where both individuals were inclined, on the vignettes, to attribute negative intent to each other. The next highest incidence of coerciveness occurred with dyads where the mother's attributions (but not the son's) were predominantly negative.

Damon (1989) and Selman (1980) have argued that the child's lower level of conceptual development contributes to a mismatch between adults' and children's concepts of relationships and, thus, to their scripts for how interactions should proceed. The sources of difference may lie also in a child's changing sense of what he or she is entitled to. For example, a script whereby children make self-disclosing statements to parents, but parents do not disclose private information about themselves to children, may be typical and tacitly agreed during early and middle childhood, but not in adolescence. At this older age, children are likely to withhold certain information about themselves and to recognize the parents' right to do the same. Parents may also move to a script of mutual privacy, or they may continue to expect the one-sided self-disclosure of earlier years (Miller, 1986; Selman, 1980).

Cognitive–behavioural treatments, an amalgam of cognitive and behavioural approaches, have proved to be effective in treating psychological disorders of childhood. Cognitive–behavioural theory is closely allied to social learning theory (e.g. Bandura, 1977). This theoretical perspective stresses the importance of the environment while also seeking to incorporate 'inner' processes as mediators between the outer world and overt behaviour.

There is a wide range of cognitive–behavioural procedures but they share a common assumption: that children (and their parents) can be taught to eliminate their maladaptive behaviours by changing external contingencies and by challenging their irrational beliefs and faulty logic; also by encouraging them to instruct themselves in certain ways (Table 5 illustrates the stages in a cognitive–behavioural formulation).

IMPLICATIONS OF DIFFERENT THERAPY MODELS

Webster-Stratton and Herbert (1993) make the point that the different therapeutic models come with different sets of assumptions about the therapist's role with clients, the causes of problems, family dynamics and the level of responsibility the client or therapist assumes for resolving problems. For example, in quasi-medical models such as psychoanalytic psychotherapy, clients are not thought of as 'responsible' for their problems. Nor are parents responsible for finding solutions. The therapist, who is the expert in the relationship, gradually uncovers the problems hidden in the unconscious areas of the client's psyche, in past experiences, and/or in the dynamics of family life. He or she interprets them to the individual client, or to the entire family in the case of psychodynamic family therapy. The client is seen as a relatively passive recipient of the therapist's analysis—unlike the active partnership encouraged in behavioural work.

Table 5 Stages in a cognitive–behavioural assessment for intervention

Stage	Aims and rationale	Procedures
(1) Taking an inventory of the client's problems.	To compile a comprehensive picture of the client's difficulties.	A semi-structured interview to draw up a problem profile.
(2) Selection of target behaviour(s).	To focus on problem areas to change.	Collaborative negotiation of goals.
(3) Identification of replacement actions.	To emphasize positive objectives.	Operationalizing of goals.
(4) Design of data recording method.	To obtain pre-treatment baseline.	Instructing client; charting.
(5) Identification of problem-controlling conditions.	To identify contingencies, beliefs, attributions, etc., preceding and following the occurrence of problem(s).	Charting (recording) ABCs of behaviours/beliefs indicative of problem(s).
(6) Assessment of environmental resources/influences.	To identify possible resources/significant influences in the client's problems.	Interview of client and significant others (genogram/social support systems).
(7) Formulation of a cognitive–behavioural intervention plan.	To select appropriate methods, i.e. the the most effective programme for change.	Familiarity with the literature. Analysis of the *function* of dysfunctional behaviour (i.e. social learning implications and meaning of the problem).
(8) Implementing of programme.	To change behaviour/cognitions by means of methods carried out in a collaborative context (e.g. Webster-Stratton and Herbert, 1994).	Applying cognitive–behavioural methods/techniques.
(9) Monitoring progress and outcomes.	To be sensitive to difficulties in the progress of therapy and to obtain information about effectiveness.	Gathering appropriate data.
(10) Planning for generalization and maintenance of change.	To achieve generality of improvements and stabilization of change.	Using the environment for maintenance; planning generalization strategies (e.g. self-reinforcement)

Chapter 2

CLINICAL ASSESSMENT: PRACTICE ISSUES

Rigorous assessment is the *sine qua non* of effective intervention. The formulation, which bridges these activities, depends upon the clinician's practice, wisdom and skill in 'mining' for the data with which the formulation is constructed. The different stages of the ASPIRE process leading towards a formulation involve many practical decisions and actions.

CONDUCTING A FORMULATION

Flow chart 1   Beginning an assessment

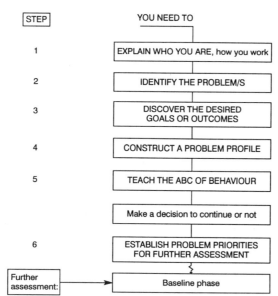

Further assessment   Phase II

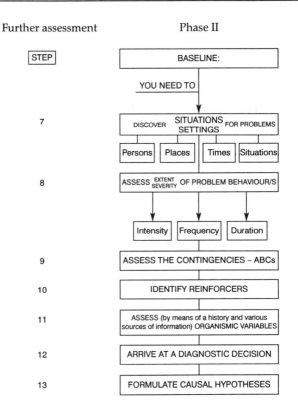

STEP

BASELINE:

YOU NEED TO

7

DISCOVER SITUATIONS SETTINGS FOR PROBLEMS

| Persons | Places | Times | Situations |

8

ASSESS EXTENT SEVERITY OF PROBLEM BEHAVIOUR/S

| Intensity | Frequency | Duration |

9   ASSESS THE CONTINGENCIES – ABCs

10   IDENTIFY REINFORCERS

11   ASSESS (by means of a history and various sources of information) ORGANISMIC VARIABLES

12   ARRIVE AT A DIAGNOSTIC DECISION

13   FORMULATE CAUSAL HYPOTHESES

The Intervention

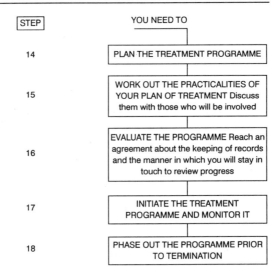

STEP   YOU NEED TO

14   PLAN THE TREATMENT PROGRAMME

15   WORK OUT THE PRACTICALITIES OF YOUR PLAN OF TREATMENT Discuss them with those who will be involved

16   EVALUATE THE PROGRAMME Reach an agreement about the keeping of records and the manner in which you will stay in touch to review progress

17   INITIATE THE TREATMENT PROGRAMME AND MONITOR IT

18   PHASE OUT THE PROGRAMME PRIOR TO TERMINATION

PRACTICAL ISSUES: ASSESSMENT

Hepworth and Larsen (1990, pp. 155–166) define assessment as the process of

> gathering, analyzing, and synthesizing salient data into a formulation that encompasses the following vital dimensions: (i) the nature of clients' problems, including special attention to the roles that clients and significant others play in the difficulties, (ii) the functioning (strengths, limitations personality assets, and deficiencies) of clients and significant others, (iii) the motivation of clients to work on the problems, (iv) the relevant environmental factors that contribute to the problems, and (v) the resources that are available or are needed to ameliorate clients' difficulties.

A large variety and number of methods have been employed to assess children's level of developmental and behavioural adjustment:

- questionnaires; checklists;
- structured or unstructured interviews;
- structured and unstructured observations.

The contributors to these assessment methods include parents, teachers, peers, siblings, children, and clinicians—all potentially valuable sources of information. The context of assessment may vary from naturalistic observations to structured play situations in laboratory or clinical settings.

Observational Techniques (see Dadds, Rapee and Barrett, 1994)

Bates and Bayles (1984) are of the opinion that parental reports of children's behaviour consist of objective, subjective, and error components. They found support for an objective component through significant mother–father and parent–observer convergences in ratings of children's behaviour. Moderately high inter-parental correlations are found in most studies in the literature. In a review of assessment issues in child psychopathology, Achenbach (1978) concluded that the most accurate observations of children's behaviour are related to the context in which they were made.

The continuities of child behaviour in a given situation and the discontinuities across situations appear to derive, in large part, from the various social roles children imitate or have thrust upon them. Even by 6 or 7 years of age, children begin to adopt behavioural roles which vary with the context in which they are functioning. Thus a given child may exhibit difficult behaviour at home but modulate his or her behaviour at school. Such a behavioural repertoire would result in there being relatively stable behaviour within a given situational context but relatively little agreement between behaviour in different situations (Fergusson and Horwood, 1987). Yule (1989) has a caveat against rejecting the concept of personality traits and leaving them out of an assessment. There is increasing evidence that introverted children respond differently from extraverted children to different regimes in the classroom and even to different styles of therapeutic intervention. He adds that evidence is mounting that personality (or temperamental characteristics) affect how a child will respond to a particular situation.

Interviews (Angold, 1994; Silverman, 1991, 1994)

Parents, teachers and other caregivers, adolescents and children, are most often the subjects of the clinical interview. In order to learn about the behaviour and problems of other persons, the three principal methods are through observation and questioning, and giving them a sympathetic 'hearing'.

Interviewing, because of the opportunity it gives to 'see them', 'question them' and by no means least, 'listen to them', becomes a prime instrument of assessment, investigation, intervention and evaluation. Verbal report, based upon clinical conversations, may be a fairly good predictor of real-life behaviour, but it can also be very misleading, and therefore, unreliable. Do not rely entirely on it (and that means the interview) for your data. Clients may not notice things, they may misperceive events, they may forget significant details and emphasize irrelevant points. Embarrassment or guilt may lead to errors of commission and omission in information-giving. If the crucial behaviour consists of overlearned responses, the client may be quite unaware ('unconscious') of his or her actions. So go and look for yourself and/or train the clients to observe so that you can see things through their informed eyes.

The guided (semi-structured) interview is the main vehicle for the preliminary assessment. Such interviews provide chiefly two kinds of information:

(1) They afford an opportunity for direct observation of a rather limited sample of behaviour manifested during the interview situation itself (e.g. the individual's speech, his or her style of thinking, competence, poise and manner of relating to the child).
(2) The interviewer seeks to secure directly as much information of a factual or personal nature from the client as is relevant to the purpose of the interview (e.g. information about the problem, opinions, relationship, parental skills, experience). A particularly important function in a clinical or social work setting is to elicit life-history data. What the individual had done in the past is thought to be a good indicator of what he or she may do in the future.

Children are not always very good at expressing their fears, frustrations or uncertainties. They cannot always tell their parents, let alone a comparative stranger, how they feel, but they have a language that adults can learn to translate—the language of behaviour and fantasy. What they do (in a direct sense in everyday life) and say (indirectly through play or story-telling) can be most revealing. It is easy to forget that children are not simply little adults and it can therefore come as a surprise when they don't interview like adults. They often fidget, become alarmingly restless in their movements, tic, look out of the window, or fiddle endlessly with a button, when they find the interview uncomfortable. And there may be many good, objective reasons for their discomfort, and for the series of blank looks or 'don't knows' that meet the interview's queries. Style is important. A patronizing, insincere tone will soon be picked up and responded to negatively. An artificial ('this is my voice for children') style is also counterproductive.

The child may not comprehend the question, especially when he or she is cognitively immature, and the question is abstract and global. The double-barrelled (two-in-one) question, laced in jargon, is also likely to floor the older child. The child may simply not know the answer to the question. Interviewers and questionnaire designers often assume that clients must know the answers to their questions, if only they'd speak out.

Children, especially those with low self-esteem, may be afraid to give their opinions because they think the interview is like a test, with right or wrong answers. They may be afraid to say anything out of loyalty to their family and/or fear of the consequences of their answers for themselves and their parents. They may put too literal an interpretation on questions, and their egocentricity, when young, may prevent them from seeing another's point of view. Then again, cognitive immaturity may not allow them to see or understand the causal connections you are seeking.

Shyness about the topic of investigation may also inhibit responses to questions. All of these emotions: fear, embarrassment, loyalty, and others, require a delicate approach in the interview, the establishment of rapport, and carefully judged reassurance where necessary.

Adjuncts to the Child Interview (see Finch and Politano, 1994)

The advantage of using projective techniques (which include play, puppets, dramatic creations, completing stories or sentences) for assessment, is that they involve relatively unstructured tasks that permit an almost unlimited variety of responses. The client has to fall back on his or her own resources rather than stereotyped, socially desirable answers. The techniques (as psychometric instruments) have their critics, but are invaluable if used cautiously as aids to communicating with children. The caution refers to interpreting the protocols—the statements about feelings and attitudes toward various members of the family. It is thought that children identify with the central characters in their stories, project their own feelings (especially unacceptable or difficult-to-acknowledge impulses or attitudes) onto the fantasy figures, and attribute various motives and ideas that are essentially their own, into the play or other creative situations and plots.

Where the child is too loyal, too frightened or ashamed, or too inarticulate to speak about feelings (or painful events in the family) it may be possible to express these things in the evolving story (you can make up the basic structure, leaving spaces for the child to fill in) about a boy or girl of similar age. Thus the therapist begins, 'Once upon a time there was a boy/girl. What did he/she most like doing?' . . . 'What did he/she not like doing?' . . . (The therapist gradually introduces, among neutral themes, topics such as secrets, fears, worries, preoccupations, family tensions, parental behaviours, and so on.)

Sentence completions are useful:

'I like to..'
'What I most dislike ....'
'My best friend..'
'I wish ....'
'My dad ....'
'My mum ....'
'If only ....'
'In my home the nicest thing is..'
'The worst thing is..'

With stories told as a response to pictures the therapist needs (as always) to be cautious about their interpretations. There is a tendency to find what one hopes to find or to superimpose our 'theories' onto the projective protocols. The safest use of these instruments is not as psychometric devices—they are too unreliable—but as a means of eliciting *clues* to important themes, which are then investigated further. With these caveats in mind, play, drama (with puppets or miniatures) or stories are undoubtedly an invaluable adjunct to work with children. The psychologist would do well to have a store of miniatures, drawing materials and pictures available.

Interviewing parents (see Cox, 1994)

There are many investigations (e.g., Yarrow, Campbell and Burton, 1968) which point to the consistent and persistent biasing of maternal reports in the direction of cultural stereotypes. The idealized picture of the happy family is one of the most potent in modern society and any failure to live up to that image rebounds on the parents, particularly on the mother. Sigmund Freud said that the sins of the children would be visited on the parents. Not surprisingly, parents complaining about 'deviant' behaviours of their children are very conscious that the complaints reflect back on them. Yarrow (1960) makes the point that, stripped of all elaboration, mothers' interview responses represent self-description by extremely ego-involved reporters.

The finding of bias in maternal reports is particularly high when they are giving retrospective reports: the passage of time dims the memory and what memory cannot provide imagination elaborates, an elaboration that is often in a direction that is socially desirable. Reports of here-and-now events and practices are more accurate and reliable. The parent presumably finds it more difficult (certainly not impossible) to falsify the present: it is much easier to rewrite history.

Reliability studies (e.g. Yarrow, 1960) have shown that there are wide discrepancies between the reports of the same mother at different times or of the same mother with a different interviewer. When data is obtained from more than one source there is again a lack of consensus. How, then, can one improve the reliability of parental reports? According to the evidence, if the mother is asked for a statement on *current* beliefs and practices, then the reports reach a satisfactory level of validity and reliability. When parents are asked to describe rather than interpret, reliability and validity measures can reach satisfactory levels.

Achenbach and his colleagues (1989) suggest that variations in assessment between different informants can be viewed as a function of different experiences with children, and that multiaxial assessments could account for situational variability in children's behaviour. While maternal and teacher ratings of particular children are only modestly correlated, there is quite marked stability in their ratings over time; in other words their individual judgements tend to be consistent, even if they do differ somewhat. There is evidence to suggest that rater-specific as well as situation-specific factors may influence behaviour ratings. In particular, maternal mood and notably maternal depression appear to influence the mother's ratings of the child.

The form of any assessment approach involves some important assumptions about behavioural attributes. Behaviourally orientated psychologists tend to view behaviours with, say, aggressive or anxiety attributes, as instances or samples of response classes rather than as outward and visible signs of internal or underlying dispositions. The language of personality, to the extent that it is used by behaviourists, is employed descriptively rather than inferentially. Conventional trait attributions are thought by critics to represent nothing more than giving two names to the same class of behaviour. Thus, if a child is seen to hit another child, there is no reason to infer that the child who does the striking is not only aggressive but also has a 'need for aggression'. Behaviours with aggressive attributes would be considered to be members of the same response class if it could be shown that such attributes entered into the same functional relationships with antecedent, concurrent and consequent stimulus conditions, rather than because they co-existed or co-varied in a group of persons. Wiggins (1973) notes that:

> . . . Issues of stability and generality become empirical questions rather than assumptions. Given a change in stimulating conditions, particularly conditions of reinforcement, the frequency, intensity, or duration of the response class of interest should be predictable from a knowledge of the functional relationships between these attributes and the stimulus conditions which control them. Under these circumstances, it is more important to determine whether or not an individual is capable of performing a response, rather than trying to estimate the typical or characteristic level at which he responds.

When it comes to 'abnormal' aspects of personality, there seems to be a minority of children whose behavioural characteristics generalize in their maladaptive aspects over both time and situation: these are among the children who turn out to cause most concern in the wake of their 'high profile' behaviour disorders. The presence of such children would account for the fact that parent and teacher ratings do show some modest positive correlations.

Psychometric testing (see Berger, 1994)

To test or not to test; that is the question faced by clinical child psychologists, especially when it comes to the issue of assessing IQ. It has been, and remains, a controversial issue. Part of the problem is that people (including some psychiatrists) tend to equate assessment with psychological tests only; tests designed to measure anything and everything from brain damage and maladjustment to personality attributes such as extraversion, self-esteem and fantasy life.

Anastasi (1982), doyenne of writers about psychometrics, defines a psychological test as 'essentially an objective and standardized measure of a sample of behaviour'. Tests of intelligence, personality and academic achievement in children are *standardized* on the assumption that the tester will be able to make comparisons between the child being tested and the sample of children on whom the test was developed. The conditions and procedures by which the test is administered, scored and interpreted are held constant for all test-takers. Such tests are called 'normative' and such comparative approaches are referred to as 'nomothetic'.

There have been debates about the extent to which tests measure *traits* and *states* which are generalized attributes, stable across time and situations, or *situational*, the person varying in his or her behaviour depending upon different contextual factors or situations (see Mischel, 1968). Rejecting polarized positions are the *interactionalists* (e.g. Bowers, 1973) who propose that people do manifest trait characteristics that determine their behaviour, but that situations always exert a strong influence to modify or moderate the effects of traits.

IQ Testing (see Howe, 1997)

Child clinical psychologists are sometimes put under pressure to provide—for a variety of reasons—a statement about a child's 'intelligence' and its implications. Many refuse, or are very reluctant, to put a numerical answer to such a request. Berger (1986), in a valuable and novel review of the issues, puts two main reasons for the negative ethos surrounding the measurement of IQ:

> First, there is the now well-documented historical and contemporary association between IQ testing and allegations of discrimination, racial, educational, or otherwise . . . Second, philosophers, many psychologists—especially those in the developmental and cognitive fields—as well as others are, to say the least, sceptical if not contemptuous and dismissive of IQ tests being paraded as devices that can generate a measure that in turn encompasses something as remarkable, complex, and subtle as human intelligence.

Berger passes judgement on this last point. He argues, from the evidence, that I.Q. tests do not index intelligence, or at least 'not the type of intelligence that any self-respecting person would like to lay claim to'. Furthermore, he argues that IQ tests do not *measure* in any meaningful sense of the term measurement. You might well ask: what is left? What remains is that they provide a numerical expression of performances; and tests, in his view, are useful insofar as they provide data that can be interpreted in ways that are relevant to clinical problems. Psychological tests are administered not because psychologists wish to produce a score, but because knowledge of the score enables certain clinically relevant statements to be made or hypotheses to be formulated or validated. And, of course, it is useful to have instruments that produce reasonably robust scores. The question of the suitability of a test for indexing performance and interpreting scores can usually be decided on the basis of expectancy tables or regression equations.

What kind of performance, then, is indexed by some of the popular tests? We know that IQs are quite good predictors of school achievement for *older* children. There is a direct association between a child's IQ score and later adjustment (prognosis) for infantile autism (DeMyer, Hingten and Jackson, 1981) and mental handicap. When combined with other variables such as socioeconomic status, family conditions and the presence of learning disabilities, IQ is an important factor in predicting academic success and adult outcome, for children with attention deficit disorder (see Wing, 1971a). Rutter and Yule (1970) have found high correlations between academic deficits and the conduct disorders.

For very young children, intelligence tests are helpful, uncovering developmental delays, but they have little predictive validity for school performance or the likelihood of behaviour problems. There is sufficient evidence—and the examples mentioned above represent only a few— that IQs have non-chance (i.e. statistically reliable) associations, concurrent and predictive, with a wide range of behavioural phenomena that are important in clinical practice in elucidating developmental, academic and behavioural problems. This, Berger (1986) acknowledges; the question for him is not *whether* to use IQ tests but *how* to do so.

Classical Test (Reliability) Theory

For critics of the mystique of scientific respectability that attaches to psychological testing as symbolized by statistical paraphernalia (e.g. standard errors of measurement, reliability coefficients, validity coefficients), *specificity* has been the 'trojan horse' to subvert classical test theory, especially with regard to the repeatability of scores *and* their interpretation. As Berger (1986) points out, general statements (e.g. reliable or unreliable) about any test are inappropriate, mainly because altering one aspect of a reliability estimation study can lead to marked variations in the reliability coefficients (and the same can be said for validity coefficients) as *specific* to the sample test, circumstances of testing, and computational procedure. The implication is that the robustness of scores must be ascertained at least for each major variation in application.

Expectancy tables, it is argued, can be constructed from any investigation that generates numerical data. With appropriate studies it is possible to draw up expectancy tables which provide the information required to decide whether a test is *suitable* as a procedure and as an instrument allowing interpretations that are relevant to the purpose of testing. There need be no recourse to reliability theory or dubious assumptions about what tests 'measure' (see Kaufman, 1980).

This is not the place to consider, in depth, the many aids to description and measurement for formulation purposes, that are available. Useful guides to the psychometric and evaluative literature are available in Barclay, 1990; Berger, 1996' Ollendick and Hersen, 1984; Scott, 1996; Webster-Stratton and Herbert, 1994.

THE ANALYSIS OF CAUSES

The tendency for clinical child psychologists to work in multidisciplinary teams which include, *inter alia*, psychiatrists, speech therapists and social workers, or in close collaboration with medical colleagues (for example, GPs and pediatricians) is understandable when we look at this complexity of physical, social, economic and psychological influences on psychopathology. Behaviour results from the interaction of psychosocial and biological determinants. The important caveat in relation to clinical formulations is not to neglect, through a commitment to a psychogenic model of biogenic theory of psychopathology, the possibility of complications from the other side of the causal equation.

Behaviour problems may be apparent immediately after birth, stemming from prenatal or perinatal complications of one kind or another. They may appear in infancy, taking the form of feeding or sleeping difficulties or excessive crying, reflecting biological dysfunction and/or deficiencies in the care babies receive, or the sheer absence of affection. Problems may emerge during the preschool years, reflecting emotional and social difficulties such as fears, excessive temper tantrums or shyness: they may be manifested as conduct problems like aggressiveness, hyperactivity or poor concentration. In any particular case they are likely to reflect the influence of psychosocial factors interacting with inborn factors of the kind described in the previous chapter.

A typical history would take account (inter alia) of the following information:

- *Prenatal and perinatal factors*
- *The home background*
  (i) family composition
  (ii) living conditions
  (iii) financial position
- *The child's background*
  (i) health
  (ii) growth and development
  (iii) school
  (iv) life events

(v) interests
(vi) friendships
- *The family background*
  (i) parents ────────────→ (a) personal details
  (ii) siblings ──────────→ (b) attitudes to child
  (iii) extended family ←─────   care/discipline
  (iv) cohesion in the family ──→ (c) problem areas

The complexity of psychiatric and psychological problems has led to great confusion in the analysis of causes. There is an all-too-human tendency to oversimplify and think of causality in linear, univariate terms: A causes B; B is the effect of A. However, there is no limit to the analysis of causes. One finds, not a single antecedent, not even a chain of antecedents, but a whole interlacing network of them. This complexity appears to obtain in Fielding's not untypical formulation of an adolescent patient's obsessional anxiety (Fielding, 1983) (see Figure 4).

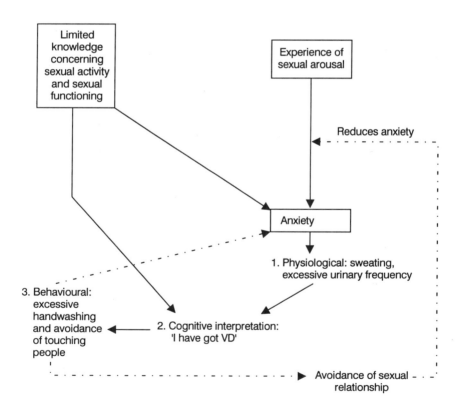

Figure 4   Clinical formulation of obsessional hand-washing in a 16-year-old male adolescent. From Fielding (1983). Reproduced by permission

One point of agreement that appears to emerge from the welter of findings about problems like these is their multicausality. Mayer-Gross, Slater, and Roth (1955) make the point that in medicine it is necessary to deal with causes of all kinds, not just those that are both necessary and sufficient. In searching for a cause of some phenomenon, we are really searching for a quantitative relationship. If A is the necessary and sufficient cause of B, then there is a one-to-one relationship between A and B. If A is necessary but not sufficient cause of B, then there is no B without A, but A may be combined with X or Y, instead of with B. If the variety of these X's and Y's is great, the causal relationship, though it still exists, is thereby attenuated. If A is neither necessary nor sufficient, then there are A's without B's and B's without A's, and the strength of the causation will depend on the proportionate relationship between AB to A on one hand and B on the other.

Mayer-Gross and colleagues observe that it is not difficult to founder in a causal network. We are less likely to do so if we take into account the quantitative aspect of causation. It is at this point that so much psychological thinking loses cogency and direction. Quantitatively important causes are tangled in a knot of others with only slight or entirely unknown quantitative relation with the effects we are interested in. These could be direct (proximal) and indirect contemporary (contextual) influences, as well as indirect predisposing (organismic) and historical (distal) influences.

A consistent theoretical framework is of vital importance to the clinical child psychologist trying to make sense of, predictions about, and intervention plans for, the dysfunctional behaviours and interactions of children and/or their parents—the all-important clinical formulation.

THE FORMULATION: THE 'WHY' QUESTION

The formal or main phase of assessment can be said to be over when the clinician has a reasonably clear picture of the clients' difficulties, strengths, history, social setting and background. It should also be reasonably clear why the problems developed and how they 'look' against a framework of normal development. Relevant intrinsic attributes of the child have been assessed. The problem is formulated usually in systemic terms, that is to say as it impinges on a *family or school system* rather than an individual alone.

The formulation provides a summary of the salient information collected: it is 'formulated' in the sense that the practitioner puts forward an 'explanatory story' (hopefully a valid one) to impose meaning on the data collected. It consists of a series of hypotheses which are statements about how the problem arose, when and where it occurs, and why it is maintained.

A particular skill is one of editing. It involves the identification of the *important* influences and *controlling* variables—among, potentially, so many—in order to plan an effective intervention. The principle of parsimony is helpful here; one invokes those causal factors that are sufficient to facilitate such an intervention. There is a balance between the wastefulness and risks of overinclusiveness (that is to say excessive complexity) and also of simplistic theorizing.

The trouble with the search for causal reasons is that there are several levels of explanation which may apply to a particular problem. This is illustrated by a young child who has a learning problem which is affecting her ability to read. On top of this, she has certain behavioural problems, as constant failure is causing her morale to sink lower and lower. Diagnostic tests carried out by the psychologist show that she has a visual–perceptual handicap. Remedial treatment is available to help her overcome her reading problem. The remedial teacher could teach her to recognize words and their meanings through the medium of her other sensory modalities. Here, the visual handicap is one explanation of the reading difficulty. Some clinicians would rest content with this level of causal explanation— the so-called *instrumental* level of explanation. The explanation is sufficiently precise to be instrumental in planning some therapeutic measures to mitigate the cause–effect sequence of events. Or it may simply be instrumental in providing the individual with a satisfactory ('Oh! That makes sense') rationale.

While this explanation provides an account of an important antecedent condition in the problem—in this case the visual-perception handicap— others might claim that the diagnostician should search for 'original' or 'deeper' causes. In this case they would feel it necessary to determine whether the visual problem is due to organic causes.

One way of reviewing some of the etiological influences in childhood on a broad canvas (detailed accounts for specific conditions appear in other chapters) is to look at a developmental–behavioural framework of assessment. This framework requires measures of behavioural, cognitive, and physiological responding as well as a determination of the social and cultural context within which the problem occurs. The strategy is to begin with a broad-based assessment of the child and his or her environment (e.g., family, school, peers) and then to obtain information regarding specific stimulus features, response modes, antecedents and consequences, severity, duration, and pervasiveness of the particular problems. The assessment utilizes a multimethod, problem-solving approach to obtain as complete a picture of the child and his or her family as possible, and one that generates a treatment plan.

Bromley (1986) describes the required steps for the explication of the individual case:

(1) State clearly the problems and issues.
(2) Collect background information as a context for understanding (1).
(3) Put forward *prima facie* explanations (conjectures/hypotheses) and solutions (programme formulation) with regard to the client's personality and predicament—on the basis of information available at the time, and on the basis of the *principle of parsimony*. Examine the simple and obvious answers first. They may, of course, have to be rejected if they don't stand up to critical examination. This provides a guide for the next stage.
(4) Search for further/additional evidence. New hypotheses/explanations will have to be formulated and examined.
(5) Search *again* for, and admit for consideration, sufficient evidence to eliminate as many of the suggested explanations (hypotheses) as possible; the hope is that one of them will be so close to reality as to account for all the evidence and be contradicted by none of it. The evidence may be direct or indirect; but it is vital that it should be admissible, relevant and obtained from competent and credible sources.
(6) Enquire critically into the *sources* of evidence, as well as the evidence itself. Bromley (1986) makes the point that in the case of personal testimony, this is analogous to cross-examinations in a court of law; otherwise it amounts to checking the consistency and accuracy of all items of evidence.
(7) Examine carefully the internal logic, coherence and external validity of the entire network of associations and hypotheses formulated to explain the client's predicament and proposals to solve the problems.
(8) Select the 'most likely' interpretation, provided it is compatible with the evidence. (Some lines of argument will be obviously inadequate whereas others will be possible or even convincing.)
(9) Work out the implications of your explanations for intervention/ treatment or some other action (or, indeed, inaction).

Always ask yourself about the implications (e.g. the risks involved) of making Type I as opposed to Type II errors in your assessment. Is it more damaging to your client if you risk Type I errors (i.e. asserting relationships falsely) than if you risk Type II errors, which deny relationships that do actually exist? The academic psychologist tends to minimize errors of incautious assertion at the expense of relatively common Type II errors. The clinician often acts on the basis of weakly supported propositions because of the dangers of ignoring potentially significant associations. But of course there may also by some risks in presuming relationships which do not have any basis in reality.

This step requires that you

(10) Work out the implications in *specific* terms.

Ultimately, the professional judgement of a client's behavioural/psycho-social/mental status is made in individual terms, taking into account his or her particular circumstances. It involves an estimate of the consequences that flow from the clients' specific thoughts, feelings and behaviours and general approach to life, with particular reference to their personal and emotional well-being, their ability to form and maintain social relation-ships, their ability to work effectively and (in the case of children) learn academically, and their accessibility to socialization.

The different stages of the ASPIRE process leading towards a formulation (described at the beginning of the chapter), involve a sometimes daunting array of practical choices, decisions, actions and caveats. Not infrequently, incoming data—sometimes as far forward in client contact time as the intervention—demands a reformulation and possibly a rethink of the therapeutic programme.

The assessment of causal influence should, in an ideal world, inform the choice of therapeutic strategy or some broader-based community inter-vention. Only too often the assessment data, like the occupants of Procrustes' bed, are made to fit the favoured therapeutic model. There is an implied suggestion that a particular approach can be applied to all problems. Sadly, faith, rather than evidence, is mostly what is on offer.

Chapter 3

CLINICAL PSYCHOLOGY: INTERVENTIONS

The task of helping a family—following a formulation of the causes and implications of their problems—can be a daunting one, encompassing a wide range of concerns stretching from, say, the need for day care for a child, developmental or marital counselling for parents, to systematic desensitization for a phobic child. The clinical psychologist's role can vary from case to case, including that of resource-mobilizer (which implies a knowledge of available facilities, also when and where to refer), adviser, teacher, therapist, counsellor and problem-solver.

Such diversification calls for a remarkably flexible professional response on the part of the practitioner; it also requires a clear-headed grasp of what goals are salient to the client. The scope of the analysis and level of intervention can also range widely, from the large grouping (the community) through the small group (the family), the couple (parents and partners) to the particular individual (say, child). It might also involve working with managers in monitoring policy, getting involved in planning and increasingly, of late, teaching other professionals (e.g. nurses, care staff) psychological skills where applicable to their work. The latter is of great significance. The number of children and adolescents requiring help is extremely large; the number receiving psychological therapy is relatively small.

Emotional and behaviour problems tend to be identified by parents and teachers. From home the child is likely to be referred to a general practitioner. There is likely to be a substantial proportion of cases (perhaps a quarter of child consultations with GPs) with a psychological component to the presenting problem. If the problem is serious the doctor will refer to a child and family psychiatric clinic either in the community or situated in a hospital department.

PROVISION OF SERVICES

Psychiatric Provision

Here is found a multidisciplinary team consisting of psychiatrists, psychologists, social workers and (in the London area) a psychotherapist.

Children with severe problems can be referred to a psychiatric day centre or to an in-patient unit. There are in-patient units specifically available for the treatment of pre-adolescent children, but also taking some adolescents of school age and older adolescents. There are also residential psychiatric units in England and Wales which cater specifically for adolescents. Regional adolescent teams also provide specialist back-up to other services (Hollin, Wilkie and Herbert, 1987).

Educational Provision

From school the child is likely to be referred to an educational psychology service. In some areas this service will be part of a multidisciplinary team, in others it may liaise with a hospital service (e.g., paediatric units). There is a wide range of special educational provision for children with emotional and behaviour problems, including tutorial classes, units for disruptive children (e.g. persistent truants), special day and residential schools for maladjusted children, and day and residential schools for autistic children.

Severe retardation in reading ability in children of normal intelligence is usually provided for in part-time remedial classes in ordinary schools. However, some local education authorities run separate remedial education units which children usually attend on a part-time basis.

Social Welfare Provision

There is also a range of social welfare provision for children with emotional and behavioural problems, especially intermediate treatment centres and community homes with education. Attendance at these facilities usually follows criminal or care proceedings in a juvenile court.

MOBILIZING HUMAN RESOURCES

Professional resources are not the only source of help. A psychologist can put his or her clients in touch with people, clubs and specialized self-help groups. As social networks, personal ties and contacts promote psychological well-being, it is important for the psychologist to identify their presence or absence for the client (see Brown and Harris, 1978). Intimate or close relationships of the type provided by primary groups (those people with whom one has face-to-face interaction and a sense of commitment) are the most significant sources of support (Brown and Harris, 1978). The supportiveness of relationships is reflected by the availability of:

- emotional support (the expression of liking, respect, etc.);
- aid (material assistance, services, guidance, advice);
- social companionship;
- affirmation (the expression of agreement);
- social regulation (appropriate role-related support such as mothering, fathering, partnership—husband/wife/companion, etc.).

COUNSELLING AND GIVING ADVICE

Counselling has, as its main aim, the production of constructive behavioural and attitudinal change. Such change emerges from a relationship of trust and confidentiality, one which emerges from empathetic non-judgemental conversations between the professionally trained counsellor and the client. Professionals have recently shown more interest in preparing couples for parenthood as a means of preventing later difficulties that flow from faulty child management (e.g. Hawkins 1972; Herbert, 1985b). This may be utopian but it does reflect a fruitful area of intervention (see Chapter 11) as is the counselling for parents following separation and/or divorce (Edelstein, 1998).

Crisis Counselling

Children are referred often to child and family psychiatric clinics at times of crisis for themselves and their families. Skilled counselling and/or therapy have been shown to be invaluable following traumatic situations such as surgery, bereavement, sexual abuse, divorce and increasingly, major disasters.

People are most susceptible to help during periods of rapid change, and adolescence is a period of transition and dramatic change. At times of crisis parents too, are particularly receptive to advice. Yet high on their list of complaints about professionals are failures of communication. These failures involve:

- insufficient information;
- inaccurate information;

- an indigestible overload of information at any one time;
- information that is difficult to comprehend because of technical jargon or poor presentation.

Of particular value to clients is the provision of the factual data or know-how about how to get access to information that helps them to make informed choices and decisions. There are many stages throughout parenthood during which well-founded psychological advice, developmental and personal counselling can help to alleviate distress and prevent the development of further difficulties. An example is pregnancy; some mothers-to-be can be shown to be at high risk of having a handicapped child. Sophisticated obstetric techniques (e.g. ultrasound scanning, amniocentesis, and various blood tests) contribute to screening for handicaps such as Down's syndrome, spina bifida, or anencephaly. Where a disability is detected, the mother may be offered a therapeutic termination of her pregnancy. Many women are not psychologically prepared to deal with the conflicts that surround these decisions and moral issues. The availability of psychological advice is likely to enhance the quality of the service being offered to them. This also applies where a couple already have a handicapped child: there is a need for genetic counselling and advice on appropriate contraception.

Hospitals have run antenatal classes for years. Parents appear to benefit from good preparation for labour and delivery. In addition to educating prospective parents about what to expect during labour, most classes teach some form of relaxation as an aid to delivery. There is evidence that systematic desensitization may be even more effective than general psychoprophylactic methods in shortening labour and lowering the intensity of pain (Kondas and Scentricka, 1972). A good preparation during pregnancy is associated with easier deliveries, the use of fewer drugs in labour, and fewer complications (Doering and Entwistle, 1975; McNeil and Kaij, 1977). A psychologist may know people who can offer objective, matter-of-fact information or guidance to the client. Giving clients an understanding of the *stages* of adaptation that follow particular crises (e.g. bereavement) can facilitate the restoration of personal equilibrium, especially when accompanied by a sympathetic hearing (Herbert, 1995; Worden, 1996).

A major theoretical and practical contribution by psychologists to the alleviation of suffering and solution of problems has been the development and evaluation of psychological therapies. They might include the child (seen alone) the parents and child (seen concurrently) or the family as a unit. The proponents of psychodynamic theories are likely to give priority to an exploration of the child's inner life, in the form of individual psychotherapy. Behaviour therapists might also opt for focused individual work on, say, a child's phobic fears. Those who still uphold the long-lived aphorism 'there are no problem children, only problem parents' (a myth that refuses to die!) would tend to inculpate parents as most in need of remediation by counselling or training. The skills deficit model which informs behaviour parent training is sometimes at risk of affirming this oversimplification.

THE EXPERT VS COLLABORATIVE MODEL

There is an important general consideration: the perspective, 'style' or model of help to be adopted. In the expert model the professionals view themselves as very much in charge because of their monopoly (or near-monopoly) of expertise, responsibility and therefore decision-making. The client is relatively passive as a recipient of advice, 'prescriptions' (about health or how to behave), or possibly therapy of one kind or another. At the other extreme clients (say parents) are viewed very much as consumers of the professionals' services, with the right to select what *they* believe is most appropriate to their needs. Decision-making is ultimately in the parents' control; professionals acting as consultants with negotiation and discussion playing a large part in the client–practitioner relationship. The formulation is very much a self-directed, demystified process.

In between, lies the collaborative or partnership model. Here the professionals perceive themselves as having expertise but sharing it and imparting it to parents and other non- or para-professionals so that *they* facilitate much of the training/therapy of the child.

Technical Therapeutic Input

There is an agnostic school of thought (the members tend to be eclectic) that is of the opinion that the technical claims of the diverse schools have never been adequately vindicated. Such a view, that there are minimal differences between therapeutic approaches with regard to outcome, is disputed by other researchers/practitioners—especially when it comes to *child psychotherapy* (Kazdin, 1988; Kolvin, *et al.*, Yule, 1989).

Nevertheless it is the kind of assumption put forward by Bergin and Lambert (1978), that led Jerome Frank (1973) in his book, *Persuasion and Healing,* to argue that the 'active ingredients'—the effective 'therapeutic processes'—are the same for all treatment paradigms. He identifies as the common components of all types of influence and healing: warmth, respect, kindness, hope, understanding, and the provision of 'explanations'. These attributes are stressed in the Rogerian client-centred literature and their effect is related to fairly global aspects of the client's well-being (e.g. self-esteem) (see Axline, 1947; Truax and Carkhuff, 1967).

Whether a trained professional has special access to these qualities (or some unique deployment of them) is thrown into doubt (surely even for those who give most weight to the relationship factor in therapy) by the absence of substantive differences in the results of professional as opposed to non- or para-professional therapists (Durlak, 1979).

The arguments and counter-arguments about effectiveness are confounded by individual differences in the therapeutic qualities and skills of therapists. In addition, some are antitherapeutic, indeed noxious, in their effects upon clients. Another difficulty arises from the sheer number of experimental comparisons that would be required if all of 230 alternative psychosocial treatments (an estimate by Kazdin, 1988, of what is available to children and adolescents) were to be evaluated.

It would be only too easy for the 'hardheaded' manager of clinical services, husbanding scarce resources, to dismiss the claims of child therapists as rhetoric. Where is the evidence that a massive injection of therapeutic (notably psychotherapy) services directed at children's problems would do anything to dent the prevalence rates? Which of the many available treatments—be they physical (pharmacological) or psychological—is most deserving of support? Are there 'horses for courses' in the sense that we can match specific therapies to particular problems? If so, is this confidence based on hard evidence rather than wishful thinking and special pleading? The issue of 'rigorous evaluation' in the ASPIRE process (page 13) is dealt with in excellent fashion by Berger (1996).

THE EFFECTIVENESS OF PSYCHOLOGICAL THERAPIES

Kazdin (1988) provides background reading on this topic. Reviews of multiple techniques bearing the superordinate title 'psychological therapy' or 'psychotherapy' (e.g. Hersen and Van Hasselt, 1987; Tuma, 1989; Weisz *et al.*, 1987) certainly suggest that *psychotherapy is better than no treatment* for a large number of childhood problems, including anxiety, hyperactivity, social withdrawal and aggression (see Kazdin, 1988 for an excellent review). This may be reassuring to know, even if it has to be hedged in with many reservations; but it is still far too crude and ambiguous a generalization. There is a more specific set of requirements which is put in the following way in Paul's much quoted question: '*what* treatment, by *whom*, is more effective for *this* individual with *that* specific problem, under *which* set of circumstances?' (Paul, 1967). We still cannot provide precise answers to this question posed over two decades ago; yet it continues to be relevant, especially if we maintain that psychotherapy is a general term that encompasses many different treatments.

VARIETIES OF TREATMENT

See Rutter, Taylor & Hersov (1994) for a background discussion on this topic.

The task of making a case for more resources, to increase the psychological input for children with problems, is not made easy (and this is also the case in adult work) when there are so many competing claims from so many different approaches, to be the true faith. There is also, often, an implied suggestion that a particular approach can be applied to all problems. Sadly, faith, rather than evidence, is mostly what is on offer to support the more Panglossian prospectuses.

What also tends to undermine confidence is the fact that there are considerable variations in the theoretical ideas that inform even similarly named treatments. Different theories of family processes generate different schools of family therapy (see Walsh, 1982; Vetere and Gale, 1987). Behavioural work is no longer a monolithic enterprise built upon a narrow reading of experimentally based learning theory.

Family Therapy (see Herbert, 1998b)

The family therapies applied to children's psychological problems have become 'a growth industry in contemporary Child and Family Centres' (Hoffman, 1995). In America, where family therapy has recently been recognized at the Federal level as a legitimate profession, there are some 17 000 therapists affiliated to the American Association of Marriage and Family Therapy and well over 300 family therapy training programmes. There is no one therapeutic entity one can refer to definitively as 'Family Therapy', but several schools or paradigms. For example, there is the structural school which has its roots in the 1960s work of Salvador Minuchin and his colleagues, originating in a residential institution for ghetto boys in New York (Minuchin, 1974). Strategic family therapy has its origins in the Palo Alto research group led by Gregory Bateson in the early 1950s—working, *inter alia*, on family communication as it affected schizophrenics (e.g. Bateson *et al.*, 1956). Humanistic, existential therapies of the 1960s, such as Gestalt therapy, psychodrama, client-centred therapy and the encounter group movement, influenced the theory and methods of various experiential family therapies—challenging the positivistic tenets of the more problem-focused schools of family therapy.

What unites most family therapists as they engage in their divergent treatment strategies is a perspective which requires that children's problems be understood as the consequence of the pattern of recursive behavioural sequences that occur in dysfunctional family systems. The goal of treatment is therefore the improvement of family functioning. The members are encouraged by a variety of therapeutic strategies and homework tasks, to understand the alliances, conflicts and attachments that operate within the family unit and to look at themselves from a fresh perspective and to seek alternative solutions to their dilemmas (see Family Life Map).

At the dependent variable end of the therapeutic equation, emphasis can be placed on symptom reduction/removal alone (called first-order change), or a more systemic level of family transformation (second order change) adopted. Second order change is empirically and conceptually difficult to identify and quantify. Bennun (1986) comments that 'if one assumes that systems constantly balance or calibrate themselves to maintain an equilibrium, one may question whether it is possible to obtain first-order change without the consequent second-order change'.

The technical elements in family therapy have been summarized by Dare (1985) as follows:

(1) making a direct contact with each family member in the meeting or joining;
(2) engaging children and adolescents;
(3) making the parent(s) feel respected and at ease;
(4) eliciting a detailed description of the presenting problem;
(5) facilitating direct interaction between family members;
(6) helping families develop new strategies to 'solve' their problems;
(7) drawing up a family tree;
(8) devising in-session tasks to facilitate realignment of family structure;
(9) devising between-session tasks;
(10) linking the formulation to appropriate interventions,

the therapeutic sequence might look something like this:

● *The joining stage.* The family and the therapist are originally isolated from each other, but the therapists use their skills to enable them to become absorbed into the family through a process of accommodation. This process creates a new system—family and therapist—which may take several sessions to create.

TIM: 22 months of age	ANNE: age 10 years	PETER: age 14 years	MOTHER: age 38	FATHER: age 45	GRANNY: age 66
LIFE TASKS	**LIFE TASKS**	**LIFE TASKS**	**LIFE TASKS**	**LIFE TASKS**	**LIFE TASKS**
• develop motor skills • develop self-control • elaborate vocabulary • explore his world – make 'discoveries'	• cope with academic demands at school (underachieving) • developing her sense of self • learn to be part of a team	• adjust to physical changes of puberty • and to sexual awareness • cope with the opposite sex (shyness) • deepen friendships (intimacy)	• review her life and commitments • adjust to loss of youth and (in her perception) 'looks' • cope with an adolescent as a patient and caring parent	• review commitments in mid-life • develop new phase in relationship with wife • face physical changes – some limitations on athletic/sexual activity	• deal with increasing dependence on others • come to terms with old age/death • cope with loss of peers
LIFE EVENTS	**LIFE EVENTS**	**LIFE EVENTS**	**LIFE EVENTS**	**LIFE EVENTS**	**LIFE EVENTS**
• parents insist on obedience now • adjust to temporary separations when mother goes to work • not the centre of attention and 'uncritical deference' as much as previously	• afraid to go to school (cannot manage maths and other subjects) • bullied by a girl in her class • jealous of attention Tim gets (calls him a spoiled brat) • worried about father's health	• worried about his skin (acne) and the smallness of his penis • has a girlfriend – his first • upset by his parents' quarrels • complains that his mother is always watching him	• coping with late child – an active toddler • has taken part-time job to relieve feeling of being trapped • feels guilty • bouts of depression • no longer enjoys sex	• threat of redundancy • high blood pressure • worried about drifting apart from his wife • had a brief affair • feels unattractive	• poor health • gave up home when bereaved (may have made a mistake!) • enjoys the little one, but • feels 'claustrophobic' with all the activity and squabbles
TODDLERHOOD	PREPUBESCENCE	ADOLESCENCE	MIDLIFE	MIDLIFE	RETIREMENT

Figure 5 Family life map

- *The middle therapy stage.* This is the phase during which the major restructuring 'work' occurs. Restructuring interventions are made during sessions and consolidating homework tasks are set between sessions.
- *The termination stage.* This phase tests the family's ability to 'fire' the therapist and do it themselves. The 'ghost' of the therapist is left behind by getting the family to simulate its ability to solve new problems and to deal with old problems if they recur.
- *The follow-up.* A follow-up session after three months, six months or a year enables the therapist to evaluate the impact of therapy and test whether it has been successful in achieving second-order change, which means enabling family rules and family functioning to change in such a way that the family generates effective solutions to problems.

When we come to techniques, there are dozens to choose from. Piercy *et al.* (1986) describe 54 technique skills for the major family therapies. This, perhaps, is the reason why the results of effectiveness in outcome studies of family therapy (where there are so many different levels of therapist expertise and mixed treatment packages) fail, so often, to generate firm conclusions. Among the methods used are:

- *Boundary clarification*—the creation or clarification of boundaries between family members is a feature of structural work. A mother who babies her teenager may hear with surprise her daughter's answer to the question 'How old do you think your mother treats you as—three or thirteen?'
- *Changing space*—i.e. asking clients in the therapy room to move about—can intensify an interaction or underline an interpretation being made about a relationship. For example, if a husband and wife never confront one another directly but always use their child as a mediator or channel of communication, the therapist blocks that manoeuvre (called triangulation) by ensuring that the child is not placed between the parents. Here the therapist may comment: 'Let's move James from the middle so you can work it out together.'
- *Reframing* is an important method in fulfilling the objective of helping clients change in a covert—less directed—manner. It is an alteration in the emotional or conceptual viewpoint in relation to which a situation is experienced. That experience is placed in another 'frame' which fits the facts of the situation as well (or more plausibly), thereby transforming its entire meaning. Giving people different 'stories' to tell themselves about themselves or about events—stories that are less self-defeating or destructive—is also a feature of behavioural work.

An example of the use of refraining with parents who abuse their children might be altering negative schema or attributions. There is a conceptual difficulty for some parents whose attributions reflect an axiom that assumes (at least in their own case) that 'there are no problem parents, only problem children'. Problematic behaviours are reified into entities which reside within the child. ('There's a little demon in him'; 'He's always trying to get at me'; 'It's his father's bad blood'.) The parents do not share, in any way, in the 'ownership' of the problem. Such a disengagement from any role in the child's negative behaviours can be risky for the child (punitive attitudes are encouraged); it is also very difficult to deal with clinically. It might be possible by means of reframing (cognitive restructuring) to modify such attributions—by encouraging parents to make 'connections' ('Do you see anything of yourself in your child's behaviour?' 'Were you like her at her age?'), and to think about behaviour sequentially and contingently.

Problems are not unidirectional; there is two-way traffic—powerful reciprocal influences in the interactions between parents and children. A family therapy perspective illuminates this fact. Behavioural and systems approaches to family therapy are often viewed as being incompatible. Despite their epistemological differences there are several significant similarities. Both approaches:

- focus on interactional rather than intrapsychic causation, i.e. how the problem behaviour of one person meshes with the behaviour of others;
- seek to discover regularities or repetitive sequences in interpersonal processes;
- emphasize observable behavioural events rather than unobservable subjective events;
- view the presenting problem as representative of broader classes of interactional patterns;
- utilize behaviour interventions aimed at changing dysfunctional patterns of interpersonal behaviour.

Dare (1985) concludes, on the basis of a review of outcome studies which involved children, that approaches which employed social learning theory and techniques, as well as a systems approach, were effective in reducing intra-familial behavioural problems (for example, aggressive behaviour in children) and in improving family interactions.

Behavioural Family Therapy (see Dadds, 1995)

During the late 1960s and early 1970s behaviour therapists established that parents could be taught to use behavioural principles to bring about positive change in the behaviour of their conduct-problem children (the subject of Chapter 11). The work of Gerald Patterson in Oregon was part of, and the inspiration for, a rapid proliferation of family-orientated research. In view of the relatively high levels of clinical effectiveness claimed for the approach it is necessary to elaborate the discussion on behavioural methods to be found in Chapter 5 by considering their application as a family therapy paradigm. This approach is in large part about the assessment and recruitment of naturally occurring environmental influences, specifically those occurring within the family between parents, siblings and child, in order to modify deviant behaviour and teach new skills and behaviour repertoires. Behavioural family therapy—as its name implies—tends to operate much more at a *systemic* level than parent training (Wahler, 1976) where the main emphasis is on the parent–child (which usually means the mother–child) dyad rather than the family. Being mainly home-based it reduces—in theory—the problem of generalizing improvements from the consulting room to the outside world. The issue of temporal generalization remains a difficult technical problem; nevertheless, parents and teachers— as primary mediators of change—are *in situ*—most of the time, and are in a position to apply contingencies and inductive methods of training, in a variety of situations and over the 'long haul' required especially in treating antisocial, aggressive children.

Parent Training (see Webster-Stratton and Herbert, 1993)

Parent training, on an individual or group basis, has proved a fruitful enterprise in work with families (see Patterson, 1982; Webster-Stratton and Herbert, 1994). This subject is dealt with in detail in Chapter 11.

The Behavioural Therapies (see Herbert, 1994b, 1998b)

Learning theories are aligned with behaviour modification (Ollendick and Hersen, 1984); cognitive theory with cognitive therapy (Brewin, 1988, Spence, 1994) and cognitive–behavioural theory with cognitive behaviour modification (Hollon and Beck, 1994). It would be overstating the case to suggest that there are clinical techniques which are the sole province of any one style of intervention: although it is fair to say that, depending on their theoretical view, practitioners use the techniques and explain their effects in very different ways. Clearly, learning processes do not sufficiently explain much abnormal behaviour, including anxiety disorders. At the tactical level of behavioural methods as techniques, the link between behavioural theory and the treatment methods of choice can be somewhat tenuous. For Erwin (1979) principles of learning serve a heuristic rather than a logical function in generating tactics for bringing about change.

Power (1991, pp. 22–23) argues that it is essential that behaviour therapy develops a sounder philosophical base that can genuinely represent the constructs with which skilled behaviour therapists work. He believes that the tacit philosophies that inform behaviour therapists at present are somewhat contradictory in nature. For example, he cites the combination of

> ... determinism (contingency of reinforcement plus learning history) and non-determinism (a causal role for mental states), reductionism (psychological states reducible to physiological ones) and non-reductionism (a causal role for mental states), associationism (belief in the traditional laws of learning) and constructivism (that attitudes or schemata alter perception).

Whatever the justice or overstatement of such comments, psychologists are still uncertain, for example, why *precisely* systematic desensitization is so successful. And this uncertainty persists despite many years of experimentation.

Fortunately, this state of affairs does not mean that a behavioural approach is valueless in such conditions. The approach can work without being tied to a theory about the origins of the behaviour. Indeed, it is one of the strengths of behavioural work that treatment does not necessarily depend (as we shall see) on the discovery and understanding of the historical causes of the problem. Indeed, some methods are like the use of aspirin, in that they are empirical rather than rational treatments. Aspirin tends to alleviate headaches of *various origins,* but it is not necessary to ascribe their success to a deficit in acetylsalicylic acid. Relaxation, incidentally, has been described with some justice (given its ubiquitous and benign applications) as 'behavioural aspirin'.

THE CHOICE OF PROCEDURES/TECHNIQUES

Procedures are chosen on the basis of one's knowledge of their therapeutic effects and acquaintance with the literature on the modification of particular problems (see Tables 6 and 7). The choice of therapeutic approach will depend not only on the nature of the target behaviour to be modified and the stimuli which maintain it, but also on the circumstances under which the child manifests the problem behaviour, and the aspects of the environment which are subject to the therapist's influence. There are two basic learning tasks that are commonly encountered in child therapy:

(1) the acquisition (i.e., learning) of a desired behaviour in which the individual is deficient (e.g. compliance, self-control, bladder and bowel control, fluent speech, social or academic skills);

(2) the reduction or elimination of an undesired response in the child's behavioural repertoire (e.g. aggression, temper tantrums, stealing, facial tics, phobic anxiety, compulsive eating) or the exchange of one response for another (e.g. self assertion in place of tearful withdrawal).

Each of these tasks may be served, as we have seen, by one or a combination of four major types of learning: (a) classical conditioning; (b) operant conditioning; (c) observational learning; and (d) cognitive learning. Furthermore, they can be analysed (and a therapeutic intervention planned) in terms of antecedent events, consequent events, organismic and self variables.

Methods for Increasing and Decreasing Behaviour

The methods shown in Table 6 are designed for the child (and sometimes parent or teacher) whose responses and/or skills are absent from his or her behavioural repertoire, or too weakly, or too inappropriately represented.

Behavioural methods for reducing unwanted, excess problems are described in Table 7. Violent, persistent temper outbursts constitute an *excess* problem. Extreme shyness would be an example of a *deficit* problem in, say, an adolescent boy or girl. An instance of *anomalous* behaviour is the uncontrollable utterance of obscene words—a problem associated with Gilles de la Tourette's syndrome.

Table 6   Methods for increasing behaviour

Procedure	Method
Positive reinforcement.	Present a positive stimulus (a rewarding event or object) following the desired behaviour.
Negative reinforcement.	Remove a stimulus (an aversive or noxious event) following the desired behaviour.
Contingency management in the token economy.	
Differential reinforcement (including discrimination training and method of successive approximations).	Reinforce appropriate behaviours in the presence of the S^D; leave them unreinforced in the setting of inappropriate circumstances, S^Δ
Provide an appropriate model.	Get someone suitable to model the desired behaviour.
Remove interfering conditions (e.g. aversive stimuli).	Remove stimuli that are incompatible (interfere) with the desired behaviour.
Stimulus control and change (including cueing and prompting).	Determine (or develop) appropriate discriminative stimuli for the desired behaviour.

Table 7 Methods for reducing behaviour

Procedure	Method
Extinction.	Withhold reinforcement following inappropriate behaviour.
Stimulus change.	Change discriminative stimuli (remove or change controlling antecedent stimuli).
Punishment.	Present mildly aversive/noxious stimuli contingent upon (following) inappropriate behaviour.
Time out from positive reinforcement (TO).	Withdraw reinforcement for X minutes following inappropriate behaviour.
Response-cost (RC).	Withdraw X quantity of reinforcers following inappropriate behaviour.
Overcorrection	Client makes restitution plus . . .
Positive reinforcement:	
(a) Reinforcing incompatible behaviour (RIB)	Reinforce behaviour that is incompatible with the unwanted one.
(b) Differential reinforcement of other behaviours (DRO).	Reinforce behaviour other than the undesired one on a regular schedule.
Skills training	Various approaches.
(e.g., behaviour rehearsal).	Simulate real-life situation in which to rehearse the child's skills and to improve them.
Gradual exposure to aversive stimuli (e.g., desensitization).	Expose child gradually to feared situation while secure and relaxed.
Avoidance (e.g., covert sensitization).	Present (*in vivo* or in imagination) to-be-avoided object with aversive stimulus.
Modelling.	Demonstrate behaviour for child to copy.
Role-playing.	Script a role so client can rehearse behaviour and/or a situation.
Cognitive control (cognitive restructuring including problem solving).	Teach alternative ways of perceiving, controlling, solving problems.
Self-control training.	Various approaches.

The treatment of 'neurotic' and stress disorders is likely to occur in the clinic, although there is nothing absolute about such a demarcation. These problems tend to be of relatively short-term duration. Although the distinction between treatment and training is, at times, indistinct, the training model is most appropriate to the longer-term disorders and handicaps of childhood. These problems (and others) tend to be dealt with in interpersonal or transactional (systemic) terms these days, using comprehensive, multi-modal treatment packages, rather than as isolated bits of childish behaviour on which to focus one's techniques. I return to this theme in Part Four.

Part II   AGE-RELATED PROBLEMS

A feature of much problem behaviour in childhood is its transitoriness. So mercurial are some of the changes of behaviour in response to the rapid growth and successive challenges of childhood, that it is difficult to pinpoint the beginning of serious problems. According to a long-term American longitudinal study (Macfarlane, Allen and Honzik, 1954), the problems which decline in frequency with age are elimination (toilet training) problems, speech problems, fears, and thumb sucking. Problems such as insufficient appetite and lying reach a peak early and then subside. Many problems show high frequencies around or just before school-starting age, then decline in prevalence and later rise again at puberty. Among these are restless sleep, disturbing dreams, physical timidity, irritability, attention demands, over-dependence, sombreness, jealousy and, in boys, food-finickiness. Only one 'problem' increases systematically with age—nail-biting. This habit reaches a peak and begins to subside only near the end of adolescence. Among the problems which show little or no relationships to age is oversensitiveness.

THE STABILITY OF PROBLEM BEHAVIOUR

It is difficult to make confident statements with regard to longer-term prediction as there have been too few methodologically sound studies. Follow-back designs are the most common but they can be somewhat unreliable in their inferences: they involve methodological weaknesses which limit the conclusions researchers can safely make (see Yarrow, Campbell and Burton, 1968).

Generally, estimates of the continuity of preschool behavioural dysfunction vary according to the definition of dysfunction, and the age, sex, and/or environment of the child. Specific behavioural problems, symptoms, or disorders appear to vary in their rates of continuity and extent of prediction of later behavioural outcomes. Predictions become more unreliable as the period separating predictor and outcome increases. At best, preschool behavioural dysfunction exhibits low correlations with outcomes in late adolescence or adulthood, low to moderate correlations with outcomes during early adolescence, and moderate correlations with outcomes at school entry.

Recent evidence from prospective studies suggests that although many problem behaviours are *transient*, children who develop *significant* behaviour problems during the preschool period are more likely to exhibit problems at a later stage. For instance, Richman, Stevenson and Graham (1982) concluded that 61% of problematic 3-year-olds still displayed significant difficulties on a clinical rating at age 8 years. Chazan and Jackson (1974) found that 42.5% of children rated as poorly adjusted on entering school also presented with behaviour problems at around 7 years of age.

The relatively high prevalence rate for behavioural dysfunction during the preschool period is suggestive of management problems for parents and caregivers—an area in which psychologists can provide empirically based advice. To establish the developmental significance of such problems, one needs to investigate the demands (referred to by theorists as developmental tasks) that put a heavy burden on children's adjustive skills or coping strategies (be they handicapped or not) as they make progress toward maturity. The newborn infant (to take one example) is said to need to develop a sense of trust and later, a growing capacity for independence. A lasting sense of trust, security, confidence or optimism (as opposed to distrust, insecurity, inadequacy or pessimism) is thought to be based upon affection, a degree of continuity of care-giving and the reasonably prompt satisfaction of the infant's needs. Some parents may be too immature or too preoccupied by personal problems to manage this.

DEVELOPMENTAL TASKS

These are tasks which arise at a certain period of life of an individual, successful achievement of which lead to a sense of satisfaction or achievement, and to more likely success with later tasks; failure leads to distress, disapproval by society and difficulty with later tasks. Among the tasks I will be examining are the following:

(1) becoming attached to caregivers;
(2) learning to talk;
(3) learning control over elimination;
(4) developing self-control (e.g. over aggressive outbursts);
(5) restraining sexual inclinations;
(6) developing moral attitudes';
(7) mastering social and other life-skills;

(8) adjusting to school;
(9) mastering academic competencies;
(10) becoming increasingly independent, self-directed.

The developmental tasks postulated by Erikson (1965) centre very much on attitudes and behaviour that feed into the child's evolving personality, and more particularly his or her sense of identity.

Behaviour problems may be apparent immediately after birth, stemming from prenatal or perinatal complications of one kind or another. They may appear in infancy, taking the form of feeding or sleeping difficulties or excessive crying, reflecting biological dysfunction and/or deficiencies in the care babies receive, *or* the sheer absence of affection. Problems may emerge during the preschool years, reflecting emotional and social difficulties such as fears, excessive temper tantrums or shyness. In any particular case they are likely to reflect the influence of psychosocial factors interacting with inborn factors of the kind described in the previous chapter.

The question is often asked whether trauma, privations and deprivations that occur in the early stages of development are persistent in their effects and therefore of predictive significance? If so, does this indicate a fundamental 'weakness' (a vulnerability) created in the child, such that adverse experiences give rise to disproportionate psychological difficulties later in life. Does a child's early status forecast later adolescent, even adult, maladjustment?

Our knowledge base is as yet limited. This is not surprising in view of the methodological difficulties inherent in the longitudinal studies which are required to provide credible results. Such studies are time consuming and expensive and therefore relatively rare.

The implications for the provision of services are considerable. If early problems are not generally transient but do have predictive significance then intervention at an early stage could be effective in preventing or mitigating subsequent difficulties. It is important to identify the kinds of problem that are most likely to persist and the conditions that are conducive to maintaining them, if one is going to target interventive action more effectively. This raises issues regarding children's capacity for coping, their flexibility and adaptability. There is surprising variability in children's (and, for that matter, parents') response to stress. Some individuals are completely overcome by circumstances which leave others relatively unscathed.

RESILIENCE VS VULNERABILITY (see Rutter, 1990)

The question formulated in the earlier stress literature was as follows: 'what makes for a vulnerable child?' Of late this question has been turned on its head in the following manner: 'what makes for a resilient child?' At one time attention focused exclusively on victims—those children who succumbed to deprivation, maltreatment, neglect and other life stresses. Later it became apparent that not every materially deprived child—to take a well-researched example—becomes an affectionless character. As clinical impressions and anecdotal evidence gave way to empirical studies it became apparent that the *probability* of psychological pathology in institutionalized children is greater than it is in family-reared individuals. This modification of the stark 'either – or' claims of the early maternal deprivation literature (see Rutter, 1981b) parallels the situation that exists with respect to contemporary theories about other pathogenic stress factors. Their impact is moderated by many social and personal factors.

We cannot predict with certainty that a particular child will develop this or that disorder merely from a knowledge of his or her history; the moderating variables have to be added to the predictive formula before one can anticipate who will succumb and who will survive. It is the search for these other factors that increasingly occupies those concerned with children's reactions to stresses of various kinds, and it is their efforts that I will be discussing in subsequent chapters (see Chapter 13 in particular). There are, on the one hand, biological and psychosocial factors that make some individuals particularly susceptible; on the other hand there are protective influences that serve a differing function. They may be 'inside' the child (easy or difficult temperament, easy or difficult birth, good or poor health, and so forth) or 'outside' the child (e.g. cohesive or dysfunctional family, secure or insecure upbringing).

By and large it is a combination of biological and social factors that is most successful in differentiating children according to vulnerability (Werner and Smith, 1977). In the Werner and Smith study, a longitudinal investigation to which I shall return, birth complications were consistently related to later impaired physical and psychological development, but *only* when combined with persistently poor environmental circumstances. The authors stress, however, that one should not underestimate the self-righting tendencies within the make-up of children: they produce normal development in all but the most intractable adverse circumstances.

INFLUENCES ON DEVELOPMENT (see Hay, 1994; Sylva, 1994)

As a biosocial organism the child's development can be impaired by inherited and/or acquired biological defects, as well as harmful psychosocial experiences. The impact of maturational factors, those neurophysiological and biochemical changes which are a function of time and age, are so complex and many-sided that a book like this cannot hope to do the subject justice. What I can offer is a 'broad canvas' of what I believe to be important.

Maturational changes are in the direction of ever greater complexity and are qualitative shifts which allow a structure to begin functioning or to function at progressively higher levels. The disruption of such processes can have devastating effects on a child's well-being, and, in turn, the parents' peace of mind. In looking at some of these influences the logical place to begin, therefore, is at the very beginning, 40 weeks before the birth.

Genetic Influences (see Rutter *et al.*, 1990a and b)

From the moment of conception—the entry and fusion of the father's spermatozoon with the ovum produced by the mother—the new individual takes possession of a genetic blueprint containing all the information that determines the genetic aspects of development for the rest of his or her life. From conception on, the child's inherited capacities *interact* with influences emanating from the environment (the first being the mother's womb) to produce a complete and unique human being.

The mechanism of heredity is remarkably reliable, and the vast majority of infants are born within the normal range of variation. The basic chemical structure of the chromosomes appears to be particularly stable. However, genetic errors do sometimes occur and they take many different forms. The cause of abnormalities in the inherited material may be a defect of the genes or of the chromosomes as a whole. These are discussed in Chapter 9. Other more general aspects are dealt with in relation to particular mental health problems and their genetic component.

Physical Growth

Growth and development are not necessarily smooth, continuous processes; in the early months of life weight and height increase rapidly, followed by a constant rate of increase until puberty when there is another growth surge (see Tanner, 1978). Body proportions also change considerably from birth to adulthood. A newborn infant has a large head which reflects the early development of the brain as compared with other body tissues.

Tanner (1978) urges caution when measurements of growth and development are interpreted. It is important that they are looked at with reference to a *normal range* so that reliable deductions about the individuals well-being can be made. It is necessary to distinguish between *normal* and *average*. Growth is monitored from serial measurements, a single measurement only being useful if it is clearly abnormal. It is useful to know the average weight of a one-year-old, the average age at which a child walks unaided. However it is also vital to know how far from average a measurement can deviate and yet remain within what is considered the range of what is normal (for example two standard deviations from the mean).

Despite the potential hazards, the vast majority of babies emerge into the world as reasonably intact beings. The total incidence of fairly serious malformations—abnormalities of structure—due to faulty intrauterine developments is variously estimated at between 1½% and 2% of all births.
It remains a moot question as to whether, and to what extent, maternal stress can convey itself to the unborn child, that is, to a degree that has long-term adverse consequences. Much of the work on the relationship between maternal attitudes and emotions and *significant* effects on the child-to-be is beset by serious methodological problems which make it difficult to arrive at confident generalizations (Joffe, 1968).

Perinatal Influences

In any analysis of causes (for a case history) particular attention is paid to the vital period before and after birth: the perinatal period, as it is called. The term *perinatal* applied to causal influences refers to those that arise between the 28th week of pregnancy and the end of the first week after birth. Causes in this time-frame are often those associated with prematurity.

What emerges from cross-cultural studies of varied perinatal practice is that human beings are remarkably adaptable. It is this adaptability which has enabled the human species to survive and thrive in all sorts of situations. When it comes to making decisions about arrangements for birth and early child care, the primary consideration should be the safety and well-being of mother and baby. There is no need for mothers to feel anxious lest this or that practice will have dire psychological effects for years to come. Contrary to a variety of strongly held beliefs, there is no clear-cut evidence that events around and soon after the time of birth can readily or seriously either distort the development of the infant's personality or interfere with the growth of maternal love and attachment. The lack of empirical evidence has not deterred the 'experts' from being prescriptive, not to say dogmatic, with mothers.

There are discontinuities between childhood and maturity—attributes in maturity which could not have been predicted from a knowledge of the young child. For normal children, personal characteristics and, indeed, most areas of behaviour, do not begin to crystallize or stabilize until the early school years are reached. And even then, only moderate correlations (associations) with adult behaviours emerge.

Prematurity (see Lukeman and Melvin, 1993)

Prematurity is a rather imprecise concept. Infants who weigh less than 2000 g (4½ lb) are referred to as 'low birthweight' babies. Those who are born prematurely—i.e., after a short prenatal period—are known as 'short-gestation period' babies. Babies who are small considering the duration of their gestation are called 'small for dates'.

Generally speaking, this last group gives rise to most concern, but all infants who are born prematurely are likely to have some developmental delay compared with non-premature babies, at least in the first year of life. With proper care, many catch up the lost ground by the time they start attending school. However, modern technology is keeping ever smaller, more vulnerable preterm infants alive—with the possible consequence of short- and longer-term developmental difficulties.

Prematurely born infants are particularly susceptible to brain injury during birth. The skull does not provide as effective a protection to brain-tissue as is provided in the case of an infant born at full term. Serious nervous system injuries may occur. Pressure during birth may cause the fracture of bones. Should this happen in the vicinity of nerve centres, there may be temporary or permanent injury to some of them, or to the sense organs, particularly the ears and eyes. Babies who are of low birth weight for their gestational age (more than two standard deviations below the mean) are found to have more abnormalities of the nervous system than the normal population. Prematurity at birth is correlated with various later complications such as excessive distractibility, hypersensitivity to sound, personality disturbance and reading difficulties (Pasamanick and Knoblock, 1961).

The complexity of disentangling cause and effect from the masses of correlations in the literature is illustrated by the range of problems associated with prematurity. They include primiparity, maternal age, malnutrition, multiple births, vaginal bleeding, prolonged rupture of membranes, habitual abortion, previous history of infertility, acute infections, and toxaemia during pregnancy. If we consider only the last of the factors—toxaemia—we find that cases involving behaviour problems reveal a greater incidence of this complication of pregnancy in their antenatal histories than control cases (Herbert, 1974).

Leaving aside the psychological ramifications of being born, there is little doubt that the birth process is the most hazardous single event in a person's life. Many factors can affect the outcome. The neonate may show acute signs of distress, the effects varying according to the duration and difficulty of birth. Physicians in the delivery room usually make a rapid assessment of the newborn, using the so-called Apgar score named after the anaesthetist Virginia Apgar. A numerical value from 0 to 2 is assigned to each of five dimensions:

- heart rate;
- respiration;
- muscle tone;
- response to stimulation;
- skin colour.

Scores range from the perfect 10 to the very low scores (3 or 4) usually associated with intensive care for the infant. Less than perfect, middle-range scores may require further investigation.

Babies who are in a very poor condition after birth take a long time to give their first cry, and subsequently develop distressed breathing or convulsions, and are at some risk of slow development later on. The seriousness of their difficulties can be gauged by the length of time they require special care; over three or four days would indicate a matter of serious concern. Fortunately most, on recovery, will develop normally.

Complications in the process of being born that may result in damage to the central nervous system include:

- a difficult passage through the birth canal (prolonged/precipitate);
- delivery by instruments;
- breech delivery (where the foetal head is the last part of the body to emerge;
- accidental twisting of the umbilical cord.

Each of these complications can disrupt the supply of vital oxygen to the brain ('anoxia'), the resulting degree of damage depending on the duration of oxygen starvation. The Ancient Chinese, with their aphorism 'difficult birth, difficult child' were aware of the psychological sequelae of birth complications. Several studies (e.g., Pasamanick and Knoblock, 1961) have highlighted in the correlations between complications of pregnancy and birth and behaviour disorders in later childhood.

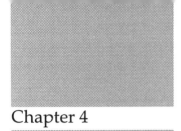

Chapter 4

PROBLEMS ASSOCIATED WITH INFANCY

The period discussed in this chapter will be taken to be from birth to approximately 18 months. So much happens to the infant in this time-span, he or she is so dramatically transformed in physical appearance and psychosocial skills from the somewhat amorphous neonate (that was) to a distinct personality of a year-and-a-half, that it seems naive to treat infancy as a unified period. The justification for doing so is the extent of the dependency of human infants during this time, and the implications this has in terms of the ability to enhance development, which is in the gift of their caregivers. The converse, of course, is the power to disrupt development.

Erikson (1965) regards early personality development as a series of stages in the development of patterns of reciprocity between the *self* and *others*. At each stage a conflict between opposite poles of this relationship has to be resolved. These are psychosocial events in the sense that they represent biological developmental processes interacting with facilitative or hindering influences in the environment, notably the family. There is potentially a sense of identity 'crisis' between trust and mistrust, confidence and doubt, initiative and guilt, and other crucial attitudes which the child will internalize as he or she grows up. Although the stages are described as if the two alternatives are complete opposites. Erikson would see persons occupying positions between the extremes, depending on the persons with whom, and situations in which, they are interacting. Generally, however, they would tend to show a predominance of one attitude if they'd been exposed to certain kinds of experience.

Danziger (1971) sees a connection between these bipolar pairs and Piaget's concepts of *assimilation* and *accommodation* (Piaget, 1953). The basic biological impetus of all living beings to adapt, by modifying the self and modifying the environment, is reflected in two interrelated processes: *Assimilation* involves a person's adjustment of the environment to him/herself, and represents the individual's use of his/her environment as he/she perceives it. *Accommodation* is the converse of assimilation and involves the impact on the individual of the actual environment itself. To accommodate is to perceive and to incorporate the experience provided by the environment as it actually is. One might say that 'mature' social development is the achievement of a balance between assimilation and accommodation, as between one's self-centred needs and an altruistic concern for others. Another way of putting this is that healthy personality development and satisfactory social relationships can be described in terms of a balance between the child's need to make demands on others, and his/her ability to recognize the demands which others ask of him or her.

At the very foundation of normal development is the child's emotional tie to his/her parents and their bonding to him/her. Erikson (1965) proposes that the essential task of infancy is the development of a basic trust in others. He believes that during the early months and years of life, a baby learns whether the world is a good and satisfying place to live, or a source of pain, misery, frustration and uncertainty. Because human infants are so totally dependent for so long, they need to know that they can depend on the outside world.

The development of a sense of trust in the world, derived from parental affection and the prompt satisfaction of need, is a major task. Mistrust and a sense of insecurity are therefore the emotional problems which, potentially, have their origins in the neglect of children's needs during this phase of life. If parents are rejecting and neglectful, the child may see the world not as a manageable and benign place, but as threatening and insecure.

VARIETIES OF PARENTING

See Sluckin & Herbert (1986); Schaffer (1996) for further reading on this topic.

It is useful to draw a distinction between generalized caregiving behaviour and specific parental behaviour. Adult human beings tend to exhibit some degree of caregiving towards young children in general. Women and men often act as temporary substitute (parents) carrying out this role most effectively. In contrast, *parental behaviour* is concerned with caring specifically for one's own, or one's adopted children. It implies parental feelings of love and an affectional attachment by parents to their children. In our society it is generally agreed that parents have the prime responsibility for meeting the basic physical and emotional needs of their children by caring for them. These responsibilities are shared with others but the extent to which others are allowed to intervene is limited. To complicate matters, the term 'parent' contains at least three components:

- *Birth-parents* give the child life, physical appearance, intellectual potential and certain personality characteristics and special talents.
- *Legal parents* carry responsibility for the child's maintenance, safety and security, and make decisions about the child's residence, education, medical treatment and so on.
- *Parenting parents* provide the day-to-day love, care, attention and discipline.

The establishment of responsive, sensitive parenting fuelled by an affectional bond between parent and child is perhaps the most critical foundation on which all social training is based (see also Hoffman, 1970). Rejection of the child, for whatever reason and at whatever level, is therefore likely to have far-reaching and harmful effects.

Responsibility as parents goes hand in hand with parental responsiveness (that is, caring attitudes) toward a child. More than the protection and nurturance of a helpless infant is at stake. There is also further responsibility—the all-important transmission of culture. This cannot be left to chance. The welfare of the individual and the continuity of the culture depend upon there being a satisfactory means of inducting the new generation into society's mores, attitudes and skills and to ensure that they, in turn, will satisfactorily hand on the culture and assume the role of another generation of parents.

The interactions between parents and children (particularly the early ones involving communication between mother, mother-figure and baby) are of crucial significance in the child's development (Hinde, 1979). Personal factors can interfere with these intricate processes. To take the extreme case: a mother suffering from depression may find it difficult to 'tune in' to her child in a sufficiently sensitive manner to be able to construct with him or her a mutually beneficial and stimulating sequence of interactions (e.g. Cohn and Tranick, 1983).

Parenting is made up of a series of far-from-simple skills, part commonsense, part intuition and part empathy, the ability to see things from another's point of view. An assessment of caring parenthood might take account of the following provision:

- safety
- shelter
- space (which includes space to play, and, particularly in older children, privacy)
- food
- income
- physical care
- health care.

In addition to basic survival functions, responsible parents meet vital psychosocial needs, including the child's requirements of

- love
- security
- attention
- new experiences
- acceptance
- education
- praise.

Infant care practices are subject to fashions, not to say fads. It has been generally assumed that it matters a great deal how the infant is handled, and that unless it is handled correctly, its future could be blighted. The plain fact is that, despite much study, there is little hard evidence concerning the relationship between specific early child-rearing practices and subsequent personality development. Thus, we do not really know how early breast feeding and bottle feeding compare as regards their psychological consequences, or whether indeed, they make any difference. Likewise, we cannot be sure whether on-demand feeding is, or is not, better than feeding at fixed intervals, and we do not know whether early or late weaning makes a difference to the child's personality development. Indeed, the evidence suggests that one of the crucial features of child rearing is the general social climate in the home—the attitudes, expectations and feelings of the parents which provide the backdrop to the specific methods of child care and training which they use. Mothers who do what they and the community to which they belong *believe* is right for the child are the best mothers.

It is not only in infant care that we find cultural variations: child care practices with older children have varied throughout history and vary a great deal at the present time (Aries, 1973; Liddiard, 1928). It is important for the practitioner to remember that ethnocentricity in clinical practice can lead to much individual suffering if methods offend against cherished cultural and/or religious beliefs. Notwithstanding variations in family pattern and style of parenting, all societies seem to be broadly successful in the task of transforming helpless, self-centred infants into more or less self-supporting, responsible members of their particular form of community. Indeed, there is a basic preparedness on the part of most infants to be trained— that is, an inbuilt bias toward all things social (Stayton, Hogan and Ainsworth, 1971). The baby responds (for example) to the mother's characteristic infant-orientated overtures in a sociable reaction. He or she also initiates social encounters with vocalizations or smiles directed to the mother which cause her in turn to smile back and to talk to, tickle or touch him or her. In this way she elicits further responses from the baby. A chain of mutually rewarding interactions is thus initiated on many occasions (Schaffer and Collis, 1986). Parents and child learn about each other in the course of these interactions; they develop attachments.

Schaffer and Collis (1986) observe that

> . . . it is curious that reciprocal influence suffered so long from neglect as a topic of empirical investigation, as even extreme environmentalist theories of development involve two-way processes. For example, Skinnerian principles imply, on the one hand, that the behaviour of the child is conditioned by virtue of contingent responsiveness on the part of the parent . . . and on the other hand that parental behaviour can be conditioned by virtue of contingent responsiveness on the part of the child.

However, as Hinde (1979) makes clear, the principle of two-way responsiveness goes beyond the boundaries of conditioning theory. It is the essence of *social interaction* that individual X does something to individual Y who in return does something back to X and so on and on. What happens as one point of the interaction influences subsequent interactions between X and Y and probably also the interactions of X and Y with other individuals.

A few studies have indicated that the mother's attitudes, measured before the child's birth, can affect mother–child interaction. Positive attitudes toward infants have been found to be related to maternal responsiveness to the baby's crying and to his or her social behaviour in the early months of life. Mothers who are highly anxious during the pregnancy have also been evaluated as having less satisfactory interactions with their babies at eight months than mothers who had been low in anxiety (see Robson and Powell, 1982, for a review of studies).

PARENTAL BONDING

Much of the thinking about bonding has been preoccupied with maternal attachment, and it has been influenced by, and confused with, research into attachment between the infant and mother. In this work, *proximity seeking* has commonly been utilized to index attachment; not surprisingly it also finds its way into key measures of maternal attachment. Behaviours which imply close contact, such as smiling, face presentations, cuddling, kissing, vocalizing, and prolonged gazing, are taken as indices of bonding. Research workers have tended to focus specifically on the mother's behaviour (for example, touching, cuddling), recording the amount of time spent in such activities, and in doing so, they have neglected the contribution of the other member of the dyad—the infant. To parody that old song 'It takes two to tango', it takes two to interact and bond.

Babies' response to their world is much more than a simple reaction to their environment. They are actively engaged in attempts to organize and structure their world. Parents are not the sole possessors of power and influence within the family. What is being suggested is that inter-actional sequences of mother–child, child–mother behaviours are likely to provide a better measure of the parent–infant relationship than a one-sided account. The notion of a dialogue (or 'conversation') between two individuals has been used as an indicator of the quality of attach-ments and gives rise to a definition of 'good' relationships expressed in terms of the reciprocity of interactions between the partners. Both mother and child are active concurrently, each for part of the time. The 'good' mother is *responsive* to her baby and continues to respond until she is satisfied; she also *initiates* activity with her infant (that is to say, she is *proactive!*).

Maternal Bonding

According to the American paediatricians, Klaus and Kennell (1976), the intimate mother–infant contact in the postpartum sensitive period gives rise to a host of innate behaviours; in their own words, 'a cascade of reciprocal interactions begins between mother and baby (which) locks them together and mediates the further development of attachment'. Such 'bonding' implies a special and focused relationship towards the mother's own offspring. But what is the quality of specialness? One cri-terion might be the mother's own report of her attitudes and feelings towards the infant. Indeed, interviews and self-rating scales have been used to this purpose. The mother is adjudged 'attached' to the infant if she consistently, over an extended period of time, reports that she loves her child, feels responsible for it, and has a sense of their mutual belong-ing. Conversely, the markers for an absence of bonding might be mater-nal reports of detachment, indifference or hostility towards the baby, and of having a sense of the child being a 'stranger', or separate from her emotionally.

Observers might be more impressed by a mother's behaviour than by her rhetoric. By this token, a mother would be considered to be 'bonded' to her infant if she looked after him or her well (being aware of the child's needs and responding to them), gave him or her considerable and consid-erate attention, and demonstrated her love in the form of 'kissing, cud-dling, and prolonged gazing'.

Mother-to-infant attachment is usually inferred, in the scientific literature on bonding, from *observations* of just such behaviour, and additionally smiling, vocalizing, touching and face presentations. The trouble with these indices is that they belong to a range of so-called 'infant-elicited social behaviours' which are not only displayed naturally by caregivers, almost at a level of unawareness, but also by many strangers. They tend to occur together in one co-ordinated package. The mother performs a facial display, while vocalizing, while gazing, and within the framework of a discrete head movement coupled with a face presentation.

Mother-to-Infant Attachment

Put briefly, the maternal bonding theory proposed that in some mammalian species, *including our own,* mothers become bonded to their infants through close contact (e.g. skin-to-skin) during a short critical period, soon after birth. This is an awesome claim considering that no other adult human behaviour, and a complex pattern of behaviour and attitude at that, is explained in such 'ethological' terms. To spell it out, the suggestion is that sensory stimulation from the infant soon after its delivery is essential if the mother is to fall in love with her baby. During the critical hours following birth, tactile, visual and olfactory stimulation of the mother by her baby is thought to be particularly significant.

The close-contact, critical-period bonding theory is said to be justified on two grounds (see Klaus and Kennell, 1976). One is rooted in studies of animal behaviour. The ethological support for the bonding doctrine, derived from early experiments with ewes and goats (olfactory imprinting) has not stood the test of time. Nor has evidence from human longitudinal studies comparing mothers who, after giving birth to a baby, have either been separated from it or have been allowed extended skin-to-skin contact with it, supported a 'sensitive' period, 'ethological' explanation. The impact of the doctrine upon the thinking of practitioners in obstetric, paediatric and social work fields has been considerable, particularly in relating bonding failures (allegedly due to early separation experiences) to serious problems such as child abuse.

These clinical applications have also been challenged (see Herbert and Sluckin, 1985; Sluckin, Herbert and Sluckin, 1983). It seems more likely that exposure learning, different forms of conditioning, imitation and cultural factors, all influence the development of mother-to-infant (and, indeed, father-to-infant) attachments and involve a process of learning gradually to love an infant more strongly—a process characterized by ups and downs, and one which is often associated with a variety of mixed feelings about the child.

INFANT-TO-PARENT ATTACHMENT

We can only speak of a child as a person when he or she becomes aware of her/himself as a separate individual, a social being. Later, to become a person in their own right, they must detach themselves, at least in part, from their mother's protective cocoon and develop a point of view of their own. Like a spaceship which has to force itself out of the earth's gravitational pull in order to make its journey, children must move out of safe orbit around their mothers and strike out to find their own place in the world.

By about four months old, infants generally behave in much the same friendly way towards people as they did earlier, but will react more markedly to their mother. They will smile and coo and follow her with their eyes more than they will other people. But although they may be able to recognize her, the bond has not yet developed which makes them behave in such a way as to maintain close proximity *to her in particular*— the real meaning of attachment. Attachment behaviour is best demonstrated when the mother leaves the room and the baby cries or tries to follow her; it is also evident when not just anyone can placate the infant. At six months about two thirds of babies appear to have a close attachment to their mothers, indicated by separation protests of a fairly consistent sort. Three quarters of babies are attached by nine months. This first attachment is usually directed at the mother, and only very occasionally towards some other familiar figure.

During the months after children first show evidence of emotional bonds, one quarter of them will show attachment to other members of the family, and by the time they are a year and a half old, all but a few children will be attached to at least one other person (usually the father), and often to several others (usually older children). The formation of additional attachments progresses so rapidly in some infants that multiple attachments occur at about the same time. By one year of age the majority of children will show no preference for either parent, and only a few retain their mother-centredness. Schaffer (1977) writes that the child, by his first birthday:

> ... has learned to distinguish familiar people from strangers, he has developed a repertoire of signalling abilities which he can use discriminatively in relation to particular situations and individuals, and he is about to acquire such social skills as language and imitation. Above all, he has formed his first love relationship: a relationship which many believe to be the prototype of all subsequent ones, providing him with that basic security which is an essential ingredient of personality.

INFANT ATTACHMENT PATTERNS

Each individual infant can be assessed for the quality of attachment to the parent. This is based on the infant's behaviour in the Ainsworth 'strange situation': throughout pre-separation, separation and reunion with the parent. The final assessment of infant to parent attachment can be described using four broad categories of the infant's response to the presence and absence of the mother (adapted from Ainsworth *et al.*, 1978):

● *Anxious/avoidant infants* (Insecurely attached Type I) show high levels of play behaviour throughout and tend not to seek interaction with the parent or stranger. They do not become distressed at being left alone with the stranger. On reunion with their parent, they frequently resist any physical contact or interaction.
● *Independent infants* (Securely attached Type I) demonstrate a strong initiative to interact with their parent and to a lesser extent, the stranger. They do not especially seek physical contact with their parent and are rarely distressed on separation. They greet their parent upon reunion by smiling and reaching.
● *Dependent infants* (Securely attached Type II) actively seek physical contact and interaction with their parent. They are usually distressed and often cry when left alone with the stranger. On their parent's return, they reach out and maintain physical contact, sometimes by resisting the parent's release. Generally they exhibit a desire for interaction with the parent in preference to the stranger.
● *Anxious/resistant or ambivalent infants* (Insecurely attached type II) show low levels of play behaviour throughout and sometimes cry prior to separation. They demonstrate an obvious wariness of the stranger and intense distress at separation. They are also more prone to crying while left alone with the stranger. They are ambivalent and frequently mix contact-seeking behaviours with active resistance to contact or interaction. This is especially evident on the parent's return: on reunion, these infants continue to be distressed as usually the parent fails to comfort them.

ASSESSING THE QUALITY OF PARENTING

See Herbert (1991) for further reading on this topic.

Ainsworth *et al.* (1978) have examined the relationship between the infant's response to separation and reunion and the behaviour of both mother and child in the home environment. Their findings suggest that maternal sensitivity is most influential in affecting the child's reactions. In the homes of the securely attached infants, sensitive mothering was exhibited to the infant's behaviour, while insecurely attached, anxious and avoided infants were found to have their interactive behaviour rejected by the mothers. It was suggested that the enhanced exploratory behaviours shown by these infants were an attempt to block attachment behaviours that had been rejected in the past. In the home environments of the insecurely attached anxious and resistant infants a disharmonious and often ambivalent mother–infant relationship was evident. The resistant and ambivalent behaviours shown were seen as a result of inconsistent parenting.

Attachment can be assessed and identified within four dimensions of caretaking style:

- *Sensitivity/insensitivity.* The sensitive parent meshes his/her responses to the infant's signals and communications to form a cyclic turn-taking pattern of interaction, whereas the insensitive parent intervenes arbitrarily, and these intrusions reflect his or her own wishes and mood.
- *Acceptance/rejection.* The accepting parent accepts in general the responsibility of child care, demonstrating few signs of irritation with the child, The rejecting parent, on the other hand, has feelings of anger and resentment that eclipse his or her affection for the child, often finding the child irritating and resorting to punitive control.
- *Cooperation/interference.* The cooperative parent respects the child's autonomy and rarely exerts direct control. The interfering parent imposes his/her wishes on the child with little concern for the child's current mood or activity.
- *Accessibility/ignoring.* The accessible parent is familiar with his or her child's communications and notices them at some distance, hence he or she is easily distracted by the child. The ignoring parent is preoccupied with his or her own activities and thoughts, often failing to notice the child's communications unless they are obvious through intensification. He or she may even forget about the child outside the scheduled times for caretaking.

Paternal Bonding

The bonding doctrine would seem to imply that paternal love is of a different order and quality from maternal love. The fact that a female gives birth does not necessarily mean that she invariably cares for the baby. This is so even in some animal species; male marmosets, to take one example, carry the infant at all times except when the infant is feeding. There have been variations among human groups. Anthropologists tell us that children may not be the special responsibility of their parent at all in some societies; they may be reared by all the members of a group living together under one roof or in a small compact housing unit. Contemporary western society is witnessing a massive increase in the number of single-parent families, in some of which the father is the caregiver.

Fathers, of course, *do* become engrossed in their infants and develop powerful bonds of affection. Commonsense, personal experience, and experimental evidence tell us so, and it happens (in most cases) shortly after birth without the benefit of skin-to-skin contact. Father-to-infant attachment is actually not so different in kind from maternal attachment. Certainly paternal behaviour soon after the birth of a baby very often resembles, in many details, maternal behaviour. Paternal attachment, however, often (but not invariably) appears to be less strong than maternal attachment. There are several suggested reasons for this.

In the first place, general responsiveness of the human male to infants tends to be less marked. It would not altogether surprise us if there were genetic factors responsible for this. In many, but not all, species of primates, males are less nurturing to the young than females, although males tend to be protective both towards the females and their young. Undoubtedly, however, the role of the human male in relation to the young is enormously influenced by culture, custom and convention. Until relatively recent times in western and central Europe, men were not expected to perform certain domestic duties, including the feeding of young infants, changing nappies, and so on. The situation in this regard is at present changing rapidly, and it may be that without the cultural overlay, men's feelings and responses towards babies would not be all that different from women's. Given the undoubted changes in social attitudes, researchers have not been eager to see whether such changes are skin deep. For example, do babies trigger the same kind of responsiveness in males and females. They usually show men and women films of babies crying and at the same time measure their psychophysiological responsiveness, such as their heart rate and blood pressure. In general, men and women appear to react in similar ways. Second, researchers have examined the ways in which parents greet their newborns since, in many species, parental behaviour is programmed to protect newborns and enhance responsive behaviour toward the young. Again, the similarities outweigh any differences.

TEMPERAMENT

We have seen that infants are not passively reactive to stimulation; they are proactive, reaching out to affect their environment. Individual differences in temperament and styles of behaving affect parents markedly, and thus, in the course of myriads of interactions, the direction of development (Thomas and Chess, 1977).

The temperamental make-up of the majority ('easy') group of children is such that it usually makes early care remarkably rewarding. They are mainly positive in mood, very regular, low or mild in the intensity of their reactions, rapidly adaptable and unusually positive in their approach to new situations. These children frequently enhance their mothers' sense of well-being and of being 'good' and effective parents. Even these easy children, who generally thrive on the widest variety of life situations and demands, can, under special circumstances, find themselves vulnerable to adverse influences; when they adapt to inconsistent and unpredictable parental demands, their easy adaptability, usually a temperamental asset, becomes a liability.

The difficult children (referred to colloquially as 'mother killers') have inborn characteristics—irregularity in biological functions (feeding, sleeping, passing motions), unadaptability, hypersensitivity, a tendency to withdraw in the face of new situations, powerful and frequent bad moods—which make them particularly troublesome to rear (Earls, 1981; Graham, Rutter and George, 1973)

Infants who are 'slow to warm up' combine negative responses of mild intensity to new stimuli with slow adaptability after repeated contact. Infants with such characteristics differ from the difficult child in that they withdraw from new situations quietly rather than loudly. They do not usually exhibit the intense reactions, predominantly negative mood and biological irregularity of difficult children.

Temperament should not be reified in the sense of being conceptualized as a fixed unmodifiable 'entity'. Environmental factors shape the manner in which temperament is displayed as the child gets older and, indeed, changes in temperament over time have been shown to be correlated with parental characteristics (Cameron, 1978). Having said this, there does seem to be a genetic component. Identical twins are more like each other in several of the nine temperamental attributes than are the two children in a non-identical pair (Torgerson and Kringlen, 1978).

Goodness of Fit

The significance of differences in temperament (or behavioural style) is underlined by research which demonstrates the releasing effect and initiating role exerted by the behaviour of the child on his or her parents (Bell,

1971). The reciprocal interactions of parent and child are in a state of constant adjustment as each reinforces the other positively or negatively. Rewardingness or punitiveness, for example, are not qualities inherent in the parent but are called out by a particular child and its behaviour. Children's characteristics interact with parental attributes—a concept referred to as 'goodness of fit'. A mismatch of temperament can result in an extended series of mutually unrewarding interactions. They can also lead to depression in mothers (in particular) and faulty or incomplete socialization in children (Herbert and Iwaniec, 1981).

Quite apart from the emotional distress experienced by the parents, they have to cope with a child whose disorganized condition makes his or her signals more difficult to interpret and whose unusual demands cause confusion and inappropriate reactions in the parents. Pathological crying, disturbed sucking patterns, unusual waking–sleeping rhythms, distractability—these are but some of the infant characteristics with which some parents are confronted.

There is evidence (Thomas, Chess and Birch, 1968) that even as early as the second year of life, and before the manifestation of symptoms, children who were later to develop behaviour problems requiring psychiatric attention showed particularly difficult temperamental attributes (70% of the so-called 'difficult' category). Only 18% of the easy children developed such problems.

Activity level is a temperamental attribute which tends to be stable over time. Parents tend to react to a child with a high activity level in a different manner than to a child with a low activity level (Barkley, 1982).

The 'Overactive Infant'

High rates of activity and high intensities of emotional expression in the repertoire of children tend to be aversive to adults, and, indeed, are among the most frequent complaints made by adults in referring children to out-patient clinics (Herbert, 1987b). Hyperactivity is one of the specific problems dealt with in a later section of the book.

Although it might seem to be a statement of parental exculpation (or scapegoating) to propose that the stimulus characteristics of the child can constitute a sufficient or necessary provocation to maltreatment, studies do indicate that abnormal attributes in the child are at least as substantial a factor in explaining incidents of abuse and deviance in the parents (Gil, 1970). It has been reported that abused children have been ill-treated in a foster home, transferred, and then abused in another foster home.

Episodes of persistent, intense crying, or screaming by the infant, bouts of bladder or bowel incontinence in the older child (not always that old), and defiance, are frequently cited as 'immediate antecedents' of parental violence. It is important to remember that most of these incidents occur in the context of what parents (rightly or wrongly) perceive as 'disciplinary' encounters (Wolfe, 1987).

DAILY ROUTINES AND PARENT–CHILD CONFRONTATIONS

Confrontations between disobedient children and their parents tend to be associated particularly with bedtime, bathtime and mealtime routines.

Bedtime and Sleeping Difficulties

The effect of the exhaustion and stress on parents of intensive night-time disturbance on the part of their young children should not be underestimated or treated in a complacent manner. Richman's survey of 771 children with sleep disruption found that 10% in the 1–2-year age range had severe, that is to say, problematic, rates of waking (Richman, 1981). There are differences, of course, in the annoyance or tolerance threshold of their hapless parents; some become very distressed and angry, others seem resilient and/or forbearing.

An infant's *pattern* of sleeping is as individual a matter as the uniqueness of his or her developing personality. This basic 'sleep cycle', as it is known, is 'given' (not learned), and as such, cannot be altered by parents or the baby. The sleep cycle of infants is biologically determined; it is regulated by a system of neurones situated in the core of the brain.

In the first half year of life, or so, the pattern of sleeping reflects the child's individual biological development. Nevertheless, this is no reason for inaction: parents can begin *gradually,* to instil routines—the foundation stones of good sleeping habits. Their expectations can have a powerful influence on how their child's sleep routines develop with age. So it is best to avoid 'labels' such as 'She's a poor sleeper' or 'He needs hardly any sleep'. If the parents' assumption is that the child is incapable of changing and they act on it—the 'self-fulfilling prophecy'—they could allow their child to develop poor sleep habits. Ferber (1985) states that:

> Because . . . parents were led to believe their child was just a poor sleeper and there wasn't anything they could do about it, they allowed their baby to develop poor sleep habits; they did not believe there was anything they could do to help him develop good ones. As a result the whole family suffered terribly. Yet I have found that almost all of these children are potentially fine sleepers and with just a little intervention can learn to sleep well.

'Normal' Sleep Patterns

Going back to the very beginning, the foetus in the womb is thought not to be truly awake, alternating between *active* sleep and *quiet* sleep. Newborn (full term) babies spend some 75% of each 24 hour period asleep. They usually have (*on average*) about 8 periods of sleep a day, often in snatches. How long they sleep varies from baby to baby. Newborns typically sleep for 2 to 4 hours at a time (note the wide range). Their need for sleep also varies widely: from 11 to 21 hours in any 24 hour period. By 6 months of age babies are spending some 50% of each 24 hour period asleep.

Night Waking

Brief periods of night waking are quite the usual thing in infancy. By the end of the first month most babies are waking up twice a night to eat. Two-month-old infants spend, on average, some 9% of the night's sleeptime actually awake: by nine months of age the time awake reduces to about 6%. Infants usually settle themselves and go back to sleep again. Sometimes they cry out. The extent to which parents are conscious of infants' waking depends on whether he or she sleeps with them, how often they monitor whether the child is asleep, and their sensitivity to the crying. There are two types of sleep:

- *REM or rapid-eye-movement sleep.* An *active* period of sleep when we do our dreaming, and
- *Non-REM sleep.* The kind we usually think of as 'sleep', a *quiet*, deeper kind of sleeping without body or eye movements. Most of the restorative functions of sleep occur in this phase; there is little, if any, dreaming; there is a regular pattern of breathing and heart-rate.

REM sleep appears in the foetus at about 6 or 7 months' gestation, and non-REM sleep between 7 and 8 months. At birth, a full-term baby will have 50% of its sleep in REM state (premature babies 80%); 35% by age three; and 25% for late childhood, adolescence and adulthood. REM sleep, thus, seems most important in the early months as the foetus and baby develops. Babies make frequent transitions between the two states. During the periods of light/active sleep a baby is easily awakened. About half of a newborn baby's sleep (as we have seen) is spent in each of these active vs. quiet states. As children mature they develop—at their own pace—the ability to pass through periods of light sleep more rapidly. Some babies sleep relatively little; many need more sleep. They will get all the sleep they need—provided they are not left hungry, are not in pain, or constantly interrupted.

Daytime Napping

The move from round-the-clock sleeping to a daytime napping schedule happens largely on its own. By the second month, infants are awake more during the day. By the third to sixth month parents' lives are enjoying some regularity again, as the baby may have developed a routine of two longer daytime sleeps. Many babies don't sleep through the night until they are 6 months old. At this age a majority (83%) do so.

An unending series of sleepless nights can bring some parents to the point of abusing their children. Among the many causes of sleep disturbance, particularly in toddlers and older children, are factors associated with behavioural problems in general, some of which present themselves alongside the bedtime problems. Extreme disobedience is a noteworthy example. Behavioural management techniques applied to settling and waking difficulties have been found to be successful in 90% of children between 1 and 5 years old (Richman *et al.*, 1985). These are discussed in detail in Chapter 5.

Eating and Mealtime Difficulties

Typical mealtime activities that cause concern are refusing food, fiddling with it, leaving the table, tantruming, crying and complaining. The mealtime setting should provide an important opportunity for children to learn social interactive skills and yet it seems a prime time for preschool children to engage in disruptive behaviour.

Psychologists sometimes have to explore the social and emotional context in which the infant or child feeds, for example in cases where they fail to thrive (Iwaniec, Herbert and McNeish, 1985). Parental responsiveness is important in something as apparently basic as providing growth-enhancing sustenance to a baby. Typically, feeding times must be adapted to the cycles of hunger and satisfaction expressed by the infant and responded to by the parent. During the feeding sessions parents should preferably be calm, and sensitive enough to respond from moment to moment to changes in the baby's behaviour. For example, they commonly respond to pauses in the child's sucking at the breast by nudging the baby. They will gaze back at the baby and talk to it. They will be alert to the child's changing needs for nourishment as it matures, by altering its diet.

Failure-to-Thrive (Iwaniec, 1995)

Failure-to-thrive is described in the literature as a failure to grow and develop healthily and vigorously. The child's weight (*inter alia*) is significantly below the norms on developmental charts. Only a few decades ago, when growth began to be studied scientifically, was it realized that failure-to-thrive is not a clear-cut disease but a symptom (or more accurately a syndrome) which has many causes: they include inadequate nutrition, malabsorption, chronic infection, major structural congenital abnormalities, metabolic and endocrine defects. However, there are some infants and young children who fail to thrive, in whom none of the above factors is obvious and whose present management and well-being is problematic.

A search of the literature on failure-to-thrive reveals a paucity of good studies. The term failure-to-thrive (once referred to as marasmus) has been applied to conditions caused by organic illness and those due (allegedly) to failure of the environment to provide appropriate nurturing, i.e. psychosocial causes. The more specific term 'non-organic failure-to-thrive' as a diagnosis becomes significant in the sort of society in which one can presume that food will be available to all its children, and where knowledge of paediatric disease and normal growth and development have become sufficiently precise to define the reasons for growth failure.

The hypothesis of a psychological aetiology for the non-organic failure-to-thrive syndrome has its historical roots in the extensive literature on the effects of institutionalization (hospitalism) and 'maternal deprivation' in infants. The early descriptions of the failure-to-thrive syndrome (but by a different name) were those of Spitz (1945, 1946). The disorder of 'hospitalism' as Spitz termed it, occurred in institutionalized children in the first year of life, and the major manifestations involved emotional disturbance, failure to gain weight, and developmental retardation. The term 'anaclitic depression' was applied to the sad, bereaved and apathetic demeanour of these infants, one of extreme mourning and melancholia (see Bowlby, 1981; Freud, 1917). A significant aetiological factor, according to Spitz, was the quality of maternal love and nurturance available to the infant; and, in particular, its discontinuation.

The early studies of failure-to-thrive were conducted in hospitals and institutions. The investigation of failure-to-thrive in the child's own home is a more recent phenomenon (e.g. Iwaniec, Herbert and McNeish, 1985). Of course it is taken for granted these days that a baby needs a close, confident and caring physical and emotional contact with the parent, be it mother (or mother surrogate), or father, in order to be healthy and to develop vigorously. The absence of such continuing nurturance and physical intimacy can bring about anxiety in the child, fretting and disruption of biological functions.

It is notoriously difficult (not to say dangerous) to infer causal relationships from retrospective data, and from largely correlated antecedents.

Correlations do not necessarily imply causation although they may be suggestive. One can speculate on the basis of findings carried out at the University of Leicester, on a serious of 34 organic and non-organic failure-to-thrive children and their families (and a control group of normally developing ill children), that there are several routes to the failure-to-thrive disorder (Iwaniec, Herbert and McNeish, 1985). An original organic lesion may heal but the subsequent emotional overlay continues to disrupt eating, which in turn affects the mother–child relationship because of the worry and conflict that ensues. Maternal resentment and ambivalence is, in a sense, secondary. Maternal rejection—when it is primary—is quite likely to be expressed in rough, hostile feeding patterns which lead to phobic avoidance (food aversion) on the part of the child.

A Treatment Programme for Children who Fail to Thrive (see Iwaniec, Herbert and Sluckin, 1988)

Stage I. Feeding is tackled in a highly structured (and thus directed) manner. Mealtimes have to be made more relaxed. Mothers (and/or fathers) are asked (and rehearsed) to desist from screaming, shouting and threatening the child over meals (self-control training). The period of eating is made quiet and calm. The mother is asked to talk soothingly and pleasantly to the child. It is extremely difficult for mothers to achieve and maintain this pattern of behaviour. It is helpful if the practitioner models the feeding; she may feed the child a few times and then help to reassure the child; she may have to prompt the mother to help the child to eat, in a gentle manner, when there is difficulty. The mother is encouraged to make contact by looking, smiling and touching. If the food is refused, the mother has to accept this if she can't encourage or coax the child by play or soft words. The food should be arranged decoratively to look attractive. She should never feed the child when feeling acutely tense or angry.

Stage II. This phase is discussed in detail; rationale and methods are explained to both parents. In most cases a contract is drawn up specifying the mutual obligations and rules for the family and practitioner. What might happen in situations where interactions are aversive is that mother (and/or father) is encouraged to play exclusively with the child each evening for 10–15 minutes during the first week, for 15–20 minutes during the second and third weeks and 25–30 minutes during the fourth and subsequent weeks. After the mother's session with the child the rest of the family might join in for a family play session. The way the mother plays and the toys she uses may have to be demonstrated and rehearsed with her. She is encouraged to talk in a soft, reassuring manner, encouraging the child to participate in the play.

The mother is also encouraged to look and smile at the child, holding hands and stroking, and giving praise for each positive response. This may require successive approximations if the child's behaviour is very timid. (The tentative approaches towards the mother are shaped by a series of reinforcements for mini-steps towards the goal, i.e. successive approximations). After a few days or even weeks, the mother is guided to seek proximity by hugging briefly and holding him or her on her lap for increasing intervals of time, eventually holding him or her close but gently, while reading aloud, looking at and describing pictures, etc.

This picture of therapy requires a lot of support for the mother and the whole family. Frequent visits and telephone calls should be made to monitor the programme. It could take three months of hard work to bring a mother and child closer together to the point of beginning to enjoy each other.

Stage III. The final stage is planned to include two weeks of deliberately intensified mother–child interaction. The mother is to interact with the child as much as possible. She should chat as much as possible, regardless of whether or not the child fully understands what she is doing and saying. She should make a lot of eye contact, smile, cuddle, hug the child. This is a period of 'over-learning'. Apart from having the child with her for everyday activities, she should spend time playing with all her children, encouraging the target child to participate in the play with his siblings. A bedtime story for all children might be introduced.

The formal programme is faded out gradually (over a period of several weeks). The case is terminated when there is evidence of the child's stable growth (measured by a paediatrician) and evidence of improved family interactions, maternal feelings and attitudes towards the child (these are always carefully monitored).

Behavioural Interventions

Less life-threatening feeding difficulties—of which there are many—are amenable to behavioural interventions which are described in Chapter 5. For an overview of infant psychopathology from the dual perspective of developmental psychopathology and clinical disorder, see Zeanah, Boris and Scheeringa (1997).

Chapter 5

PROBLEMS ASSOCIATED WITH EARLY CHILDHOOD

For the purposes of this chapter, early childhood is defined as the pre-school period (from 18 months to about 5 years). The major developmental task during this period is hypothesized by Erikson (1965) to be the achievement of 'initiative': vigorous reality testing, imagination, and imitation of adult behaviour. The psychoanalytic (Freudian) concept of identification, in which the child 'incorporates' his or her parents as an ego-ideal, finds a close parallel with an increase in the child's global 'imitation' of the parent followed by more selective attention to 'good' and 'role-appropriate' attributes (Lee and Herbert, 1970). In the Freudian canon the resolution of the Oedipus complex brings in its wake the formation of the super-ego, establishing both the child's sex-role identification and his or her moral standards. These events are thought to occur around the age of five.

Kohlberg's account is similar in its timing (Kohlberg, 1978). In the case of cognitive developmental theory, however, identification is not a fixed, rigid personality structure which depends on a specified relationship with the parents. Kohlberg suggests that children's behaviour is motivated by an intrinsic need for mastering the environment; adult approval for their behaviour is an indication that a satisfactory level of competence has been reached. Children seek and are increasingly dependent on adult approval. Kohlberg (1978) states that:

> ... it is more correct to say that the child wants to secure rewards or approval as a sign that he has performed the task competently rather than to say that the child wants to perform competently in order to obtain situational rewards and approval.

An increasing awareness of self-identity typically leads to a 'negativistic crisis' around the age of 2—the 'terrible twos'. Children who have previously accepted assistance in their efforts without fuss insist on doing things themselves and displaying their own competence: they also resist parental request and commands. Discipline becomes a very real issue in the child's second year of life, although the foundations for good disciplinary practices should have been laid down much earlier. Notions of right and wrong, a code of behaviour, a set of attitudes and values, the ability to see the other person's point of view—all of these basic qualities which make an individual into a socialized personality—are nurtured in the first instance by parents.

Patterson (1975) states that by the age of 2 most toddlers have advanced to the point of possessing an important range of verbal and motor strategies to replace their more coercive responses of former times (crying and screaming). He traces the developmental history of coercive behaviours. They display a steady decline in performance rates from a high point in infancy down to more moderate levels at the age of school entrance. The highest rates of negativistic–disruptive behaviours occur before the age of 3; 2- and 3-year-olds display high rates of whining, crying, yelling, and high-frequency behaviours, as well as high rates for most other coercive actions. By the age of 4, there are substantial reductions in negative commands, destruction, and attempts to humiliate. By the age of 5, most children used less negativism, non-compliance, and negative physical actions than younger siblings (Reynolds, 1982). Hartup (1974) also notes a significant decrease in aggression from the ages of 4 through to 8 in his study of classroom behaviour.

PREVALENCE RATES

(See Campbell (1995) for background reading on this topic).

Richman, Stevenson and Graham, (1975), using a screening questionnaire and interview with the mothers of over 800 preschool children, found that 7% had moderate to severe and 15% a mild category of behaviour problems. Similar prevalence rates were reported by Richman, Stevenson and Graham (1982) in 705 non-immigrant 3-year-old children—a 1 in 4 random sample from a borough in London—again using a parent screening questionnaire and interview with parents. These problematic children were more likely than the 'normal' children to attend a child clinic, were more accident prone and showed more signs of developmental delay. The rate of language delay was found to be in the region of 2–3%. Children with such delays were more likely to come from large families and the families were more likely to have suffered stressful circumstances over the previous year. The quality of the parents' marital relationship was associated with the presence or absence of behaviour problems in the children. In the control group, nearly one in five children had parents whose marriage was rated as poor, while in problem children the rate was nearly twice as high (37%). The proportion of women working (about 20%) was almost exactly the same in both the problematic and non-problematic children.

Earls and Richman (1980a) compared the prevalence of behavioural problems in 3-year-old children of West Indian-born parents with children of British-born parents, using a semi-structured interview with parents, together with a 12-item behaviour screening questionnaire. The children of West Indian-born parents were all born in the UK and the parents were all working in the UK for less than 20 years. The children of West Indian families were living in poorer housing and had experienced more separations but did not show higher rates of behaviour problems. A one year follow-up (Earls and Richman, 1980b) showed that the prevalence and pattern of behaviour problems were very similar in the two groups. The global rating of severity of behaviour adjustment suggests that behaviour problems might be more frequent as well as more severe for the children of British-born parents. In an American epidemiological study of 110 3-year-olds, using the same behaviour screening instruments while applying a correction formula, Earls (1980) estimated a prevalence rate of 16.5% with a cut-off score of 11.

Richman, Stevenson and Graham, (1982) reported that 37% of their sample exhibited nocturnal enuresis more than three times per week; over 10% displayed eating problems, sleeping problems, overactivity and restlessness, several fears, poor sibling and peer relations, difficulty in being controlled, and encopresis. Less than 10% of 3-year-olds were reported to exhibit poor concentration, high dependency, frequent temper tantrums, unhappy moods, and several worries. Earls (1980) reported similar patterns for an American sample; however, the American 3-year-olds were less likely to display eating problems, overactivity, and worries.

Of course, babies can be 'difficult' as we have seen in the section on temperament; but it is not until about the age of 3 that epidemiological studies begin to report the behaviour problems of children as belonging, in a sense, to them as individuals. During the earliest stages of life—say the first year or two—problems are not so much *of* them, but rather problems created *for* them, difficulties—organismic and environmental—which can impede their development and blight their contentment. At this stage they're absolutely dependent and, as such, to be viewed in clinical assessments (if there is to be an understanding of what is going wrong) as part of caregiver–infant attachment systems.

In a clinical context children are sometimes referred to as being 'oversocialized' in their style of behaviour. Reasonable conformity (contrasted with slavish or blind conformity) enables the child to learn the patterns of prosocial behaviour that will guarantee social acceptance, which in turn leads to good personal and social adjustments (Herbert, 1974). Non-conformity, on the other hand, is as prejudicial to good adjustment as extreme conformity. The child who refuses to conform to the accepted standards of the group is likely to find himself or herself a social outcast. This is serious for social development because he or she is deprived of the satisfactions of belonging to a group and of the learning experiences which come from a sense of belonging and the feelings that go with comradeship.

OVER-CONTROLLED BEHAVIOUR

It is a fairly reliable generalization that punishment leads to self-control only when children are on the side of the person doing the punishing. Since they love their parents the children are on their side. Because of this identification they join in with the parental disapproval of the behaviour. Although such attachment is a condition which makes the development of conscience possible, it also gives parents a power which can be detrimental to the child. And this brings us to one of the problems of over-socialization. If children are strongly and exclusively attached to parents who set impossibly high standards and are deeply 'hurt' when their offspring fail to live up to them, it is quite likely that they will acquire a sense of conscience so severe and restrictive that their spontaneity and emotional life will be crippled, and much of their creative energy remain unused (Wright, 1971).

The risk comes particularly from authoritarian, restrictive parenting (Baumrind, 1966). Authoritarian parents attempt to shape, control and judge the behaviour and attitudes of their children according to unbending standards of conduct, usually absolute standards, often determined by theological considerations (Baumrind, 1966). Such parents value obedience for obedience's sake, in other words as a virtue; they favour punitive, forceful measures to curb self-will at those points where the child's actions or beliefs conflict with what they think is proper conduct. Children should be indoctrinated with such values as respect for authority, respect for work, and respect for the preservation of traditional order. They do not encourage verbal give and take, believing that the child should accept unquestioningly that *they* know best. Kagan and Moss (1962) have demonstrated that maternal restrictiveness with older boys is associated with high levels of aggression but this does not hold for young boys or for girls. In the case of paternal punishment, Eron *et al.* (1963) have shown that the consequences depend on their occupational level. Punitive fathers with high status appear to be much more likely to have aggressive sons than low-status punitive fathers.

NON-COMPLIANCE AND TEMPER TANTRUMS

The display of non-compliant behaviour is often associated with temper tantrums and aggression. The origin and development of oppositional behaviour in children has been the subject of considerable theoretical speculation. Patterson (1982) suggests that oppositional behaviour is a learned 'coercive' strategy by means of which the child exerts control over parental behaviour. The oppositional child if commanded by an adult in authority is quite likely to react with rage—a frightening display of temper. The parent insists, so the child escalates the aggravation. A vicious circle can be set in motion. If the tantrum is intense or persistent enough, the parent or teacher may concede to the child. Giving in to the child's non-compliance tends not to occur on every occasion, producing what is, in effect, an intermittent schedule of reinforcement for coercive, non-compliant actions. The parent's capitulation is also reinforced by the termination of the child's tantrum. This process of reciprocal reinforcement by the removal of aversive stimuli has been described as the 'negative reinforcer trap' (Wahler, 1969). The implications of this theory for practice are discussed in Chapter 11.

AGGRESSIVE AND VIOLENT CHILDREN

There are many different definitions of aggression, most of them betraying assumptions about its nature and origins. In the case of violence the term implies extremes of aggression to some theorists and carries emotive overtones. According to Lorenz (1966), aggression is an instinct—an atavistic but autonomous impulse—to be tamed, exorcised or sublimated in the child as soon as possible. Aggression, and its particularly anti-social manifestations (violence), are explained in terms of the vicissitudes of innate or inborn tendencies and the control systems which evolve to cope with them. Learning theorists, in contrast, point to the fact that as progress is made up the evolutionary scale living creatures depend increasingly less on reflex or instinctual patterns of behaviour and more on experience and learning; hence the many variations in human behaviour, and the optimism about the possibilities of change. Aggressiveness, in this view, is a learned habit or appetite.

These issues of definition and attribution have been described and critically reviewed by many (notably Bandura, 1973; Browne and Herbert, 1997). They lead one to conclude that aggression is a generic term for a variety of complicated and many-sided phenomena which include (for example) aggressive actions (behaviour); so-called 'states of mind' such as rage; anger or hostility (subjective feelings); aggressive drives, inclinations, thoughts and intentions (motivations), and conditions under which aggressive behaviours are likely to occur (environmental stimulation). Reference to aggression may be admiring ('he's an aggressive batsman') or pejorative ('these aggressive teenage hooligans').

A Social Learning Approach

The social learning approach treats childhood aggression as a learned event that takes place usually in a social context, and that produces *injurious and destructive effects* as well as *social labelling processes* (i.e. the social judgements that lead people to name certain acts as 'aggressive' or 'violent'. The term *destructive* is applied to children who destroy, damage or attempt to damage an object. *Disruptiveness* is applied to interference with another person so that he or she is prevented from continuing some ongoing activity or is caused displeasure. *Physical attack* is a term applied to an actual or attempted assault on someone of sufficient intensity potentially (or actually) to inflict pain. *Verbal abuse* occurs when children scream or talk loudly enough for this to be unpleasant to another person if carried on for a sufficient time, with sufficient intensity, or when the content of their speech is abusive.

Although biological factors do influence aggressive behaviour, children are assumed not to be born with the ability to perform the *specific* complex acts of aggression; this ability must be acquired through learning, either by direct experience or by observing the behaviour of other people (Bandura, 1973). While new forms of aggressive behaviour can be shaped by selective reinforcement of successive approximations to it, much complex behaviour is acquired by watching the behaviour of exemplary models. These may be what the child observes in everyday life, or they may be symbolic models that are read about or observed on television or in films.

Aggressive actions tend to occur at certain times, in certain settings, towards certain objects or individuals and in response to certain forms of provocation; children rarely show aggression in blind, indiscriminate ways. People become aggressive at certain times because of current conditions and influences. There are two categories of contemporary influence to consider in planning treatment: contemporary circumstances which *instigate* aggression (i.e. physical or verbal attacks, deprivation, frustration, conflict and exposure to aggressive models) or *maintain* aggression (i.e. direct, vicarious and self-reinforcement).

The interactions between parents and child go a long way (as we have seen) towards shaping aggressive behaviour because of the reinforcing consequences inherent in their behaviour. Children are likely to generalize what they learn about the *utility* and *benefits* of aggression to other situations. In these circumstances they have to put to the test the consequences of being aggressive. For example, they may try being aggressive because it produced results with siblings or with the peer group in the playground at school. Of course, aggressive behaviour which has been acquired may not be performed, either because appropriate instigating conditions do not occur or because the consequences of aggressive acts are likely to be unrewarding or unpleasant.

Among the most common instigating conditions for aggression are various forms of aversive experience, such as physical assaults, verbal threats or insults and any frustrating conditions which prevent the child from getting what it wants (Bandura, 1973). Although such aversive experiences do sometimes generate aggression, this is not always the case; the anger they evoke may be accompanied by other alternative responses. Various incentives (as we have seen) may also act as instigators of aggressive behaviour. Here, the instigation is the *pull* of expected reward rather than the *push* of aversive experience. Thus aggressive and alternative responses are selected for performance on the basis of their anticipated consequences.

The probable nature of these consequences is conveyed to the child by means of various informational cues or discriminative stimuli. For instance, he or she might be told that acceptance into a gang depends on the successful performance of a certain aggressive act, or the presence of a weak potential victim may facilitate aggression, whereas a stronger victim might be conducive to an alternative response. Exemplary models also influence the performance of previously learned aggressive responses.

There is a confidently expressed consensus that aggressive behaviour in children can be related to long-term attitudes and child-rearing practices. To summarize the findings (see Herbert, 1987b), parental permissiveness of aggression is said to increase the child's tendency to behave aggressively. More precisely, a combination of lax discipline combined with hostile attitudes in the parents produces very aggressive and poorly controlled behaviour in the offspring. The lax parent is one who gives in to children, acceding to their demands, indulging them, allowing them a great deal of freedom, being submissive and inconsistent, and, in extreme cases, neglecting and deserting them. Parents with hostile attitudes are mainly unaccepting and disapproving of children: they fail to give affection, understanding or explanations to children, and tend to use a lot of physical punishment, but not give reasons when they do exert their authority—something applied erratically and unpredictably, not to mention arbitrarily. Over a long period of time this combination produces rebellious, irresponsible and aggressive children: they tend to be disorderly in the classroom, lacking in sustained concentration and irregular in their working habits.

Modelling

The evidence suggests that children model their behaviour on that of their parents. Bandura and Walters (1963) compared families of adolescents who exhibited repetitive anti-social behaviour with those of boys who were neither markedly aggressive nor passive. It was found that the families differed in the extent to which they trained their sons to be aggressive through precept and example. Parents of the non-aggressive boys did not condone aggression to settle dispute, whereas those of the aggressive boys repeatedly modelled and reinforced combative attitudes and behaviour.

Reinforcement

There is convincing evidence (see Bandura, 1973) of the importance of reinforcement in shaping up and maintaining aggressive behaviour. The major effect of direct experience is to select and shape aggressive behaviour through its rewarding or punishing consequences. Aggressive responses which are followed by reinforcing consequences tend to be retained and strengthened, while those that are unrewarded or punished tend to be discarded. Direct external reinforcement may be of a positive kind involving the presentation of rewards such as tangible resources, attention, approval or social status.

Several theorists (e.g. Patterson, 1982) have looked at aggression in terms of the concept of coercive power. There is fairly good agreement in the clinical literature that there are two major types of aggressive response: (1) hostile or angry aggression, in which the only objective of the angry individual is to harm another person by inflicting some injury; and (2) instrumental aggression, in which the occurrence of harm or injury to another person is only incidental to the individual's aim of achieving some other goal. Bandura (1973) points out that hostile aggression is also instrumental, except that the actions are used to produce injurious outcomes rather than to gain status, power, resources or some other goal. In either case, the 'aggressor' exercises coercive power against another person. Coercive power involves the use of aversive stimuli, threats and punishments to gain compliance, and can be used offensively to take something away from another person. It can also be used defensively to avoid doing something. Patterson (1982) has developed the concept of 'coercive' families to describe events in which parents, caregivers or other people, interacting with the child, become involved in supplying reinforcers for aggressive behaviours. He postulates negative reinforcement as a mechanism to strengthen the behaviour of the aggressor and, in some instances, of the victim as well. It is also hypothesized that some exchanges become extended, and that when this occurs there is likely to be an escalation in the intensity of the painful stimuli. Theorizing of this kind has come into its own in the assessment and treatment of child abuse in the context of violent families (Herbert, 1988).

It is assumed that family systems which permit behaviour control by the use of pain are quite likely to produce children who exhibit high rates of noxious actions. Patterson (1982) observes that *negative reinforcement* is most likely to operate in certain closed social systems where the child must learn to cope with aversive stimuli. In such a family, for example, children's aggressive behaviour will be supported by both positive and negative reinforcement. Their hitting terminates much of the aversive stimulation. In addition, as many as a quarter to a third of their coercive behaviours are likely to receive positive reinforcement for deviant behaviour as well.

Patterson (1982) lists the following possibilities for the child's failure to substitute more adaptive, more mature behaviours for his/her primitive coercive repertoire:

(1) The parents might neglect to condition pro-social skills (e.g. they seldom reinforce the use of language or other self-help skills).
(2) They might provide rich schedules of positive reinforcement for coercive behaviours.
(3) They might allow siblings to increase the frequency of aversive stimuli which are terminated when the target child uses coercive behaviours.
(4) They may use punishment inconsistently for coercive behaviours.
(5) They may use weak-conditioned punishers as consequences for coercion.

Antecedent Control

We have found, as have others, that there are several methods for reducing aggression based on a modification of the antecedent side of the ABC 'equation' (see p. 33).

- *Stimulus change: reducing discriminative stimuli for aggression.* Certain stimulus conditions provide signals to the child that aggressive behaviour is likely to have rewarding consequences. Treatment programmes are planned to reduce *discriminative stimuli* for such aggression.
- *Providing models for non-aggressive behaviour.* Acceptable alternatives to aggression may be enhanced by exposing youngsters to prestigious or influential children or adolescents who manifest alternative non-hostile behaviours, especially when they are instrumental in obtaining pleasing outcomes for the models.

- *Reducing the exposure to aggressive models.* Exposure to other people behaving aggressively may facilitate the imitation of such behaviour by the observer. An attempt to reduce the exposure of children to such models (e.g. aggressive peers) is likely to decrease the likelihood of their behaving similarly.
- *Reducing aversive stimuli.* Violent reactions may be instigated by a large variety of aversive stimuli: it is reasonable to expect that a reduction of such aversive stimuli might be accompanied by a decrease in aggression. One technique is to resolve conflicts before they flare up into violence. Another involves the defusing of aversive stimuli by diminishing their power to arouse anger in the child. This can be achieved by using humour, by cognitive restructuring (reframing 'provocative' stimuli), or by using desensitization procedures.
- *Conflict resolution* ('settling differences'). There are two broad approaches to conflict resolution: (a) arbitration or mediation of specific conflicts, and (b) modification of communication processes (see Herbert, 1988). Behavioural contracting is the most common example of the negotiation and arbitration approach; it involves the therapist in the role of a mediator or arbitrator who facilitates discussions to seek compromises and mutual agreements between opposing parties. Contracts about reciprocal exchanges of specific behaviours and reinforcers can be drawn up to enhance the likelihood of a positive outcome (see Kirschenbaum and Flanery, 1983).
- *Desensitization.* O'Donnell and Worell (1973) provide examples of the effectiveness of three procedures applied in order to reduce anger: systematic desensitization, desensitization with cognitive relaxation and desensitization in the absence of relaxation training. (Chapter 13 contains further discussion of these techniques.)
- *Communication training.* Verbal instructions, practice and feedback are the major techniques used to modify communication processes (Kifer *et al.*, 1974). Their emphasis is more on learning new adaptive behaviours rather than eliminating problem behaviours; the techniques are primarily educational rather than therapeutic. Much of the misunderstandings, 'sound and fury', and negative messages that abound in the homes of conduct-disordered children can be traced to extremely poor or faulty communication skills.
- *Self-instruction.* Self instruction training—the development of children's skills in guiding their own performance by the use of self-suggestion, comments, praise and other directions—has proved invaluable with hyperactive, aggressive (impulsive) children (Meichenbaum and Goodman, 1971; Schneider, 1973).

    More cognitively orientated methods have proved useful with older children and adolescents, e.g. self-control training (assertion and relaxation training, role-play, behaviour rehearsal (Craighead *et al.*, 1983).

- *Cognitive change (with regard to antecedent events).* The instigation of aggression may be influenced by antecedent cognitive events such as aversive thoughts (e.g. remembering a past grudge), being aware of the probable consequences of aggressive actions, or being capable of solving problems mentally instead of 'lashing out' reflexly.

  The youngster's search for various possible courses of action in the face of provocation and frustration can be made more flexible by attention to the thinking processes that precede, accompany and follow violent actions. A skill that hostile children sometimes lack is the ability to identify (i.e. label) the precursors, physiological, affective and cognitive, to an aggressive outburst, so that they can bring into play more adaptive solutions to their problems.
- *Skills training.* (see Herbert, 1986; also Chapter 11). Children often lack (due to a variety of experiences of social deprivation) the skills to choose between alternative courses of action in person-to-person situations, and, in addition, knowledge of actions ('solutions') which they can take, plus some means of choosing between those they do have. Alternatively, they are locked into narrow, rigid and perhaps self-destructive modes of action, aggression being a classic example. Thus the therapeutic aim is to increase the child's or caregiver's repertoire of possible actions in person-to-person situations, making their relationships with others both more constructive and more creative.
- *The problem-solving model.* The assumption here is that some children are unskilled or deskilled (i.e. lose proficiency at problem-solving) due to lack of opportunity to practise them in various situations (see Bornstein and Kazdin, 1985; Spivack, Platt and Shure, 1976). It is crucial to unravel the situational factors that operate in (say) a social deficit problem (a complicated social interaction), to analyse it and to generate alternative solutions to the self-defeating strategies so far adopted. Those adopting a cognitive–social learning model view effective social functioning as being dependent upon the client's (a) knowledge of specific interpersonal actions and how they fit into different kinds of person-to-person situation; (b) ability to convert knowledge of social nuances into the skilled performance of social actions in various interactive contexts; (c) ability to evaluate skilful and unskilful behaviour accurately and to adjust one's behaviour accordingly.

Outcome Control

Extinction

There is sound evidence that procedures based on reduction of reinforcement, identified as maintaining aggressive behaviour, can reduce its frequency and/or intensity. In some studies, aggressive behaviour is consistently ignored; in others it is ignored while a competing pattern of pro-social conduct is rewarded. In other cases pro-social behaviour is positively reinforced, but aggression is punished (Herbert, 1989a).

- *Time Out* is an effective extinction procedure. It consists of:
  - *Activity time out*, where the child is simply barred from joining in an enjoyable activity but still allowed to observe it—for example, having misbehaved he or she is made to sit out of a game, or
  - *Room time out*, where he or she is removed from an enjoyable activity, not allowed to observe this, but not totally isolated—for example, having misbehaved, sitting in a 'time out' chair at the far end of the sitting room or a classroom, or
  - *Seclusion time out*, where he or she is socially isolated in a situation away from the reinforcing contingencies.

Time out may last from three to five minutes. In practice, 'activity' or 'room' time out should always be preferred before any form of 'seclusion' time out. The child is warned *in advance* about those behaviours that are considered inappropriate and the consequences that will follow from them. It is helpful to discuss with parents *in advance* the range of issues that may arise from the use of time out.

Time out is not, however, a method without complications. If it is to be used effectively, it requires painstaking explanations for the child and parents, preemptive warnings for the parent of what can go wrong, and a prompt 'trouble shooting' response to the difficulties, if they do arise (see Webster-Stratton & Herbert, 1994). To take one example, time out is quite likely to lead to tantrums or rebellious behaviour such as crying, screaming, and physical assaults. With older, physically resistive children, the method may simply not be feasible. When the behaviour to be eliminated is an extraordinarily compelling one that all but *demands* attention (reinforcement) from those present, or when time out is difficult to administer because the child is strong and protesting, an equivalent of time out may be instituted by removing the sources of reinforcement from him/her. So if the parent is a major source of reinforcement, he or she should remove her/himself, together with a magazine, to the bathroom when the child's temper tantrums erupt, coming out only when all is quiet.

- *Response–cost*. The use of response–cost procedures involves a penalty being invoked for failure to complete a desired response. This may involve the forfeiture of rewards currently available—as for example, when failure to complete homework results in the loss of television privileges. It is a feature of the *collaborative approach* (recommended by

Webster-Stratton and Herbert (1994)) that with this, as with other methods, we ask parents to help us problem-solve—that is, to come up with appropriate costs and rewards. In the following case, a hyperactive boy, Matthew, was extremely disruptive and noisy. He made life miserable for his older brothers and sisters while they read or watched television by constantly interrupting them—making loud humming and wailing noises and also banging things. The response–cost method was explained to the parents in the following way: 'To stop your child from acting in an unacceptable way, you need to arrange for him to bring to an end a *moderately* (but significantly unpleasant) consequence, by changing the behaviour in the desired direction.' The parents worked out the following scenario for Matthew.

A bottle of marbles representing his weekly pocket money, plus a bonus, was placed on the mantelpiece. Each instance of misbehaviour 'cost' a marble (the equivalent of a specific sum of money). In a good week, Matthew could increase his pocket money quite substantially; in a bad week it could be reduced to zero. Of course, the 'cost' of transgressions was highly visible to the boy. As always, sanctions were to be balanced by rewards, since punishment alone—as it is put to parents—tells children what not to do, not what they are expected to do. An extension of the range of rewards for therapeutic interventions is enshrined in the Premack principle, where a preferred behaviour is made contingent on correctly performing a non-preferred behaviour. This principle, when worked out by the parents, required Matthew to play quietly for set periods, timed with a kitchen timer, and if he did this successfully, he was rewarded by stickers. These could be exchanged for time on a computer game.

- *Natural consequences.* If parents ensure (within limits of safety) that the child is allowed to experience the consequences of his or her own actions, this becomes an effective means of modifying behaviour. If a child is destructive with a possession and, for example, it breaks, he or she is more likely to learn to be careful if he or she has to do without it. If parents always replace the toy he or she is likely to continue to be destructive.

Unfortunately, from the point of view of the parents' 'self-interest', children are frequently not left to experience the consequences of their own misdeeds. Against their own and the child's best interests they intervene to 'protect' their offspring from reality. Potentially educative (though punishing) reality is replaced by a kind parent; the result, however, of this kindness is that the implications (outcomes) of the situation often do not become apparent to the child and they go on committing the same misdeeds over and over again. A good deal of discussion and debate with parents (particularly over-protective ones) is required here. The issue is, to what extent (particularly with toddlers and teenagers) parents should intervene ('interfere'?) to protect the child from the inevitable risks of life? To what extent is the child allowed to learn from experience (i.e. 'the hard way')?

- *Self-management training.* In order to engender or strengthen self-control, techniques have been developed to change the parent's or child's instructions to him/herself. Training involves raising the client's consciousness of the circumstances in which he/she gets angry; it then moves through a series of stages: first the therapist (or parent) models the performance of a task, making appropriate and positive self-statements (e.g. 'Think first, act afterwards'; 'It's not worth losing my temper'. I'll count to ten and stay calm.'). The child then practises the same behaviour, gradually moving to whispered, and eventually silent self-instruction. Children are encouraged to use self-statements so that they can observe, evaluate and reinforce appropriate overt behaviours in themselves.

- *Contracts.* We have seen that in coercive families the cues or messages are frequently negative ones. Communication between members may be not so much aversive as impoverished or practically non-existent. Where family systems include behaviour control by the use of verbal and/or physical pain, they are likely to produce children who exhibit frequent ('high rate') aggressive actions. Coercive interactions, maintained by negative reinforcement, are most likely to operate in closed social systems where the child must learn to cope with aversive stimuli such as incessant criticism.

This is where contracts come in. They can be used to 'open' closed systems somewhat. And certainly one way of increasing positively reinforcing communications while reducing punitive interactions is by sitting down to work out a contract with members of the family. The discussion, negotiation and compromise in such therapist-led situations introduces the family to an important means of resolving interpersonal conflicts and tensions, and to enhanced communication, which they may have experienced only rarely.

The following guidelines might be followed in planning the contract:
— Keep the discussion positive. Recriminations are unavoidable, but the volume should be kept down and negative complaints turned into positive suggestions.
— Be very specific in spelling out desired actions.
— Pay attention to the details of privileges and conditions for both parties. They should (a) be important, not trivial, and (b) make sense to the person/s involved.

CHILDHOOD FEAR AND ANXIETY

Children experience a wide variety of 'normal' fears as they grow up (King, Hamilton and Ollendick, 1988; Morris and Kratochwill, 1983). Young infants are afraid of loss of support, loud noises and strangers, as well as sudden, unexpected, and looming objects. One- and two-year-olds show a range of fears including separation from parents and fear of strangers. During the third and fourth years, fears of the dark, being left alone, small animals and insects emerge. Fears of wild animals, ghosts and monsters come to the foreground during the fifth to sixth years; and fears of school, supernatural events, and physical danger emerge in the seventh and eighth years. During the ninth to eleventh years, social fears and fears of war, health, bodily injury, and school performance become more prominent.

When is an emotional 'problem' really a problem? This question underlines the importance of a developmental context for explaining a child's fearfulness (anxiety has been called 'fear spread thin'). The question arises from the essential normality of these emotions. Anxiety is not wholly a maladaptive condition. It is, in fact, a fundamental and universal response to a wide range of life events and a normal adaptation to particular environmental circumstances. Indeed, it is *functional* in the sense of having positive survival and reward value, 'driving' the individual to maximum efficiency for 'fight or flight' in the event of extreme threat or toning him or her up for peak performance in activities such as examinations, acting and athletics. For many aspects of human performance, an 'inverted U-curve' relationship is postulated between efficiency and level of anxiety. Parents also make use of the child's fear in teaching the child to avoid danger, and anxiety (about the loss of love or approval) is vital for ensuring compliance and the internalization of rules and values in the task of socialization (Wright, 1971).

What, then, is abnormal fear or dysfunctional anxiety? Context is one criterion. Is the fear proportionate to the objective threat inherent in a particular situation? The physiological accompaniments of the fight or flight response to threat, if they are chronic and unresolved by action (given the constraints of life at home and at school and the fact that many of the threats are symbolic rather than real), many contribute to the etiology of psychophysiological disorders (Herbert, 1974).

Context for childhood fear is a wider criterion than that for adults. Fears are so widespread at different ages and stages of development that at one time or another a given fear may be said to be or not to be age-appropriate. An analysis of children's fears suggests that certain types of situations tend to evoke more worries at one particular phase of development than at another. Up to the age of about six or seven months, a baby will probably show no concern about being with strangers, but from then on it is quite common for this to change. Babies gradually learn to discriminate between familiar people, like mother, and the other—unknown—people in the world. In many infants, the first fear of separation from mother is quickly followed by a fear of people who are strange or new to them. This fear may generalize, becoming a temporary but widespread fear of the unfamiliar and unknown.

Later, the situations that the pre-school child fears are still mainly those linked to a sense of security and apprehensions over strangeness and suddenness. Things beyond control are typically feared by youngsters.

Night-Time Fears and Worries

There are times when children say they do not want to go to bed, or wish to come to their parents during the night, because they are afraid of the dark, of being left alone, or some other thing. All children, as we saw earlier, experience fear as they grow up, many of the specific fears being about separation. It is possible to see how some of them might be related to anxieties about going to bed (e.g. fear of the dark, ghosts, being alone). Some children lie awake at night worrying about school, about death, their own or their parents' health, or other matters.

Fear of the Dark

Many youngsters learn to fear the dark and this causes bedtime problems. To be left in the dark is not initially an unpleasant experience for a young child. Sooner or later, however, when in pain with a tummy ache, frightened by a dream, hungry, cold or miserably wet, the child will cry for mother. She comes hot foot to the rescue, putting on the light as she enters the room, and soon eases the distress. What better conditioning model could there be for unwittingly associating darkness and distress, and light with positive reinforcement in the form of a consoling mother?

What she might do is to enter the room without putting on the light, chatting and reassuring the child until she has ascertained the trouble, and then, if essential, switching on the light to remedy the situation. This sequence of events ensures that there is no direct and recurrent relationship between the arrival or presence of mother and the light. If the child has learned to fear the dark because of terrifying tales from peers about ghosts and burglars, punishment is obviously quite inappropriate.

Overcoming Fear

The contagious effect of calmness and lack of fear has been used in extinguishing fears. Nursery school children who were afraid of dogs were treated successfully during eight brief sessions by observing unafraid children playing happily with a dog. The most effective methods used by adults to help their offspring are those which:

- help the child develop skills with which he/she can cope with the feared object or situation;
- take the child by degrees into active contact with the feared object or situation;
- give the child an opportunity gradually to become acquainted with the feared object or situation under circumstances that at the same time provide the opportunity either to inspect or ignore it.

Methods that are sometimes helpful in enabling the child to overcome fears include:

- verbal explanation and reassurance;
- verbal explanation, plus a practical demonstration that the feared object or situation is not dangerous;
- giving the child examples of fearlessness regarding the feared object or situation (parents frequently quote the example of other children who were not afraid);
- conditioning the child to believe that the feared object is not dangerous but pleasurable.

Self-help

It has been found that, even without help, children can overcome fears, either as part of the general process of growing up or by using the following techniques:

- practising overcoming their fear by enlisting the help of adults, fantasy characters (e.g. Superman) or favourite toys;
- talking with other people about the things they fear;
- arguing with themselves about the reality or unreality of dreaded imaginary creatures or fantasized events—say death—that they fear.

Bad Dreams

Aggressive children tend to have more hostility in their dreams (which can be frightening) than gentle youngsters; anxious children have more unhappy, worrying dreams. Children who have been separated from their mother by a long stay in hospital are more likely to be prone to nightmares subsequently—though there is no noticeable effect on the dreams of children who are separated from their mothers *but* remain in their own home. Unpleasant dreams tend to increase when a child is in poor health, with vivid nightmares about death, illness and other morbid topics.

Nightmares often set in after trauma (bereavement, an accident)—and for short periods when a child, particularly a sensitive child, is unsettled or worried by a change of school, a move to a new town or the trial of examination. If he or she has emotional problems—for instance cannot come to terms with parents' separation, or a new stepfather—there may be recurrent nightmares, often on the same theme as the daytime worry. Disturbing dreams tend to become a problem for children around the ages of ten to eleven; one third or more experience them. For a girl, nightmares peak in their incidence at six or seven years of age. They become less frequent as she gets older.

BEHAVIOUR PROBLEMS AT BEDTIME

(See Ferber, 1985)

Among the many causes of sleep disturbance, particularly in toddlers and older children, are factors associated with behavioural problems in general, some of which present themselves alongside the bedtime problems. Extreme disobedience is a noteworthy example. Going to bed may become a problem with a wilful toddler; keeping him/her there may be an added ingredient of misery for parents. Some children simply aren't sleepy when their parents think they should be; others 'fight' sleepiness as if it were the enemy!

The bedtime problem may take one of four forms. For example:

- *The bedtime battle.* Here the child flatly *refuses* to go to bed at the allotted time and defies all requests/instructions/pleas/demands to go to bed by ignoring/arguing/running away/or throwing a violent temper tantrum.
- *The bedtime 'game'.* In this variety the child dreams up a variety of ploys to *delay* bedtime: for example, requiring just a few more minutes to see the TV programme; needing to say goodnight to all the pets in the house; wanting just one more story.
- *The 'summons'.* Some children may go to bed readily, but later repeatedly ask for parents to come to them, escalating a form of 'emotional blackmail' by crying or screaming if the summons is not obeyed.
- *Coming to mother's bed.* For a variety of reasons children fall into the *habit* of getting into their parents' bed. Even when fear is not involved it can be a difficult habit to 'break'.

Behavioural management techniques like the ones described earlier for aggression, but applied to the bedtime difficulties, have been found to be successful in 90% of children between 1 and 5 years old (Richman *et al.*, 1985). Douglas and Richman (1984) have produced a manual which has been successfully used by health visitors (68% improvement rate) (Farnes and Wallace, 1987) and in a community clinic (Thornton *et al.*, 1984).

In conducting an assessment it is important to remember that children who refuse to go to bed or who wake early are often responding to inappropriate cues about how they are expected to behave. Getting ready for bed may have become disconnected from actually going to bed and falling asleep. There can be a gap of several hours of play between getting changed and falling asleep. The cues for falling asleep may be linked to the parents going to bed.

The child needs to learn a set routine which is relatively brief (up to half an hour) of getting ready for bed and falling asleep. A regular and relatively brief sequence of wash, change, drink and story. Parents sometimes, from sheer exhaustion and despair, let the child stay up until he or she falls asleep in the sitting room. The child is then carried to bed where the confrontation is quite likely to begin all over again. Some parents sit for ages by the child's bed until he or she falls asleep. Others accede to the demand that the child sleeps in Dad and Mum's bed, and perhaps even end up going to bed early for the sake of 'peace and quiet'. What parents are unwittingly teaching their children is that their coercive actions, be they refusals, temper tantrums or 'cunning ploys', if sufficiently intense and/or prolonged, will in the end get them their own way.

Asking parents to keep a bedtime behaviour and sleep diary provides a picture of the child's sleep pattern and is vital in planning an effective intervention. Some children will play up at bedtime. Some will still be having daytime naps which interfere with a prolonged sleep at night, so the pattern over twenty-four hours is helpful. The chart records the total time that the child is awake during the night, including the frequency of waking and the duration of time awake; also what he or she does on waking—for example, coming to the parents' bed, and the parents' reactions to the waking behaviour.

The following points are important to convey to parents:

Step 1: Preparing for bed. This should be made a pleasant, reassuring time for your child, with a well-established time and routine.

Step 2: Preparing for sleep. This should occur with the child in bed. A story or two can be read together and you will probably wish to chat a little. Explanations of the new routine should be given at this time. The final part of this stage includes tucking him or her in and a kiss, saying calmly but firmly: 'Good night, have a good sleep, see you in the morning.'

Step 3: During the first hours. If he or she cries or calls out ignore it—unless there is a note of urgency or panic—until he or she gets out of bed. If he or she does get out of bed and comes to the room where you are (and you have assured yourself that there is nothing wrong), take him or her back, without fuss, to the bedroom. Put him or her to bed in a matter-of-fact way. Then say, 'You must stay in bed: I have things to do. If you come out, I will take you right back.'

Step 4: This action needs to be repeated *consistently* whenever the child gets out of bed. Provide as little reinforcing attention (for example, chats and cuddles) as possible for these activities during the night.

Step 5: Pin up a 'bedtime chart' which is marked out in squares for every night of the week. If the child does not get out of bed, tick the appropriate square and put a happy face or some other sticker on a chart or let him or her colour in one section of a picture. Every success receives a lot of praise. Promise a special treat at the end of the week, such as having a friend to tea or an extra trip to the park, when the chart or picture is completed. The chart or picture is moved from the bedroom and pinned up in a place of honour in the sitting room. If he or she does get up on any night, repeat Steps 3 and 4 with *unremitting persistence.*

BEHAVIOUR PROBLEMS AT MEALTIMES

Typical difficulties are: 'bad table manners', refusing to eat or eating painfully slowly, getting up from the table, finicky eating habits, faddiness, tantruming and crying. The setting for a family should (or could) provide an important opportunity for children to enjoy family life, and learn interactive skills; instead, it seems only too often (especially with pre-school children) to become the occasion for open warfare.

Prevalence (see Douglas, 1989)

In a London study of 3-year-olds, 16% were judged to have *poor appetites,* while 12 per cent were considered to be *faddy.* There were no sex differences in the rate of difficulties, but the problems were found to persist for one year in about two thirds of these children and to continue for over five years in about one third. In a study of 5-year-olds, over one third of the children were described as having mild or moderate *appetite* or *eating* problems. Two thirds of these were considered to be *faddy* eaters, while the remainder were thought not to eat enough.

Personality theorists (notably the Freudians) have always emphasized the importance of early satisfying feeding experiences in the development of personality traits (e.g. oral optimism v. pessimism) and parent–child relationships. During the early weeks after birth, many of an infant's waking hours involve feeding. The feeding situation is an important component of the bonding process between parent and child (see Sluckin, Herbert and Sluckin, 1983). While it is not contentious to suggest that the development of positive feeding patterns is significant to the child's physical and psychological well-being, the fuss made by early theorists about the long-term effects of scheduled versus unscheduled feeding or early versus late weaning on personality development proved to be totally unjustified (Lee and Herbert, 1970). Which is not to say it is not important to make an infant's feeds as relaxed and pleasant an occasion as possible.

Parents frequently make of mealtimes (like bedtime) a rod for their own backs. They fail early on to established *routines* which are (as habits) the means to put the child on autopilot at such times. They may give the child too much choice. There may be too many distractions (e.g. TV or family rows). They may have little idea about how much the child's appetite matches the helpings on the plate, thus provoking conflict when the child picks at the food or refuses to empty the plate.

Assessment of Feeding Problems

- *Keeping a Food Diary.* Parents are asked to keep a detailed record of what exactly the child eats over the course of a day or, if possible, a week. This should include details of the amount and type of food eaten, including all snacks and drinks, as well as the time and place. This record is particularly important where obesity is a problem. A precise record of the quantity of food eaten is critical.
- *Height and weight charts.* Height and weight records are useful in assessment and treatment as they aid the practitioner in deciding on the health implications of the child's eating problem. There are variations in the food children require. At certain ages, children have less need for calories. Between the ages of one and five, most children gain four to five pounds a year but many will go three to four months without any weight gain at all, resulting in a decline in appetite.
- *Disruptive behaviour.* Disruptive mealtime behaviours can include stealing food from others, eating spilled food, aggressiveness towards others at the table, destructive acts such as throwing food, drink, plates and cutlery, screaming and throwing tantrums.
- *Childhood psychological problems.* Anxiety, depression or reactions to adverse (perhaps abusive) relationships within the family may cause the child to stop eating and thus fail to thrive.

Douglas (1989) recommends a mixture of behaviour management skills, nutritional help, reassurance, confidence-building and monitoring, in the task of helping parents cope with feeding difficulties. Behavioural methods have a proven track record (see Herbert, 1987b; 1994a). For instance, children learn much of their behaviour by observing how parents react, and this also applies to mealtime situations. They learn from noticing how their parents eat, talk and behave at the table.

An Example of a Management Programme:

- *Offer limited choice.* If your child is a faddy eater, resisting most of the usual family fare, he or she might be given the option of eating what the family eats, or instead, one type of preferred nutritious food. The choice should be made well before each meal, so that you are not forced into last-minute preparations. By offering an alternative, you give your child a face-saving way out of conflict. A limited choice introduces the idea of compromise; offering choices indicates that you are willing to give your children some room to negotiate in a responsible way.
- *Reward good eating and table manners.* For example, you could praise the child for staying seated, using cutlery properly and talking quietly. If and when a disruptive child is eating in the desired manner, you should be prompt in acknowledging the fact. You might say, 'You're doing so well by eating your dinner,' or 'I'm really pleased that you can eat your food in such a grown-up way.' When parents pay attention to good manners rather than bad, children will learn that there is little pay-off for behaving badly.
- *Having time-limited meals.* Some children drag mealtimes out by eating slowly, complaining at every mouthful and playing with their food. Instead of letting meals drag on and on, negotiate a reasonable amount of time in which the child has to finish eating, perhaps 20 to 30 minutes. Explain ahead of time that when a timer goes off, their plates will be removed. A star or sticker chart, where a star or sticker is awarded for eating well, should provide a powerful incentive.

TOILETING PROBLEMS

An important developmental task for the toddler (and one whose failure has been reported to lead to specific incidents of child abuse in some families) is the achievement of continence in toilet functions. The control of elimination means the inhibiting of processes which are, at first, completely involuntary. The baby's muscles must mature until they are strong enough and coordinated enough to hold back the waste products that are trying to emerge from his or her body. Of all the muscles in the trunk region, those which control the organs of elimination are the slowest to come under voluntary control. Children are expected to achieve satisfactory bladder control during the day by the time they start school. Parents and teachers may tolerate occasional lapses in the infant school but, thereafter, an incontinent child is likely to come under increasing social pressure. Bladder control comes somewhat later than bowel control.

'Potty training' is the phrase commonly used to describe the steps parents take in helping children to develop bowel and bladder control (a physical achievement) and teaching them where to put faeces and urine (a social skill).

Control of the bowels is attained before bladder control. The developmental sequence is *generally* as follows:

- First, bowel control *at night*.
- Next, bowel control *during the day*.
- Then, bladder control *during the day*.
- Finally, bladder control *at night*.

The sequence may vary; some children achieve bowel and bladder control 'simultaneously'. Girls tend to be quicker than boys in becoming continent, i.e. developing control.

There is much variation in the age at which control is achieved by children *in different cultures* and most likely *within our own culture* depending on the expectations of their parents. Weir's (1982) study of 706 three-year-olds in an outer London borough, showed the following:

- 23% of boys and 13% of girls were wet by day (wetting more than once a week).
- 55% of boys and 40% of girls were *wet by night*.
- 21% of boys were *'soilers'* (i.e. had soiled at least once during the previous month); in the case of girls it was 11%.

Tierney (1973) provides a breakdown of toileting skills. The development of each of these abilities can be broken down usefully into training stages or steps, as illustrated in Figure 6.

The order in which children achieve the different skills is variable. Some learn quickly, others slowly. The early steps are facilitated by:

- anticipating the child who is regular (sitting him/her on the potty at the expected time or when the telltale signs (e.g. a red face) are visible;
- making a sit-on-the-pot part of the morning routine (before dressing) and evening routines (at bedtime);

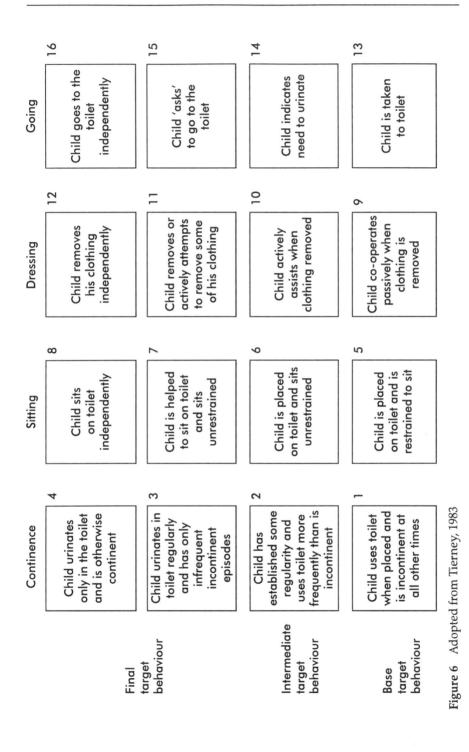

Figure 6 Adopted from Tierney, 1983

- praising success (and effort);
- gradually increasing the frequency of sessions on the potty (avoid force and over-long and boring 'sittings');
- encouraging the child to let caregivers know when he or she has urinated or passed a bowel motion. The awareness of *having* wet or soiled precedes the awareness of *impending* urination or bowel movement!
- eventually leaving off nappies;
- teaching the child to help (and eventually manage) in the putting on and taking off of pants;
- reminding the child to ask for the potty (this means having it handy as there may be a rush to sit him or her on it);
- making liberal use of praise and encouragement for trying and success. Avoid criticism and punishment. Move eventually to using the toilet.

From birth onwards, children become dry for gradually increasing periods. At about 15 months they will point to wet pants and puddles. They may wake at night and cry to be changed. They usually have a word which is used for both urine and faeces. By between 18 months and 2 years of age most children report to mother when they have soiled themselves. Their vocabulary now distinguishes between urine and faeces. By two-and-a-half, about 90% of girls and about 80% of boys make known their need to urinate. By about 3 years of age, children commonly go to the toilet by themselves. The difficulty of the exercise in self-control depends on the child's degree of maturity when training begins. Once the child has had a dry night then we know that the necessary physical control mechanisms are present. After a month of completely dry nights it is fairly safe to assume that the maturational and training processes are complete. Delayed continence is one of the biggest problems encountered in mental handicap.

Chapter 6

PROBLEMS OF MIDDLE CHILDHOOD

Middle childhood is taken to mean the period ranging from about 5 to 11 years of age.

DEVELOPING A NEW INDIVIDUALITY

The years of middle childhood are notable as a period in which youngsters' interactions with the people in their home and school environments help them to shape their personality, their individuality. The seriousness with which life is approached through work, and a preoccupation with what can be achieved, assist them to develop a sense of industry. In Erikson's framework of psychosocial development, the theme of this period of life is in a sense of duty and accomplishment—laying aside fantasy and play and undertaking real tasks, developing academic and social competencies. Crises are likely to be related to attitudes pertaining to 'industry' as opposed to feelings of 'inferiority'. The culture of childhood at this time in life is geared to a preoccupation with 'making things', especially with other children. Toys, which are still acceptable and desired, are of the type that help children to achieve a sense of success and accomplishment in making things. Not surprisingly, construction kits are especially popular.

Elkind (1967) describes the pragmatic–optimistic nature of school-aged children. The pragmatism shows itself in their concern with how things work and how to produce things of meaning and value that will receive the approval of others. Success in small endeavours feeds a sense of optimism about mastering new skills and acquiring new abilities. A source of this optimism for children, according to Elkind, is their belief that there is an unlimited number of years in which to attain their goals and master the skills necessary to become an adult. The pragmatism that accompanies this optimism about themselves results in an attitude that persistent effort at a task eventually ends in its accomplishment. Achievement motivation is one of the earliest and most stable attributes displayed by children (McClelland, 1961).

The ever-increasing importance of social and extra-familial influences in the child's life has been discernible in the earlier developmental phases described in previous chapters. In order to achieve, trust, autonomy and initiative it was necessary for the child to mix with an increasing number of people. Now, by going to school, his or her social universe is significantly extended. Where previously the parents and family were the main agents of socialization, in middle childhood, teachers, friends and peers now become important social influences. There are fairly crucial implications in the balance of power between parents and peer-group in the socializing of the child, as he or she grows older. Children at this stage tend to choose friends from those who live in the same neighbourhood or who are in the same class at school, also those who are about the same age. Even at this tender age children tend to choose friends who have the same status as themselves. In choosing friends, primary school children (after the age of 8 or so) prefer members of their own sex.

PREVALENCE RATES

The age bracket of 5–10 years is the most vulnerable age grouping, particularly if the stressor involved a period exceeding six months of separation from parents, siblings and the family home. Emotional disorders constitute just under half of the overall prevalence rate of children in their middle school years and early adolescence: conduct disorders constitute a similar proportion (Rutter, Tizard and Whitmore, 1970). In a recent survey (Cohen et al., 1993) of a general population sample of ages 10–20, age and gender patterns for several disorders suggest developmental stage-associated risks. These include oppositional disorder in both genders, and conduct disorder and major depression in girls. Major depression shows a pattern suggestive of vulnerability at the onset of puberty (see Tables 8 and 9).

Yule (1981) provides a useful guide to the prevalence and type of childhood problems of the school-going period. He notes that handicapping problems are very common in the 9–11 age range. In the studies of over 2000 children in this bracket in the Isle of Wight in the early 1960s (Rutter, Tizard and Whitmore, 1970) there was a very strong relationship between school failure and behavioural problems. By the end of their junior schooling, 16% in the 9–11 year age group were handicapped to a significant extent. In an epidemiological longitudinal study (Esser, Schmidt and Woerner, 1990), 356 out of 399 8-year-old German children were re-examined at age 13. The authors found that prevalence rates for psychiatric disorders in 8- and 13-year-olds lay in the range of 16–18%. Between one quarter and one third of these children manifested serious disturbances (see Plomin, 1995; for a discussion of the genetic influences).

Table 8 Emotional disorders of childhood and adolescence

| | Prevalence per 100 youths | | | | | |
| | Overanxious disorder | | Separation anxiety | | Major depression | |
	Girls	Boys	Girls	Boys	Girls	Boys
Age 10–13:						
260 girls, 281 boys						
No. cases	40	36	34	32	6	5
Prevalence	15.4	12.8	13.1	11.4	2.3	1.8
(SE)	2.2	2.0	2.1	1.9	0.9	0.8
Age 14–16:						
262 girls, 246 boys						
No. cases	37	13	12	3	20	4
Prevalence	14.1	5.3	4.6	1.2	7.6	1.6
(SE)	2.2	1.4	1.3	0.7	1.6	0.8
Age 17–20:						
224 girls, 222 boys						
No. cases	31	12	4	6	6	6
Prevalence	13.8	5.4	1.8	2.7	2.7	2.7
(SE)	2.4	1.5	0.9	1.1	1.1	1.1
Odds ratio (95% confidence limits)						
Gender	0.51 (0.39–0.71)*		0.77 (0.50–1.18)		0.44 (0.24–0.82)*	
Age	0.92 (0.87–0.97)*		0.74 (0.68–0.80)*		1.03 (0.94–1.13)	
Age^2	1.00 (0.98–1.02)		1.00 (0.98–1.03)		0.99 (0.96–1.02)	
Gender by Age	0.90 (0.80–1.00)*		1.02 (0.86–1.20)		1.01 (0.82–1.23)	
Gender by Age^2	1.01 (0.97–1.04)		1.06 (1.01–1.12)		1.07 (1.00–1.14)*	

Table 9 Disruptive disorders of childhood and adolescence

| | Prevalence per 100 youths | | | | | |
| | Attention deficit disorder | | Conduct disorder | | Oppositional disorder | |
	Girls	Boys	Girls	Boys	Girls	Boys
Age 10–13						
260 girls, 281 boys						
No. cases	22	48	10	45	27	40
Prevalence	8.5	17.1	3.8	16.0	10.4	14.2
(SE)	1.7	2.2	1.2	2.2	1.9	2.1
Age 14–16						
262 girls, 246 boys						
No. cases	17	28	24	39	41	38
Prevalence	6.5	11.4	9.2	15.8	15.6	15.4
(SE)	1.5	2.0	1.8	2.3	2.2	2.3
Age 17–20						
224 girls, 222 boys						
No. cases	14	13	16	21	28	27
Prevalence	6.2	5.8	7.1	9.5	12.5	12.2
(SE)	1.6	1.6	1.7	2.0	2.2	2.2
Odds ratio (95% confidence limits)						
Gender	1.90 (1.33–2.70)*		2.27 (1.60–3.22)*		1.05 (0.78–1.41)	
Age	0.88 (0.82–0.93)*		0.98 (0.92–1.03)		1.01 (0.96–1.06)	
Age^2	0.99 (0.97–1.01)		0.98 (0.96–0.99)*		0.96 (0.94–0.98)*	
Gender by Age	0.90 (0.79–1.01)		0.90 (0.80–1.01)		1.00 (0.91–1.10)	
Gender by Age^2	1.02 (0.98–1.07)		1.06 (1.00–1.11)*		1.01 (0.97–1.05)	

FEARS AND PHOBIAS

Both the number and intensity of fears reported by children and adolescents *decrease* with age (King *et al.*, 1989; Ollendick, King and Frary, 1989). Using the *Fear Survey Schedule for Children—Revised*, Ollendick (1983) found that 7- to 10-year-old children reported significantly more fears than 11- to 13-year-olds or 14- to 16-year-olds, who did not differ from one another. The *Fear Survey Schedule for Children—Revised* consists of 80 stimuli to which the children are asked to indicate the extent of their fear: 'none', 'some', or 'a lot'. The younger children, on average, reported having a lot of fear for 17 of the stimuli, whereas the two older groups reported a lot of fear, on average for 13 of the items. Eight of the ten most feared objects or situations were the same regardless of age: being hit by a car or truck, not being able to breathe, bombing attacks, fire, getting burned, falling from a high place, a burglar breaking into our house, earthquakes and death. For 7- to 10-year-old children, the remaining two most frequently reported fears were getting lost in a strange place and being sent to the (school) principal. For older children and adolescents, however, the remaining two fears consisted of getting poor grades and failing a test. Overall, it is evident that children and adolescents between 7 and 16 years of age reported realistic and specific fears and that eight of the top ten fears were the same across these age ranges. Consistent with Bauer's (1976) developmental analysis, however, it is clear that the additional fears reported by younger children were of separation and punishment whereas those of the older children and adolescents were of a social–evaluative nature. Unlike the 'normal' fears of childhood, phobias are likely to be intense, durable, and not age-specific.

Determining an accurate estimate of the prevalence of phobias in children is difficult despite the various ways of determining such figures. On the basis of test questionnaires, observations and interviews, Agras, Sylvester and Oliveau (1969) retrospectively classified the fears of children as common fears, intense fears, and phobias. Common fears were abundant; however, the rate of intense fears was about 8% while the rate of phobias was about 2%. In an extensive survey of 9–11-year-old children on the Isle of Wight, Rutter, Tizard and Whitmore (1970) found fewer than 1% of the children to have clinically significant phobias. However, as noted by King, Hamilton and Ollendick (1988), this may be an underestimate since children with single phobias were not included in these estimates. Based on these studies and others, it appears that Miller, Barrett and Hampe's (1974) suggestion that 'the most typical response pattern approximates a J-curve in which 84% or more of the children show no fear of the stimuli while 5–15% show what parents consider to be normal fear, and 0 to 5% show excessive fear.

While it may be the case that some highly fearful and phobic children 'outgrow' their condition over time (e.g. Agras, Chapin and Oliveau, 1972), it is probable that many do not and that, for those children, fears persist and develop into phobias (Ollendick, King and Frary, 1989).

Fears of Attending School

Among the most worrying fears of childhood are those that produce a reluctance or refusal to go to school. We take for granted the early-morning routine of seeing the children off to school. So when a child refuses to go any more, it is a shock to realize just how dependent we are on the voluntary cooperation of youngsters for the smooth running of the daily household round. As with real 'rebellions' (parents tend to think of the refusal as rebellious), school refusal tends to catch those in authority by surprise. There is the age-old problem of what to do about the rebel once we have exhausted all the usual methods of persuasion. And there is the same feeling of impotence for, when the problem becomes really serious, the school refuser remains implacable in the face of threats, entreaties and bribes. Short of carrying the offender forcibly to school and chaining him or her to the desk, there seems little more that harassed parents and teachers can do.

King, Ollendick and Tonge (1995) quote a mother, illustrating her sense of bewilderment and helplessness.

> It's so hard as a single parent . . . what can I do? I leave to go to work in the morning before the school bus arrives, and he just refuses to get on the bus. Nanny (maternal grandmother) can't make him go, neither can Papa (maternal grandfather). What can I do? I need to work and can't be there in the morning. Sometimes I wonder if he's mad at me and trying to get back at me for something I did. But I don't think so—we really have a good time together. We've been through a lot; we're buddies most of the time.

Assessment

Let us begin with a definition in the form of guidelines for identifying children who refuse to go to school:

- severe difficulty attending school, often resulting in prolonged absence;
- severe emotional upset, including excessive fearfulness, temper outbursts, or complaints of feeling ill when faced with the prospect of going to school;
- staying at home with the parents' knowledge when the youngster should be at school;

- absence of antisocial characteristics such as stealing, lying and destructiveness.

This last criterion explains why it is inappropriate to label 'school refusers' as opposed to 'truants' as rebels.

Prevalence

In the case of school refusal it is low, but estimates in different studies vary. School refusal, which is frequently associated with anxiety disorders, and is differentiated from *truancy* (which tends to be associated with conduct disorders), occurs throughout the entire range of school years with high peaks at 5–6 and 11–12.

To distinguish between school refusal and other forms of absenteeism (reluctance and mild/moderate variants of non-attendance difficulties) and 'severe' school refusal, King, Ollendick and Tonge (1995) suggest the criteria: absence from school 40% of the time or more over a 4 week period.

Children who refuse to go to school usually manifest excessive anxiety and a variety of maladaptive fears. For example:

- fear of separation from their parents (usually the mother);
- fear of some kind of harm befalling their parents;
- fear of bullying by peers;
- fear of punishment by teachers;
- fears of taking tests;
- fears of undressing for sports or PE;
- fears of going to a new school.

In making an assessment of a complex problem like school refusal it is helpful to have a conceptual framework—a guide to the factors that require investigation. You might, for example assess the push–pull factors in school attendance. Many children feel reluctant at times to go to school. Their parents 'push' them into going, sometimes simply by their being there, i.e. they do not have to exert undue pressure (see Mitchell and Shepherd, 1966). But there are 'pull' factors: the authority of the school, the presence of friends at school, the interest provided by a good school (and conversely the boredom of being at home or elsewhere on one's own). In any assessment of persistent non-attendance at school the presence or absence, strength or weakness of these push–pull factors need to be evaluated. As a background to this analysis, it is helpful to list the potential crisis points in getting a child to school and keeping him or her there. It is useful to view this chronologically (see Figure 7). Thus it is quite useful to look at the process (as set out there) involved in a child getting ready for school, going and staying there, then returning home—and the things that potentially can go wrong, thus disrupting his or her attendance.

Indicators

We can first of all state the obvious: that, in such a case, the parents will have been trying unsuccessfully, and for some time, to get the child to go to school. In addition, the child is likely to be suffering from anxiety in connection with a number of other topics, which most children cope with fairly well; like quicksilver, his or her anxiety is apt to move about, changing shape—now attached to one object (say, his mother's health), now jumping to another (perhaps a sarcastic teacher), and then another (possibly the playground bully). His/her apprehensions are not soothed by reassurances. They have recurrent physical symptoms, which tend to clear up at weekends, or even (and this is particularly maddening) shortly after parents have reluctantly agreed to keep them at home. Are they, then, malingerers or rebels? The answer is neither.

Let us look at Thomas, who is refusing to go to school. This pale and tremulous child is experiencing all the mental and physical suffering of an anxiety attack—no less real because his parents feel that his fears are unreasonable or imaginary. He is the antithesis of the defiant rebel. The child does not *choose* to stay away from school; the fact of the matter is that he *cannot* go, because of some overwhelming dread of the school-going process. Research shows that it is certainly not mere *dislike* of the place that causes school refusal. There is no difference between the attendance records of children who like school and those who dislike it; the cause must be something much more serious and fundamental. Thomas displayed some of the typical physiological changes—pallor, breathing irregularities, tremulousness and muscular tension—signs of sympathetic nervous system arousal. He also displayed, again typically, complaints of physical illness (stomach pains and headache) for which there was no organic cause. The tearfulness, verbal excuses and protests, tantrums and other resistive behaviours, are also par for the course.

Some school refusers display *depressive* features, including dysphoria, irritability, feelings of worthlessness, weepiness, guilt and sleep problems. Such problems are most often found in adolescent school refusers.

Social skill deficits—problems of interacting with peers, loneliness and social isolation—are fairly common. Low self-esteem is often a significant factor. They may suffer from any of the anxiety disorders listed in DSM-IV (American Psychiatric Association, 1994):

- separation anxiety disorder;
- simple phobia (e.g. social phobia);
- over-anxious disorder;
- avoidant disorder;
- panic disorder;

Has to wake up on time → Get bathed, dressed, breakfasted → Leave the house on time → Make a journey → Enter the school gates → Go to assembly → Stay in the school → Go home at appropriate time

School phobia?

(1) Does he wake on time? If not, why not?

(2) Does he get enough sleep? If not, why not (going to bed late; lying in bed unable to sleep because of morbid pre-occupations, tense, depressed)?

(3) Anyone to structure his day at home, e.g. supervise his getting ready ('push')?

(4) Is he sick/anxious/panicky?

(5) Any reason he needs to be at home (care for a sick member of the family; parents keep him at home to look after siblings, etc.)?

(6) Is he afraid to leave home because concerned about his mother's health, afraid of an accident befalling her (preoccupation with death, separation, anxiety)?

(7) Is he depressed, overwhelmed by apathy, helplessness, inertia?

Truancy?

(8) Is he teased/bullied on the way to, or at, school?

(9) Claustrophobia/clothing (adequate for school)/homework?

(10) Is there anything to keep him at school (interests, friends, teacher)?

(11) Deviant models (peer group) for truanting

(12) Other 'pull' factors absent? (Is he under-achieving grossly at school, bored?)

(13) Does anyone really know him or take an interest in him at school?

Figure 7

- obsessive–compulsive disorder;
- post-traumatic stress disorder;
- generalized anxiety disorder.

These should be routinely explored for their possible presence in school-refusing children and adolescents. The first two are the most frequently observed diagnoses (together with depressive disorder) in school refusers. What is clear from various diagnostic studies is that the formulation of school refusal is complex, variable, and highly individualized.

Duration

For some children the school refusal episode is acute and shortlived; for others it persists over years. SR children show a normal distribution of intelligence. Some are at risk of a continuation of psychopathology in later, adult life.

Assessment: A Multimethod Approach

A wide range of procedures is used to assess school refusal:

- behavioural interviews (e.g. Ollendick and Cerny, 1981);
- diagnostic interviews (Silverman, 1994);
- self-reports e.g. Fear Schedule for Children (Ollendick, 1983);
- ratings of significant others (e.g. Child Behaviour Checklist, Achenbach, 1978);
- self-monitoring (e.g. Beidel, Neal and Lederec, 1991);
- behavioural observations (e.g. Gardner, 1997; Hartmann, 1982).

The strategy (King, Ollendick and Tonge, 1995) for assessing school refusal is to begin with a broad-based assessment of the child and his/her environment (e.g. family, school, classroom, peers—see Figure 3) and move on toward obtaining specific information about stimulus features, response modes, antecedents and consequences, severity, duration, and pervasiveness of the school non-attendance. In essence, this is a problem-solving approach.

It is important to remember, as a backdrop to school refusal, that childhood is notable for fears of many remote and improbable circumstances. Much later—at adolescence—the fears which arise are more immediate and personal, such as those concerning relationships with the opposite sex. The age of eleven tends to bring about an increase in the fearfulness of children. This may be due, in part, to separation from old friends, familiar routines, with the move to secondary school. Among eleven- and twelve-year-olds, worries connected with *school* are nearly half as many again as worries about home matters.

Causation

Many causal influences (determinants) contribute to the development and continuation of school refusal. Among the factors mentioned in the literature are:

(1) constitutional (inborn) vulnerability, emotional reactivity;
(2) temperament (behaviourally inhibited, shy, fearful);
(3) stressful life events at home and/or school (e.g. change of school; illness, accident, operation requiring absence from school/hospitalization; illness, death, departure of parent); bullying; harsh teacher;
(4) an accumulation of life stresses (see Blagg, 1987).

Given that many children are not enamoured of life at school, why do only certain children carry their reluctance to go to school right through to the point of adamant refusal? Much will depend on the intensity of the stresses in a particular school situation, but the normal range of stressful school situations, whatever they are, precipitates drastic reactions in a minority of children only. For most children school fulfils several important needs, providing a stimulating and reasonably happy environment most of the time. Despite the inevitable complaints and the occasional reluctance (expressed to suspicious—sometimes complaisant—parents) which are part of the ups-and-downs of any child's school-going career, surveys show that most children enjoy school life once the routine becomes established. Mitchell and Shepherd (1966) reported that in Buckinghamshire about 5% of boys and 3% of girls under the age of 12 disliked going to school; yet their attendance was very little different from those who liked school. They say that 'this would seem to indicate that, during the primary school years, children may achieve regular attendance under firm parental pressure and regardless of their own inclinations.'

The 50 school-refusing children Hersov (1960) studied gave different explanations for their refusal; the commonest (34%) was a fear of some harm befalling mother while the child was at school; next in importance were fear of ridicule, bullying, or harm from other children (18%); next, fear of academic failure (28%); then—rather less frequently—the fear of a strict, sarcastic teacher (22%). Hersov found overt anxieties about menstruation in six girls and concern about puberty and masturbation in three boys.

Several of children's anxieties at school—in a general sense—may figure in the school refuser's worries. They include the size and routine of the school; examination stresses; experiences of classroom failure; disturbed relationships with teachers and schoolmates; parental pressures and expectations; and intellectual disability. Sixth-grade American schoolchildren, aged eleven, worry about the following school situations, in order of frequency: failing on a test; being late for school; being poor in spelling; being asked to answer questions; being poor in reading; getting a poor report card; being reprimanded; not doing as well as other pupils; being poor at maths and drawing. The point about a 'phobic reaction' is that it is disproportionate to the objective 'distressing' situation. Most children manage to cope with the difficulties listed above without refusing to go to school. But the phobic child may not really be worried about any of these things. In many instances, it is a fear of leaving mother rather than something at school that is bothering him or her.

Those at Risk

Why should only certain children escalate an initial reluctance to go to school to the point of refusal? There are many predisposing causes at work which produce a *vulnerable* child, one who is unable to meet stressful challenges (which are bound to arise from time to time in the school situation) with resilience and flexibility. Studies of children with attendance problems show many of them to be neurotic, a large proportion of them being timid, fearful and inhibited when away from home. A majority of these apparently timid children show the *reverse* behaviour at home, being wilful and demanding, even dominating their parents by their stubbornness. Generally, school refusers are anxious because for some reason they cannot cope outside the home. When they *do* go to school, such children are well-behaved, conforming (again, not rebels), and hard-working (some being successful, others failing), but usually they are socially maladjusted.

Treatment

Most cases of school refusal respond to treatment. Many experts believe that the child and family consultation clinic is best placed to offer the broad-based treatment strategy, including therapy and counselling, which is required for such a problem. An assessment of the child's attainments at school by an educational psychologist may uncover specific learning difficulties.

Cooperation between parents and school is, of course, of great importance. The type of individual therapy programme to be instituted will be determined by the exact nature of the child's disturbance. The information revealed by a thorough psychological, educational, and psychometric investigation will suggest what procedures should be followed. Remedial education can be provided when necessary; a change of class or school may be arranged, referral made to a specialist unit dealing with school attendance problems, or individual therapy applied.

School refusal is pervasive in its ill-effects on the child's life; it isolates him or her from so many learning experiences—social as well as academic. Thus, the primary criterion of a successful intervention is the child's return to school. Some of the treatment possibilities include the following.

Family Disturbance

It is important not necessarily to give a school refusing child 'sole ownership' of the problem. Various forms of neurotic disorder and other forms of psychiatric disturbance have been found in parents of these children (e.g. Last *et al.*, 1987). Parents may be highly anxious and overprotective. Whole families can become 'infected' by the heightened arousal and frustration surrounding the non-attendance. Behavioural family therapy (see Herbert, 1987b; 1988) may be appropriate in such cases or even, perhaps, adult counselling/therapy for the parents.

Medical Check/Intervention

Viral infections and other medical conditions can contribute to the onset of school refusal. Liaison with the family doctor is important.

School Visits

Liaison with the school should be close and informative. Network meetings between those involved: education welfare officer, psychologist, teacher(s), headteachers and others of significance to the case will be vital for planning the intervention—vital because the intervention so often is multilevel, and requires coordination. Issues such as whether to return to the present school, enter a new one, or attend a special non-attender's treatment/educational unit will require careful thought and discussion. Fences may have to be mended if relationships between the parents and school have become difficult.

Pharmacotherapy

Pharmacotherapy is sometimes used in an adjunctive role, especially where the child suffers from separation anxiety and/or depression to a serious degree. This is a contentious area and requires more space to consider the issues than is available in this guide. However, see King, Ollendick and Tonge (1995).

Behavioural Treatment Strategies

(See Herbert (1987a, 1994a) and King & Ollendick (1997) for the theoretical background.

These behavioural management strategies consist of:

(1) relaxation training (see Knoeppen, 1974);
(2) systematic desensitization;
(3) emotive imagery;
(4) modelling (see Esveldt-Dawson *et al.* 1982);
(5) cognitive restructuring (Kendall, 1993);
(6) shaping and contingency management.

'Desensitization techniques' offer a promising compromise between the difficulties of enforcing an immediate reintroduction of the child into school and the dangers of further delays (see Chapter 13). An example of a desensitization technique is provided by the case of ten-year-old Jimmy who suffered from a school phobia. He and his therapist would go to the school early in the morning when no one else was present. Jimmy was asked to report any feelings of apprehension. As soon as he did so, the therapist immediately took Jimmy back to the car and praised him for what he had achieved so far. The therapist and the child approached the school together in a series of steps graded from the least anxiety-provoking situation (sitting in a car in front of the school) to the most anxiety-provoking condition (being in the classroom with the teacher and other pupils present). At the end of a twenty-day period of desensitization treatment, Jimmy had returned to school completely. The presence of the therapist (with whom Jimmy had a good relationship) was considered as a strong positive stimulus evoking a positive emotional response. The graduated re-entry into school-life was so designed that Jimmy's confidence in the therapist would counteract any fears aroused by each new step forward in the treatment programme.

In the case of Barry, an only child aged 15, the author had to intervene over a wide spectrum as many of the push–pull factors in his life were absent or minimal. This meant, *inter alia,* enlisting the help of a kindly neighbour to wake him up. When his mother was alive she'd had to 'drag' him out of a deep slumber. The father was on early shifts with a bus company and could not supervise the early morning routine. A series of school visits was also required to mobilize the personal interest of a teacher and educational psychologist in the fate of this lonely boy. The school was an extremely large and impersonal place. The programme also involved discussions with the boy about his future plans, his social life (he was introduced to a youth club) and his grief over the loss of his mother. Joint meetings were arranged between the author, Barry and his father to iron out misunderstandings, to work out a rota for household chores, and to arrange a contract (see Figure 8) involving a loan for a moped if Barry returned to school and gave proof of his intention to attend regularly.

In the case of two girls, aged fourteen and fifteen respectively, a central theme in their problems was a sense of helplessness (see Seligman, 1975), purposelessness, and apathy. A carefully structured 'timetable' of events and activities was constructed in order to help them to face life again. Incorporated within this was a controlled and gradual re-entry into school. Social skill training helped the girls to overcome their lack of social confidence.

Lazarus and Abramovitz (1962) illustrate the use of emotive imagery in the treatment of Stanley, a phobic 14 year old boy. He had suffered from an extreme fear of dogs for nearly three years. He would take two buses on a

---

Contract

Between   Barry K. and Mr K.

Son agrees to:

(1) Get up and make ready for school when aroused by the next door neighbour (every weekday).
(2) Catch the 8.00 am village bus to school.
(3) Stay at school during school hours.

Father agrees to:
(1) Lend Barry £20 toward the purchase of a moped.

Both parties agree to the following conditions:
(1) The loan will be paid after Barry has been back at school for 1 month.
(2) The penalty for missing school after that date will be the loss of the use of the bike for each day missed (unless there is a legitimate reason for absence from school).
(3) The money will be returned at the rate of £1.50 per month out of Barry's paper round money.

Signed...
                        Father

Signed...
                        Son

Figure 8

circuitous route to school rather than risk an encounter with dogs on a direct 300-yard walk. Because he was not responsive to relaxation training, the therapists applied a technique called 'emotive imagery'. Children are required to visualize elaborate fantasy situations involving their favourite heroes, activities or desired goals, and aspects of the phobic stimulus are woven into the fantasy in a gradual manner. It is hoped that the pleasant features of the situation will counter the aversive ones. In Stanley's case, he had a powerful ambition to own an Alfa Romeo and race it at the Indianapolis 500. The therapists instructed him to close his eyes and imagine as vividly as possible that his wish had been fulfilled. The first scene involved the sports car standing outside his house, where Stanley could picture how beautiful it was. Next he imagined going out for a drive in it. Then he would stop in a little town; people would admire the car, and so on. Into this highly pleasurable situation was introduced a large dog which would come up and sniff at the car. If the boy felt any anxiety, he would, as in systematic densitization, immediately signal, and the image would be 'erased' from his mind. This technique led closer and closer to the previously frightening stimulus and proved successful in combating his phobia.

COGNITIVE DEVELOPMENT AND SCHOOL ACHIEVEMENT

Getting on toward 7 years of age children begin to solve problems concretely, using a variety of cognitive strategies which were not available to them in their earlier years. It is no accident that the child can cope with school at about the same time he or she can see events from different perspectives and think conceptually about complex relationships (see Inhelder and Piaget, 1964).

Another significant finding is that developmental changes on a variety of intellectual tasks indicate that between 5 and 7 years of age there is a dramatic increase in the quality of performance on problems requiring focused and sustained attention. This generalization seems to hold for several cultures (Mussen, Conger and Kagan, 1984). The child under 5 years of age seems easily distracted and lacks the ability to select, shift and direct focus like the over-fives. By the end of middle childhood we begin to see the fundamental difference between concrete operational thinking and the cognitive capabilities of the next stage which Piaget calls 'formal propositional thinking'.

The Slow Developer

We know that children develop at different rates in a variety of spheres of life; there is a wide range of differences which is quite normal. However, the really slow developer—be it physically, intellectually or emotionally— may face special difficulties in adjusting to school life. And these difficulties of adjustment are not necessarily confined to the opening phases of school life. The school environment is one which, all the time, is evolving towards greater complexity. It therefore continually increases its demands upon the child, demands of greater and wider mastery of intellectual, social and physical skills.

If children are going to be successful at school they must desire *and* strive to do what is required of them by their parents and teachers, and also to do it well. Eventually they develop their *own* standards of excellence. When this incentive to do well comes into play—the child is not born with it—it is called achievement motivation. By the time children are at primary school, they show (as teachers are well aware) marked differences in their need to achieve, and in the areas of endeavour in which they show it. The pressure for success and for 'results' in our competitive society is enormous; the price of failure is a heavy one. To mention the words 'academic success' in some circles is to generate a heated debate. Some schools are criticized for their tunnel vision of success, based—as we have seen— upon a narrowly conceived and exam-orientated curriculum. If unrealistic standards are set at home or school, it is not long before children become self-conscious about the discrepancy between their performance and the expectations of adults.

All of this begs the question: what is success? It is surely inadequate to judge academic success solely by means of relatively narrow educational criteria (such as exams) which largely determine occupational skills. Many other advantages are provided by schools' personal relationships, social skills and attitudes—and these too may have a marked influence on people's careers. Academic success might also be defined by psychological criteria, in terms of experience, incentive, knowledge and intellectual skills outside the remit of the examination curriculum. Success does involve more than attainment; it involves curiosity about the world, the opening of minds, the motivation to *use* and capitalize on one's education, to develop toward higher levels of maturity. Maturity is a value judgement and therefore impossible to define in absolute terms. However, the mature person in western culture is thought to be capable (relative to his/ her age) of:

- being flexible in the face of new situations—able to change when it is necessary;
- developing a point of view; his/her own outlook on things; being him- or herself and capable of independent action and thought;
- showing a sense of humour;
- accepting reality;

- accepting him- or herself, showing respect and liking (not narcissistic love) for him- or herself, plus self-awareness;
- Enjoying human relationships (i.e. able and willing to form affectionate, lasting and altruistic emotional attachments to other people).

Research tells us that young people who do well at school tend to enjoy good health, have average or above-average intelligence and well-developed social skills. They are likely to have a good opinion of themselves, the ability to gauge accurately their effect on others, and to perceive correctly the quality of others' approaches and responses to themselves. Early maturing boys and girls have many advantages in terms of capability and self-confidence.

Social status—rightly or wrongly—depends to a large degree on occupation. Occupation, in turn, is associated very much with academic qualifications. If academic success is going to be measured in terms of the social status to which it opens doors, then the main criteria are likely to involve the level, grade and number of formal qualifications obtained by the student. Inevitably, however, competition, selectivity and discrimination enter the educational equation, much to the disadvantage of some youngsters. The absence of opportunity too often occurs well before school life begins.

The differences which occur between individual children on measures of educational attainment are strongly related to the children's social background and ethnic origin. Studies in the UK and the USA have consistently found that children from lower social class groups achieve lower scores than those from middle-class backgrounds. For example, the National Child Development Study in the UK followed up all children born in one week in 1958 throughout their school careers. Detailed information was collected about their educational progress, home background and psychological development at the ages of 7, 11 and 16 years. The data revealed a very close relationship between social class and educational attainment. On tests of arithmetic and reading, for example, the proportion of children with poor test scores was much higher in children from manual working-class homes that in those of non-manual, middle-class homes.

Cultural Deprivation

This kind of finding has frequently been explained in terms of the idea of educational disadvantage, or 'cultural deprivation'. Children from lower-class homes are more likely to live in families with a large number of children, and with a single parent, to have a low family income, and to live in poor housing. All these factors combine to restrict the cognitive and linguistic stimulation which children receive in the home and this, along with any lack of parental encouragement, gives rise to underachievement at school and poor performance in tests.

Along with this explanation came the view that 'cultural deprivation' could be remedied: that remedial education programmes could be provided which could compensate for the effects of a disadvantaged background. Appropriate intervention ought to be able to reverse the effect. The outcomes of the compensatory education programmes which were mounted in the USA ought to provide crucial tests of these predictions.

Compensatory Education

Among the best-known compensatory education programmes are *Project Head Start*, which began in 1965, and the Milwaukee project carried out by Heber and his colleagues at the University of Wisconsin. The idea was to give preschoolers from disadvantaged homes a 'head start' by providing them with educational experiences which were likely to be absent from their homes. In particular, attempts were made to remedy their cognitive and linguistic deficiencies. A variety of local programmes were instituted across the USA, and these varied quite widely in their content and duration, and in the age, socioeconomic and ethnic composition of the children. A radical interpretation of the generally disappointing results is that the 'cultural deprivation' model on which the intervention programmes are based might be inappropriate.

An alternative view, the 'difference' model, is that because schools and educational institutions tend to be permeated with white, middle-class values and attitudes, children from different backgrounds may simply fail to adapt to them. The black working-class children in these studies may not be 'deprived' in relation to their middle-class counterparts; they may simply be 'different', and it may be at best patronizing, and at worst racist, to assume the former. If this is true, there is no reason why compensatory programmes *should* produce any increase in intellectual ability—e.g. IQ scores and scholastic attainment.

Authoritative (not authoritarian!) parents are most likely to facilitate the development of competence and self-reliance in young children by enhancing responsible, purposive and independent behaviour. McClelland (1961), who devoted many years to research on influences on motivation and achievement in America, maintains that what is desirable is an emphasis on the child meeting certain achievement standards between the ages of 6 and 8. The young person, later on in development, is likely to be highly motivated if, in addition, he or she is held in warm regard by both parents, who are ambitious for their offspring but not too dominating, and who have a strong, positive attitude towards education.

There can be little doubt that hereditary factors are also a major source of individual differences in attainment. Environmental factors too can enhance, stunt or distort attainment. Parental background plays a part in what children achieve. Social-class differences in attainment increase as children grow older. A study by Douglas and colleagues of a large random sample of all children born in Britain in one week in 1946 found that differences between the average attainments of the offspring of manual and non-manual workers increased between the ages of 8 and 11. Irrespective of the level of attainment, significant differences appeared at age 11 between children of the two classes who had been equal at age 8 (see Douglas, Ross and Simpson, 1968).

Social class is also closely related to school-leaving age; according to the 'Youth in Transition' study, working-class children in the USA are less likely to stay on at school for a sixth-year course. By the age of 18 more than half of those who had left school early had failed at least one grade in school, compared to only 27% of the high-school graduates. Students gave as their reasons for dropping out statements which were consistent with low academic ability. As one put it, 'I was mostly just discouraged because I wasn't passing.' Students who were lower in academic ability, as measured by standardized tests of ability, were more likely to drop out.

Locus of Control

Students in the 'Youth in Transition' study were given a personality test to measure what is called 'locus of control'. Those students who scored high on the scale ('externals') believed that forces controlling their lives were external to themselves, in the hands of fate or chance. The students who were high 'externals' were more likely to drop out of high school than those who scored low on this attribute ('internals').

An internal locus of control is correlated with satisfactory school achievement. If children are allowed to experience a degree of control over their learning environment, then they will learn more effectively. Obviously we have to be careful here. If by helping children to internalize their locus of control we lead them to believe that whenever they fail in anything it is their fault, then we will be doing more harm than good.

Schools are in a powerful position to exert influence on their students because, in essence, they have a 'captive audience' for some 15 000 hours. This is the average amount of time spent by British children at school. They enter an environment providing work and play for nearly a dozen years during a formative period of development. Children spend almost as much of their waking life at school as at home. And it is an influence not only because it transmits academic and technical skills and cultural interests. The school introduces boys and girls to social and working relationships and to various forms of authority which they would not experience in the family. The areas of particular influence— academic success, social behaviour, moral values and occupational choice—represent major themes in the socialization of young people (see Sylva, 1994).

Schools are a microcosm of the society they serve. No matter how good they are, they can only do so much for the young people who have been severely disadvantaged or emotionally disturbed by the circumstances of their lives—sometimes from their earliest years. These children are programmed for failure, unless the opportunity arises to reverse or remedy destructive influences. Fortunately, for many children who have been condemned to failure at school, the great release comes when they go out into the adult world and have to earn a living and perhaps support a family. They find new incentives and rewards for their efforts, and they surprise and delight themselves with the unsuspected capacity for hard work and application which they discover.

Failure in a success-orientated world has significant consequences for the well-being of adolescents, not only at school, but in other facets of their lives. There is a strong association—as we have seen—between emotional disturbance and under-achievement at school—a perennial matter of concern to both teachers and parents. Emotionally disturbed adolescents tend to distract and harass their teachers, and disrupt and anger their more conscientious fellow students.

Under-achievement

Chronic under-achievement in boys of above-average aptitude may begin in the primary school. It is not so likely to show itself in girls until they reach secondary school. Adolescents who fail at school may be of lower than average IQ, but intellectually well-endowed young people can also do poorly. It is rare to identify academic failure in isolation from a range of other problems, particularly disruptive activities in the school setting and/or disturbance in relationships between the adolescent and other members of the family. Although the learning problems of adolescents in the school setting may sometimes be causally linked to attentional and other specific learning deficits, academic failure arising from such problems is much more likely to be manifested during the infant primary school years (Torgesen, 1975). Studies (e.g. Trites and Fidorowicz, 1976; Peter and Spreen, 1979) indicate that specific deficits in reading persist through adolescence into adulthood with the youth falling further and further behind. These effects seem to be most marked for female adolescents.

Children with specific difficulties in learning manifest a variety of emotional and conduct problems, ranging from aggressive and disruptive behaviour, to anxiety, poor motivation and low self-esteem (Yule and Rutter, 1985). These are referred to by staff in many care and educational establishments as 'challenging' behaviours. There is also evidence that many such children fail to develop appropriate social skills (LaGreca, 1981).

Specific Learning Difficulties (Reading Problems)

This problem is fairly common and is usually found in boys. Using a criterion of two standard deviations (or about two years retarded) below expected reading age, specific retardation of reading has been found in some 10% of inner-London children (Berger, Yule and Rutter, 1975). In the Isle of Wight survey (Rutter, Tizard and Whitmore, 1970) 4% of the children were found to be reading at least 28 months below the level expected on the basis of their age and intelligence. They were all children of normal intelligence. Many backward readers were found to be clumsy and delayed in their speech. The backward readers showed difficulties in telling right from left. They also suffered from what is called motor impersistence. That is to say they couldn't hold any movement, such as shutting their eyes, for very long. They also had general difficulties in concentrating. Reading backwardness often goes hand in hand with difficulties in arithmetic and spelling, and it is not uncommon for there to be a family history of reading difficulties. The causes are probably multifactorial and include (notably) poor home situation, inadequate teaching, lack of home–school cooperation and genetic factors. Emotional problems are frequently associated with backwardness in reading; a third of the children with severe reading backwardness also exhibited marked antisocial behaviour.

SCHOOL ORGANIZATION

There is a mass of research evidence emphasizing the importance of the influence of organizational features of the school. The school that does well on examination results (in the UK) also does well on social measures (e.g.

low delinquency rates; low truancy rates). The school atmosphere, if good, creates good social responses and good academic responses from students. *The two go together!* After all, *academic* development and *personal–social* development are the two major purposes for which schools are created.

Rutter *et al.* (1979) demonstrate very convincingly that children do better at school—in all sorts of ways—when the curriculum and approaches to discipline are agreed to, and supported by, the staff acting together. Attendance at school is better and delinquency less frequent in schools where there is such accord and where courses are planned jointly. Group planning provides opportunities for teachers to support and encourage one another; continuity of teaching is also enhanced. Much the same is found with regard to standards of discipline. Exam successes are more frequent and delinquency less common in schools where discipline is based on *general* expectations set by the school (or house, or department) rather than left to individual teachers to work out for themselves. School values and norms appear to be more effective if it is clear to all that they have widespread support. Discipline is easier to maintain if the pupils appreciate that it relates to generally accepted approaches and does not simply represent the whim of an individual teacher.

Assessment: Organizational Aspects

Fontana (1986) lists the *organizational* features that characterize successful classroom activities:

- The school rules are few in number but are clear, well publicized, and consistently applied.
- Rules are sensible, are related to the needs of the school community, and are seen by children as being fair and appropriate.
- Rules, moreover, are subject to change and development in response to the changing and developing needs of the children and of society generally.
- The school has clear and efficient lines of communication between pupils and teachers at all levels, and equally effective lines of communication between the staff themselves.
- Decisions taken by the headteachers and by staff generally are never arbitrary, but are related to the procedures, standards and values which the school is seen by all its members to be operating.
- Where possible, the school provides opportunities for democratic debate on important issues. At the very least, pupils and teachers are allowed to feel that there are opportunities to make their views known within the school system, and that such views will receive sympathetic attention.

- The school provides effective classroom teaching, related successfully to the children's academic and social goals.
- The school makes it clear, by word and deed, that it is there to help children with both their personal and their academic achievement problems. No individual or group within the school is made to feel that they are less important to the community than are any of the rest.
- The school offers stimulating and adequate provision for cultural, sporting and leisure pursuits, and indicates that these are an integral part of school life.
- Close and sympathetic links are maintained with the local community, including parents, and full participation by the community in the life of the school is encouraged.
- There is a set and workable procedure for assessing children with special needs, and for helping them to meet these needs.
- Children receive clear guidance at points of academic and vocational decision, such as when deciding on options between available subjects, making vocational choices, and preparing for interviews and job applications.
- The school is seen by pupils of all ability groups to be preparing them for the realistic opportunities and challenges of the outside world, and to be a source of information and guidance in relation to this world.

THE INFLUENCE OF TEACHERS

In terms of the individual teacher, the important point to remember is that the teacher needs to see what kind of sense the experiences that are being offered actually make to the class. Are the children responding to and interpreting these experiences in the way in which the teacher wishes? Is it even possible for them to do so? Can the children see the application of these experiences (their relevance) to their own lives and to their daily concerns? An important aspect of that experience is discipline.

Discipline and Management in the Classroom (see Cooper, 1993; Goldstein, 1995)

There is a subtle but important distinction between managerial and educational outcomes of different disciplinary approaches. Both are important, and they overlap, but it is crucial to move beyond mere control. Since it cannot be assumed that quiet, orderly pupils are necessarily working in a productive or appropriate manner, discipline must arise not only from 'outer' control and from firm management, but also from 'inner' control resulting from the pupil's interest and enthusiasm.

Here are two questions for teachers regarding their strategies for keeping order in the classroom:

- As a result of these strategies, is the children's behaviour such that I can now go on to teach them something?
- To what extent are these strategies making a direct contribution to the task of helping pupils to be successful in their learning and to develop an intrinsic interest in curriculum activities?

The style of discipline adopted by teachers has a marked effect on whether or not the pupil manifests acceptable behaviour. There is evidence that a humane approach to control, which is characterized by skilful *group* management, enhances pupil interest, motivation and achievement. It is particularly important for teachers to adopt strategies which convey purposefulness and seriousness, providing clear procedures for helping pupils and making pupils accountable for completing work on time. The particular rules which are set and the specific disciplinary techniques which are used are probably much less important than the establishment of some principles and guidelines which are both clearly recognizable and accepted by the school as a whole. For all that, rules—or better, *thoughtful rules*—are crucial.

Cues (rules) inform the pupils about what is required of them. Here are a few guidelines for teachers:

- Negotiate rules. Discuss the rules and the reasons for them, with children who are old enough to participate in such a process. Rules are more likely to be obeyed if they are perceived as fair and seem to have a purpose. It is surely not demeaning (where possible) to engage pupils in the formulation of *their* classroom rules.
- Negotiate a set of classroom objectives and clarify the part played by rules in facilitating these objectives.
- To be effective rules should elicit responses which the pupils are capable of making.
- Emphasize rules that offer beneficial outcomes for appropriate actions.
- Select a few essential rules only—ones that can be enforced and reinforced.
- Praise pupils who follow the rules, identifying the precise grounds for the praise.
- Rules *alone* are unlikely to be effective. Ground and/or individual reinforcers (privileges) might be built into the curriculum.

Disruptive Behaviour (see Fontana, 1984)

In large part, what teachers (or parents) define as 'disruptive' activity depends upon their view of the essential nature of children in general, and pupils in particular. Teachers perspectives range over a wide spectrum and often seem polarized: at one extreme is the view of the 'good' student as deferential and docile—one who passively receives the wisdom of, and correct answers from, the teachers. At the other extreme, the pupil is regarded as an active partner in the learning process—figuratively speaking, the 'fire to be lit' rather than the 'vessel to be filled'. In this child-centred (as opposed to teacher-centred) approach, the child may be thought of as deviant if passive, whereas, in the other view, passive receptivity is the desideratum of the good pupil. Not surprisingly what one teacher calls disruptive may not be so for another.

The perceptions of parents must also be taken into account. In order to bring young children to the professionals' attention, one or more of his or her parents must come to the view that their problems merit such a referral. However, parents may inaccurately label their children as deviant due to their own problems of adjustment (e.g. marital dissatisfaction, depression, anxiety) (Webster-Stratton, 1988, 1989).

DEVELOPMENTAL–BEHAVIOURAL ASSESSMENT

Behaviour that is disruptive at school tends to occur in particular situations, between:

- pupil and authority (lateness, absenteeism, truancy, non-compliance);
- pupil and work (repeated failure to do homework or produce written work, opposition to projected work);
- pupil and teacher (the use of abusive and foul language, persistent interruption of the teacher, refusal to carry out instructions, disruptions of the teaching situation);
- pupil and pupil (bullying, intimidation, violent assault, extortion, theft).

Specificity

In many respects disruptive actions tend to occur at certain times, in certain settings, towards certain objects or individuals and in response to certain forms of provocation: children rarely show antisocial behaviour, be it aggression or defiance in blind, indiscriminate ways. There are two categories of contributory influence to consider in an assessment:

(1) *Contemporary circumstances*. For instance, physical or verbal attacks, deprivation, frustration, conflict and exposure to disruptive models which *instigate* or *maintain* (by direct, vicarious and self-reinforcement) antisocial activities.

The interactions between parents and child go a long way (as we have seen) towards shaping disruptive actions in the home, because of the reinforcing consequences inherent in their nature. Children are likely to generalize to other persons and situations what they learn about the utility and benefits of being 'difficult' with parents. In these circumstances they put to the test the consequences of being antisocial and disruptive.

For example, they may try being aggressive because it produced results (e.g. much needed kudos) with siblings or with the peer group in the playground at school. Of course, deviant behaviour which has been acquired as part of the child's repertoire may not necessarily be performed often, either because appropriate instigating conditions do not occur, or because the consequences of such acts are likely to be unrewarding or aversive.

(2) *Early learning.* But it is not only the 'here-and-now' current influences that must be taken into account in a clinical assessment. Early learning and development are important and knowledge of such factors may well influence the line taken in planning an intervention.

We know that continuity or stability varies according to *type* of behavioural disturbance. This is highlighted by the findings of Fischer *et al.* (1984) (see page 18). The longitudinal investigation by Robins (1966) of American children suggests that by ages 7 or 8 the child with *extreme* antisocial aggressive patterns of behaviour is at quite considerable risk of continuing on into adolescence and indeed adulthood with serious deviancy of one kind or another. Knowledge of the long 'incubation' period for many of the more serious antisocial childhood manifestations has implications for policy with regard to preventative work and for the credibility of applied social learning theory. Can this approach break through and interrupt the pattern of persistent antisocial behaviour?

The implication of a long and gradual (as opposed to relatively 'acute') onset of problems, is often that of a 'long-haul' intervention and a clinical formulation that includes the family system (not only the child) as client. I shall return to this theme.

CLASSROOM MANAGEMENT

The amount of formal punishment applied makes little difference in producing 'good behaviour'. In fact, too frequent disciplinary interventions are actually associated with increased disruptive activity in the classroom. Demeaning teaching behaviours such as corporal punishment, sarcasm or ridicule are notorious for militating against whatever educational out-comes are desired; in fact they tend to aggravate bad behaviour, and bring about alienation from school authority. There are parallels here with parental discipline (see Herbert, 1989b).

Pointing out a pupil's prosocial/on-task behaviour when it occurs, rather than focusing endlessly on the bad, and providing ample approval at appropriate times, will be of inestimable value to teachers who wish to foster cooperative attitudes and actions in their charges. Teachers, in gen-eral, find fault more than they praise. If teachers pay attention to a pupil who is working well, this will tend to strengthen such activity and make it likely to recur. Building on this principle is what is called 'contingency management'. It embodies one of the main characteristics of behavioural approaches to classroom management; the systematic application and/or withdrawal of reinforcement.

The aim is to increase the desired academic-related actions and reduce the disruptive activities which are such a trial to everyone but the offender. For some under-achievers, the claim of that actress who said 'Rather bad publicity than *no* publicity at all!' seems to apply in the form: 'Rather neg-ative attention (scolding) than no attention at all!' Teacher attention in the form of criticism and shouting can reinforce disruptive behaviour in cer-tain children and is thus self-defeating. It is less likely to have this unde-sirable effect if it takes the form of a 'soft reprimand'; a quiet, perhaps whispered caution, does not place the pupil in the limelight of attention from classmates.

Psychologists have applied principles of operant conditioning to supplant inattentive (and disruptive) behaviour by strengthening socially and aca-demically acceptable activities that are incompatible with the undesirable 'off task' behaviours such as squirming, fooling, talking, tapping and walking around the classroom. Differential reinforcement is used to strengthen attending ('on task') actions, such as looking at the book, work-ing out the maths problems, or listening to—and communicating with—the teacher, at appropriate times. Appropriate behaviour is rewarded (with praise, privileges, etc.), while inappropriate actions are ignored (if possible) or penalized.

There is a caveat to all of this. Teachers are often advised without qualifi-cation to reward pupils for their good behaviour rather than punish them for their bad behaviour. Rewards handed out indiscriminately carry the risk of undermining intrinsic motivation—the inherent interest and reward of the task itself. As Samuel Johnson observed, 'He who praises everybody praises nobody.' Verbal praise, as distinct from tangible rewards, tends to enhance rather than reduce intrinsic interest. This is because verbal praise can provide youngsters with information ('feedback') about their performance. The language of praise is crucial. The words 'I like the way you are using trial and error to solve that problem' are more fruitful, in their specificity, than monosyllabic approbation such as 'Great!', 'Good', or the more prolix 'Well done!' Rewards are more likely to increase youngsters' curiosity, desire to respond to a challenge and satisfaction with their work if they are sincere, justified and made contingent on real achievement.

Psychologists have been able (by systematically varying teachers' attention) to change an initially well-behaved class with an average rate of disruptiveness of 8.7% to one in which disruptiveness reached a level, on average, of 25.5 per cent. This increase was made possible by getting the teachers to withhold approval when pupils were being attentive. When the old conditions were restored, disruptiveness decreased to 12.0 per cent. It rose to 19.4 per cent on return to these non-approval conditions, and then soared to 31 per cent when teachers strongly and frequently disapproved of disruptive behaviour. Fortunately, normality was finally reinstated when the experiment was terminated. These are not ephemeral or frivolous results. They have been replicated many times and they enshrine an important principle: 'Catch the child in good behaviour.'

This emphasis on the 'positive' is not a recipe for letting children 'get away with' deviant behaviour. Judicious ignoring can work for certain subliminal or barely perceptible infractions which are designed to attract attention. More serious transgressions would lead to chaos if they were simply ignored, and if nothing else were done. Teachers who are most effective in managing their classes tend to spot disruptive actions very early on and then nip them in the bud firmly but with minimal drama. The net effect is negligible interruption of the class and minimum 'pay-offs' for offenders from their classmates. An atmosphere of unremitting disapproval increases the likelihood that youngsters will show hostile behaviour.

Because educational failure tends to have so many repercussions, the extent of the difficulties should be assessed in interviews with the young person, the parents and teachers. School reports, giving details of the student's work and examination performance, may have to be augmented with a psychometric assessment of cognitive and attainment skills, direct observation of the youngster's academic behaviour in the classroom, and assessment of his or her social behaviour in the educational setting.

Giving older children responsibility for looking after school books and equipment conveys teachers' expectations that they will behave responsibly; young people can similarly be taught to behave responsibly at home. It should always be remembered that they are responsible for their own behaviour—good and bad. In the final analysis the teacher cannot control, or be responsible for, a young adult's actions. If the teacher's attitude implies that adolescents are not ultimately in control of their own behaviour, they will be tempted to opt out of their responsibilities. It is important to achieve a subtle balance between the teacher's authority and the teenager's self-direction and accountability.

Pupils have very clear ideas about what offends their dignity, self-respect and self-esteem. They react against teachers who seem inhuman or too straitlaced, and who interpret their role as teachers too literally and rigidly; those who treat pupils as anonymous, or as members of a horde, rather than as individuals in their own right; teachers who are 'soft' and/or inconsistent; and those who are 'unfair'. By contrast, pupils describe a 'good teacher' as someone who is able to keep control (paradoxically, this attribute in particular); who is able to 'have a laugh' with pupils; who can generate warm, friendly relationships and who understands pupils; who is fair, treats them as equals or with respect; and who allows a degree of freedom.

The reactions to teachers who are felt (fairly or unfairly) to assail and affront pupils may involve strategies called 'equilibration' and 'reciprocation'. In the former, pupils use tactics to restore their sense of dignity and self-esteem; they most often take the form of truanting. The latter is a strategy which includes disruption; it is a form of 'paying back' in kind, insult for insult, blow for blow.

Three major tactics of reciprocation have been identified:

- *Subversive ironies* include the ridiculing of teachers by name-calling, writing insulting graffiti or playing tricks on them.
- *Confrontational laughter* includes the sort of remark which raises the laughter of the entire class, at the teacher's expense.
- *Symbolic rebellion* has been described in an example provided by Peter Woods (described in Herbert, 1987b). A class of fifth-year 'non-examination' boys were given the task of repairing and making functional two dilapidated glasshouses. The job took them a whole term. They destroyed their work, when completed, in the space of a few minutes. This act seems like a comment on the pointlessness of school as far as they were concerned.

Teachers may be able to pre-empt or control such actions by looking out for vulnerable pupils—resentful young people who are predisposed to overract to real or imagined insults.

CLINICAL SCHOOL-BASED INTERVENTIONS

Cognitive–behavioural interventions for issues of serious academic concern have become increasingly popular in recent years (Wong, Harris and Graham, 1991). Examples of programmes used with school children and adolescents are the Anger Coping Programme (Lochman *et al.*, 1989), the Problem Solving Skills Training (PSST) Programme (Kazdin *et al.*, 1987), the Programme for Academic Survival Skills (PASS) (Greenwood *et al.*, 1977), the Practice Skills Mastery Programme (Erken and Henderson, 1976) and the Good Behaviour Game (Barrish, Saunders and Wolf, 1969).

These interventions provide operational definitions of appropriate and inappropriate behaviour and draw on different combinations of methods for their promising results (see Braswell, 1995). The main components are those which train young people to use self-talk, adaptive attributions, problem-solving/techniques and self-instruction/self-control skills, in order to modify their dysfunctional classroom activities.

A significant approach to classroom disruption involves the triadic model of providing consultations to teachers, on the assumption that they are the persons best placed to bring about behavioural change in students, and, indeed, in their own attitudes, behaviour and curricula (see Goldstein, 1995, for a review of the literature on classroom interventions).

An example of a programme for treating aggressive adolescents is that of Feindler and Ecton (1986). They provide aggressive adolescents with a rationale for cognitive restructuring that includes the analogy of rebuilding thoughts as does a carpenter rebuilding some area of faulty construction. The rationale also emphasizes the importance of learning to moderate extreme negative thinking that could trigger actions that might ultimately lead to a loss of personal power. The self-assessment process involves the following steps: (1) identify the tension, (2) identify what triggered the tension, (3) identify the negative thought connected to the tension, (4) challenge or dispute the negative thought, and (5) tone down or rebuild the thought or substitute positive thought in place of a negative one.

The school-based programme of Sarason and Sarason (1981) is an interesting example of a problem-solving intervention at the high-school level. Working with students identified as at-risk for continued delinquent actions and possible dropping-out from school, the authors designed an intervention that was presented as a special unit within a required course. The training content emphasized modelling both the overt behaviours and the cognitive antecedents of adaptive problem solving and included many opportunities for classroom behaviour-rehearsal. At the end of the programme, the students participating in the intervention class were able to generate more adaptive solutions for addressing problem situations than control subjects, and were able to give improved self-presentations in the context of a job interview for summer employment. The students were unaware of the fact that their interview was being evaluated with regard to the outcome of the intervention. At one-year follow-up, treated students had fewer absences, less tardiness, and fewer referrals for problematic behaviour than controls.

Reid and Borkowski (1987) have attempted to develop appropriate effort-orientated attributions in hyperactive schoolchildren. Such children have been reported as having a highly externalized locus of control. They are thus more likely to view what happens to them as being the result of external influences. The authors paired self-control training following a curriculum like that of Kendall and Braswell (1985) with instruction in effort attributions for both success and failure. In this training, failure was presented as the result of not using the treatment strategies, and success was considered to be the result of the child's active commitment to the strategy. The self-control plus attribution training group displayed a more reflective cognitive style than the group receiving self-control training only, and an increased sense of personal causality. At 10-month follow-up, a notably hyperactive subgroup displayed more positive teacher ratings of prosocial actions than previously.

Chapter 7

EARLY ADOLESCENCE

Adolescence is a biosocial construct—it begins in puberty and ends in a cultural definition of independence—and as such, is a moveable feast. The notions of childhood and adulthood are clear enough. Children are wholly dependent upon their parents for love, nurturance and guidance; adults are required to be independent and able to care for themselves. Somewhere between the immaturity and the hoped-for maturity of adulthood lie the six or seven years referred to as adolescence.

Adolescence is not a homogeneous stage of development. The differences between eleven and eighteen year olds can, depending on individual development, be the difference between someone who, in body and mind, is still a child, and a person who is, in most respects, an adult. Developmental tasks and preoccupations, and, indeed, their cognitive maturity, vary to an extent that requires us to consider assessment and treatment in terms of early, middle and late adolescence: the first (from about 11 to 13 years of age) being closer to childhood in its ramifications, the third (the late teens) overlapping with adulthood. Childhood ends, loosely speaking, with adolescence; the term 'adolescence' refers to the *psychological* developments which are related broadly to the physical growth processes defined by the term 'puberty'. Figure 9 provides some of the markers for the transition from one stage of development to another. Of course, the professional responsibility of clinical child psychologists transcends these somewhat arbitrary 'frontiers'. Indeed many clinical (psychology and psychiatry) posts are advertised in terms of combined child/adolescent specialisms.

By the time puberty arrives, triggered by an interaction between the sex hormones and certain cells of the brain, psychosexual development and differentiation between males and females in their identity with gender are well developed and largely irreversible. Immense changes occur in puberty, and the maturing of the sex glands is of great consequence at this stage. Even more important, however, is the convergence of critical emotional and social developments which have been taking place since childhood, and which

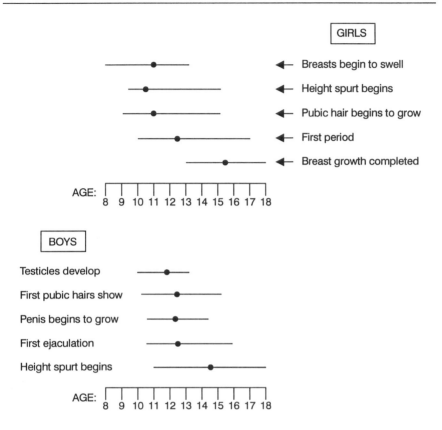

Figure 9   The age *range* for the onset of physical developments at puberty
(● = average age).

reach maturity now. The attainment of sexual maturity has a profound effect upon adolescents' status among those of their own age (see Herbert, 1987a; Rutter, 1979b, for reviews). Early-maturing boys and girls look grown up for their age and are thus given more responsibility by adults. They are likely to become leaders and to participate widely in school clubs and activities. They find it easier to compete and win at sport. Their self-confidence is boosted and so is their popularity. Yet sometimes the strain of being different, of being expected to behave in a 'grown-up' manner, begins to tell.

THE EARLY ADOLESCENT

Why, it must be asked, has adolescence been 'insulated' from the rest of development and given—relative to other stages—such a bad name? The popular (and professional) notion that adolescence is different from the whole of development which precedes it and the whole of development which follows it is of relatively recent origin. Among the early proponents of this view was Hall (1904). As the title of his magnum opus suggests, this was a weighty, and indeed, influential work.

His belief that adolescence is necessarily a stage of development associated with emotional turmoil and psychic disturbance was to become so deeply rooted, reinforced by a succession of psychoanalytically orientated writers, that it persists to this day. The 'storm and stress' story (built on eagerly by journalists in sensational items about feckless teenage hooligans and vandals) has filtered down to street level as a veritable 'demonological' theory of adolescence. Small wonder that so many parents await their child's adolescence with foreboding, and given the potency of self-fulfilling prophecies, the 'confirmation' for some of their worst predictions.

Certainly, the professionals had tended to take a jaundiced view of adolescence, attention being drawn to neurotic- or psychotic-like features: hysteria, regression, mood swings and disintegration. Hutter in the 1930s described adolescence in Alice in Wonderland terms as a period of development 'in which normally abnormalities so often happen it is abnormal that everything passes normally' (Hutter, 1938).

Not much had changed by the 1950s. Anna Freud writing on adolescence in 'Psychoanalytic study of the child' said it was 'abnormal' if a child kept a 'steady equilibrium during the adolescent period ... The adolescent manifestations come close to symptom formation of the neurotic, psychotic or dissocial order and merge almost imperceptibly into ... almost all the mental illnesses' (Freud, 1958). In the 1960s, in 'Foundations of child psychiatry', the child psychiatrist, Gillespie, wrote that 'the astonishing contrasts and contradictions which are so characteristic of adolescence produce so strong an impression of instability as to lead sometimes to a mistaken suspicion of a schizophrenic illness' (Gillespie, 1968).

As a final illustration of the medical view of adolescence as pathology and one which almost brings us up to date, we have Van Krevelen writing in the 1970s that 'adolescence is a period of life, which by its disintegrative character may seem a psychosis in itself ... it is difficult to discern in this stage a pathological process from normal development' (Van Krevelen, 1971).

But are psychiatric symptoms, alienation, the generation gap, and identity crises really the norm? Take the storm and stress concept of adolescence: this phase, although certainly not immune from its share of pain for those growing up (and for those guiding the growing-up process), is not unusually characterized by severe emotional disturbance. Although there may be problems, their overall significance and extensiveness have been exaggerated. Psychological problems are probably a little more common during adolescence than during middle childhood, but the difference is not very great (Graham and Rutter, 1973; Rutter *et al.*, 1976).

PARENTAL ATTRIBUTIONS

Why have parents been so prepared to believe the worst of teenagers? Doubtless the reasons are many and varied. Certainly, the context of raising teenagers is an important factor: parents are facing shifts at this time in their own personal development, from youthful maturity to early middle age. We cannot consider adolescents and their problems without considering the manner in which they interact with their parents, who are not without their own preoccupations and anxieties. Most parents are over 30 years old when their first child reaches puberty. Indeed, there are many parents whose children reach their teens when they are in their forties or even fifties. Parents sometimes feel vulnerable as they survey their own bodily changes, reappraise their identity and achievements and look forward, with some apprehension, to the future. To some extent their preoccupation with self- and body-image, their changing, sometimes disturbing, thoughts about the meaning of life, the directions they have taken, and the choices put upon them, converge with those of their teenage children. This may well contribute to the ambivalence of parent–adolescent relationships.

ALIENATION BETWEEN GENERATIONS

The much beloved (by the media) and feared (by parents) 'generation gap' is not as pervasive in adolescence as is generally thought (Herbert, 1987c). Distancing is not a typical pattern. Most adolescents are still attached to their homes in a positive way, and they continue to depend upon the emotional support, goodwill and approval of their parents. The family continues to be of critical importance to them as it was in earlier, less mature years; indeed, concern and supervision (as long as it is not oppressive, or too intrusive) can be demonstrated to be vital during a phase when youngsters are experimenting with life by 'trying on' different personae.

It is exceptional for teenagers to feel torn between their two 'worlds' of parents and peers, certainly on the more important issues of life. There are more likely to be differences of opinion on minor issues such as hairstyle, fashion, social habits and privileges, where parental views are likely to be rejected in favour of the standards of their offspring's friends. Where major issues are concerned, it seems that only a minority of adolescents radically depart from their parents' views; there is little evidence that secondary or higher education in itself causes changes in the political attitudes that young people absorb from their parents (Herbert, 1987c, Rutter, 1979b).

A majority of adolescents share their parents' attitudes towards moral and political issues, and are prepared (by and large) to accept their parents' guidance on academic, career and personal issues. If anything, it could be said that the generations are drawing together rather than apart (Hill and Aldous, 1969). Teenagers and their parents tend to agree on the important issues more than do parents and *their* parents (grandparents). Although the evidence is meagre, it does appear the rebelliousness and alienation are more likely in young persons who, in spite of considerable maturity, remain dependent on their parents economically or in other ways—such as students in higher education (Rutter, 1979b).

Another popular belief about adolescence is that an inevitable crisis over personal identity occurs, producing all or some of the symptoms of stress: anxiety, depression, a sense of frustration, conflict and defeatism. The development of identity does not always proceed smoothly, but what evidence we have calls into question the belief of Erikson (1965), that adolescents usually suffer a crisis over their identity. Most teenagers actually have a positive but not unrealistically inflated self-image and this view of themselves tends to be fairly stable over the years (Coleman, Wolkind and Ashley, 1977).

Although adolescents have become more accepting in their attitudes to premarital sex, this does not imply, as the media like to suggest, a massive rise in casual sexual relationships. Young people, and particularly girls, continue to emphasize the importance of love and stable emotional attachment in premarital sex, although intended marriage or an engagement is not so often seen as a prerequisite of such relationships. The emphasis tends to be on a stable relationship with one sexual partner at a time—so called 'serial monogamy' (Rutter, 1979b). Girls do, however, display more conservative attitudes to these issues than boys.

Most young people wish to get married and have children. Certainly, a committed relationship is generally thought to be essential for the rearing of children, and, although a majority of British adolescents would wish such a longstanding commitment to take the form of marriage, a substantial minority reject such a view (Rutter, 1979b; Schofield, 1973). An American study (Sorensen, 1973) indicated that a majority of teenagers expect sexual fidelity after marriage, even though they do not expect it before then.

COGNITIVE DEVELOPMENT

It is during adolescence (roughly the years from 11 or 12 to 15) that the child begins to free his or her thinking from its roots in their own *particular* experience. They become capable of *general* propositional thinking, i.e. they can propose hypotheses and deduce consequences. Language is now fast, versatile, and extensive in its use. It is public, so that adolescents not only gain from their own thoughts but also from the articulated thoughts of many others. Their world has become larger and richer, socially, intellectually and conceptually. Both opportunity and training are essential to the development of logical and rational thinking and problem solving. It is not an innate characteristic; it depends upon the right sort of environmental stimulation and encouragement (particularly in the preschool period) and it also depends on natural growth processes. Logical thinking or rationality is an important requirement for adjusting to life's demands; it is also a vital criterion of mental health. It can also constitute a 'trial' for parents as teenagers flex their intellectual 'muscles' by asking 'why not?', and questioning parental social and moral values.

PROBLEMS OF ADOLESCENCE

As a major period of transition and change it would be surprising if there were not more serious problems than these, associated with adolescence; there are, but what is really surprising is that contrary to popular opinion adolescence does not, in fact, appear to be a markedly more vulnerable stage of development than others. Nevertheless, about one in five adolescents do experience significant psychological problems. Among these problems are:

- depression (and suicide attempts, a much later phenomenon, with a peak at 15–19 years);
- anxieties (particularly fears about school and social situations);
- conduct problems;
- eating disorders (anorexia nervosa, bulimia nervosa);
- substance abuse.

What *is* different is that the youngster is at greater risk; the implications of errors of judgement, foolhardy risk-taking, experimentation with adult predilections, tend to be more serious.

Boys tend to cope with early maturing more easily than girls; their early maturity puts them on a par with girls of the same age. Girls, in particular, may find that their early maturity is perceived as sexually provocative by some. They may be self-conscious about their precocious sexual development, especially their body image and the fact of menstruation. Premature sexual development seldom means premature sexual experience of an adult kind. In general, premature puberty leads to an increase in sexual arousal, but psychosexual behaviour tends to remain roughly in line with the child's actual age and social experience.

Late maturers look childlike for their age. They are more likely to be teased by their peers and thus beset by feelings of inferiority and a sense of social isolation. Girls are likely to suffer less than boys because they are on a par with most boys of their own age, but they may worry about late breast development and the onset of their periods, particularly if under pressure from their more physically advanced peers. Boys who are late developers seem to feel the most pressure and lack most in self-confidence.

Adolescent Identity

We have seen earlier that there is a popular but erroneous belief in an almost inevitable adolescent identity crisis which is accompanied by symptoms of stress, such as anxiety, depression, frustration and defeatism. Erik Erikson's views on the development of identity have been very influential. Erikson (1965, 1968) sees adolescence as a stage in the life-cycle with a particular challenge or task to be met. For the teenager it is the challenge between 'identity' and 'identity diffusion'—in a sense, one set against the other (see Figure 10, which is an adaptation of Erikson's ideas about the vicissitudes of identity development, put in the form of a flow chart).

In leaving behind their childish roles (stage 1), adolescents are thought to become preoccupied with finding for themselves a satisfactory answer to the question 'Who am I?' They may 'try out' a variety of identities in their search for answers; they seek experience in different roles and through a variety of relationships (stage 2). It is self-exploration through experimentation. Some settle for an immature self too soon ('foreclosure'). Others are too late; thus it is suggested that if boys and girls fail to clarify and give substance to their personal identity they are likely to experience depression and even despair. These feelings, plus a sense of meaninglessness and self-depreciation, are the indications of what Erikson calls 'identity diffusion'.

A reasonable agreement between the self-concept ('myself as I am') and the concept of the ideal self ('myself as I would like to be') is one of the most important conditions for a favourable psychological adjustment—at school and in other aspects of the child's life (Ausubel et al., 1954). Marked discrepancies (i.e. negative self-concepts) are likely to arouse anxiety, unhappiness and a sense of dissatisfaction with life (Crandall and Bellugi, 1954). Under-achievers at school have been found to have poorer self-concepts

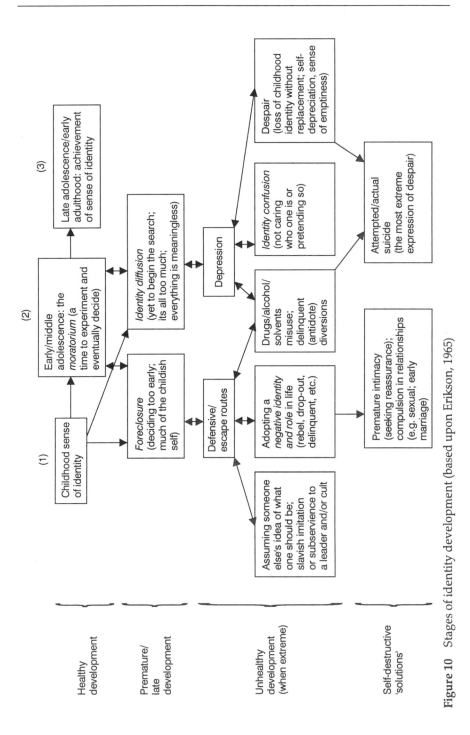

Figure 10   Stages of identity development (based upon Erikson, 1965)

than normal achievers and reflect feelings of defensiveness, loneliness, and being unduly restricted in their freedom (Ausubel *et al.*, 1954). It is clear that self-attitudes—as central and organizing aspects of personality—provide a gauge of the child's adaptation to his or her life-situation; they involve their meaning for others, how they want to be seen by others, and also what they wish to be like. Positive self-attitudes are the basic ingredients of positive mental health, and negative self-concept among the critical predispositions to maladjustment (Coopersmith, 1967). Young people with the latter tend not to suffer from feelings of anxiety. They seem to trust their own perceptions and reactions, and are confident in the likelihood of success in their endeavours. Their approach to other persons is based upon the expectation that they will be well received Their general optimism is not misplaced, but founded upon accurate assessments of their own abilities, social skills, and personal qualities. They are not self-conscious or obsessively preoccupied with personal problems. They are much less frequently affected with psychosomatic disorders (insomnia, headaches, fatigue, intestinal upset) than are youngsters of low self-esteem.

Those with low self-esteem present a picture of discouragement and depression. They tend to feel isolated, unlovable, incapable of expressing or defending themselves and too weak to confront or overcome their deficiencies. They are anxious about angering others and shrink from exposing themselves to the limelight in any way. In the presence of a social group, be it school or elsewhere, they remain in the shadows as audience rather than participants, sensitive to criticism, self-conscious, preoccupied with inner problems. This dwelling on their own problems not only exacerbates their feelings of malaise but also isolates them from opportunity for the friendly relationships such persons need for emotional support.

The boys tend to gauge their individual worth primarily by their achievement and treatment in their own interpersonal environment, rather than by more general and abstract norms of success. A correlation of +0.36 was found between positive self-concept and school achievement. Self-esteem and popularity correlated +0.37. The teachers, in the main, judged these youngsters very much as they judged themselves.

The DSM has a category for problems relating to identity (see below). The essential feature of what is called 'identity disorder' is an inability to integrate various aspects of the self into a coherent and acceptable sense of self, causing considerable subjective distress, e.g. depression, anxiety or self-doubt.

The diagnostic criteria for identity disorder include severe subjective distress regarding uncertainty about one or more issues related to identity, including at least *three* of the following:

(1) long-term goals;
(2) career choice;
(3) friendship patterns;
(4) sexual orientation and behaviour;
(5) religious identification;
(6) moral value systems;
(7) group loyalties.

Depression figures a good deal in this theory of identity crisis and, as a relatively common feature of adolescence, is a possibility requiring vigilance on the part of the psychologist carrying out an assessment.

Depression (see Williams, 1997)

Depressive reactions are often mentioned in the literature as concomitants of school refusal and truancy; they also figure in discussions of problems such as failure-to-thrive, substance abuse and delinquency. But depression has only recently achieved the status of a problem of childhood in its own right, a syndrome rather than a predictable response to loss or deprivation (Cantwell and Carlson, 1983). Because of its undermining effects and the risk of suicide, childhood (and, indeed, adolescent) depression has become an increasing concern of people in the helping professions (Kazdin, 1990).

Assessment. Anxiety and depression—which both come under the 'internalizing problems' category—have nevertheless been treated, generally, as separate disorders in young people. But they can, and do, occur together. Depression is more likely to be manifested in children and adolescents with severe symptoms of anxiety (Bernstein and Garfinkel, 1986). This means that any assessment must be comprehensive enough to allow for the possible coexistence of depression and anxiety.

The checklist below contains the main signs of depression:

- a demeanour of unhappiness and misery (more persistent and intense than 'the blues' which we all suffer from now and then);
- a marked change in eating and/or sleeping patterns;
- a feeling of helplessness, hopelessness and self-dislike;
- an inability to concentrate and apply oneself to anything;
- everything (even talking and dressing) seen as an effort;
- irritating or aggressive behaviour;
- a sudden change in school work;
- a constant search for distractions and new activities;
- dangerous risk-taking (e.g. with drugs/alcohol; dangerous driving, delinquent actions);
- friends being dropped or ignored.

The problem with the list is that almost everyone seems to experience these 'symptoms' at times and to some degree. Whilst most people are spared the more severe forms of depression, few of us are not familiar with the milder forms. These often accompany loss, failure or disappointment in one or more areas of life, such as achievements, relationships, employment, status. Many people know only too well the depression which accompanies bereavement. This often lasts, where the attachment was close, for at least one to two years, but frequently for longer.

Depression is one of the notable disorders that beset adolescents (Herbert, 1987c). Depression can be masked by a constant search for distractions and new activities, also dangerous risk-taking and sometimes delinquent activities in adolescence. The following questions will help you in your screening of the client's conditions. Your mental alarm bells should be ringing loudly if the answers to the following questions are in the affirmative.

- Are there several of the signs (listed above) present in your client?
- Do they occur frequently/intensely?
- Have they persisted for a long time?
- Do they cause *extensive* suffering?
- Do they stand in the way of ongoing life tasks (e.g. socializing, working efficiently, enjoying leisure activities).
- Do they get in the way of relationships with others?
- Do they cause distress in others?

The main dimensions considered in contemporary adult/young adult practice are:

- *severity*   — mild, moderate or severe;
- *type*   — depressive, manic, mixed;
- *special features:*   — with neurotic symptoms;
                     — with psychotic symptoms;
                     — with agitation;
                     — with retardation or stupor;
- *the course*   — unipolar or bipolar;
- *aetiology:*   — predominantly reactive;
                     — predominantly endogenous ('out of the blue'/organismic).

By focusing in an assessment on these dimensions each person's circumstances and experiences can be appraised individually, rather than according to a rigid, generalized taxonomy.

The milder form of depression may show itself as a lack of physical energy and well-being. In its more severe manifestations children and adolescents tend to be irritable and bad-tempered, and, when it is at its worst, they sleep poorly, lack an appetite, and are always dejected, apathetic and lifeless. Adolescents who are (for whatever reason) depressed feel helpless, sad and useless and find it sometimes impossible to meet the challenges of life. They cease to strive and to use their full effectiveness in whatever sphere of activity they find themselves.

The apathy of a young person with depression is often mistaken for laziness. Depression can be masked (particularly in adolescence) by frenetic, often antisocial, risky activities, and is thus not easily detected. Another difficulty for the clinician is that any item in the list above can occur normally in adolescence without in any way indicating a depressive disorder.

The measurement of depression in children. Kovacs (1980) has devised *The Children's Depression Inventory (CDI)*, a self-report measure which assesses the severity of depression in school-aged children. It consists of 27 items that describe a variety of affective, cognitive and behavioural symptoms. A cut-off score of 19 identifies the highest 10% (clinically depressed) of this population.

Causation. It seems paradoxical that the high standards which many pre-adolescents and adolescents set themselves also create problems for them. The evidence indicates that many young people who are highly self-critical tend to be anxious, insecure, depressed and somewhat cynical. Sometimes they lapse into feelings of despair (Herbert, 1987c).

There is a bewildering number and variety of aetiological models to sift through in the quest to understand and explain the phenomenon of childhood and adolescent depression. They range from the biological (biochemical, neuroendocrinal and genetic), through the psychosocial (behavioural, cognitive, family process, learned helplessness), to the psychodynamic. (See Kazdin, 1990, for an excellent guide to this complex literature.)

- *Developmental influences.* Developmental factors contribute to depression. Researchers have highlighted the vulnerability to depression which may be induced by the *early* loss of important relationships and the associated feelings of helplessness.
- *An integrated causal model.* Akiskal and McKinney (1975) have integrated the many variables which research has suggested as being involved in depressive disorders, into a multifactorial model (Figure 11). The emphasis is upon interacting variables which converge into a 'final common pathway', reflecting changes in brain biochemistry and experienced by the person as depression.

Depression can be either very severe or less severe, with major depression at one end of a continuum, and at the other end mild depression joining the anxiety disorders.

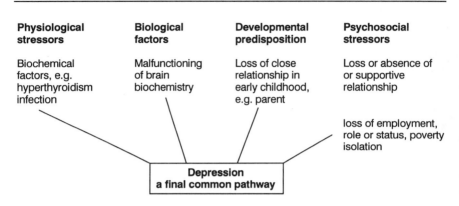

Figure 11   Final common pathway to depression.

The loss of a parent is one of the foremost precursors of depressive problems. Van Eerdewegh *et al.*, (1982) studied a sample of children of young widows and widowers, and the children of controls. The children's reactions to the parental death were recorded one month and thirteen months after the event in a structured interview with the surviving parent. They found the persistence of a minor form of depression; an increase in bedwetting; and a significant degree of impairment in school performance for older children. There were no significant increases in behavioural problems. Losing a parent of the same sex (particularly for boys) appeared to be a significant risk factor for depression.

Their results suggested several risk factors, including the following: mental illness in the surviving parent; financial deterioration of the family after the death of the parent; the sex of the child and of the surviving parent; the stability of the home environment prior to or after the death; the quality of the marital relationship before the death, the coping capacity of the surviving parent; and the quality of the support system of the family after the death.

In a more recent investigation, Van Eerdewegh, Clayton and Van Eerdewegh (1985) found that dysphoria, falling school performance and withdrawn behaviour were significantly increased in bereaved children of both sexes at all ages, while temper tantrums, bed-wetting and depressive syndromes only increased in the age and sex categories normally associated with these conditions. The highest symptom scores for both sexes were associated with having a mentally ill (more often than not depressed) mother. They found that bereaved daughters of mentally ill mothers had the highest scores. The investigators suggest that the delay between the time of the death and the onset of psychiatric difficulties in the child makes it less likely that the death itself is the sole factor leading to psychiatric problems.

In depression one of the most important risk factors is the absence of a close confiding relationship. Such a factor seems also to be of importance in taking up drug use. There is some evidence to suggest that drug takers, especially those who develop a problematic use, exhibit common characteristics such as low self-esteem, high levels of anxiety and depression (see Herbert, 1987c; Weiner, 1970).

Suicide and Parasuicide

Depression is a common feature of suicide and attempted suicide. These two forms require definitions:

- *Suicide* contains two main components: that the person brought about his or her own death, and that this was done knowingly.
- *Parasuicide,* or attempted suicide, involves any non-fatal act of self-injury or taking of substances in excess of the generally recognized or prescribed therapeutic dose. By convention, alcohol intoxication alone is excluded.

Research on suicide is still relatively sparse. There are many unanswered questions: for example, are all people who commit or attempt suicide to be regarded as depressed, or are some suicidal behaviours the impulsive activities of people hitherto not in a depressed mood. Suicide is extremely rare in young children. The rate in early childhood per thousand appears to be around 0.001 per 1000 at age 10 (Shaffer, 1974). However, it merits a brief mention here as it begins to appear in puberty, and increases in prevalence, reaching its highest levels in the late teens (Lumsden-Walker, 1980). Suicide rates rise sharply during adolescence so that it comes to rank among the half-dozen most common causes of death among older adolescents. (The figures are still well below those for adults, and only a minute fraction of the suicide rate in old age.)

Attempted suicide is very much a late adolescent phenomenon—the peak being among 15–19 year olds. There has been a tenfold increase in such incidents since the 1960s among adolescent boys and a fivefold rise for girls. Nevertheless, the rate of attempted suicides for adolescent girls far exceeds that for boys—3 to 1 (Weiner, 1970).

A survey by Hawton (1982) of a sample of 50 adolescents admitted to hospital after self-poisoning revealed that suicide attempts commonly follow episodes of ill-health (such as asthma or juvenile arthritis), rows with parents, friends or teachers, or admission into care of the Social Services Departments. Of these 50 adolescents, fewer than 20% made a repeated self-poisoning attempt in the same year.

The aetiology of suicidal behaviour in adolescents is commonly associated with substance abuse. Another common pattern of influence is the setting of an example of suicidal behaviour by family members or friends (Toolan, 1975). Adolescents who commit suicide tend to show a combination of depression and conduct disorders.

Intervention

The need for a broad-based intervention with depressive problems seems to be the conclusion of recent studies (e.g., Puig-Antich *et al.*, 1985). Tricyclic medication, counselling, psychotherapy, behaviour therapy, cognitive therapy and group therapy are the main options, singly or in combination. In serious cases the young person may have to reside in an adolescent psychiatry unit or a social services home. (A useful account on the pros and cons of pharmacotherapy is given by Campbell *et al.*, 1989).

Depression in older children (and adolescents) lends itself to a cognitive-behavioural approach. Most depressed clients manifest a high rate of intrusive negative thoughts, including selective ruminations about past negative events, and thoughts about the hopelessness of the future and their helplessness in the face of their perceived dilemma (Seligman, 1975).

Seligman's formulation of clinical depression is in terms of learned helplessness—a feature of many hard-pressed parents with difficult children (Herbert, 1988). A sense of helplessness, it is posited, leads to cognitive and motivational deficits and emotional disturbance. These learned helplessness effects are determined in large part by the attribution which the client makes when he or she experiences a persistent 'disconnection' (independence) between their behavioural responses and their outcomes (see also Abramson, Seligman and Teasdale, 1978). What people tell themselves about their experience affects their behaviour. For example, some clients may tend to attribute the causes of what happens to them to forces beyond their control, while others may see themselves as having a major influence and say on the unfolding events of their life.

This notion (locus of control) generates practice methods which have proved very promising with, for example, parents with low perceived self-efficacy—methods (e.g. 'cognitive restructuring') that include the attempt to alter overt behaviour by modifying thoughts, assumptions, and interpretations. Multifaceted or integrative cognitive–behavioural interventions have proved successful for treating childhood depression (Fine *et al.*, 1991; Kaslow and Rehm, 1982; Kendall, 1984; Reynolds, 1984). Reynolds and Coats (1986), following an initial screening of high-school students, randomly assigned 30 moderately depressed adolescents to one of three conditions: cognitive–behavioural therapy, relaxation training, or waiting-list controls. Students on medication for depression or related disorders were excluded. In addition to the initial screening, subjects were tested on three occasions, i.e. pretreatment assessment, post-treatment assessment, and a five-week follow-up assessment.

The cognitive–behavioural programme stressed training in self-control skills including self-monitoring, self-evaluation, and self-reinforcement. The relaxation training condition involved progressive muscle relaxation exercises, and the application of relaxation skills to tension-provoking situations. Both treatments were administered to small groups of participants for ten 50-minute sessions over a five-week period. The interventions were evaluated on measures of depression (self-report and interview), self-concept (general and academic), and anxiety (State-Trait Anxiety Inventory-Trait Scale).

Both cognitive behaviour therapy and relaxation training were found to be effective in the treatment of the depressed adolescents. Compared to the waiting list control condition, both treatments resulted in a significant reduction in depressive symptomatology. Further, these improvements were maintained at the five-week follow-up assessment. Of interest were the findings in relation to measures of anxiety. On this criterion the greatest changes occurred for the relaxation training subjects, especially from post-treatment to follow-up assessment. In relation to general self-concept, there were no significant differences between the groups at post-test and follow-up. Both treatment groups, however, reported higher levels of academic self-concept at post-treatment relative to the control group. Yet at follow-up, only the cognitive–behavioural group showed a significantly greater level of academic self-concept compared to the waiting list control group.

Social skills training has been successfully applied to depressed children who often exhibit poor social skills. Frame *et al.* (1982) focused on behaviours such as inappropriate body position, lack of eye contact, and poor speech, in their treatment of a depressed boy.

Drug Abuse

Drug abuse was relatively infrequent among children in the not-too-distant past, but now it is far from being as rare as it used to be; it becomes quite common during the years of adolescence. Most young people who try drugs out of curiosity do not continue to use them regularly. Those who take drugs tend to do so infrequently and give them up altogether after a year or so.

The terms 'drug abuse' and 'drug misuse' refer to the observation that a particular form of drug-taking is a harmful (abuse) and/or socially unacceptable way of using that substance (misuse). 'Users' are likely to develop 'tolerance' for a drug, which means that their body has adapted to the repeated presence of the drug so that higher doses are required to maintain the same effect. The body may react with 'withdrawal effects' to the sudden absence of a drug to which it has adapted; they involve severe physical discomfort. When this occurs and leads to a compulsion to continue taking the drug so as to avoid these symptoms, we speak of 'physical dependence'. The more important and widespread problem of 'psychological dependence' refers to an irresistible psychological compulsion to repeat the stimulation, pleasure or comfort provided by the drug's effects.

The key factor in drug-taking is opportunity—the availability of drugs and people to tempt and 'prompt'. Users have generally been exposed to drugs by their peers or by people (not infrequently family members) whose values incline towards nonconformity or even deviance. Rebelliousness, low self-esteem, a poor sense of psychological wellbeing (including depression) and low academic aspirations are among the characteristics commonly found in adolescent drug users. The boredom and hopelessness of unemployment also play their part. Substance abuse (for example, glue-sniffing) presents a similar picture. High-risk drug-taking is defined as uncontrolled use, whether or not it is already demonstrably harmful. A person is also taking an unacceptable risk if he or she is a regular user, that is to say taking drugs at predictable intervals.

Ira Mothner and Alan Weitz, the authors of *How to Get Off Drugs* (Harmondsworth, Penguin, 1986), maintain that, while the occasional use, in a social or intimate setting, of a substance such as cannabis would seem to be a low-risk activity, there are people whose sensitivity to the drug is so great that even this involvement is very risky. Nevertheless, for large numbers of users, the occasional social use is within the low-risk range. (See Table 10 for a list of the most common drugs, their potential for addiction/dependency, effects, and risks.)

The Institute for the Study of Drug Dependence, in Britain, lists the following risks:

1. *Overdoing it*
(a) Taking too much at one go could lead to a fatal overdose or an extremely distressing experience.
(b) Taking high doses frequently may impair mental and physical functioning and normal development
(c) Financing drug purchase can lead to a deterioration of diet and housing, and the degradation of a person's lifestyle.

Table 10 Drug effects and dangers (dependence/addiction: H = High; M = Moderate; L = Low)

Most common substances	Effects most drugs produce	Complications/dangers
Alcohol (M)	• Temporary pleasant mood	• Sexually transmitted diseases
Nicotine (H)		
	• Relief from anxiety	• Severe infections (e.g. endocarditis, hepatitis, blood poisoning) (from intravenous injections)
Marijuana (L to M)		
	• False feelings of self-confidence	
Amphetamines (H)		
Barbiturates (M to H)	• Increased sensitivity to sights and sounds (including hallucinations)	• Malnutrition
Cocaine (H)		
Opiates (e.g. heroin, morphine, methadone) (H)	• Altered activity levels (sleeplike, stupor – frenzy, agitation)	• Accidental injury to self
		• Overdose leading to death
Psychedelic drugs (e.g. mescaline; LDS) (L)		• Alienation of family and friends
	• Unpleasant or painful symptoms when drug is withdrawn	
Volatile substances (e.g. glue, solvents, paints) (L)		• Irreversible damage to bodily organs
Tranquillizers (e.g. Valium, Tranxene) (L)		

2. *Wrong time, wrong place.* In moderate doses most psychoactive drugs impair attention, reaction time and motor co-ordination, thus affecting studying and other activities.

3. *Adulteration and mistaken identity.* Drugs offered on the illicit market are likely to contain impurities and adulterants with unpredictable, possibly dangerous effects.

4. *Doubling up.* Doubling up drugs, loading one drug on top of another, multiplies the risks of a harmful outcome. Some users take several drugs; complex interactions can occur which may prove fatal.

5. *Injection.* This is the most hazardous method of taking drugs (opiates, sedatives and stimulants). The major dangers are from overdose, infections (e.g. hepatitis, AIDS), abscesses and gangrene.

6. *Pregnancy.* The foetus can be damaged by drug use in the pregnant mother.

7. *Drug laws.* The user and supplier of drugs are at risk by breaking drug laws.

8. *Individual differences.* Drug effects vary with individual's body weight and psychological make-up. The young person who is likely to

become addicted is very often the same kind of individual who is at risk of serious mental illness in late adolescence, and the same sort of background tends to be common to both: a broken home, parental strife, and a dominating or ineffective mother or father—parents who provide little by way of example or standards. It is, in fact, quite exceptional to come across a young person addicted to drugs who has not had quite severe family problems. That is not to say that these problems are the actual *cause* of addiction, but rather that drug-taking is one of a number of ways of dealing with apparently intractable personal problems, a peculiarly contemporary way.

The motives for seriously using drugs in the long term are many and varied. There may be an element of defiance in it, doing what the parents disapprove of and fear; there may be a special attraction if the adolescent knows that this is something the parents have never experienced. There is pressure to conform in experiencing new sensations and sharing them with other members of one's own age group. The elements of risk and excitement certainly exert a strong pull towards experimenting with drugs. But, however much these various factors may contribute to the decision to take drugs, the chief motive for a great many teenagers is their wish to escape from precisely those problems which make adolescence, for them, such a difficult and stressful period of life.

Perhaps we should not be too surprised that disadvantaged adolescents—looking to a future with little hope and facing economic, social and racial discrimination, enduring degrading living conditions, often with untreated physical ills, suffering disintegration in their social environment and in their own families—give up the search for meaning and personal identity, and seek escape in the oblivion of narcotics.

It is important for parents and practitioners to be on the lookout for signs that may lead them to suspect drug use. It is not easy, because some of the signs are not uncommon in adolescence generally. There is often a gradual change in the adolescent's habits and a general lethargy. Other signs include: aggression; loss of interest in school work, sport, hobbies and friends; furtive behaviour and frequent lying; bouts of drowsiness or sleeplessness; unexplained disappearances of money and belongings from the home.

Heroin addicts usually stop bothering about their appearance, their speech may become halting, and they tend to drop old friends and take up with new ones. Users of heroin may receive unexplained messages or telephone calls, followed by an immediate and unexplained departure. Spots of blood may be noticed on their clothes, and (most important) needle marks on the back of the hand and the inside of the elbow. There may also be thickened brownish cords under the skin, which are veins, solidified as a result of the injections.

There is a tendency for the addict to be hostile to society, and therein lies part of the trouble when it comes to treatment and rehabilitation. A hospital too often epitomizes society in the mind of the addict. More informal methods are therefore required, and in most countries clinics run on 'non-institutional' lines within the community, and more casual in style, are being set up. Sadly such agencies and local drug advice centres are thin on the ground in the UK.

Most promising seem to be those communities which are run by ex-addicts. The addict who is desperate for drugs has an uncanny instinct for putting the most subtle and painful pressures on families and doctors alike, but these tactics are familiar to ex-addicts and therefore get nowhere with them.

Prevention of drug abuse is, of course, the best way of helping. Shock tactics, such as horror stories about the dangers of smoking, drinking or drug-taking, have not proved effective as deterrents; in fact they can be counter-productive. Calm, objective education is more likely to forewarn teenagers of the risks. The school, with its access to so many young people, seems an obvious place to inform them about drugs and, by providing accurate information, meet their natural curiosity about the subject. It must not be an amateurish ad hoc business. Any educational programme requires skilful teachers and a sophisticated curriculum (see Pagliaro and Pagliaro, 1996, in Further Readings).

Sexual Orientation and Identity (see Money and Ehrhardt, 1972)

This is one of the areas of childhood and adolescent development capable of causing much distress and anxiety, depression and uncertainty — and, not surprisingly, it is listed as one of the DSM-III-R criteria of an identity disorder. The 'problems' related to sex, in the secondary school, are likely to be due to sexual curiosity and ignorance. Even in our supposedly enlightened age, one is impressed by the anguish and disappointment caused by widespread misinformation, misconceptions, myths, fears and inhibitions about sex.

In pre-adolescent individuals, sexual interest and behaviour are intermittent, casual and not very intense. Sexual experimentation, mainly sex play between children of the same sex, rises in incidence as youngsters get older. Homosexual play usually takes the form of handling each other's genitals. This occurs in roughly 30% of 13-year-olds (Herbert, 1978c). We know from surveys that about one in two adults is likely to have had one or more sexually tinged experiences involving someone of the same sex, and that at least half of those who haven't, have felt some sexual attraction to someone of their own sex. Usually the attraction or contact is a 'one-off' or transient matter which mainly occurs during adolescence.

Conduct Problems

Conduct disorders are three times more common in boys than in girls (Rutter, Tizard and Whitmore, 1970). Such a male predominance is further underlined in the case of delinquency (West, 1980), where male delinquents outnumber female delinquents in a ratio of up to ten to one. In the United States the ratio is smaller, with a higher increase, of late, in female as compared with male cases.

Three main conduct problem areas can be isolated: serious antisocial behaviour, overactivity, and aggression. We analyse the first of these in this chapter, as childhood and adolescent antisocial problems constitute such a central and broadly coherent developmental and clinical theme. Youngsters with conduct and delinquent disorders demonstrate a fundamental inability or unwillingness to adhere to the rules and codes of conduct prescribed by society at its various levels. Such failures may be related to the temporary lapse of poorly established learned controls, to the failure to learn these controls in the first place, or to the fact that the behavioural standards a child has absorbed do not coincide with the norms of that section of society which enacts and enforces the rules.

The problem for the therapist carrying out an assessment is that all children are disobedient some of the time—a fact of life all parents have to contend with. At what point is non-compliance maladaptive? This is a sensitive issue given the lip service paid by society to individualism: a precarious balance is required by society between 'reasonable' conformity and 'unreasonable' or slavish conformity. There are also other types of behaviour which come under the heading of conduct disorders. They include, as we saw, disruptiveness, boisterousness, fighting, attention seeking, restlessness, negativism, impertinence, destructiveness, irritability, temper tantrums, hyperactivity, profanity, jealousy and uncooperativeness. Again, most children manifest these 'problems' to some extent. The diagnostic problem lies in the fact that there is no clear-cut distinction between the characteristics of 'abnormal' children and other children; the differences are relative—a matter of degree. Like it or not we are in an area of social value judgements rather than objective scientific criteria. Behaviour problems, signs of psychological abnormality, are, by and large, exaggerations, deficits, or handicapping combinations of behaviour patterns common to all children.

Take 'delinquent acts' as an example. A 6-year study was conducted by the Survey Research Centre of the London School of Economics (Belson, 1975) on a random sample of 1425 London youths between the ages of 13 and 16 from all social levels. They were encouraged to reveal their antisocial secrets during the intensive interviewing. Belson wished to find out whether they had ever been guilty of any of 44 different types of theft, ranging from keeping something found to stealing a car or lorry. Belson's study is unusual because it used a population which included non-delinquents and undetected delinquents, as well as boys already known to police and courts. So much research in the delinquency area is rendered useless because it is based on young people who have come before the courts or are inmates of penal institutions. The detected offender is almost certainly a biased sample of the delinquent population in general. And such bias makes it impossible to draw valid inferences about the characteristics of offenders in general or about the motives for their offences. Nearly all the London boys of all backgrounds and classes admitted to some stealing—mainly petty—at some time or other. In this sample, 98% admitted having kept something that they had found (but in only 40% of these cases was the article in question worth more than £1; 70% had stolen from a shop; 35% from family or friends; 25% from work, and from a car, lorry or van; 18% from a telephone box; while 5% admitted having stolen a car or lorry, and 17% had 'got in a place and stolen'. Apparently boys from all classes are given to thieving but *what* they steal varies. Boys from the private sector tend to specialize in thefts from their relatives or from changing rooms, while their state school contemporaries are more disposed to stealing cigarettes or sweets from shops and also find great temptation in motor vehicles. Clearly, a majority of the boys in this study had indulged in at least one offence which, if detected and prosecuted, would have swollen the official statistics bearing on 'delinquency' rates.

Diagnostic Decision Making

This finding highlights the difficulty of deciding when problem behaviour is sufficiently serious to merit further investigation and therapeutic intervention. The remarkable thing about this by no means untypical survey (see Elmhorn, 1965; Malewska and Muszynski, 1970) is that these were ordinary boys of school age, most of whom had never been suspected of being juvenile delinquents. It cannot be assumed that youths who have been found guilty of an offence are the only ones committing antisocial or delinquent acts.

This begs the question: what is antisocial? In a sense young children are all antisocial and, judged by adult criteria, 'delinquent'. Even 'innocent' toddlers lash out at each other, inflicting pain; they 'steal' each other's possessions and appear to show no remorse after transgressing the rules. In a sense they do not need to learn 'delinquent' behaviours or attitudes. These tendencies occur quite spontaneously and to the child they have an internal logic which is dazzling in its simplicity.

What happens, as the child matures, is that he has to learn to avoid certain behaviours; that is to say, he must be trained to check certain impulses and to regulate his behaviour in terms of certain informal and formal rules of conduct (including the law).

This socialization process is a slow continuing process, involving countless 'lessons' from parents, siblings, peers, and adults in authority over the child. To a significant degree the rules continue to be flouted by a wide range of young people, some in a minor and relatively painless manner. Others give vent to their impulses in a blatant and highly aversive fashion. As this kind of child gets older and ranges more widely outside the confines of his home, the implications of his conduct become more serious. His misdemeanours are quite likely to take him and his parents into the juvenile courts. In other words, his acts are legally defined as delinquent and, in the manner society has of categorizing and labelling people, he becomes a juvenile delinquent. This process of labelling is highly selective. Certain children are more likely than others to avoid detection. Children who attend a school which is conscious of its good name are, if caught stealing, likely to have the incident dealt with privately between headmaster and parents. A boy who is caught shoplifting is more likely to be dealt with leniently if he is known to come from a 'respectable' middle-class home. Issues like these make it impossible to draw an ambiguous line of demarcation between delinquents and non-delinquents.

Delinquent behaviour is often no more than a transitory incident in the pattern of a youth's normal development. We know that although a large number of young people commit isolated crimes, few develop into career offenders. After a steady increase in the frequency of delinquent acts during childhood, reaching a peak in later adolescence, there is a fairly sharp decline in the delinquency rates in the early twenties. The large majority of delinquents gradually merge with the law-abiding population—settled down perhaps by the responsibilities of a job, marriage, and family life—and do not appear before the courts again. Among delinquent youths brought to court, half are never reconvicted. Many of these youngsters are essentially normal and do not have a conduct disorder in the sense used in this book. Given the poor prognosis for an early established conduct disorder, there is an onus on the clinician to know the developmental evidence (and particularly data from longitudinal studies) before making a diagnosis. We know that *isolated* antisocial or delinquent acts are common and therefore of relatively little diagnostic significance.

What is apparent from facts like these is that early identification of conduct disorders may be a crucial matter, but that diagnostic decisions rest on somewhat vague criteria. However, there is an intensity/frequency dimension which can be taken into account. Ryall (1968) examined in depth the characteristics of some 150 consecutive entrants to a fairly typical community school (approved school) which admitted boys aged 13 and 14 years, mainly from small- to medium-sized conurbations. At the time of committal they were routinely offending at least once a fortnight. The level of delinquent activity was so high that it was impossible to determine accurately the average total number of offences which had been committed by the boys; a minimum estimate would be about 100 for each boy, but the true figure was probably several times higher. The great majority of the offences were acts of theft and many were relatively minor offences of shoplifting. However, it was easier to estimate more accurately the quantity of breaking and entering offences which had been committed and the average number of these far more serious offences was well over 20 per boy. The population also contained a minority of boys whose offending was of a rather different nature (e.g. those who specialized in taking and driving vehicles), but for these boys the frequency and intensity of offending was just as great as for the majority who indulged in more generalized forms of antisocial behaviour. Ryall notes that the peculiar feature of approved school children was the *quantity* of their law breaking. He emphasizes that the *intensity* of the offending of the persistent delinquent is at the centre of the treatment problem. For these boys delinquent behaviour had become a habit or, more precisely, a self-reinforcing learned behaviour pattern. Each delinquent act was producing excitement, peer-group status, and possible material rewards, thus generating the motivation for further offences.

Delinquency (see Farrington, 1995; Rutter and Madge, 1976)

It is important to make the distinction between delinquent and antisocial behaviour. For example, vandalism and burglary are clearly antisocial in their effects on people. Illegal acts such as smoking marijuana or truanting are not directly antisocial but deleterious to the person committing the delinquent acts. While some delinquency is antisocial in nature, its distinguishing characteristic—as compared to, say non-compliance, school disruption, or other conduct disorders—is that it involves acts by young people ('young' as defined by a given legal system) expressly forbidden by law. In addition, the young person should not be suffering from mental disorder (again as legally defined).

In terms of clinical intervention with delinquents, however, it is the techniques associated with behaviour modification and cognitive behaviour modification which predominate: the recent enthusiasm for cognitive therapy appears, from the literature at least, not to have infected those who work with young offenders. The use of behavioural techniques with offenders generally (Morris and Braukmann, 1987) and young offenders specifically (Hollin, 1990; Stumphauzer, 1986) is well documented in the literature. There are reviews of interventions with young offenders based specifically on social learning theory (Nietzel, 1979); indeed this is a field which has received a great deal of attention, from both researchers and clinicians.

COGNITIVE–BEHAVIOURAL THERAPY

A cognitive-based intervention can be defined as a treatment approach that aims to alter specific perceptions, images, thoughts, and beliefs through direct manipulation and restructuring of faulty, maladaptive cognitions. A growing number of practitioners acknowledge the significance of the cognitive representation of events and experiences in the development of the conduct disorders and other antisocial manifestations (e.g. delinquent activities) of children and adolescents.

The cognitive–behavioural approaches to interventions for children and adolescents consist usually of techniques which have been adapted from adult work (see Hollon and Beck, 1994; Bream and Cohen, 1985; Ollendick, 1986; Ollendick and Cerny, 1981). Some have their roots in cognitive therapy (e.g. socratic questioning, persuasion, challenging, debate, hypothesizing, cognitive restructuring, verbal self-instruction and internal dialogues). Others are drawn from behaviour therapy.

Anger-Control Training (Cognitive Change)

There are anger management programmes designed specifically for adolescents (Feindler and Ecton, 1986), many drawing heavily on the research and procedures published by Novaco (1975, 1979, 1985). Most of them consist of three stages: cognitive preparation; skill acquisition; and application training. The intention is to lower the likelihood of aggressive behaviour by increasing awareness of the signs of incipient hostile arousal and techniques to encourage self-control. The performance of aggressive, antisocial behaviour may be influenced by antecedent cognitive events such as aversive thoughts (e.g. remembering a past grudge), being unaware of the probable consequences of aggressive actions, or being incapable of solving problems mentally, rather than 'lashing out' automatically. D'Zurrilla and Goldfrie (1971) identify the processes which often precede and guide adaptive behaviour in different circumstances as follows:

- being able to recognize problematic situations when they occur;
- making an attempt to resist the temptation to act impulsively or to do nothing to deal with the situation;
- defining the situation in concrete or operational terms and then formulating the major issues to be coped with;
- generating a number of possible responses which might be pursued in this situation;
- deciding on the course(s) of action most likely to result in positive consequences;
- acting upon the final decision and verifying the effectiveness of the behaviour in resolving the problematic situation.

Adolescents with conduct problems are helped to identify their aggressive behaviour and recognize the conditions which provoke and maintain it. The problem situation is analysed, broken down into its component parts, and represented in a manner most likely to lead to a solution. A number of procedures are available for this purpose. They include self-recording by the adolescent of his or her hostile activities, together with observations of the circumstances in which they occurred and their consequences. Lochman (1992) reported a three-year follow-up of aggressive young adults (males) participating in a school-based anger control programme. The results were encouraging: the treated group had lower rates of substance abuse and higher levels of self-esteem and social problem-solving skills than untreated controls. There was no evidence, however, that the programme had a significant long-term effect on delinquent behaviour. A study by McDougall *et al.* (1987) with 18 institutionalized young offenders found that the anger control programme assisted in lowering the level of institutional offending.

CONFLICT

One of the factors contributing to the delinquency of many young people is their inability to cope with conflict situations involving authority figures. Discipline becomes a very real issue in the child's second year of life, although the foundations for good disciplinary practices should have been laid down much earlier. Notions of right and wrong, a code of behaviour, a set of attitudes and values, the ability to see the other person's point of view—all of these basic qualities which make an individual into a socialized personality—are nurtured in the first instance by parents.

Mothers and fathers need to be firm and unbending at times, tough as well as flexible at crucial moments. They also need to know when to move from one modality to the other. This blend fits the recommendations of child-rearing specialists who are concerned with fostering the sort of children who are socially responsible and outgoing, friendly, competent, creative and reasonably independent and self-assertive (Baumrind, 1971).

Not surprisingly, adolescents are likely to complain and compare their lot with other teenagers when the limits are set down and insisted on. However, there is clear evidence to show that children realize their parents are firm *because they care*. They know, deep down, that they cannot cope alone. They need to know someone has charge of their lives so that they can learn about and experiment with life from a safe base. Children who get their own way all the time tend to interpret such laissez-faire permissiveness as indifference; they feel nothing they do is important enough for their parents to bother about.

Conflict situations are those interpersonal situations in which the youth and authority figure (such as a parent or teacher) have opposing wishes or plans. The youth may want to buy a motor bike, but his mother wants him to purchase an old car because she thinks bikes are dangerous and will get him into bad company. Youngsters often make inappropriate responses to conflict situations (such as fighting, withdrawing, tantrums or destructive behaviour); a serious escalation of conflict may bring them into contact with clinics, court and other agencies.

PROBLEM-SOLVING

Problem-solving skills provide parents and their adolescent children with a general coping strategy for a variety of difficult situations. They could help teenagers taught by psychologists (in more serious circumstances) or by parents to deal more effectively with a variety of conflict situations, such as choosing between alternative courses of action, arriving at mutually acceptable decisions with parents, developing cooperation with the peer group. The particular advantage of the problem-solving approach is that it teaches people how to think and work things out for themselves. There are four steps to provide parents with:

(1) *General orientation*. This is by way of an introductory scene-setting exercise; trying with the young person's help to gain some perspective about the nature of the problem, putting it into the context of why, when and how it occurs. It is important that he or she should be able to recognize the problem and the 'danger' signs. The youngster might think back over the events that have given rise in the past to the problem situation. If this sheds no light on the difficulty you might encourage your daughter or son to monitor future circumstances that prove problematic (e.g. a diary of events).

(2) *Problem definition and formulation*. Define all aspects of the problem as explicitly as possible, in concrete terms rather than in vague and abstract language. This helps you to unravel what looks like a complicated problem and, perhaps, to simplify it. Here is an example (an agoraphobic adolescent): 'It is a terrible effort to shop at the centre. I begin to get butterflies in my stomach when I go into the shopping centre. I feel nervous if there is a large crowd milling about. I can just about cope with small shops if I stay near the door. I really begin to panic if I have to shop in the large shops, well in or away from the door. Before long I feel paralysed, I can't move; I feel as if I might faint.' And here is an example for parents: 'I get angry with my son David. My muscles tense up. I want to lash out at him when he is cheeky. But what do I mean when I say he's cheeky? It's when I feel that my dignity is threatened, especially when my friends are present, or that my authority is demeaned. It's something about his manner, dumb insolence I call it, unfriendly. And then, eventually, I explode in a torrent of recrimination and abuse. Perhaps he also feels provoked by my manner. I must think about that.'

Next you might categorize the salient features of the particular situation in a way that identifies your main *goals* and the *obstacles* that get in the way of fulfilling these goals. For example, the agoraphobic teenager wishes to be able to shop normally, i.e. without anticipatory dread (her goal). To do that she will have to overcome her anxiety (the barrier). David's mother wishes to improve her relationship with her son (the goal), her interpretation of his motives and manner and possibly her own attitude towards him (if he says she is patronizing, this may be a barrier to her objective). This stage is a further clarification of what may be going wrong and why this should be so.

(3) *Setting goals*. Setting goals is at the centre of the attempt to solve problems: parents' help in this matter could be invaluable to their youngsters. A *workable* goal is an accomplishment that helps the individual manage problematic situations. The goal is achieved when he or she has acquired new skills, practised them, and actually used them to solve or manage the situation causing all the difficulties. This accomplishment is often referred to in counselling as the new (or preferred) scenario.

Here are some scenarios based on questions adolescents can usefully ask themselves:

Q   What would the problem situation be like if I could cope better?
A   I'd be able to talk to others without feeling awkward and tongue-tied; I would not spend so much time on my own.
Q   What changes would take place in my lifestyle?
A   I'd go out with a nice girl. I'd be more ambitious; take an interest.
Q   What would be happening that is not happening now?
A   I'd go to concerts, the cinema and plays instead of always moping in front of the TV.

Scenarios and set goals can help young adults in difficulty, in four ways:

(1) They focus the person's attention and action. They provide a vision which offers hope and an outlet for concentrated effort.
(2) They mobilize energy and help pull the worries out of the inertia of helplessness and depression.
(3) They enhance the persistence needed for working at the problem.
(4) They motivate people to search for strategies to accomplish their goals.

If you can help adolescents to the point of defining goals, they are, in essence, on the first stage of 'recovery'—orientating themselves to face life rather than turning away from it, embracing optimism rather than resignation. Egan (1975) writes that goals should preferably be:

(a) *specific,* a necessity if they are to be converted into actions;
(b) *measurable,* that is, capable of providing feedback that change is occurring and, eventually, verifying that the objective has been accomplished;
(c) *realistic,* in the sense that the adolescent has the resources to achieve them; that external circumstances are not bound to thwart their accomplishment: that the goals are under the control (potentially) of the teenager: and the cost of obtaining them is not too high;
(d) *pertinent to their problem* and not simply a partial solution or even a diversionary move;
(e) *the adolescent's own goals* and not those he or she simply adopts because someone expects them of him/her, or they are the line of least resistance;
(f) *in keeping with his or her values;*
(g) *achievable within a reasonable time.*

The problem-solving approach is geared to the present and the future rather than being preoccupied with past wrongs, mistakes and 'complexes'.

> *Example.* Graham, aged 18, who saw his friend—a pillion passenger on his motor bike—badly injured while he was unharmed is tortured by remorse. He drinks heavily and obsessively asks himself whether the accident was his fault. His studies at university have suffered and his social life has dwindled to nothing. He spends all his free time at the hospital where his friend is making a slow and painful recovery, but one which will never allow him to be the promising athlete he was. The friends avoid talking about the accident.

Graham is helped to spell out a scenario in which he makes his peace with his friend by raising the painful subject of the accident, and by expressing his sorrow (and sense of responsibility) for what happened. He will visit his friend regularly but not 'hound' his bedside in the guilt-ridden, self-punishing way that has been his previous practice. He will begin to pick up the threads with his other friends, and apply himself to his studies as a counter to the obsessive thoughts he has when sitting around indulging in morbid introspection.

(4) *Action.* In taking action to deal with a problem there are three sub-stages which help parents or their youngster to make the right move and to verify that they have done so.

(a) *Generation of alternatives.* Work out as wide a range of possible solutions as you can think of in terms of general strategies (what to do) and, later, specific tactics to implement the general strategy (how to do it). Brainstorming—freely, and, at first, uncritically generating as many ideas as possible—can be a help. For example: the phobic girl can continue to try to solve her problem on her own, but she has done this to no avail. She can consult a clinical psychologist. Let us look at the way David's mother puts the alternatives:

(i)   I could punish David more severely.
(ii) I could ignore him.
(iii) I could try to engage in a calm debate with him.
(iv) I could turn the issue over to his father.
(v) I could penalize him (take away a proportion of his pocket money each time) without getting into an interminable debate.
(vi) I could negotiate an agreement with him covering the perennial issues we argue over.
(vii)I could look into my own attitudes and feelings toward him. Do I get *him* going as much as he does me? Am I at fault in some way?

It might be useful to ask others how they would react, or imagine how others might react, if requested to solve a similar problem (e.g. how would his father, aunt or his teacher approach this problem?).

(b) *Decision-making.* Work out the likely consequences of the better courses of action you have put forward. What is the utility of these consequences in resolving the problem as it has been formulated? For example, with regard to the proposed solutions:

(i)   Punishment doesn't seem to work; in fact it seems to make David more intractable.
(ii) He'd probably follow me around, arguing more forcibly. Like me, he can be very stubborn.
(iii) Sounds good, but I find it so hard to keep cool. And we may not be able to resolve things in the heat of the particular confrontation.

(iv) My husband won't thank me for that; he'll say, 'It's your problem'. I have to cope in *my* way when David is disobedient.

(v) This may work but it could also generate trouble, sulking and tantrums.

(vi) Sounds a possibility; David can be reasonable when he's in a good mood. The trick is to catch him at the right time.

(vii)This is painful, but he may have a point when he says he wishes I could hear myself talk to him as if he's an idiot or baby.

Part III   SPECIAL NEEDS: DEVELOPMENTAL DISORDERS AND HEALTH PROBLEMS

Now that psychologists are so involved with paediatric assessment clinics, general practice, and well baby clinics, they are required to assess and intervene in a wide variety of developmental problems. Particularly in the early preschool years, young children present a wide range of difficulties in sleeping, eating, and elimination. Delays in speech and language are likely to be brought to the notice of family doctors and are likely to be referred on for specialist help. By their very nature, many of such developmental difficulties disappear over time, but they can cause untold worry in the interim. And it is worse when the advice 'Just ignore it, it'll go away' or 'He'll grow out of it' proves to be incorrect. The ability to differentiate short- and long-term problems is crucial.

THE IMPACT OF CHILDREN WITH SPECIAL NEEDS

See Beresford (1994) for further reading on this topic.

Children who are disabled (intellectually and/or physically) or chronically ill are more likely to have behavioural and emotional problems than healthy children—a fact that puts an additional strain on parents struggling to cope with the disability/illness in its own right. Davis (1993) points out how each disability/disease presents specific problems to the children and family:

'When children are hurt, ill or disabled, they need physical and personal attention, and this has consequences for all members of the family. At a relatively trivial level, one of the parents has to stop cooking, reading or watching television to see to the child, to cuddle him or her or kiss a bruise better. If the child is sick, parents become worried, arrangements have to be made to look after him or her while one parent takes the other children to school or they have to make time to go to the GP. Time may be lost from work, and the other children lose attention. Such consequences are a routine part of family life but, in chronic disease, they become a way of life. Anxiety may be the norm, outside commitments may be impossible and childcare duties are increased, including appointments with professionals and even periods away from home for hospital admissions.'

Davis describes how parents are profoundly affected by illness in their children, with as many as 33% of parents of children with cancer, even in remission, having such severe depression and anxiety that they require professional help. In a study conducted by Davis with one of his students, 31% of mothers of children with diabetes were found to have stress levels that would have benefited from a professional mental health intervention. Communication and relationship problems are reflected in increased marital distress, sometimes in divorce. There is evidence of increased disturbance in siblings.

Interventions (see Evans, 1989)

It is not possible to detach the discussion of the 'management' of intellectual or physical disability from an ideological–political context of civil rights expansion to handicapped persons. Radical changes are taking place under the impetus of the normalization and deinstitutionalization movements, more options being available as behavioural technology lifts the self-help skills and aspirations of this group. Clinical child psychologists have extended their interventions from the hospitals out into the community where they work with handicapped children and adolescents in their own homes, in sheltered accommodation, hostels and training centres. Evans and Meyer (1985) propose a three-component model for the design of behavioural interventions with children who are handicapped: interventions which either manipulate natural consequences (contingency strategies), teach alternative behaviours (curricular strategies), or modify environments (ecological strategies). A good deal of attention has been given to speech training, the results of which have been somewhat disappointing (Ager, 1985). The success of many behavioural interventions which tend to be biased to the *non-verbal,* and the general preference of persons with severe learning difficulties for coding information in a *visuospatial modality,* has led to increasing use of non-vocal teaching strategies.

Developmentally impaired children learn maladaptive behaviours in the same way as children who are not handicapped, but there are some important differences:

(1) Parents may consider the child to be 'ill' on a long-term basis, and so not expect more reasonable behaviour from their child—'After all, he is handicapped, we can't expect him to stop banging his head on the walls'.

(2) Because intellectually (and some physically) impaired children learn more slowly, procedures which would have been successful if continued tend to be abandoned because there is so little improvement in the short term (i.e. the parallel situation to teaching new developmental skills).

Teaching the child new ways of behaving requires a more structured approach than is necessary with the normal child. This structure, naturally enough, seems to go against the grain for many parents, who quite understandably prefer to rely on a less formal, more intuitive approach to their normal children.

For most parents, the idea of the expert handing out advice on child-rearing *ex cathedra* was always doomed to failure. It is now recognized that parents have a considerable expertise which needs to be mobilized in cooperation with specialists so that a jointly agreed programme may be evolved. There are several schemes available providing help and support for parents of disabled children. They may take the form of parent groups (e.g. Mencap) or training groups with specialist members, or home visits by specialists. The latter is of importance because intellectually/developmentally impaired children, like all children, perform to their best when relaxed, and in familiar surroundings with familiar people present. Assessment in hospital, or clinic, can yield quite misleading results. The past history of a child's problem behaviour can also prove unreliable if relied on to the exclusion of the parent's record of the child's behaviour—as and when it occurs.

Parent training is now seen as a standard ingredient for early intervention programmes with mentally/developmentally handicapped children (Bidder, Bryant and Gray, 1975; Jeffree, McConkey and Hewson, 1977; Revill and Blunden, 1979). Home-based assistance is available through the Portage project which began in Wisconsin in 1969. A trained person visits the family at frequent intervals and works with the parents and child. During these visits, the parents and the Portage visitor agree on what skills the child needs to acquire next and how the parents can achieve this by working with the child each day (e.g. Daley *et al.*, 1985); these methods have proved to be extremely valuable (Clements *et al.*, 1979; Revill and Blunden, 1979; Scaife and Holland, 1987).

Another service of help is the Education of the Developmentally Young (EDY) project started by the Hester Adrian Research Centre at Manchester University. This was designed to teach those working with young handicapped children the skills for modifying the behaviours of these children (e.g. Farrell, 1982). Targets set to help them learn better speech, manual dexterity or social skills, must be realistic. The goal should be beyond the child's present attainment, so as to provide a challenge, but not so far ahead as to reinforce a sense of failure. Clear instructions and patience are required in any learning situation. Coercion should be avoided. Handicapped children are likely to encourage their parents to be too protective, both because they *are* more helpless and because they often like routine and letting things be done for them. If parents do too much for their children the message they are giving them is that they are incapable of doing things for themselves. They are teaching them to be helpless.

Although the problem of handicap has always been with us, a number of developments in our society have re-emphasized its importance. One is the increasing complexity of society and the demands it makes on its members, and another is the emphasis on compulsory education. Both of these have served to alter the definition of intellectual impairment and to bring within the category persons who would not previously have been considered handicapped. Recently, the growing realization by educators that more than 50% of the jobs in our society do not require schooling beyond primary level has meant a growing emphasis on the integration of the less severely handicapped youngsters into the community to which they rightly belong—a theory and, indeed, a policy referred to as 'normalization' (Wolfensberger 1980).

Hudson (1982) makes the point that very little research has focused on the issue of the most appropriate formats for training the parents of developmentally handicapped children. With this in mind he carried out a component analysis of a group training programme for parents in Melbourne, Australia. The sample consisted of the mothers of 40 developmentally handicapped children, who were randomly allocated to one of four treatment groups: verbal instruction, verbal instruction plus teaching of behavioural principles, verbal instruction plus the use of modelling and role-playing, and a waiting list control group. Using multiple outcome criteria it was found that (a) the inclusion of the teaching of general behavioural principles did not improve the performance of parents, and (b) it was necessary to include techniques that directly shaped the parents' behaviour (modelling and role playing) in order for them to learn to be effective teachers of their children.

Much of the literature and comment in the past emphasized the debilitating effect of a handicapped child on his or her home, upon the brothers and sisters (Gath, 1972) and even more upon the marriage. However, all is not gloom (see Allen and Affleck, 1985; Blacher, 1984; Hewett, 1970); many families meet the challenge of handicap with courage, resilience and common sense. Many of them are not 'just coping' but are positively happy. It is necessary to avoid the extremes, a Panglossian view of handicap and its effects on everyone concerned, on the one hand, and a pessimistic or fatalistic view on the other. Many parents cope on their own, a few break down under the strain; others are supported by social workers from the local authority, or clinical psychologists with counselling skills and expertise in the ramifications (personal, practical and social) of having a child who is impaired in body and/or intellect. This is truly vital work.

In today's legislation a child is taken to be in need if (a) he or she is unlikely to achieve or maintain, or to have the opportunity of achieving or maintaining, a reasonable standard of health or development without the provision for him or her of specified services by a local authority or (b) he or she is likely to be significantly impaired, or further impaired, without provision of such services; or (c) he or she is disabled. A child is disabled if he or she is blind, deaf or dumb, or suffers from mental disorder of any kind or is substantially handicapped by illness, injury, or congenital deformity.

CHILDREN IN NEED (see Herbert (1993) on the Children Act)

Each child should be assessed in terms of:

- physical well-being and physical care;
- mental health;
- social and intellectual development;
- emotional development—the quality of parental care—and behaviour.

CRITERIA FOR ASSESSING HEALTH AND DEVELOPMENT

All criteria relate to a child similar in age, gender and from a similar cultural, racial and religious background.

- *Reasonable standard.* A child is determined as *not* achieving or maintaining a 'reasonable standard' of health or development when their conduct, presentation or care detrimentally sets them apart.
- *Significant impairment.* The health and development of a child is to be regarded as 'significantly impaired' where there is objective evidence (developmental assessments, child protection events, etc.) that the child's development is being adversely and avoidably impaired through lack of parenting skills resources.
- *Disability* (see checklist in Table 11). Is there visual impairment, hearing impairment, serious communication difficulties, substantial handicap stemming from illness, injury or congenital conditions?

- *Significant risk.* Whether a child is 'significantly at risk' needs to be determined by a child protection case conference. Some children may be at risk and in turn 'in need' even if there is no evidence that they are not achieving or maintaining a 'reasonable standard of health and development'.
- *Significant harm.* A child's health and/or development is being 'significantly harmed' through acts of omission or commission on the part of the parent(s)/carer(s) or because the child is beyond parental control.
- 'Development' means physical, intellectual, emotional, social or behavioural development; and 'health' means physical or mental health.

In this last item lies a major part of the professional's dilemma. What is a standard of development? And what constitutes physical or mental health? It has taken over a decade of debates before terminology relating to abnormality, dysfunction, and disadvantage could be codified in WHO (1980). Fryers is of the opinion that there is hope now that in scientific writing and serious discourse the confusion brought about by a plethora of terms and concepts can be overcome.

The WHO definition of impairment incorporates a functional as well as a structural component:

- 'Impairment: in the context of health experience, an impairment is any loss or abnormality of psychological, physiological or anatomical structure or function.'
- Disability is seen as the limitation of personal activity consequent upon impairment: '. . . any restriction or lack (resulting from an impairment) of ability to perform an activity in the manner or within the range considered normal for a human being.'
- Handicap is the resulting personal and social disadvantage: '. . . a disadvantage for an individual, resulting from an impairment or disability, that limits or prevents the fulfilment of a role that is normal (depending on age, sex and social and cultural factors) for that individual.'

Developmental disorders are coded on Axis II in the DSM-III-R classification because some of them are chronic and may persist into adult life without remission. Their essential feature is a disturbance—general or specifics—in the acquisition or retention of motor, language, cognitive or social skills. They include (*inter alia*):

- elimination disorders (functional encopresis or enuresis);
- developmental receptive language disorder;
- developmental expressive language disorder;
- pervasive developmental disorder (autistic disorder);
- speech disorders (not elsewhere classified) (elective mutism, stuttering);
- gender identity disorders.

Table 11   Disability checklist

Hearing
Moderate to severe: hearing difficulties even with hearing aids; has or is likely to have persisting difficulty with language and communication sufficient to impair development.
Profound: little or no hearing, with little or no benefit from hearing aids.

Vision
Moderate to severe: partially sighted, visual difficulties sufficient to impair everyday activities and/or development despite the use of aids.
Profound: blind, no useful vision.

Speech and/or Language
Moderate to severe: difficulties communicating through speech and language, and as a result unable to participate in the normal activities of a child of similar age.
Profound: no meaningful speech or language, therefore unlikely to use speech as the primary means of communication.

Physical
Moderate to severe: physical difficulty (for example, motor) or chronic illness resulting in long-term impairment of health or development, even with the provision of drugs, diet or aids.
Profound: difficulties with all basic functions. of such severity that assistance is likely to be required.

Learning
Moderate to severe: A permanent learning impairment sufficient to prevent the child from fulfilling roles or performing activities which are generally understood to be within the capacity of children of that age and cultural background.
Profound: profound or multiple learning difficulties.

Behavioural and emotional
Moderate to severe: emotional and/or behavioural difficulties likely to be long-term, and such as to impair the quality of the child's life, resulting in underachievement in normal social contexts (for example, school or workplace), with failure of social development and integration.
Profound: emotional and/or behavioural difficulties likely to be so severe in the long-term that they seriously impair the quality of the child's life, resulting in inability to function in normal social contexts or constituting a risk to themselves or others.

Chapter 8

DEVELOPMENTAL PROBLEMS

ELIMINATION DISORDERS

Faecal Soiling (Encopresis)

When stool enters the rectum, causing it to stretch, sensory nerves are stimulated. These nerves send a message to the brain telling us we are full and need to evacuate. However, when the child withholds (for whatever reason) stool, his/her rectum enlarges slowly over weeks and months. Eventually it becomes so large that it can no longer be suddenly stretched by the passage of stool into the rectum. At this point the child no longer knows if the rectum is full or not. Because the appropriate messages are not getting through, a large, hard impaction of stool forms in the rectum. The constipation becomes so severe that it leads to a partial blockage of the bowel. Some of the motions liquefy and leak around the impacted area, soiling the child's underwear. Children with encopresis due to rectal impaction cannot prevent themselves from soiling. They are unaware of their blockage and unable to prevent the leakage.

To summarize: the soiling occurs because the child has lost the normal anal reflex through excessive constipation and subsequent dilation of the bowel. This problem is referred to as *retention and overflow*. Sometimes (after about one to three weeks, when the rectum is so loaded that messages get through) a stool (a large hard lump of faecal matter) is let out when the child's muscle relaxes. The child usually doesn't realise that it is happening until it is too late. Some children, fearing ridicule or punishment, hide the evidence—the soiled clothing.

A Definition of Soiling

There are different definitions of encopresis in different text books. Because research suggests that soiling (and children who soil) cannot meaningfully be compartmentalized, into disorders with physical, as opposed to psychological, aetiologies, or into any other recognizable groupings, a broad and simple definition will do:

A soiling child refers to any child over the age of four and under the age of 16 who regularly soils his/her underwear and/or bed.

Background Information

- it is not an uncommon problem.
    - Three in every 100 children entering primary school at five years will still be soiling.
    - Between 7 and 8 years, about two out of 100 children are soiling.
    - At 12 years, about one in every 100 boys (and some girls) are still soiling.
- Because of the shame felt about this problem, and the attempt by many families to keep the soiling a secret, the figures quoted above may be underestimates.
- Constipation, or hard bowel movements, cause pain, irritability and a decreased appetite.
- A child's emotional state (due to stress/trauma) can affect the functioning of the bowel. Thus, soiling may result from distressing individual and/or family life-events.
- Many parents are likely to think (shamefully) that their child has a unique problem because most parents have never heard of another with a soiling problem.
- Some children have *never* established bowel control ('primary encopresis'). When bowel control has been established for at least 6 months before the soiling begins, the soiling is referred to as 'secondary encopresis'.
- Soiling is not a unitary symptom, but a many-sided syndrome.
- For example, it can lead to fear, embarrassment and a lowering of self-esteem in the child, which leads on to yet other social ramifications.
- He or she is quite likely to be taunted, teased, even bullied at school because of the problem. (Children have been suspended from school because staff find soiling so difficult to manage.)
- For the family, there are feelings of bewilderment, frustration, failure, revulsion and anger. Soiling tends to engender negative responses from parents. It is one of the most common precipitants of physical abuse incidents (see Clayden and Agnarsson, 1991).
- Soiling is sometimes associated with behaviour problems such as non-compliance and defiance.
- More boys soil than girls.
- Children of all levels of ability soil.

- Children from all walks of life soil.
- There is a highly significant association between enuresis and encopresis.
- There is a relationship between soiling and low birth weight.

Most children have successfully *learned* bowel control between the ages of two and four, irrespective of the training methods used or how early they were applied. The learning task is quite a daunting one.

Dollard and Miller (1950) have this to say:

> Within a relatively short space of time the toddler must learn, under pain of losing his/her mother's esteem, 'to attach anxiety to all the cues produced by excretory materials to their sight, smell and touch . . . to deposit faeces and urine only in a prescribed and secret place, and to clean its body. It must later learn to suppress unnecessary verbal reference to these matters.'

Anthony (1957) elaborates the point thus:

> From the child's eye view, the toilet ritual, as practised by the adults of our compulsive communities, must sometimes appear as an exacting and complex ordeal far removed from the simple evacuations into the nursery pot. It is his business with maternal prompting, to become aware of defecation cues in time, to stop his play in response to this, to suppress the desire for immediate excretion, to search for and find an appropriate place for the purpose, to ensure adequate privacy for himself, to unfasten his clothes, to establish himself securely on the toilet seat . . . to recognize an end-point to the proceedings, to cleanse himself satisfactorily, to flush the toilet, to re-fasten his clothes, to unbolt the door and emerge successfully to resume his interrupted play at the point where he left off.

This guide does not deal, as its main emphasis, with early failures of training (i.e. 'primary encopresis'). The point of the two quotations is to highlight the complex *social learning* (i.e. psychology) involved in the control and social response to an essentially physical activity (defecation). If the learning occurs under stress it may break down under stress.

Causation

There is no uniform causation for all cases of soiling; it comes about in different ways and for quite differing reasons. Rigorous assessment is therefore crucial. The search for antecedent influences which may be linked with the problem produces a list of factors ranging from the intellectual (such as learning disability); the physical (for example, constipation); the psychological (fear of the toilet) or social (neglectful or coercive training in toilet habits).

Psychological Determinants

The psychological factors associated with soiling may be secondary to the soiling—an 'emotional overlay' which *contributes* to the onset, maintenance or exacerbation of the symptoms. They include:

- coercive training/punitive remedies on the part of parents;
- the role of anxious/overprotective mothers: overly strict fathers (Bellman, 1966);
- a tendency of soilers to be nervous (Bellman, 1966);
- a tendency of soilers to be food refusers (Bellman, 1966);
- a tendency of soilers to suffer from learned helplessness (Sluckin, 1981).

Environmental Factors

Among the predisposing environmental influences are:

- stressful environments (Butler and Golding, 1986);
- poor toilets at home or at school;
- separation (and other traumatic) experiences;
- dietary factors: eating a diet deficient in fibre (and drinking excessive milk) can cause constipation in older children.

Physical Causes

The vast majority of cases of soiling are a result of chronic constipation and stool withholding. Not surprisingly, then, our particular interest in this book is with *retention and overflow*. When they feel the urge to have a bowel movement, they are afraid of experiencing pain and respond by holding the stool in. The role of the colon and rectum is to absorb water from the stool, so the longer the child withholds, whether voluntarily or involuntarily, the harder and more painful his/her bowel movements become. A 'vicious cycle' is created of stool withholding, causing more painful bowel movements, causing more stool withholding, and so on *ad nauseam.*

When the bowel is frequently overloaded, the rectal muscles become *over-active* while concurrently the anal muscles relax reflexly in response to the rectal activity (Clayden, 1988). Thus, as the muscles go on churning to eliminate the blockage, the child has no voluntary control over what happens below, and he or she soils. No wonder a child said to me, 'It's not me who soils, it's my bottom'. His bottom seemed to him to have an independent existence!

Other Physical Conditions

These include undiagnosed Hirschsprung's disease, intestinal obstructions, congenital abnormalities, gastrointestinal disease, brain injury and developmental delay, and can be read about in Clayden and Agnarsson (1991).

The Assessment

Points to remember are as follows:

- Parents and child are likely to be deeply embarrassed.
- You need a common language to discuss toileting and soiling issues with them. Most families have their own words (e.g. loo, toilet, lavatory, potty; poohs, No 2s, big jobs).
- The collaborative approach stresses the desirability of discovering what the child and his/her parents wish to do about the problem. Respect their views and give them time to express them.
- It also puts an emphasis on empowering the parents by providing them with knowledge and skills, and by sharing your thinking with them. Engage them in an active partnership during the assessment and (later) the intervention. (Incidentally, sharing information reduces the number of clients who drop out of therapy—a particular problem in the case of soiling).
- The assessment is not only about soiling; it is about a child with an embarrassing, restrictive problem; a child with feelings, and a child with a family which is also experiencing powerful emotions and attitudes about the child's 'failure'.

Steps for Assessing the Problem

Step 1:   Ask for precise details of the soiling and any other behaviour problems.

Step 2:   Use the ABC Model (see Figure 12) and the Soiling Behaviour Checklist to systematize data.

Step 3:   Formulate hypotheses about the pattern of causes and determinants in this case of soiling from this checklist:

- passing a motion is painful;
- abnormal appearance/consistency of motions;
- faecal masses (severe constipation);
- diarrhoea;
- anal lesion;

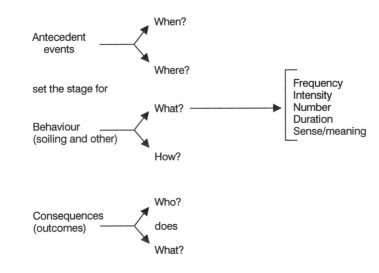

Figure 12   The ABC approach to assessing behaviour

- failure to teach child bowel control;
- early bowel training stressful (punitive, coercive, too early);
- toilet arrangements unsatisfactory;
- diet inadequate/inappropriate;
- stressful/traumatic life-events (at present);
- stressful/traumatic life events (around time of onset of soiling);
- teasing/bullying at home or school in connection with soiling;
- behaviour problems present;
- high emotional arousal surrounds the bowel function (anger, resentment, despair, shame) at home;
- fear of going to the toilet;
- abnormal response to bowel function (hiding, smearing, hiding underwear);
- refusal to sit on the toilet;
- refusal to talk about the problem;
- loss of confidence by the child (low self-esteem);
- depression (child);
- defiance of a general kind (child);
- parental attitudes dysfunctional (overprotective, punitive, rejecting);
- family attitudes/relationships dysfunctional (coercive, punitive, hostile);
- loss of confidence (parent);
- learned helplessness (parental depression);
- marital conflict;
- abuse (physical/sexual/emotional).

Intervention

The intervention has four strands to it:

(1) *Medication.* Laxatives are used to ensure effective rectal emptying and, eventually, the recovery of sensations related to defecation and continence.
(2) *Food.* A high fibre diet helps to ensure continuance of rectal emptying.
(3) *Routine.* Routines are established to facilitate the timing of defecation and to establish toileting habits in the child.
(4) *Training.* Behavioural methods are used to facilitate the child's learning or re-learning.

(1) *Medication*
   (a) Docusate and picosulphate are used to get rid of the old, hard stools by softening and 'dissolving' them. Enemas may have to be used in some cases.
   (b) Medication is required to help send the stools along more quickly and make the rectum contract more. Senokot is commonly used for this purpose.
   (c) There are medicines which provide roughage and keep the stools soft (e.g. Lactulose).

(2) *Food*
   (a) Some foods slow down the movement of the bowels (e.g. milk) or put the child off his/her food because they are filling (e.g. sweets).
   (b) High fibre foods help to keep stools soft.

(3) *Routines*
   (a) The body requires routines (regular rhythms of eating, sleeping, passing a motion).
   (b) The judicious use of senna, plus the routines prescribed in the behavioural programme, may provoke the passage of a stool at a time convenient for the child.

(4) *Training*
   This brings us to the use of behavioural programmes.

   Preliminaries
   (a) If the child is fearful about going to the toilet/passing a motion, you will need to desensitise his/her fears (see Herbert, 1987b).
   (b) It is hard to pass a motion if the child is tense. You might suggest music, a comic, pictures or a toy to help the child relax—just so long as they do not distract him/her from the primary task!
   (c) Children often need reminders to go and make an effort on the toilet. Parents *and* child may need reminders (e.g. a script) for keeping to the programme.

(d) Praise and encouragement and more tangible rewards (reinforcers) will facilitate learning and make the sometimes unpleasant
toileting activity less burdensome for the child. Reward effort *and*
success.

(e) Before initiating the programme ensure that the constipation is
under control; if not failure will ensue.

(f) Remember: failure breeds failure; success breeds success.

The Programme

The steps the programme might follow include:

(1) initiating the treatment plan on the basis of a *negotiated* working
agreement;
(2) moving toward simple early goals applying methods that are ethically
acceptable and which have been explained to parents and accepted
by them;
(3) collecting data as measures of change (e.g. ratings of behaviour, interactions, diary writing);
(4) using and interpreting data as a basis of monitoring.

Designing the Individual's Programme

Every child is an individual, and unique. So is his family. Bowel movements
are also individual; there are considerable variations in the need to defecate.
Bowel movements can occur in healthy children several times a day, several
times a week, or only a few times a month. Even the child's constipation has
its individuality; each soiling problem is made up of its own particular mixture of predisposing causes, contributory precipitating influences, and
social consequences. This means that there is no one behavioural formula,
no set-piece programme to fit all cases. Each soiling programme needs to be
individually designed, discussed and negotiated with the family. It is vital
to involve the parent/s *and* child in all aspects of the work.

It may be helpful to see the 'script' (usually typed out for parents) of a
fairly typical kind of programme.

Peter's Programme

Organiser: Peter's mother: Sally Brown

Helper: School nurse: Mary Smith

Now that Peter's constipation has been cleared the agreement is to carry
out the following plan that we have jointly agreed to:

(1) To keep a record in the event diary of:
   (a) his medication
   (b) his going to the toilet and the results.
(2) Peter will have a hot drink with each meal (his diet has been discussed).
(3) Because the most likely time to be successful is after eating, he will go to the toilet about 15 minutes after each meal.
(4) Peter will sit there for at least 10 minutes. There will be some comics and his Walkman to keep him amused. However, he has promised:
   (a) To try pushing, every so often, imagining (as we have practised) that he is blowing a balloon.
   (b) He will have a box to rest his feet on to help with the pushing.
   (c) Even if he passes a small stool, he will go on trying, off and on, to pass yet another.
(5) *Incentives.* Peter's reward for cooperating so well and helping himself will be:
   (a) A happy face for his merit book for trying (and staying the full 10 minutes).
   (b) A further *two* happy face stickers for producing a pooh.
(6) The family will look at Peter's charts and offer him encouragement (never criticism) and praise for trying.
(7) When Peter has collected X happy faces his Mum and Dad will take him to Y for a treat.
(8) Mrs. Smith will stay in touch and review the progress of the programme in Z days/weeks.

Enuresis

Whether a child has been wet all his or her life, or has more recently lost bladder control, he or she needs special help in the difficult task of learning control. (This applies to children *over the age of five*—the age at which the majority might be expected to be continent at night.) Nocturnal enuresis is usually defined as repeated involuntary passage of urine during sleep in the absence of any identified physical abnormality in children aged above five. The child will usually (and preferably) be examined first by a doctor in case there is a physical cause for the bedwetting, although organic aetiology (that is, physical or medical causation) is somewhat uncommon. When a child wets the bed, it seems that his or her brain is not properly aware of the amount of urine in the bladder, allowing it to empty automatically while he or she is sleeping.

The likelihood that a child will become continent spontaneously over a 12-month period is reduced sharply after the age of four (Shaffer, 1994). Nocturnal bedwetting at least once a week occurs in approximately 13 per cent (boys) or 14 per cent (girls) of five-year-olds (Rutter, Tizard and

Whitmore, 1970). while some estimates (Morgan, 1984) make the rate higher! The prevalence rate is 1–2% for youngsters over fifteen and for adults. Enuresis is a very common occurrence amongst children in residential establishments.

Nocturnal Enuresis

Nocturnal enuresis is one of the commonest reasons for families seeking help from general practitioners and clinical child psychologists. The problem was referred to as early as the 16th century in *The Boke of Chyldren* by Thomas Phaire, in a chapter with the delicate title 'Of pissing in the bedde.' Fortunately this ancient problem is very responsive to expert intervention today (Smith and Smith, 1987).

According to Baller (1975) nocturnal enuretics

(a) involuntarily wet the bed;
(b) show no evidence of urinary, organic pathology;
(c) are three and one half years of age or more;
(d) have simply continued the night time wetting habits of infancy ('primary enuresis') or have fallen into a pattern of bed-wetting ('secondary enuresis') that averages more than twice a week.

Morgan and Young (1972) say of enuresis that it is not only a source of embarrassment to the sufferer, often invoking ridicule or punishment, but it can place an intolerable burden upon intrafamilial relationships—especially in those large families living in overcrowded conditions, where several children may wet the bed. For the majority of enuretics, to be a bed-wetter carries adverse emotional consequences, and they tend to exhibit some degree of reactive disturbance. They make the point that even when this is not apparently the case, enuresis imposes a limit on the child's choice of activities; few enuretics can happily go camping or stay with friends. In own-homes and residential establishments, the daily wash of bedlinen is unpleasant and onerous; all too often both natural parents and house-parents are forced into a fatalistic acceptance of enuresis as an inevitable correlate of child upbringing.

Assessment

- *Primary enuresis.* This problem represents a behavioural deficit. The child has never gained control of nocturnal wetting.
- *Secondary enuresis.* Here the child reverts to bed-wetting after a period of being dry. Onset is most common between the ages of 5 and 7 but uncommon after age 11. The child's control may, anyway, have been tenuous at best. As many as 25% of preschoolers who have been conti-

nent for at least 6 months will start to wet again (Ferguson, Horwood and Shannon, 1986). A period of stress may produce the regression.

A further distinction can also be made between children who are regularly and those who are intermittently enuretic.

Causation

The origins of nocturnal enuresis would seem to be multi-factorial. Enuresis may have its origins in faulty learning. Because the peak age range for the emergence of continence is between one-and-a-half and four-and-a-half years of age, it could be said that there is a 'sensitive' period for the emergence of night-time dryness. Harsh pressurizing of the child or (conversely) complacent neglect of training may lead to a failure of this development. Emotional problems are then superimposed when the child is made to feel acute shame at his or her 'babyish' ways. Only too often, as I have already mentioned, they have to endure punishment, scorn and ridicule at home and at school. Other contributory causal influences may be urological and medical factors, such as small functional bladder capacity, genetics, maturation.

Surveys suggest 10% of all cases of enuresis are the result of medical (physical) conditions, most commonly urinary tract infections. Approximately one in twenty female and one in fifty male enuretics have such an infection. Other uncommon physical causes are chronic renal or kidney disease, diabetes, tumours and seizures. Such potentially important causes make an expert physical examination a matter of routine. Enuresis runs in families; some 70% of clinically referred enuretics have a first-degree relative who was enuretic as a child.

Emotional Influences (Anxiety)

Children who wet the bed may also tend to be anxious or nervous children; what is not certain is the precise nature of the relationship between feeling anxious and wetting the bed. A popular view is that emotional disturbance is associated with bed-wetting. This idea is supported by the fact that several studies have shown that after the successful treatment of bed-wetting there is usually a decrease in anxiety and an improvement in the way the child feels about him- or herself. This explanation seems plausible when we think about the problems of being a bed-wetter. The child is often ridiculed by brothers and sisters and may even be ridiculed by parents. Staying at a friend's house or going on school camps is not possible. It is even very difficult to hide the problem from neighbours, given the frequent appearance of sheets and blankets on the clothes line. It is not surprising that the bed-wetter becomes very anxious about the problem.

Treatment (see Morgan, 1984)

Over the years a number of methods have been suggested for the treatment of enuresis. Some of these have been based on scientific theory and research while others are merely 'old wives' tales'. A particularly common, but unsupported, belief is that bed-wetting is related to depth of sleep—children wet the bed because they sleep deeply. Because of this unsupported idea, some parents in the past have implemented what could only be described as harsh regimes, for example making children sleep on hard beds to prevent deep sleep.

Many physicians turn to medication to treat their enuretic patients. A favourite drug is a tricyclic antidepressant, imipramine hydrochloride (Tofranil). Certainly, an increase in urinary control tends to occur in about 25–40% of cases in the first two weeks of treatment, but there is up to 95% relapse following the withdrawal of medication. There is no clear theoretical rationale for the use of this drug. More sure, but more onerous and time-consuming, is the approach based on a training paradigm; treatment, in such cases, can be thought of as the teaching of new and more effective skills and more appropriate responses to stimuli.

Synthetic antidiuretics (e.g. desmopressin) have been used alone and in combination with the alarm system described below. The effects are comparable to those of the tricyclic antidepressants (Shaffer, 1994).

The Enuresis Alarm

The device known as the 'enuresis alarm' has been developed to help children (with the supervision of a professional) to overcome the problem of bed-wetting. Basically, the alarm is made up of a pair of detector mats on the bed, connected to a buzzer next to the child's bed. As soon as the child begins to wet during sleep, the buzzer sounds. The use of the alarm produces two actions—stopping the stream and waking—whenever the child's bladder begins to empty automatically during sleep.

Gradually the brain learns to connect these two actions with the feeling of a full bladder. After a time the brain becomes more aware of the amount of urine in the child's bladder, and begins itself to take the two actions of contracting the muscles and waking the child when the bladder is full. Eventually the child is able to sleep without wetting, waking up unaided to use the toilet at night.

Mini Body (Pants) Alarm

Pants alarms for night-time and/or daytime toilet training are miniature portable versions of the apparatus used in the treatment of bed-wetting. A sensor is attached to the child's pyjama or underpants and the alarm is carried on a wrist band or in a pocket. The device delivers an auditory signal to the child.

The evidence for the superiority of the alarm method (with rates of remission between 80% and 90%) over no-treatment and other-treatment control procedures is well documented for nocturnal enuresis (see Shaffer, 1994). While Doleys' (1977) data based on over 600 subjects revealed an average relapse rate of 40%, nearly 60% of those returned to continence after booster sessions.

Incentive Systems

Because of the ease of producing some change in the child's motivation to be dry by offering rewards (reinforcement) for dryness, this is probably a good place to start for the parent of the bed wetter.

- *Rewards.* One method is to provide a *special* reward for achieving a given (a *gradually* increasing) number of consecutive dry nights. The usual number of dry nights the child is expected to have to be considered 'trained' is fourteen in a row. If fourteen in a row are achieved the child is less likely to go back to wetting.
- *Star/sticker charts.* Night (and day) wetting can sometimes be brought to an end by the use of a simple star or sticker chart for dry beds (or pants). When a negotiated number of stars is achieved, the child receives a special treat or privilege, or exchanges them for small items such as crayons, plasticine and so on at a fixed tariff. A record is kept on a chart—a little like a calendar, with a space for each day. Each time the child has a dry night a gold star (or colourful sticker) is placed in the appropriate place on the calendar and the child can see how well he or she is going by the number of stars on the chart. Sometimes this will be enough to motivate the child to be dry more often; it can then be backed up by making sure that some other reward, such as an outing or TV viewing, is available only if a certain number of stars is earned each week.

This method results in a marked reduction, and in some cases a cure, in up to 20% of enuretics (Devlin and O'Cathain, 1990).

A child may continue to wet the bed because he or she is simply not motivated enough (or perhaps *encouraged* enough!) to learn to be dry. Indeed some instances have been observed where the child is able to wake up and go to the toilet when required but instead *chooses* to wet the bed. This is particularly likely to occur in the middle of winter, or if the route to the toilet is long and dark. Here it is important for parents to provide the necessary motivation for the child and to change the situation in some way so that going to the toilet and keeping the bed dry is more attractive than wetting the bed. However, there are problems associated with sanctioning/penalizing the child for wetting the bed as the problem may not be simply motivational and the child may be being punished unfairly. The punishment may lead to an increase in anxiety associated with wetting the bed.

A preferable alternative is to increase the child's desire to be dry and to make being dry a very attractive option. This means that the parent provides incentives for the child being dry and, at the same time, ignores those occasions on which the child wets. The easiest (and often most effective) strategy is to make sure that the child gets lots of praise and attention when a dry night is achieved.

Daytime (Bladder-Stretching) Training

There is some evidence to suggest that bed-wetters may have smaller bladder capacities than non-bedwetters. Training children to hold greater and greater amounts can increase the bladder capacity.

Daytime training involves having the child signal on first feeling the need to go to the toilet. He or she is then asked to hang on for five minutes before going. After five minutes are up he or she is allowed to go and is praised extensively for these efforts. When the child can hold on easily for five minutes the length of time is gradually increased by five minute intervals, until the child can hang on for up to thirty minutes. This method helps to increase the capacity of the bladder so that he or she can get through the night without having to go to the toilet.

This procedure certainly increases bladder capacity but its effectiveness in treating bed-wetting has not been firmly established at this stage. It is a useful way of dealing with the problem of urgency of urination.

Training the child to hold greater and greater quantities of fluid can increase bladder capacity. The child is encouraged to drink as long as possible. He or she is asked to urinate in a measuring cup and record how much was passed. Each day the child tries to break the previous record and a reward is provided for success. (The bladder has a capacity of 140–200g (5–7 oz) on average in the six year old.)

The 'start and stop' method while urinating (holding and letting go of the flow of urine) strengthens the muscles' and bladder valve's ability to inhibit urine flow.

Diurnal Enuresis Treatment Programmes

The use of incentives for habit-training and portable body alarms also play their part in the treatment of daytime wetting.

PROBLEMS OF COMMUNICATION (DEVELOPMENTAL LANGUAGE DISORDERS)

Communication in spoken language is the latest, most complex and probably the most valuable of man's and woman's evolutionary achievements. To communicate is to convey meaning from one individual to another in an intelligible code. Such a code is provided by language. In learning a language, infants are assimilating their culture's conceptual categories for thinking, perceiving and reasoning. Given that the basic needs of children are fulfilled by interaction with adults and other children, it is not surprising that serious emotional problems flow from children's inability to express themselves meaningfully or to comprehend others. Cantwell and Baker (1985) distinguish between:

- *Pure speech disorder.* 'Impairment (including delay and deviance) in the articulation or fluency of production of speech sounds' and
- *Pure language disorders.* 'Impairment (including delay and deviance) in the receptive or expressive use of words to convey meanings.' The relationship between speech and language dysfunction and behavioural disorder is substantial; the fact is that 50% of speech-and-language disordered children also display psychopathology of sufficient intensity to warrant a 'diagnosis' (Piacentini, 1987).

Developmental Aphasia

Disturbance in the ability to produce and comprehend speech are referred to as aphasic conditions (aphasia). The *aphasia* disorders are those that are thought to be directly linked to brain dysfunction in language processing. The *acquired aphasias* result from postnatal brain damage.

The distinction between congenital and developmental aphasias is usually based upon whether a family history is present (indicating developmental aphasia) or neonatal brain damage was indicated (congenital aphasia). The true developmental aphasias are rare; estimates of 1 in 10 000 for receptive developmental aphasia and 1 in 1000 for expressive developmental aphasia have been obtained in community surveys (Rutter and Schopler, 1992).

Much of the information that enables the individual to understand or express himself or herself in speech appears to be stored in the left parietal cortex in right-handed people (Penfield and Roberts, 1959). The use and understanding of language may be impaired in several ways, and such impairments lead to associated difficulties in mastering that all-important skill of reading. Penfield and Roberts are of the opinion that there are no really pure forms of language defect. However, they present evidence that relatively small lesions may in some cases produce impairments where one aspect of language is much more disturbed than others. The commonly quoted examples of this are expressive impairments of speech associated with lesions in the region of the Rolandic fissure, and dyslexia, usually accompanied by dysgraphia, associated with parieto-occipital lesions.

Executive Aphasia

It is fairly common for there to be a developmental delay in language expression in the case of intelligent children with unimpaired comprehension and normal adjustment. There is usually a good prognosis in such cases of developmental speech retardation. Many of these children will enjoy normal speech by six years of age. However, this sort of problem shades into the more serious syndrome of executive aphasia. Here there is usually evidence of perceptual difficulties indicative of brain injury. The comprehension of language may be normal or relatively less impaired than the ability to speak.

Receptive Aphasia

This syndrome is rare in its more serious form. The milder form of impairment may involve an inability to localize sounds although the child can respond to some of them in an undifferentiated and gross manner. Such a deficit makes it impossible for the youngster to process the complex series of sounds which make up language. At the other extreme are those individuals who are 'word deaf' and, in fact, totally inattentive to sounds, although special techniques indicate that there is no peripheral or cochlear hearing loss to account for their deafness. The problem may occur in early childhood following or preceding a series of epileptic attacks.

These children with receptive and executive aphasia often have the particular language difficulties (and also suffer from other disabilities) which present features seen in sufferers from autism. There are children whose clinical features reveal them to be in the hinterland between autism and aphasia and there are aphasic children who, under stress, temporarily preoccupy themselves with the same obsessive rituals and avoid making interpersonal relationships in a manner analogous to autistic children. Aphasic children shed these habits on removal from stressful conditions, unlike autistic children.

The assessment and treatment of aphasic children requires the involvement of speech and language therapists. Estimates of the prevalence of such language delays vary, but a recent review of three separate epidemiological surveys suggested a prevalence figure in the range 3–5% for three-year-olds showing significant delay in their language development: (Stevenson, 1984). Longitudinal studies demonstrate that children with language delays are markedly at risk for continuing educational or behavioural difficulties; many language problems (e.g. delay in speech) are linked with other basic disabilities (see Rutter, 1977). To take one example, children with profound hearing loss will require specialist help to acquire adequate communicative abilities. Children with partial transient hearing loss may also experience speech and language disturbances. Thus an audiological assessment should always be considered for children with language delays or speech abnormalities.

Many of the factors causing delays in the normal rate of language acquisition are broadly connected with psychosocial disadvantages including poor parent–child relationships, institutionalization, many siblings, deaf parents and maternal depression.

Semantic–Pragmatic Disorder

Rapin and Allen (1983) introduced the term 'semantic–pragmatic disorder' as part of developmental language disability. This condition, being manifested in inappropriate social and communicative behaviour, shares many features with autism and Asperger's syndrome. Where the boundaries are, or whether there are any, is a matter of debate and disagreement (e.g. Bishop, 1989; Smith and Leinonen, 1992; Wing, 1988).

Bishop (1989) recognizes the overlap between this disorder and the autistic and Asperger syndromes, but considers it clearer to keep the conditions separate. The term is used for children who are not autistic on conventional criteria but who initially present with a picture of language delay and receptive language impairment and who then learn to speak clearly and in complex sentences, with semantic and pragmatic abnormalities. Semantic–pragmatic problems tend not to be taken seriously until well after five years of age. There is no test or assessment battery which reliably incorporates these children into a diagnostic procedure.

Although this disorder predominates among verbal autistic preschoolers it is also encountered occasionally in non-autistic children with developmental language disorder and in some non-autistic hydrocephalic children. At pre-school, these irritatingly verbose children initiate more verbal interactions than normal children but do so inappropriately. They may repeatedly ask questions to which they know the answer and perseverate with favourite topics and phrases. Bishop (1989) analysed conversions of 14 8–12 year old children with semantic–pragmatic deficit disorder, comparing them to the conversations of 20 normal children and of 43 children with other developmental language disorders. The interpretation was that the inappropriacy of these children's language was indicative of cognitive and social limitations and comprehension failures rather than a specific linguistic deficit.

Lucas (1980) makes a connection between *underlying* semantic problems and pragmatic problems which ensue, assuming (as he does) that semantic and pragmatic aspects of a person's communicative functioning are closely linked. Smith and Leinonen (1992) are of the opinion that the term 'semantic' can be envisaged, as reflecting *one* of the influences bearing upon the pragmatic component. For example, lack of semantic specificity hardly accounts for a failure to integrate literal meaning with situational requirements, nor can limitations of vocabulary account for an inability to draw together information so as to derive coherent and meaningful ideas.

In learning to communicate a child needs to know that there are many rules and meanings, social nuances, sensitives and insensitives. What then, are some of the *general* and *specific* aspects of what one needs to know about communication that allow a child to function appropriately? The general aspects of what is referred to as pragmatic 'knowing that' require (Smith and Leinonen, 1992) the knowledge that:

- Communication is based on mutual knowledge; one needs to presuppose what the other person knows.
- Communicative behaviour can be appropriate or inappropriate—in relation to contextual factors such as the status, age, sex, cultural origin or outlook of the participants, the setting and the types of discourse.
- One has a choice of communicating or not communicating with others.
- Communication is cooperative, intention-driven behaviour.
- One's communicative contribution needs to be relevant to the assumed shared topic.
- Meanings can be negotiated in communication.
- There are expectations and consequences attached to communicative behaviour.
- Intention can be expressed and interpreted directly or indirectly.

- Meanings can be shared via different signalling systems and modalities.
- When encountering a communication problem adaptive strategies can be used.

In order for communication to progress responses need also to function as initiations.

- One's own communicative behaviour has an effect on the mental state of others, and oneself.
- Different contexts and situations have different communicative conventions associated with them.
- Communicative behaviour can be judged successful or unsuccessful by oneself or others.
- Meanings expressed in communication can have personal significance for oneself and others.
- One takes the other person's knowledge, interest and feelings into account, if one chooses.
- One can violate communicative principles intentionally or unintentionally.
- One can communicate about 'real' and imaginary objects, events and concepts.
- One can express one's opinion if one chooses and if the context permits.

Intervention

The most appropriate treatment for children with language delays has not yet been established. Simply to provide these children with a remedial language programme will not offset the continuing adverse influences (in many cases) of their social and family situations.

Howlin (1984) has reviewed a number of schemes for parental involvement in the treatment of children with language delays. These ranged from those centred on children with delays associated with learning disability and autism through to those involving expressive language delays primarily the result of inadequate or inappropriate stimulation at home. She found that although few of these approaches to treatment has been adequately evaluated, those that involved the parents in home-based activities as part of a structured programme of remedial help for the children were likely to show significant gains (see also Scaife and Holland, 1987).

Selective Mutism

The child who elects to remain silent in the presence of others, or (more accurately) selects to whom he or she will talk, is a phenomenon which was described a long way back in literature (Austin 1811), but relatively recently in clinical publications. Kratochwil (1981) gives good reasons why the earlier diagnostic term 'elective mutism', should be superseded by 'selective mutism' (SM). SM children are reported to have age-appropriate speech development, but appear 'stuck' at a stage children often pass through at about 2–3 years, which is characterized by excessive shyness. Selective silence tends to occur most frequently in school, presenting a formidable problem in the classroom (Baldwin, 1985). In 4–5-year-olds, shortly after initial school entry, the prevalence of non-speaking in school is 7.2 per thousand among a Birmingham UK sample (Brown and Lloyd, 1975). However, a sharp decline in the number of non-speakers was noted over the next 20 months, after which only one child remained totally mute. The disorder represents less than 1% of child guidance and social work referrals in the USA, an incidence which nevertheless is sufficiently high to be problematic.

Several studies (e.g. Sluckin, Foreman and Herbert, 1990) have attempted to isolate individual and demographic factors associated with, and possibly predisposing children to, selective mutism. Of particular interest is the finding that SM children have been exposed to greater family discord and a greater number of environmental stressors than controls. Moreover, they frequently come from families with a history of some form of psychopathology (Kolvin and Fundudis, 1981).

Intervention

Treatment for SM has progressed through several identifiable phases. Early psychodynamic approaches stressed infant and childhood experiences which had interfered with the mother–child relationship, hence treatment had a relatively narrow focus and little effort was made to remove the 'symptom' of restricted speech itself.

Reed (1963) was possibly the first author to propose that SM might be a learned pattern of behaviour. Thus a child's differential pattern of communication might be subjected to a functional analysis (see Figure 3) with respect to the frequency of talking (speech) in certain situations and/or to certain individuals. Using a behavioural analysis, Cunningham *et al.* (1983) point out that in response to a child's silence, adults (teachers in particular) often tend to adopt a pattern of verbal interaction which reinforces simple, non-verbal responses, while peers, in contrast, do not speak, or simply reduce their interaction with the SM child. The effectiveness of the child's non-verbal communication is said to be a major factor contributing to the persistence of the disorder. These authors found that the most fruitful treatment strategies were 'shaping' by rewarding an approximation to the goal in situations where a minimum of speech was present, by 'situation fading' and 'individual fading'. In situation fading, the child and the person he or she is willing to talk to are moved, step by step, from one place where speech is present, to another where speech is not as yet present. In individual fading, new individuals are gradually introduced into situations familiar to the child. A combination of fading and judicious reinforcement procedures leads to the child's being able to talk to an increasing number of people in a variety of situations, treatment duration positively correlating with degree of generalization of speaking. Procedures such as 'escape avoidance' and 'response cost', both of which are mildly punitive, are counter-productive since increasing anxiety might inhibit speech.

An alternative paradigm, described by Labbe and Williamson (1984) is 'reinforcement sampling'. This technique, based on incentive motivation, enables a child to sample or play with a reinforcer that can later be earned by speaking. In one case, a pet rabbit was used for this purpose. In another case, a 7-year-old SM was permitted to use a pair of skates for a period. Possession of the skates was made contingent on speaking in class and in the clinic. This procedure was said to be successful even when response shaping had failed.

Many case studies have appeared, reporting behavioural programmes and showing that such treatments are often successful not only with regard to increasing the speech but also in improving the child's overall functioning (e.g. Sanok and Stiefel, 1979). The use of behavioural techniques does not, however, always provide a quick solution to the problem.

Outcome studies evaluating particular techniques have tended to focus on the immediate post-treatment period; medium- and long-term follow-up studies of SM patients are few by comparison with those concerned with aetiology. This paucity of follow-up data is likely to reflect difficulty in keeping track of clients over a long period, the initially low incidence of the condition, and the sporadic way in which most therapists encounter it.

In a retrospective study by Sluckin, Foreman and Herbert (1990) 25 children, who had at one time been selective mutes, were followed up by means of questionnaires administered via their schools, two to ten years after referral. Eleven had been given individual therapy programmes with a behavioural content and home and school involvement. The remainder received remedial help from special needs teachers in the school setting, with routine schools psychological service support and minimal home contact. Data were gathered on the following: number of school terms spent mute, age at referral and at follow-up, referral–follow-up interval, incidence of past and present mental illness in the family, social class, Rutter (B1) score, and whether they came from an indigenous or non-indigenous background. Stepwise multiple regression revealed the importance of a history of some form of mental illness in the family as a major determinant of non-talking at follow-up. Those children receiving individual behavioural programmes had made more durable and greater improvements than those having had non-intensive, school-based programmes.

Stuttering

This problem, an example of the first subcategory is also referred to as 'stammering' and is a disorder of speech rhythms. Kanner (1953) states that 'the flow of speech is disrupted by blocks and tensions which produce hesitations and repetitions or prolongations of sounds. The continuity of diction is broken by clonic and tonic spasms of the muscles which participate in the mechanism of speech.' Stein and Mason (1968) are critical of definitions of stammering which emphasize the lack of fluency in speech because they see stammering as a disorder of communication, not of speech. They define persistent stammering as a problem 'manifest in progressive dissolution of communication. The disorder is expressive of a disharmony in the interrelation between psychic processes and the linguistic encoding process irrespective of possible neuropathological conditions.' A majority of cases have their onset between the ages of three and five years. There are no onsets, apparently, after the age of nine. Andrews and Harris (1964) in a survey of over 1000 school children found an incidence of 3%; this figure rose to 4.5% if cases of transient stammering lasting up to six months were included.

It is well known that emotional factors can affect speech mechanisms; normal speakers occasionally stutter with strong emotion and stutterers may experience a particularly severe blockage in speech in times of distress. In fact, at the best of times, there is a considerable degree of overlap to be observed in the speech features of persons classified as stutterers and those classified as non-stutterers. Three categories of stutterer have been identified by Andrews and Harris (1964):

(1) developmental stuttering, being of early onset (2–4 years) but lasting only a few months;
(2) benign stuttering, characterized by late onset (mean age 7½ years) but tending to spontaneous remission after about two to three years;
(3) persistent stuttering, with an onset between 3½ and 8 years.

Treatment

There is a substantial literature on this topic (e.g. Di Lorenzo and Matson, 1981; Ollendick and Matson, 1983) and a multiplicity of aetiological theories and therapeutic techniques are catalogued there. Behaviour therapists view stammering as learned behaviour, and, where there is no definite physical defect, as a behaviour pattern that may be directly and successfully retained by a variety of behaviour-orientated techniques. These include aversive response-contingent procedures (Flanagan, Goldiamond and Azrin, 1958); contingency management (Burns and Brady, 1980); negative practice (Case, 1960); distraction (Cherry and Sayers, 1956); the correction of the negative habits or poorly developed speech patterns (Dalali and Sheehan, 1974) and systematic desensitization of anxiety about speaking (Boucheau and Jeffry, 1973).

PERVASIVE DEVELOPMENTAL DISORDERS

A diagnosis called 'childhood onset pervasive developmental disorder' (see Johnson & Goldman, 1993) was introduced in the USA to replace the earlier version of a category called 'childhood schizophrenia'. Before being displaced it applied to children who were thought to have a form of schizophrenia which was simply an early version of adult schizophrenia. The evidence, as it emerged over the years, did not support the view that adult and childhood schizophrenia (as was) were closely related disorders (Lockyer and Rutter, 1969).

Infantile autism, a diagnosis introduced by Kanner in 1943, and childhood onset pervasive developmental disorder are now thought to represent a single category called 'Autistic Disorder'.

Autistic Disorder (see Wing, 1971a)

Wing and Gould (1979) describe a *triad* of impairments in autism and say that all three must be evident:

(1) impairment of social relationships;
(2) impairment of social communication;
(3) impairment of imagination.

Rutter (1978) proposes the following diagnostic criteria:

(1) onset before 30 months;
(2) impairment in social development;
(3) impairments in language development;
(4) insistence on sameness.

Differential Diagnosis

Autism can be differentiated from several major categories of disability, including childhood schizophrenia, developmental aphasia, mental handicap, and environmental deprivation. Semantic–pragmatic disorder is in a more ambiguous 'territorial' position.

- *Childhood schizophrenia.* Schizophrenic and autistic children share sustained impairment in social relations, resistance to change in the environment, speech abnormalities, and inappropriate affect. Nevertheless, there are features that can be used to distinguish them, notably the age of onset of the disorder. Children develop psychoses in two waves. The first wave begins to show symptoms before the age of 3, and the second between ages 5 and 15. The children who typically show the characteristics associated with autism are members of the first wave, with onset of the disorder before the age of 30 months. Children of the second wave, those who have some period of normal development before the onset of the full syndrome between the ages of 30 months and 15 years more closely resemble schizophrenic adults in symptomatology. These children may be diagnosed as childhood schizophrenics.
- *Developmental aphasia.* In developmental aphasia children either fail to develop, or are delayed in the development of, receptive and expressive language. These children share with autistic youngsters speech patterns such as echolalia, pronoun reversal, sequencing problems, and difficulties in comprehension. However, the language deficits of autistic children are more severe and more widespread than those typically seen in aphasic children.

  Unlike autistic children aphasic children generally make eye contact, achieve meaningful communication through the use of gestures, exhibit emotional intent, and engage in imaginative play.

  Language-disordered children are more likely to be of normal intelligence than are autistic children. These children may also develop problems in social relationships; they are seen as secondary to the primary language handicap.
- *Learning disability/mental handicap.* Both autistic children and children who would receive a primary diagnosis of mental handicap share poor intellectual ability that persists through the life-span. Other similarities may include echolalic speech, self-stimulation, self-injury, and attentional deficits. What differentiates the two conditions is communication. Although the ability to communicate in mentally handicapped children may be limited, their intent and motivation are apparent. Whereas intellectually impaired children are typically characterized by slow physical development, autistic children are not.

The pattern of intellectual impairments differs. Whereas it is common for children with severe learning disability to show impairments over a wide range of functioning, autistic youngsters usually display a more variable pattern. Thus, autistic children tend to score poorly in assessments of the use of language meaning and concepts (Rutter, 1978), and to score higher on performance assessments such as visual-spatial and mechanical abilities.

Autistic children are more likely to show some isolated areas of outstanding functioning in the areas of music, mechanical ability, rote memory, and mathematics. As we have seen it is the case that the majority of autistic youngsters are also intellectually impaired. When both syndromes are present, the child typically receives both diagnoses.

- *Semantic–pragmatic disorder.* The term 'semantic–pragmatic' disorder (like the terms 'high-level language disorder' and 'conversational disability') refers primarily to children with adequate linguistic skills whose problems lie in the areas of comprehension and appropriate use of language. The main difficulties appear to be in the *use* rather than the *structure* of language. Semantic–pragmatic disorder, being manifested in inappropriate social and communicative behaviour, shares many features with autism and Asperger's syndrome.

Bishop (1989) reserves the term semantic–pragmatic disorder for children who are not autistic but who initially present with a picture of language delay and receptive language impairment and who then learn to speak clearly and in complex sentences, with semantic and pragmatic abnormalities becoming increasingly obvious as their verbal proficiency increases (p. 118).

Bishop notes that the diagnosis of autism should be based on behaviour manifested before five years of age. Semantic–pragmatic problems, by contrast, tend to be taken seriously until well after that stage. Such children might also have been diagnosed as suffering from Asperger's syndrome.

Another differential diagnostic difficulty is posed by the fact that some of the behavioural manifestations of children diagnosed as 'psychotic' are similar to those of children diagnosed as suffering from 'semantic–pragmatic disorder'.

- *Environmental deprivation.* Features of autism have been likened to the characteristics of children suffering from maternal deprivation, anaclitic depression, and hospitalism which are all characterized by developmental delays resulting from abuse, neglect, and/or institutionalization. Bettelheim (1967) and Kanner (1943) have even speculated that deprivation in the form of parental emotional abuse or neglect is a contributory causative factor in the development of autism. There is now general agreement that autism is *not* caused by neglect.

Assessment (see Caron and Rutter, 1991; Cawthorn et al., 1994)

There is an extensive history of controversy over which criteria are essential for the diagnosis of autism. Not all the children who are diagnosed as autistic show all of the supposedly 'pathognomonic' behaviours. Wing (1988) emphasises that there is no clear borderline to any of the behavioural features, and that autistic behaviours are best regarded as occupying either only some or all of the diagnostic dimensions described earlier, to a varying extent and with a varying degree of severity. Whilst a minority of children with such behaviours may be regarded as 'classically autistic' and occupy all four or five behavioural dimensions, the majority are best regarded as lying on a continuum of severity on each of the four or five dimensions. The behaviours generally tend to become less severe as the child gets older. All of this makes it hard to say which children are autistic and which children are not.

It would be easy to get bogged down in a differential diagnostic debate as to the precise meaning of autism and its boundaries relative to childhood psychosis in general or childhood schizophrenia, mental handicap and brain damage in particular. Whereas 'schizophrenia' is the name given to a group of mental illnesses which usually develop after the age of puberty, and which have a characteristic pattern of clinical symptoms, and a characteristic course and outcome, there is no justification for finding analogies between it and between autism—a condition of maldevelopment in childhood—which simply has as one of its features (like schizophrenia) social withdrawal. This characteristic is shared with many other psychotic conditions, and is thought to be secondary in childhood autism to difficulties in language and communication.

The World Health Organization's International Classification of Diseases (ICD), now in its tenth version (ICD-10, World Health Organization, 1992), and the American Psychiatric Association Diagnostic and Statistical Manual (DSM), currently in its fourth edition (DSM-IV, American Psychiatric Association, 1994)—are now widely used to classify autistic children. As a result of a large international field trial their definitions of autism have become conceptually convergent (Volkmar and Schwab-Stone, 1996).

It is interesting to examine the term 'autistic disorder' in ICD-10, which defines a number of separable categories under the general heading of pervasive developmental disorders:

- *Childhood autism* (F84.0): impaired or abnormal development must be present *before* three years of age, manifesting the *full triad* of impairments in the following areas:

  (1) reciprocal social interaction;
  (2) communication;
  (3) restricted, stereotyped, repetitive behaviour.,
- *Atypical autism* (F84.1). Onset of impaired or abnormal development is seen *after* three years of age, and is shown in *one or two* of the above triad of impairments.
- *Rett's syndrome* (F84.2). A syndrome limited to previously normal girls with decelerating head growth in infancy, early autistic behaviours, severe mental handicap, hand wringing, clapping, licking or other stereotyped hand movements. Most are nonverbal, many develop epilepsy, episodic hyperventilation, muscular hypotonia, and scoliosis. Although indefinite survival occurs, there is an excess of early deaths.
- *Other childhood disintegrative disorder* F84.3 below. Appearance of autistic behaviours following completely normal development until at least age 2 years. May be associated with loss of motor and cognitive skills and with epilepsy. Must not be attributable to a defined progressive degenerative disease of the brain.
- *Overactive disorder associated with mental retardation and stereotyped movements* (F84.4) This diagnosis is used to identify individuals who show prepubertal hyperactivity, stereotyped movements and problems with attention in association with severe mental retardation.
- *Asperger's syndrome* (F84.5). See discussion below.
- *Other pervasive developmental disorders* (F84.8)
- *Pervasive developmental disorder, unspecified* (F84.9)

The DSM-IV system of classification published by the American Psychiatric Association provides the following criteria for diagnosis of autism.

- *Onset.* Onset before 3 years of delayed or abnormal function in at least one of: social interaction, language for social communication, symbolic or imaginative play
- *Social behaviour.* Qualitative impairment in social interaction (at least two of four possible criteria)
- *Language and communication.* Qualitative impairments in communication (at least one of four possible criteria).
- *Activities and interests.* Restricted repetitive and stereotyped patterns of behaviour, interests and activities (at least one of four possible criteria).

There is another issue: the question of what assessment procedures to use in order to make a diagnosis of autism. Assessments of childhood disorders have usually included a battery of tests designed to measure the child's functioning in areas such as intellectual ability, social maturity, speech and language, physical and motor development, family interactions, parental problems and emotional development. Generally, a standard battery of tests includes IQ tests such as the Wechsler test.

However, the standard assessment battery of tests requires caution in interpretation when used for an autistic population; such tests are often inappropriate for the assessment of autism as lack of motivation, non-compliance, speech anomalies, tantrums, attentional deficits, and withdrawal from environmental stimulation, interfere with accurate test scores.

Other methods have thus been developed to assess autistic children: clinical interviews with parents and informal observations of the child, checklists and observational schemes, and behavioural assessments. Information such as the developmental history of the child, social behaviour, speech anomalies, behavioural excesses (e.g. self-stimulation, self-injurious behaviour, and behaviour problems), inappropriate emotional behaviour, insistence on sameness, and other characteristics of autistic children are obtained *in* the course of conducting clinical interviews.

A detailed assessment of the clinical characteristics of the twins from the *British twin study of autism* by Le Courteur *et al.* (1996) led to the conclusion that (1) phenotypic expression extends more broadly than autism as currently defined by either ICD-10 or DSM-IV, and (2) the wide range of clinical manifestations reflects considerable variable expression of the same genotype. This suggests that a broader range of communication and social impairment (in particular) should be included as part of the concept of autism, notably for research and intervention purposes.

Rutter states that classification should take a multiaxial approach in which the following are described on separate independent axes:

- the behavioural 'syndrome';
- the intellectual level;
- the medical conditions;
- the psychosocial situation.

A further criterion involves disturbances of response to sensory stimuli. This includes 'disturbances of motility'—a wider definition of stereotypic (beyond play) behaviour (e.g. imitation, hand clapping or oscillating, body rocking, head banging or rolling and twirling objects.

Measures

The Childhood Autism Rating Scale (CARS; Schopler, Reichler, DeVellis and Daly, 1980) has a respected role as a general aid to the diagnosis of autism. This 15-item scale was first developed in 1971 as a research tool and later revised to evaluate children for treatment and education in the TEACCH programme for autistic children in North Carolina. A score of greater than 29/60 is regarded, from validation with psychiatric diagnoses, as the diagnostic criterion for 'mild autism' (Schopler and Reichler, 1979). The criterion-related validity, from comparison of CARS scores and clinical ratings in the same diagnostic session, was 0.84. When CARS scores were compared with independent clinical assessments the correlation was 0.80.

The scale has internal consistency, coefficient alpha = 0.94. Test–retest reliability over one year was 0.88 and the diagnostic test–retest agreement was 82% (coefficient κ, correcting the diagnostic agreement figure for change agreement, was 0.81). The CARS is suitable for use by 'relatively inexperienced visiting professions' the correlation of ratings between such people and experienced professional psychiatrists or psychologists 0.73, constituting 92% agreement (coefficient κ = 0.81) for diagnostic screening. The scale is also reliable when compiled from a variety of information. For instance reliability between diagnostic testing sessions and ratings from parent interview was 0.82 (diagnostic agreement = 90%, coefficient κ = 0.75), between such sessions and ratings from classroom observations was 0.73 (86% diagnostic agreement, κ = 0.86) and between sessions and case history records was 0.82 (82% diagnostic agreement, κ = 0.63).

Observations and Interview Guides

Other aids to observation and interviews include:

- *The Psychoeducational Profile* (Schopler and Reichler, 1979) (mental ages 2–5)
- *Autism Behaviour Checklist* (Krug, Arick and Almond, 1980)
- *The Autism Diagnostic Observation Schedule* (Lord et al., 1989)

Clinical Concerns

- *Preservation of sameness.* Autistic children become very disturbed over changes in their surroundings and alterations in their routines. Temper tantrums may greet the apparently most trivial change, for example, their 'regimented' toys accidentally pushed out of place. Obsessional attributes may be even more pronounced at adolescence.
- *Extreme tendency to autistic aloneness.* From early in life the infants' preference to be alone—his or her inability to relate to persons and situations—becomes noticeable. This self-absorption, the physical repudiation (drawing away) of cuddling, the lack of concern about the comings and goings of people, the preoccupation with things, soon begin to disturb his or her caregivers. This rejection of social interaction has its corollary in a retardation of development.

- *Attachments/Social behaviour.* There is a general agreement that it is the distinctive anomalies in social development that are most specific within the triad of impairments and most handicapping across the range of children with autism. Reports of autistic children indicate differences in the sorts of attachment behaviour which are characteristic of normal children. They do respond to others' emotions and they are able to form affectionate attachments (Capps, Sigman and Mundy 1994), but they do not show an intense eagerness to share, and in play they do not pretend to act like other people, except in a ritual, echolalic manner. Autistic children (to the concern of their parents) tend not to keep close by them and may not even show any acknowledgement of their return after an absence, let alone any sign of greeting. They do not seem to use their parents for comfort, although they will enjoy a game of rough and tumble. Another characteristic of autistic children's social behaviour is their failure to seek bodily contact to gain comfort or security (see Rutter, 1983).

Wing (1971) asked a group of parents about the early behaviour of their 6–15-year-old autistic children. Of the 17 children, 14 were thought to have been handicapped from birth. According to their parents, a number of these children failed to show various social behaviours at the appropriate age, or even when they were older: 10 failed to lift their arms up when their parent came to pick them up; 7 showed very little response to their mother's voice and 11 did not draw their parent's attention to things by pointing. All of these behaviours are usually part of normal social interaction.

Autistic infants are frequently described by their mothers as being non-cuddly babies who seldom laugh and who often become stiff and rigid when they are picked up. Other mothers have described their autistic infants as exceptionally 'good' babies because they were so undemanding. This lack of social relatedness is reflected in the child's later social development. Many autistic children do not develop appropriate play skills. Most autistic children also do not form normal friendships with other children. They can truly be called social isolates.

Research into the social behaviour of autism has primarily focused on eye contact and gaze aversion, the approach and avoidance of autistic children, play skills, and social skills training. Hutt and Ounsted (1966) measured the amount of time autistic and non-autistic children spent looking at either room fixtures or faces drawn on the wall. The autistic children spent significantly more time looking at the room fixtures than at any of the drawn faces. The face most avoided by these children was a smiling human face with eyes.

Autistic children may imitate, but they do so self-centredly or like an echo, without the creativity, humour and companionship that is so charming in ordinary toddlers' play. They seem not to be aware of how one normally negotiates meanings, intentions and beliefs with language.

Rutter (1983) had this to say:

> ... we are forced to the conclusion that autistic children's social abnormalities do stem from some kind of 'cognitive' deficit if by that one means a deficit in dealing with social and emotional cues ... it appears that the stimuli that pose difficulties for autistic children are those that carry emotional or social 'meaning'.

Intelligence

The majority of autistic children are intellectually handicapped as measured by standard intelligence tests. Among autistic children tested in the preschool years, 74% had IQs below 52. When these same children were tested six years later, the majority still scored in the handicapped range. Even the majority of the children who had shown the most social improvement and who had received several years of treatment and special education scored in the handicapped range. Intelligence appears to remain stable over time, irrespective of current treatment or educational input.

The intellectual impairments appear to be independent of disturbances in social relationships and of motivational factors. Rutter (1983) presented arguments for this proposition along these lines:

- If poor intellectual performance were a secondary result of social impairments, then one would expect all autistic children to score in the mentally handicapped range on IQ tests. However, approximately 20% score within the normal range.
- If poor intellectual performance were secondary to 'autism', one could predict that an improvement in the psychiatric condition of the child (a reduction in 'autism') would be correlated with improvement in the IQ. Yet, evidence suggests that this is not the case, and that the IQ remains relatively stable despite changes in the child's condition.
- Although it might be argued that the autistic child's performance on intellectual assessments may be lowered by poor motivation or by negativism, research designed to investigate such a possibility does not support this contention.

Of autistic individuals, 10–20% have special 'splinter' skills (so-called). It is only too tempting to assume that such a child has normal intelligence: usually the opposite is true. Creak (1961, 1964) called these special abilities 'islets of ability' or 'splinter skills' because these special areas are surrounded by other areas of general intellectual handicap.

Speech and Language

A defining characteristic of autistic children is their extreme deficits in speech and language. Some 50% are non-verbal and emit only a few sounds. They may acquire some appropriate speech but this depends on receiving intensive therapy. Those children who do learn to speak, before special training, usually manifest speech that is non-communicative. Of the autistic children in one study, 65% of those who had not developed language by age 5 remained mute all of their lives.

The *deficits* of verbal autistic children are characterized by adequate phonology and syntax but deficits at the level of semantics and pragmatics. Impaired pragmatics is the most significant characteristic of autistic communication. (For a detailed discussion of clinical pragmatics see Smith and Leinonen, 1992.)

Self-injurious Behaviour

Self-injurious behaviour (SIB) is defined as behaviour in which the child inflicts physical damage on his or her own body; it includes a wide variety of actions such as hair pulling, face scratching, slapping, eye gouging, and arm and leg banging. The most common forms of SIB are head banging and self-biting, usually on the hands or wrists. The sensory feedback received from self-inflicting a wound may be reinforcing. Self-injurious behaviour is similar to self-stimulation, but much more destructive and frightening.

Self-stimulatory Behaviour

An autistic child may spend hours switching lights on and off, or gazing at them, rocking, twirling, or flapping hands. All of these activities have a social and educational cost for autistic children. The problems associated with self-stimulation and self-injury include ostracism because other people are frightened or put off by them.

Self-stimulatory activity may interfere with an autistic child's attention and learning of new tasks. It may disrupt previous learning and interfere with observational learning. It may displace socially acceptable play. Studies have shown that the kinesthetic, visual, and auditory feedback received from engaging in the self-stimulatory behaviour is reinforcing. For example, when the sound associated with spinning objects (auditory feedback) is blocked (sensory extinction), the frequency of object spinning decreases. Some studies have shown that autistic children will work at one task to earn the opportunity to self-stimulate.

Austistic children engage in more self-stimulation in an unstimulating or unfamiliar environment. When tasks are frustratingly failed, self-stimulation increases and it decreases with correct responding. These findings indicate that autistic children do use self-stimulatory activities to maintain environmental regularity, by avoiding boring or unfamiliar situations, or situations in which failure is probable.

Stimulus Overselectivity

Stimulus overselectivity is a perceptual disability in which a child responds only to part of a relevant cue, or even to a minor, often irrelevant feature of the environment. Overselectivity has been studied mostly in autistic children and has been found to occur particularly in those with lower IQs. It has been suggested that stimulus overselectivity greatly hinders autistic children in learning complex discriminations in language and social skills. It may also help explain the common need among autistic children to keep their environments the same or unchanging.

A promising approach to the treatment/management of undesirable behaviour is first performing a functional analysis of what sets the stage for, or reinforces, the behaviour, and then changing the environment in accordance with contingencies. For example, Carr and Durand (1985) performed a functional analysis of SIB that revealed that some children were using their SIB as a means of communication. The treatment consisted of teaching appropriate forms of communication, which resulted in a decrease in SIB.

Prevalence

The prevalence of the autistic syndrome varies according to how it is defined: estimates vary from 4.0 to 13.8 per 10 000 population.

In 1966–68 Lotter undertook a survey of the entire population of 8–10 year olds in Middlesex and found that:

- If Kanner's criteria were strictly applied there were 2 per 10 000 population.
- If children with several typical traits were included there were 4.5 per 10 000 population.
- If children with some but not all the features were included there were 7.8 per 10 000 population.

Social Class

There appears to be little or no effect related to class.

Sex Ratio

In the same way as the prevalence varies with the diagnostic criteria used, so does the sex ratio. It is generally quoted as 4 male: 1 female. Estimates range from 16 to 1, to 1 to 1 (for low IQs).

Causation

Biological influences. Twin studies (see Folstein and Rutter, 1977) indicate that environmental causes are unlikely to have more than a minor role in the causation of autism.

There is a growing consensus that the autistic spectrum is ultimately caused by some biological fault occurring well before birth. Autism and its variants are now recognized as but one of the developmental disorders of brain function, with a variety of different aetiologies and widely differing degrees of severity. As a developmental problem it is a consequence of interactions of biological influences, some of which stem from genetic controlling factors, others from the environment that stimulates and transforms the brain as it is developing.

Biological theories have sought causes of autism in the following areas:

- *birth trauma.* No *single* birth trauma is clearly associated with autism but there is a raised incidence of such difficulties.
- *Viral infections.* Rubella (German measles) in the mother shows a raised incidence.
- *Neurophysiology.* EEG abnormality estimates range from 10 to 83%. There is an increased incidence of epilepsy (particularly in adolescence).
- *Neuropsychology.* There is a lack of replicable neuroanatomical findings in this area of research. Neuropsychological deficits are described below.
- *Neurochemistry.* Findings here have been inconclusive.

Genetic Factors. Autism probably originates in the genes or from a pathogenic influence that affects brain organization in early embryo or foetal development before birth. Twin and family findings agree in demonstrating that genetic factors are likely to operate strongly in the majority of cases of autism (Le Courteur *et al.*, 1996; Rutter, 1983). However, the effects do not appear until the brain has attained a certain level of maturity— until certain psychological functions emerge (see Trevarthen *et al.*, 1996). Autism may be a *spectrum condition:* that is, the full expression of the autistic condition may be found in one child in a family, but the siblings may also be affected, although less severely (see August, Stewart and Holmer, 1983). There are rare cases in which families have three or more autistic children (Ritvo *et al.*, 1990).

Genetic studies suggest a polygenic recessive gene model (involving many genes from both parents) as a cause for some of the cases.

The rate of fragile X in autism is estimated at about 2.5% (Bailey *et al.*, 1993) with occasional cases being associated with other chromosomal anomalies. (Screening for these anomalies is indicated for genetic counselling.) Depending on the nature and extent of the damage, autism may occur as a very 'pure' disorder, but may also occur together with other impairments. Frith (1989) states that if different handicaps can be superimposed on autism, then the immense individual variation in children diagnosed as autistic would be less puzzling. This logic fits in well with the concept of the autistic continuum, a concept based on the empirical finding that all autistic children, including the top 25%, show all three of Wing's criteria. Other brain-damaged children, e.g. Down's syndrome cases, do not have all of them.

The characteristic constellation in Wing's triad—the core features of autism to be explained in any aetiological theory—refers (as a reminder to the reader) to three kinds of impairment:

- social incompetence;
- communicative impairment;
- imaginative impairment—no spontaneous pretend play (pretend play is believed to be linked with later ability to understand others' mental states).

These impairments give rise to different kinds of behaviour at different ages and at different levels of ability.

Neuropsychological deficits. The presence of some form of organic brain dysfunction in autistic children was first indicated because of the demonstration in follow-up studies that in about a quarter to a third of cases epileptic seizures develop during adolescence (Rutter, 1970). Subsequent epidemiological research (Deykin and MacMahon, 1979) confirmed both the increased incidence of epilepsy and the oddity that it has its onset during the teenage years. (Most mentally handicapped children with epilepsy first have seizures during early childhood.)

In a few cases, autism has been found to be associated with (and presumably due to) some medical condition giving rise to brain pathology. For example, infantile spasms and congenital rubella (see Rutter, 1983) have both been linked with autism. Of course, there are medical syndromes that are also associated with general mental handicap. But it should be noted that the medical conditions that give rise to intellectual impairment differ strikingly in their links with autism. Some, such as the two just mentioned, fairly commonly lead to autism.

Observations such as these make the theory that there is some subtle brain abnormality which can be linked to the Wing triad, but not to any other handicaps, seem plausible. Whatever the primary cause, autism cannot be regarded as a haphazard collection of symptoms. Rather it is a distinct and definable disorder, despite considerable individual variation and despite inconsistencies in diagnostic practice across different centres. From this point of view it becomes an important aim—according to Frith—to identify a single cognitive deficit. Such a deficit would eventually need to be mapped onto the brain system. Frith (1989) states that although the nature and origin of any brain abnormality is unknown, it can be assumed that it involves a 'final common pathway'. The concept of the final common pathway allows one to leave open the question of primary cause while earmarking a particular brain system that, when damaged by whatever means, will always lead to a particular disorder. If there were several independent dysfunctions, then presumably researchers would not have discovered such a strong common denominator as is implied by the triad.

Competing theories. There has been considerable debate among practitioners and theoreticians over the extent to which the primary disorder in autism is emotional, social, cognitive or 'metacognitive' (see Trevarthen *et al.*, 1996). The fact is that many aspects of the causation of autism remain a mystery, but many theorists relate much of the bizarre symptomatology to deficits and/or abnormalities of cognition (see Rutter, 1983). This applies particularly to the autistic child's problems of communication. Frith (1989) observes that from the beginning, as evident even in Kanner's (1943) and Asperger's (1944) first descriptions of autism, there was the idea that by studying their language we should come nearer to understanding autistic children. We have seen how autistic children have peculiar problems of speech and language and this has attracted the attention of linguists and psychologists alike. As a result there is now an impressive number of published investigations from which, in Frith's opinion, a surprising conclusion has emerged: that the speech and language problems that can be so freely observed in autistic children are not actually at the core of the disorder, but rather, the consequences of a broader communication failure.

Communication (see Frith, 1994). Autistic children display deficits and abnormalities in communication prior to the period when language is normally acquired. Babbling is infrequent and conveys less information than that of non-autistic infants. However, they often cry and scream to indicate need. They do not use gestures (as deaf children try to do) as a substitute for speech and it has proved difficult to train them to do so.

It is significant that the autistic child's apparent insensitivity to other person's feelings and overtures appears before the child is three years old.

The point is made that the development of the child's mind fails at the time when most children begin to be extremely sensitive to and interested in other people's ideas and actions, and when speech is beginning. Nine to twelve months is a stage in development when a baby is normally changing rapidly; it is a time of the most intense communication and sharing of different ways of doing things, when children are expected to be insatiably curious and full of imagination about meanings in their play. They want to put these ideas into language. They demonstrate increases in alertness, in intelligence and curiosity, in purposeful, constructive handling of objects, in memory, and in willingness to share experiences and actions with companions.

By way of contrast the autistic child is handicapped in communicating with others in several significant ways connected with language and information-processing.

Language. Severely delayed and often very deviant language is regularly the presenting complaint of parents of preschool children on the autistic continuum. The one exception is the subgroup of Asperger's syndrome (a topic we return to). The problems are threefold:

(1) *Non-verbal pragmatics* include the interpretation and display of facial expressions, body postures, gestures, and acoustic aspects of speech (prosody) that clarify the intent of verbal communications. Autistic children are likely not to look at the person they are speaking to, not to use gestures to supplement speech, to speak in a monotonous voice with an odd robotic rhythm or in a high-pitched singsong that may make affirmative sentences sound like questions. They tend not to notice threatening facial expressions or a raised tone of voice. A telling early sign of impaired non-verbal pragmatics is failure to look up when called by name, or to point out things they want.

(2) *Verbal pragmatics* of autistic children—for example initiating communication, staying on topic, engaging in meaningful dialogue, using language as a tool to comment or fulfil needs, providing appropriate turn-taking—are seriously impaired. (Bishop and Adams, 1990). Verbal autistic children may engage in long monologues that have no discernible communicative intent, or ignore signs of impatience from the recipient of the boring, non-stop talk.

(3) *Semantic deficits* in autism refer to aberrations in the organization of word meanings (lexicon) and the retrieval of words, spontaneous speech, the comprehension of verbal utterances and the ability to put together coherent discourse.

A useful technique in order to gauge comprehension is to ask the child open-ended questions such as why, when and how. Many autistic children who can answer concrete questions appropriately and who can be shown to know the answer to an open-ended question, may answer in a manner that is quite beside the point.

Pragmatics can be said to be at the interface of language and sociability while semantics is at the interface of language and cognition. Certainly very impaired comprehension and persistent lack of expressive language are associated with poor cognitive outcome in autism. Indeed, the ability to acquire speech appears to be a crucial prediction of later adjustment in autistic children. In a follow-up study of 80 autistic children, Eisenberg and Kanner (1956) reported that 50% of the children who were able to speak by the age of 5 were rated as demonstrating fair or good adjustment while only 3% of the non-speaking children were rated in this way. This general finding of a close relationship between the ability to speak and later adjustment has been confirmed in several studies.

Like the child with 'developmental aphasia' the autistic patient has a fundamental difficulty in the comprehension of language and in addition experiences disturbance in the organization of perception. If the mechanisms in that part of the brain responsible for processing and structuring (i.e. integrating) the visual and auditory stimuli which enter the eyes and ears of the child were faulty, it would make sense of several observations concerning the autistic child. A failure to achieve order and meaningful structure from the incoming messages the child is receiving from the environment would explain his or her withdrawal, limited span of attention, intensely violent emotional reactions to certain forms of stimulation, and obsession with sameness. Hermelin and O'Connor (1970, 1985) claimed that the autistic children's inability to encode all kinds of stimuli meaningfully underlies the apparent social impairment. They conducted a series of experiments on the hierarchical organization of sensory systems and sensory dominance in the development of autistic children.

The background to their work is explained as follows: the developing child goes through a number of sequences, in the course of which alterations in the nature of the hierarchical structure of the senses occur. Thus interoceptive and visceral sensations are dominant in the infant, and this dominance is gradually superseded first by tactile and kinaesthetic, and then by auditory and visual sensory systems. Thus, in an organism in which vision represents the predominant sense mode, the other avenues of sensory input are utilized as background information against the pre-eminent visual stimulus. Once a certain stage of development has been reached, it is the meaning rather than the modality of stimuli which determines their place in the hierarchy. As Luria (1961) has put it, the second signalling system concerned with meaning and language comes to dominate and direct the first, which is concerned with the organization of direct sensory input. The hierarchical organization of sensory systems therefore functions to a very large extent to determine which aspects of the environment constitute 'figure' and which aspects constitute 'background'. One would expect that the organization of behaviour would depend on whether and how such a hierarchical structure of sensory systems has developed. The experiments performed by Hermelin and O'Connor demonstrated that this development is relatively orderly in most nonpsychotic mentally handicapped children. At a mental age of about 4–5 years visual dominance is established in the sensory hierarchy of the first signalling system. However, this visual dominance is suppressed if it competes with meaningful verbal stimulation, which then in turn assumes dominance. Down's children remain primarily responsive to visual signals.

In autistic children, even within the first signalling system, the structural hierarchy seems to be insufficiently developed. Variables such as intensity or reinforcement schedules, rather than sensory modality, seem to determine response behaviour. Their behaviour appears more random and less predictable than subnormal controls. In short, the authors demonstrated that less intellectually impaired children respond most often to words, Down's children to light and autistic children most often to the most intense signal regardless of its modality or meaning. Hermelin proposes that failure to achieve auditory dominance may be a factor in the impaired speech of autistic children. This thirty-year-old research remains relevant today (see Hobson, 1991).

There have been many brave efforts (see Kiernan's 1983 review) to teach autistic children non-vocal means of communicating. There is some evidence that even some of the most handicapped children can learn to communicate needs using signs and symbols that may assist the development of their spoken language.

Information processing (meta-cognition). The theory that autism is basically a cognitive disorder that interferes with social functioning has been reformulated by Baron-Cohen, Leslie and Frith (1985) who describe the condition as arising from a primary disorder of 'meta-cognition' or 'interpersonal perspective taking', notably *thinking on other persons' thinking.* For a person to possess 'meta-cognition' or a 'theory of mind' he or she must (it is assumed) have a higher-order cognitive–perceptual processing system, i.e. certain crucial 'inner language' processes (Hobson, 1993a, b).

False and True Beliefs

Given that a theory of mind encompasses the understanding of one's own and other people's state of mind, including wanting, believing, pretending, we need measures of this concept. There are vignettes that attempt this. For instance: Sally has a marble. She puts it in a basket to keep and then goes away. Anne takes the marble out of the basket and puts it in a box. When Sally returns where will she look for her marble? To predict this it doesn't matter where the marble really is. It is where Sally thinks it is that is important.

A three-year-old child predicts according to where the marble really is. Most four-year olds can predict Sally's mental state. Understanding mental states begins with very young children. Two-year-olds can be engaged in pretending, e.g. pretend drinking or pouring from an empty glass. This is not like having a false belief. Two-year olds understand 'just pretending'. From about 18 months children react to imaginary situations.

Research using three groups of children:

- autistic—mean age 12 years;
- Down's syndrome—mean age 10 years;
- normals—mean age 4 years,

produced the following results for the 'Sally' problem:

- normals—over 80% correct;
- Down's—over 80% correct;
- autists — 20% correct (4/20).

The Down's children responded in line with their mental ages but the autistic children did not.

Another study acted out the 'Sally' situation using real people. Autistic children were just as unsuccessful at this. Language-impaired children with a language age of 7 had 100% passes, whereas only 25% of the autistic group passed.

Other tests are:

- *The true belief test.* This is where a person knows the truth but not the whole truth. The first adult hides a coin in a basket. The second adult goes out of the room; the first adult then hides a second coin. When the second adult returns where will she look for the coin?

  All the children know the second adult saw the first coin being hidden. 44% of the autistic children predicted where she would look correctly. These were then questioned as to whether the adult knew about the other coin. Half of them failed, i.e. they did not understand 'knowing' and 'not knowing'.
- *A double false belief test.* Mary and John are at the ice cream van. They have no money and say they will go home and get some. The ice cream man says he will wait outside the school, but he then tells Mary to be

outside the park. He then meets John and tells him to be outside the park also. John wants to meet Mary. Where will he go to meet her?

Six out of ten Down's children with a mental age of 7 passed this test. None of the autistic 15-year olds passed it.

Cognitive Deficit Theory

Wing's triad has been explained in terms of a single cognitive deficit (Baron-Cohen, Leslie and Frith, 1985; Leslie, 1987). This deficit has important consequences for language and communication development. The infant comes into the world with cognitive abilities which have as their aim the representation of analysing automatically what things and people are like—building up considerable knowledge about his/her relationships to the outside world. The child forms representations of their physical appearance, properties and function with impaired efficiency. Intellectual impairment in such first-order representations in children caused by pervasive brain damage does not provide an explanation for Wing's triad of impairments; rather it is due to a fault in second-order representations. Leslie (1987) proposed that it is only from the second year of life that the normal child unequivocally displays the ability to form second-order representations. The first clear manifestation is the emergence of pretence.

More sophisticated developments take place as available knowledge extends beyond knowledge of the state of the world gained through perceptual experience: knowing that such knowledge exists. This is what is meant by 'second-order' representations; they are the critical ingredient in the ability to pretend. They are also involved in many other accomplishments such as 'mentalizing' (thinking and reasoning about the content of our own and of other people's minds). The systematic application of mentalizing arises from the individual's 'theory of mind'.

Every normal child develops such a 'theory' with profound effects on social life and on communication in general. A theory of mind allows the child to interpret overt behaviour by reference to invisible mental states. In this way he or she can distinguish 'really meaning it' from 'just pretending'. If there should be a fault in metarepresentational ability (the ability to form second-order representations), then this would be devastating for the development of a theory of mind. Without a theory of mind such everyday social nuances as pretend, deception and bluff would be incomprehensible. The idea that there is a way of knowing what 'makes people tick' would be totally alien.

Trevarthen *et al.* (1996) makes the point that the theory of metacognition is manifestly a rational one that separates the mind from the body. It does not seek evidence on bodily expressions of emotion, vocalizations, facial expressions, gestures and body movements. Such movements contain information about self–other awareness. This is the principal point of criticism of Hobson (1990a–c, 1991) who has a psychoanalytic interest in the emotional dynamics and self-regulation of infants and young children. He is of the opinion that '. . . children do not develop, nor do they need, a "theory" about the mental life of others. What children acquire is knowledge that other people have minds' (Hobson 1990b, p. 199). In his opinion a journey of three stages must be followed. First, a child acquires a concept of self; second, the individual establishes relatedness between himself and the others by means of observing others' bodily expressions; and third, develops a relationship based on analogy between his subjective experiences and the others' bodily appearances. Hobson does not agree that autistic children are able to form first-order representations for the perception and expression of emotions, and for normal social–affective responsiveness. Emotional responses may not be normal from the start of life. Autistic individuals continue to have difficulty recognising emotional states in adult life (Harris, 1989).

Trevarthen and his colleagues (1996) write that contemporary research has been looking under one particular lamp post because the light there is bright. Interest in language and thinking in autism may have missed evidence that these aspects, which can be measured only in individuals whose mental abilities are functioning at a relatively high level, are aspects of a condition which begins to affect mental functions at a more fundamental level (as suggested above). There are motives and emotions underlying words and reasons that make it possible for human beings to be conscious of, and to communicate with, one another. The language, and the processes of thought based on language (postulate these authors) are affected in autistic individuals because deeper and earlier developing functions are disturbed. The evidence comes from observations on how infants communicate before they understand language, and on the expressions of feeling and interest by which all persons make sympathetic contact.

Psychological Influences

The earliest literature on the psychological causes of autism was mainly psychoanalytic in orientation. The best-known exponent was Bruno Bettelheim who directed the Orthogenic School at the University of Chicago. Bettelheim (1967) believed that there were three basic types of autistic children, differing in the degree of withdrawal brought about by the severity of early neglect by their parents, notably their mothers:

- The mute children who have totally severed communication and contact with the real world. They treat other humans as objects and constitute the most disturbed type.

- The children who have some language and display occasional anger outbursts. They have some contact with reality, but still do not act independently.
- The children commonly labelled as schizophrenic. They have fairly good language skills and form limited social relationships; however, they have rich fantasy lives that interfere with normal functioning.

Autism, in his view, represents a fixation at the first stage of 'primary narcissism', a failure to shift to object relations (physical and social). The autistic child tries to blot out stimuli in order to avoid psychological pain. The source of this pain, he suggests, is the mother who fails to nurture the child *emotionally* although her care at the physical level is adequate.

These mothers of autistic or schizophrenic children were harshly labelled 'refrigerated' or 'schizophrenogenic' and depicted as cold, detached and rejecting with little interest in people and little human warmth. They were also described as highly intellectual (Bettelheim, 1967; Eisenberg and Kanner, 1956). It has also been suggested that autism is caused by a 'double bind' attitude of mothers who superficially give the appearance of being warm but are in reality cold and indifferent to their children.

This kind of speculation has been conclusively refuted by painstaking research (see Gelfand, *et al.*, 1985). For example, when parents of autistic children are compared to parents of children with other forms of handicap, no differences have been found on personality or interaction measures. Gelfand *et al.* (1985) make the point that psychoanalysts were never able to answer satisfactorily the question why a child would regress or become fixated in social development to such a cataclysmic degree. It is not difficult to imagine the demoralization of families and the damage to mothers' reputations and self-esteem that resulted from this stigmatizing theory of psychogenic autism.

The therapeutic methods that flowed from this psychoanalytic theory involved reducing, indeed minimizing all parental contact, while the autistic child was at the Orthogenic School. Children were regressed to relive earlier experiences in an ethos of total acceptance; treatment could last several years. There is no objective evidence that the method produced real and positive changes in the autistic problems of the children exposed to this regime.

Interestingly, it was not only the psychoanalysts who proposed a retreat by the autistic child in early development brought about by failures of parenting. The behaviourist theory of Charles Ferster (1961) postulated a kind of retreat into a self-stimulatory world because the parents do not provide enough consistent reinforcement. The severe behavioural deficits of autism are attributed to a faulty conditioning history. This theory has not been confirmed; the behaviour patterns described by Ferster have never been objectively observed in the parents of autistic children. It does not explain other symptoms of autism such as the profound cognitive deficits.

Any idea that autistic children might come from dysfunctional families has to deal with the finding that the marital stability in the families of autistic children has been found to be greater than for other disturbed children. It has been reported that 11 per cent come from broken homes as compared with 50 per cent for other types of emotionally disturbed children.

Treatment

The overall treatment of autistic children is a good example of the need for a multidisciplinary service. The following treatment goals have been suggested:

- fostering social and communicative development;
- enhancing learning and problem-solving;
- decreasing behaviours that interfere with learning and access to opportunities for normal experience;
- helping families cope with autism.

The overall treatment programme would require:

- appropriate medical care;
- special educational provision;
- family support (e.g. use of behavioural methods, counselling, respite, books);
- direct treatment (e.g. speech and language therapy, medication).

Medical care. This refers to discussions with parents about issues such as diagnosis, treatment and prognosis; genetic counselling, and the treatment of medical conditions when present.

The history of medical interventions with autistic (and schizophrenic) children is littered with ineffectual, experimental and possibly countertherapeutic methods such as psychosurgery, ECT and drug therapies using D-lysergic acid (LSD-25) (see Gelfand *et al.*, 1985). Pharmacological treatment has included the use of vitamins, antipsychotic drugs (e.g. Thorazine, Stelazine and Melaril) and stimulants (Fenfluramine), tricyclic antidepressants and Beta-blockers (to mention a few). There are risks of serious side-effects with many of these drugs. An example of this is the use of neuroleptic Haloperidol to reduce aggression and stereotypic behaviour. Even with a conservative dose about 1 in 4 cases are at risk of dyskinesia and dystonias. There is, to date, no evidence that any drug produces major improvements or affects the fundamental deficits of autism (see Campbell *et al.*, 1989; Sloman, 1991). Lord and Rutter (1994) state that 'there is no indication for their routine use' (p. 586).

Educational provision. The Warnock Report (1978), in the UK, made several recommendations for meeting children's special educational needs in both ordinary and special schools. The choice will be between a main-stream school, a special school catering for a range of handicaps and a specialist school for autistic children.

Lord and Rutter (1994) say that education has been by far the most powerful source of improvement for autistic children and adolescents in the last 50 years. With access to appropriate educational services, far fewer children are placed in long-stay institutions.

With appropriate education, more autistic children are using the intellectual skills they possess to acquire functional academic skills (see Venter *et al.*, 1992). Few, however, even among the higher-functioning autistic children, attain academic skills at their mental-age level.

Special schools. The main advantage of special schools catering solely for autistic children is that the teachers are aware of their characteristics and needs. However, because of the relatively low incidence of autism, many of these schools are residential, ranging from full-time residential to weekly boarding. Residential schools provided needed relief for families who cannot cope with the child at home. They will help accustom those autistic young people, particularly in adolescence, who will be unable to live in the community, to living away from home. However, the transition between home and school is likely to be difficult and far more disruptive when the child is residential than when the child attends school on a daily basis and lives at home.

The school environment. Wendy Brown, former Principal of the Helen Allison School for autistic children, writing in 1979 about school environment and organizations, says that schools for autistic children are for those who cannot benefit from anything less specialized. The label 'autistic' is not in itself enough when it comes to school placement. As she puts it:

> The degree of handicap in autism and the measurable IQ varies very greatly indeed. Some autistic children are SSN and have severe behaviour problems. Some autistic children are SSN and charmingly easy to have around. Some are within the normal range of intelligence and wickedly difficult. Some have the IQ comparable with ESN(M) but have no language and severe behaviour problems . . . The normally intelligent autistic child with minimal behaviour problems might rightly be placed within a normal school. At the other end of the scale is the SSN autistic child with severe behaviour problems . . . [who] may be happier in the less pressurised environment offered in the schools for ESN(S). (The Ingo Wakehurst Memorial Trust Fund Study Weekend (Autistic Children, October 1979).)

There are three crucial requirements in a school for autistic children: high staff ratio, understanding of language handicap and a positive policy of intervention. They need at least one skilled adult to lead them, to support them and to demand kindly but firmly from them—in other words continuously to intervene. Very few of them will be able to dispense with this support and stimulation. The school environment needs to be to an autistic child what the wheelchair is to a seriously physically handicapped child.

The reason, among others, is the need to supply positive motivation from the outside. Most autistic children lack motivation and a competitive drive—a lack of interest and personal satisfaction derived from a well performed task.

Family support. There are many ways in which the families of autistic children can receive their much needed support:

- local and/or national societies (e.g. the National Autistic Society);
- counselling and advice for parents (e.g. child management, genetic counselling);
- respite and other practical help;
- self-help support groups;
- specialized centres providing programme 'packages'.

Among the centres providing services to autistic children and their parents are:

- *Treatment and Education of Autistic and Related Communication — Handicapped Children (TEACCH)* is a well-validated programme based for over 30 years on the University of North Carolina. The focus is on the development of communication skills and personal autonomy. A wide variety of empirically tested methods are tailored to the individual and to improving his or her quality of life (see Schopler, Reichler and Lansing, 1980). Workshops on TEACCH principles often take place in the UK.

  A dramatic demonstration of the effectiveness of parental involvement in the TEACCH programme is reported by Schopler, Reichler and Lansing, 1980. The reported rate of institutionalization of autistic individuals range from 40–90% of the American population, depending on the study. The institutionalization rate of autistic individuals who participated in the TEACCH programme over a 10-year period was only 8%.

- *The Home-Base Teaching Project* is based in the Department of Child Psychiatry at the Maudsley Hospital, London (see Howlin and Rutter, 1987) and is an outreach programme for the families of young autistic children. The programmes are individually designed to foster language development, facilitate social development and treat behavioural problems (e.g. obsessional and ritualistic behaviours) that undermine learning and development. Parent–child interactions are seen to be of particular importance in producing results.

- *The Groden Institute* provides a full service based on behavioural lines for autistic children and their families (Groden and Baron, 1988).

Parent Training

Parent training, as we saw earlier, is essential for early intervention programmes with mentally/developmentally handicapped children. Home-based assistance is available through the Portage project in which a trained person visits the family at frequent intervals and works with the parents and child. During these visits, the parents and the Portage visitor agree on what skills the child needs to acquire next and how the parents can achieve this by working with the child each day (e.g. Daly *et al.*, 1985); these methods have proved to be extremely valuable (Revill and Blunden, 1979), as have those of the Education of the Developmentally Young (EDY) project started by the Hester Adrian Research Centre at Manchester University. This was designed to teach those working with young handicapped children the skills for modifying the behaviours of these children.

Direct treatment. Sadly, there are no treatments which produce 'cures' for autism. In the 50 years since Leo Kanner published his paper on 'early infantile autism' there have been many approaches to intervention, some emphasizing a treatment philosophy (e.g. psychodynamic therapy and medication), others a training approach (e.g. behaviour modification).

The early (post-Kanner) inculpation of intrusive, cold, so-called 'refrigerator' mothers, as causes of their children's autism, sometimes led to policies of separating children from their parents. Psychodynamic therapy was directed at the child's damaged emotions and self-image. In time, this notion of a schizophrenogenic mother was discredited, and the psychodynamic approach with autistic children found to be ineffectual at best, and at worst (scapegoated as parents must have felt) counter-therapeutic.

There was a paradigm shift such that the fault was re-located from aberrant motherhood to faulty functioning in the autistic child. Various defects were identified, notably problems in communicating. Behaviour modifications techniques were used to tackle a wide variety of behavioural and cognitive problems.

(1) *Communication training.* Howlin and Rutter (1987) have reviewed the results of language and communication training with autistic chil-

dren. Given that the language deficits characteristic of autism affect so many aspects of the child's social and personal functioning, great hopes (and numerous studies) have been invested in this area.

These studies of language training with autistic children first appeared in the USA in the mid-1960s. The main emphasis of training was on the application of operant methods to teach imitative responses or to extinguish inappropriate utterances; later on the focus was on the establishment of rule-governed speech.

Sadly, the results have not always been encouraging. However, growing sophistication and experience in this area (see Howlin and Rutter, 1987; Jordan, 1993) has led to significant successes. There remains, however, a problem with generalization of skills-teaching to other behaviours.

(2) *Behavioural management.* Behavioural methods have proved to be effective in the management of specific behaviour problems, especially, it is argued, intensive programmes begun at a very young age (see McEachin, Smith and Lovaas, 1993). Problems addressed include the following:

(a) *Social interactions.* Under some circumstances (with skilled encouragement) autistic children will interact with other people. Clark and Rutter (1981) found that, as the demands for a social response from autistic children are increased, the children are more likely to produce a social response. This kind of observation has encouraged psychologists and teachers to use behavioural methods to shape up social behaviour, skills and speech. There have been attempts to teach autistic children to verbalize affection to their parents (Charlop and Walsh, 1986); also endeavours to get normal and mildly handicapped peers to facilitate their social interactions. In one investigation, the baseline spontaneous social interactions between autistic children and non-handicapped peers at lunchtime, playtime and recess constituted 3% of all interactions. After the non-handicapped peers were prompted to act as behavioural tutors in the classroom for autistic children, the spontaneous interactions increased to over 90% in the unstructured settings.

(b) *Self-stimulation.* Self-stimulation contributes to the bizarre appearance of autistic children. It appears to be a highly preferred activity for, if allowed, they may spend most of their day engaging in self-stimulation and prefer this social interaction to playing with toys. They resist attempts to discourage their behaviour and may forgo favourite snacks for self-stimulation. When engaged in self-stimulation, the child tends to be unresponsive and is sometimes oblivious of his or her surroundings. It has been demonstrated to interfere with the acquisition of new behaviours (e.g. Koegel and Covert, 1972). Although self-stimulation remains a target of suppression, there is some indication that some children can learn even when self-stimulation is not suppressed. Also, as self-stimulation appears to be autistic children's most preferred activity, there is some evidence that it can be used as a reinforcer to motivate autistic children to learn; while not necessarily increasing its overall occurrence.

(c) *Aggression.* Behavioural techniques—notably reinforcement principles—have been used successfully to reduce aggressive behaviour.

(d) *Obsessional/ritualistic behaviour.* It may not be possible to eliminate these time-consuming, disruptive preoccupations from a child's repertoire, but they may—using behavioural methods—be shaped and transformed into more adaptive rituals or habits.

(e) *Self-injurious behaviour.* Concern over the adverse effects of self-injurious behaviour such as scratching, biting, head-banging and face-slapping, which can lead to disfigurement and blindness, has led to the application of behavioural methods (e.g. time-out, overcorrection and DRO—differential reinforcement of other/zero rate behaviour). They have been effective in reducing self-injury. Therapists have demonstrated the elimination or marked reduction of self-injury in 94% of the cases dealt with. Parents consider behavioural methods acceptable and effective for these purposes.

It hardly needs saying that behavioural techniques, although useful, are not curative. It is vital to involve parents in any interventions.

(3) *Antecedent control.* More attention is paid these days to ways of organizing and structuring the autistic child's environment so as to pre-empt maladaptive behaviours, e.g. working out simple strategies such as picture schedules in order to provide a clear warning that the context of (say) the classroom activity or home routines are about to change.

(4) *Metacognitive ('theory of mind') training.* There is, as yet, no clear-cut evidence for the efficacy of interventions rooted in the metacognitive model of autism. Baron-Cohen and Howlin (1993) refer to unpublished studies which suggest that it is possible to train verbal autistic children to pass the 'first-order' model of mind tasks (e.g. 'Sally Anne' test). There is, apparently, only limited generalization of these accomplishments and their influence on everyday functioning appears to be marginal.

(5) *Fashion and fads*. There have been many fashions and fads, some ephemeral, others long-lasting because they offered real help in the remediation of particular difficulties associated with autism. Among them are:

- music therapy (Jacqueline Robarts in Trevarthen *et al.*, 1996);
- psychoanalysis (Maratos, 1996);
- family and peer network co-training (behavioural methods) (Charlop and Walsh, 1986);
- Berard Auditory Therapy (Goldfarb, 1961);
- facilitated communication (Prior and Cummins, 1992);
- holding therapy (Welch, 1983);
- intensive movement therapy; basic communication therapy (Hogg, 1991);
- video home training (Berger, 1978);
- medical treatments (e.g. Sloman, 1991).

Prognosis and Outcome

Autism, as we have seen, is most clearly recognizable in the later pre-school years, in other words: 4 to 6 years of age. Among the crucial out-come influences for these children are knowledgeable (i.e. trained) parents and a comprehensive nationwide system of services. A compara-tive study by Lovaas (1973) of children who received treatment and were then released either to parents or institutions demonstrated that the for-mer either maintained their therapeutic gains or improved further, while the latter lost their improvements and reverted to earlier, abnormal pat-terns of behaviour.

Autistic children do not improve *markedly* as they grow older, although many show encouraging improvements in social behaviour and commu-nication at a simple level as they enter school (Harris *et al.*, 1990).

Adolescence can be very trying because of increased irritability and aggression, which generally tend to subside gradually.

Adult status. A review of 21 outcome studies suggests that only 5–17% of autistic children had good outcomes (i.e. near normal social and inde-pendent lives) (Lotter, 1978). Rutter's (1977) review indicated that 16% ultimately make a good adjustment (ability to lead an independent life), 25% an intermediate adjustment (a semi-independent life) while 60% remain severely handicapped.

The great majority of children with a performance IQ below 50 or 60 will remain severely handicapped and dependent on others for meeting their daily needs, for the remainder of their lives. For the child with a performance IQ in the normal range and useful communicative language at 5 years of age (also no more than mild receptive language impairment) there is a 50/50 chance of a good level of social adjustment in adulthood and considerable (but not complete) ability for autonomous living. Autistic adults frequently change jobs or need sheltered employment. Their inflexibility, poor work skills and obsessive rituals make for difficulties at work!

Asperger Syndrome

Hans Asperger published a paper (Asperger, 1944), which was translated and annotated by Ulta Frith in Frith (1994), describing what he called 'a particularly interesting and highly recognisable type of child'. The type had in common what he called 'a fundamental disturbance which manifests itself in their physical appearance, expressive functions and, indeed, their whole behaviour'.

After a period of neglect, his identification of a syndrome closely related to autism has become a matter of theoretical and practical clinical concern and debate. Whether or not autism and Asperger syndrome should be considered as distinct and mutually exclusive diagnostic categories, or the latter as a subcategory of the former, cannot yet be given a definitive scientific answer.

Features of Asperger Syndrome

Children with Asperger syndrome suffer, in Frith's view, from a particular form of autism; they belong to the autistic spectrum (some theorists prefer the term 'high functioning' or 'mild' autism).

- A notable feature of the syndrome is their ability to speak fluently by the age of five; the language development may be slow to begin with and also very odd in the way it is used for communication.
- They often become quite interested in other people as they grow older.
- However, they are socially inept and inappropriate.
- They show abnormalities of social imagination.
- They tend to be extremely egocentric.
- The knowledge they accumulate is fragmented, lacking in 'common sense'; they fail to learn from their experience in a manner that provides social meaning and useful guidelines for living.
- They develop obsessive interests.
- They manifest abnormal sensory responses.

CROSS-GENDER BEHAVIOUR

This can be a matter of concern for parents. Cross-gender behaviour in young children (DSM-III-R code 302.60) refers to the fact that there are youngsters whose actions, preferences, likes and dislikes do not fit neatly into society's expectations of what is an appropriate sexual identity for the sexes. There is persistent and intense distress about being a girl (or boy), and a desire to be mistaken for the opposite sex. It is not merely a matter of voicing the advantages of girlhood or boyhood. They are seen as very 'feminine' boys or extremely 'masculine' girls. This area of clinical concern is fraught with value judgements, stereotyping and confusion of terminology.

Training of sexual impulses and the nuances of 'correct' gender behaviour appear to be among the life-tasks that are universal in child-rearing. The vital process by which children learn the behaviour and attitudes culturally appropriate to their sex is called 'sex-typing'. Children learn certain sex-role standards, those psychological characteristics which are considered appropriate to one sex in contrast to the other. Physical gender is decided at conception. But the evidence suggests that, from a psychological point of view, the newborn human is not, in any essential sense, sexually differentiated. Gender identity and sexual role standards are acquired during childhood; in fact, by the age of 6 children are committed to shaping their behaviour to the cultural mould of what is 'appropriate' to their biological sex. They manifest anxiety, and even anger when accused of acting in ways regarded as characteristic of the opposite sex.

As early as the second year of life, children begin to distinguish between what is 'masculine' and 'feminine'. Preference for one sex role or the other also begins to emerge early, probably the third year. By school-going age, they have thoroughly learned the concepts 'male' and 'female'; they divide the world into male and female people and are preoccupied with boy–girl distinctions (Kagan, 1958b). Studies (Hampson and Hampson, 1961; Money, 1965) have shown that it is difficult to bring about a major realignment of sex role and gender identity after three years of age. Once the standards of sex-role behaviour are learned, they are not easily altered. The die is cast, pretty well, by the age of 6, if not earlier.

Biological Influences

Studies of abnormalities of physiology and anatomy suggest that prenatal (or postnatal) genetic or hormonal influences play only a secondary part in the process; upbringing and indoctrination into a sex role have the overriding influence (Hampson and Hampson, 1961). Girls whose mothers took synthetic progestins during pregnancy to prevent uterine bleeding were reported as being 'tomboyish' during their preschool years (Ehrhardt and Money, 1967). They had genitalia with male characteristics. Young boys whose mothers ingested female hormones when they were pregnant were reported as being less athletic as young children and less interested in rough-and-tumble play than their peers (Yalom, Green and Fisk, 1973). They were not necessarily abnormal in their gender identity but there was an associated higher than usual level of cross-gender behaviours and interests.

Psychosocial Influences

There is evidence to support the claim that upbringing and societal indoctrination play the major part in shaping gender identities (Hampson and Hampson, 1961). Theories designed to account for the way in which the child acquires sex-typed patterns of behaviour have emphasized the role of identification, referring to the processes whereby one person models himself or herself upon another. It differs from the concept of imitation in certain ways. It suggests a relatively long-lasting relationship between subject and model, and focuses attention on the fact that some models exert more influence over the subject than others—although the reasons why they do so are not adequately explained in the literature.

A subject is said to be identified with a model if he or she is more likely to match that model's behaviour than other models' behaviour. Also, the matching behaviour is more extensive than that implied in the notion of imitation. The subject behaves as if he or she were the model in situations other than those in which he or she has seen the model, and in a relatively comprehensive manner. That is to say, he or she adopts the model's values, beliefs, attitudes and style of life, as well as matching particular forms of behaviour. According to the anaclitic theory of identification, the child imitates and identifies with the behaviour of the parent who is warm and nurturant.

The view of many social learning theorists (e.g. Bandura, 1969; Kagan, 1958a; Mischel, 1970) is that children's experience with parents (particularly same-sex parents) critically determines the nature of their subsequent learning of social roles. The empirical results of the many studies which have been carried out present a somewhat confusing picture, and there is not space to review the theoretical debates in detail here.

The question of a boy's or girl's gender-identity is sometimes of concern to men who rear girls, or women who bring up boys, in the absence of a partner. What they are worried about is the possibility of an inappropriate identification. They may also worry about their child being homosexual. It is here that confusion arises because the issues of gender-identity problems and homosexuality are often mistakenly thought of as one and the same thing.

Homosexuality, transvestism and sexual inversion are independent (although sometimes overlapping) phenomena, and the failure to draw this distinction causes much misunderstanding. For example, only a small percentage of adult transvestites are homosexual (Randall, 1970), and only a minority of homosexuals are transsexuals. The direction of the individual's sexual interest—the choice of a sexual partner—is very rarely explained by chromosomal or hormonal anomalies. Early life experiences seem to play a part in many cases of homosexual inclination; poor relationships with parents, particularly the parent of the same sex, are thought to be a contributory factor (Bancroft, 1970). When one considers how many strongly heterosexual individuals have had poor relationships of this kind, such a theory is robbed of most of its explanatory value. Nevertheless, there remains strong evidence that early family relationships are, in some way, involved in homosexuality, but the precise 'hows' and 'whys' remain a mystery.

The theory most favoured by active homosexuals is a biological one: their sexual orientation has been set since birth as a result of genetic determination or prenatal development (e.g. accidental exposure to excess levels of hormones while the individual was developing in the womb), rather than deliberately chosen. Some theorists suggest that homosexuality is learned by pleasurable (early) homosexual experiences or by frightening heterosexual encounters. Again, none of these theories is supported by systematic analyses of homosexual/lesbian individuals' early (?sensitive period) experience.

Homosexuality is not considered in this book to be a clinical disorder. This is not to say that it is not a source of worry for older children and young adults (not to mention their parents) if they suspect they may be 'gay'. It is not unusual for young persons to 'get it wrong' because they have misinterpreted the significance of a homosexual attraction ('crush'), a homosexual encounter, or opposite gender (e.g. tomboyish) interests.

It is estimated that somewhere between 4% and 14% of people are attracted to others of the same sex. Precise statistics are difficult to obtain because of the continuing social stigma and reluctance 'to come out'. Then again, many individuals change their sexual expression over their lifetime; and many enjoy (bisexually) heterosexual and homosexual attachments.

Transsexualism refers to the persistent discomfort and sense of inappropriateness about one's assigned sex. There is a preoccupation with getting rid of primary and secondary sexual characteristics, while acquiring those of the opposite sex.

Chapter 9

INTELLECTUAL IMPAIRMENT

Fryers (1984) observes that there are many confusing terms in use, serving different traditions or different purposes. Currently, 'mental handicap' appears to be most favoured internationally by parents, and 'mental retardation' or 'severe learning difficulties' by service professionals. But handicap and mental retardation are not medical diagnoses, although doctors frequently refer to them in this manner. They are administrative categories from educational traditions.

Knowledge of child behaviour and development enables a clinical psychologist to be sensitive to the timetable of 'achievements' (walking, talking, etc.) about which parents become so proud or worried. Where an infant is mentally handicapped, a dawning awareness that something is 'not right' may be so gradual that parents cannot say when they began to worry. It would not be surprising if at some time during a pregnancy parents asked themselves: 'Will the baby be all right?' For most parents these anxieties are somewhat submerged in the activity of the last few months of the pregnancy. They become apparent again at the birth, but despite such apprehensions parents are never really prepared for the birth of a handicapped child.

Adjustment to the fact of handicap—if the baby is impaired physically and/or intellectually—may continue over many years, depending (to some extent) on whether the handicap was apparent at birth, or only became clear later, and whether the parents were told clearly and several times about the probable extent and nature of the child's handicap. Parent's reactions to their handicapped child are frequently formulated in the literature, in terms of a series of stages: shock or denial, guilt, despair, depression, disappointment and eventual acceptance or adjustment. However, Blacher (1984) and Allen and Affleck (1985) argue on the basis of their findings that by no means all parents experience emotional reactions to the birth of a handicapped child in such an ordered sequence; nor are they necessarily affected adversely over the longer term.

ASSESSMENT

The functional impairment has been operationalized by using measures of IQ—that most contentious quotient. The IQ has been the foundation of most classifications of intellectual impairment, and in spite of doubts about comparability, has generally been the basis of much research and many policy decisions. An IQ under 70 has usually been accepted for 'mild' impairment, in conjunction with 'social criteria'. An IQ of 55 divides 'mild' from 'severe'. An IQ of 55 is, in fact, 3 standard deviations below the mean. In practice, however, IQ 50 has proved more useful and is the most widely used convention in the epidemiological literature. Severe learning disability (IQ below 50) appears at a rate of about three children per 1000 (Fryers, 1984). The 'profound' category has achieved poorer agreement, coming into play for IQs of under 25 or 20. Fryers (1984) makes the following wise observation:

> It is obvious that no set of categories and no single system of classification is satisfactory, nor can it ever be however defined, since the group of people with whom we are concerned suffer from a ragbag of disorders, difficulties, and needs, and a varying ragbag at that, and who have been brought together almost by historical accident of educational development. They do not, and cannot, constitute an entity except we make it so. Research workers in this field must be exceptionally wary and clearheaded; more epidemiological awareness would benefit much of the literature. Service planners should try to understand the conceptual problems before applying simple criteria. To study and to plan clearly defined standard categories is essential, but whatever system of classification is satisfying to the epidemiologist or convenient to the planner or administrator should not be allowed to determine the life-style and lifetime services for any individual. Taxonomies are for groups, categories serve the needs of professionals; individual clients require thorough, multidisciplinary assessment of their individual situation, constantly updated, and a service delivery system which can respond to their changing needs and those of the family.

A multiplicity of causes—hereditary and environmental—contribute significantly to severe intellectual impairment and its sequelae, disability and handicap. To take one example, the Lesch-Nyhan syndrome which occurs in about 1 in 50 000 babies is produced by a deficiency of an enzyme essential for purine metabolism. From about 3 years of age the child's behaviour (e.g. self-mutilation, biting, head-banging) becomes more bizarre and extreme. Prevention (detection before birth) is possible, but tragically there is no known cure for the undetected disorder.

There are many other rare conditions involving metabolic defects; over 50 have been described and they continue to be discovered. Phenylketonuria (PKU), Tay Sachs disease, Neiman–Pick disease, and Hurler's disease (Gargoylism) are among the better known (see Table 12). In the overall

Table 12 Mental handicap and its ramifications (adapted from Fryers, 1984)

Handicapping disorder	Nature of disorder	Features	Detection/prevention	Intellectual implications
1. Down's syndrome.	chromosome aberrations, present at conception: (i) trisomy 21 (94% of cases); (ii) trisomy mosaics (3% of cases); (iii) translocation (3% of cases).	Highest prevalence at birth/1000 in mothers of 45–49 (56.52). Primary disorder.	Amniocentesis can indicate affected foetus.	All likely to be intellectually impaired, a majority severely so (however, much variability in trisomy mosaics).
2. Patau's syndrome (Tri. 13).	Autosomal anomalies present at conception.	Prevalence at birth: Collectively 2/1000.	Nil.	Occasionally severe, or mild intellectual impairment.
3. Edward's syndrome (Tri. 17 or 18).	Autosomal anomalies present at conception.	Primary disorder.	Nil.	Occasionally severe, or mild intellectual impairment.
4. *Cri du chat syndrome* (anom. 5).	Autosomal anomalies present at conception.		Nil.	Occasionally severe, or mild intellectual impairment.
5. Klinefelter's syndrome.	Sex chromosome disorder.	Prevalence at birth 3/1000.	Nil.	Occasionally severe, or mild intellectual impairment.
6. Phenylketonuria (PKU).	Defect of protein metabolism.	Prevalence at birth 0.05–0.2/1000.	Screening programme after birth; special dietary regime prescribed.	Extreme impairment if not treated.
7. Galactosaemia.	Defect of carbohydrate metabolism.	Prevalence at birth 0.02/1000.	Screening programme after birth; special dietary regime prescribed.	Extreme impairment if not treated.
8. Tay Sach's disease.	Defect of lipid metabolism.	Prevalence 0.04/1000, death in early childhood.	No treatment available. Genetic counselling.	Extreme impairment.
9. Epiloia (tuberous sclerosis).	Causal mechanisms are not clear.	0.01/1000.	No treatment available.	Many severely impaired.

scheme of things these conditions are so rare that they contribute minimally to the overall incidence of mental handicap.

Children may be born with abnormalities of the chromosomes. A single chromosome or part of a chromosome may be absent or duplicated, or may have moved out of place. Obviously a large number of genes can be affected, a fact often incompatible with the continuing viability of the foetus. However, some do survive to birth. One of the most common examples of a chromosome abnormality and a relatively easily recognized condition—the largest single contributor to severe intellectual impairment—is Down's syndrome. It is the result of a genetic anomaly that occurs because one pair of the mother's chromosomes fails to separate during meiosis, giving her offspring 47 rather than 46 chromosomes, the extra one at position 21.

Other, rarer, conditions, such as Klinefelter's syndrome, Turner's syndrome, and the Fragile X syndrome, occur because of an abnormality of the sex chromosomes. Phenylketonuria (PKU) provides us with an example of how an environmental intervention (dietary control) can mitigate an inherited defect. In PKU—a form of mental handicap—an enzyme necessary for normal development is not produced, owing to the abnormality of a crucial gene. (One gene is responsible for the synthesis of one enzyme.) In this case the absence of an enzyme required to convert phenylalanine into tyrosine means that phenylalanine accumulates in body tissue. This results in the interference with cerebral functioning and development. Fortunately the condition can be detected by a routine test in the first weeks of life. If the identified infant is put on a phenylanaline-free diet he or she will not become intellectually impaired.

INTERACTION OF HEREDITY AND ENVIRONMENT

A normal set of genes and an appropriate, facilitative environment are each needed for satisfactory development and the acquisition of adaptive behaviour. What appears to be the same effect can be produced by different genes (e.g. schizophrenia and a type of blindness called retinitis pigmentosa); the same genotype may produce different effects due to the influence of other genes ('modifiers') and of differing environmental experiences. This variation is termed the 'penetrance' of the gene.

In the case of epiloia (tuberous sclerosis), a form of mental handicap accompanied by epilepsy, the condition is brought about by a single abnormal gene. Because of variation in the penetrance of this gene, children could be (a) mentally handicapped but not epileptic; (b) epileptic but not mentally handicapped; or (c) neither epileptic nor handicapped but manifesting other signs of the disorder such as rashes and tumours.

Environmental factors can set limits on (or enhance) the individual's achievement of all his or her genetic potential. A youngster well endowed with intellectual potential may well be cognitively 'stunted' if starved of stimulation and the opportunity to learn.

A large number of degenerative conditions of the central nervous system are hereditary (e.g. certain types of ataxia) as are degenerations of the neuromuscular system. These disorders are determined by a variety of single genes—dominant and recessive, autosomal (non-sex) and sex-linked.

GENETIC ACCIDENTS

The mechanism of heredity, as we saw in Part II, is remarkably reliable, and the vast majority of infants are born within the normal range of variation. However, genetic errors do sometimes occur and they take many different forms. The first type of genetic error concerns the effects of mutation. Any deviation from the norm in genetic information is called a mutation. The DNA structure of the gene may be wrongly copied. Gene changes occur in exceptional circumstances such as excessive radiation from X-rays or nuclear fallout. They can occur spontaneously but this is rare—about once in 50 000 generations for any particular gene. A mutant gene can be passed on from one generation to the next in exactly the same way as a normal gene. It becomes a permanent characteristic. On the whole the effects of mutation are deleterious. The resultant pathological condition is often self-limiting owing to its severity and the inability of the affected individual to reproduce. Although deleterious genes arise by mutations or changes in the chemical structure at specific points in chromosomes, these changes cannot be conceptualized in the same way as gross morphological changes in chromosomes. This brings us to the second type of genetic error.

In the second case the abnormality is in the structure or number of chromosomes due to translocations and deletions. Errors may occur in the processes of forming sex cells and fertilization, which cause chromosomal anomalies with important consequences for development and behaviour. Chromosome abnormalities are found in approximately 1 in every 200 live births. Most, though, are found in spontaneous abortions (miscarriages).

Many characteristics in which there is quantitative variation, particularly complex ones like intelligence, temperament, stature, longevity and athletic ability, depend on the action of many genes (called 'polygenic' inheritance). Polygenic inheritance is of much greater significance to those working with behaviour problems, learning difficulties and developmental problems than are chromosomal or single-gene abnormalities. Polygenic mechanisms are believed to produce attributes which are continuous and approximately normally distributed, e.g. height, weight, blood pressure and intelligence.

INTERVENTIONS

Clinical psychologists working in this area offer their services as part of a multidisciplinary team. These may involve the following techniques.

1. *Psychoeducation*. The aim is to help parents and other family members understand their child's diagnosis and its implications for the child's development. It is difficult for parents to appreciate the implications of the diagnosis of intellectual disability. Most parents experience shock and denial (two elements of the grief process described later). Psychologists on multidisciplinary teams have a responsibility to help team members give parents and family members a clear message about the diagnosis and assessment since this is what the parents require to get on with the process of accepting their child's disability and dealing with it in a realistic way. The diagnosis/assessment should give information on the normative status of the child's cognitive abilities and adaptive skills; psychological and emotional status; biological factors; and supports necessary for the child to live a normal life. A major goal in psychoeducation is to avoid giving parents ambiguous information which allows them to maintain the erroneous belief that their child has no disability or a transient condition that will improve with maturation.

2. *Life skills training*. The portage programme offers a highly structured way of empowering parents to coach their children in the development of a variety of life skills in a systematic manner. In addition, the principles of behaviour modification may be used for designing skills development programmes and training parents and school staff to implement these to help the child develop life skills.

3. *Organization of appropriate support*. Following the comprehensive assessment and feedback of diagnostic information, clinical psychologists may have a role in organizing and arranging support systems for children with intellectual disabilities and their families. The appropriateness of these supports in meeting the changing needs of the child and the burden of care shouldered by the family require periodic review and revision. The child and family's support needs must be clearly defined in concrete terms; the precise action plans for arranging supports agreed with the family and the professional network; the precise roles and responsibilities of members of the professional network in providing supports arranged; the way in which the provision of supports will be resourced financially specified; and the timetable of periodic review dates drawn up.

4. *Challenging behaviour*. Intellectually impaired children learn maladaptive behaviours in the same way as children who are not handicapped, but there are some important differences. Teaching the child new ways of behaving requires a more structured approach than is necessary with the normal child. Interventions to reduce the frequency of challenging behaviours should be based on a thorough functional analysis of the immediate antecedents and consequences of such behaviours which maintain them. A wider ecological assessment is also required to identify both personal attributes and relatively enduring features of the physical and social environment which may predispose children and their carers to evolve mutually reinforcing patterns of behaviour that maintain aggressive and self-injurious behaviour (Evans and Meyer, 1985; Oliver, 1995).

Note. There has not been space in an already brief account of learning disability, to discuss *specific* learning difficulties in subjects such as writing, spelling and number skills. However, Margot Prior, in her book *Understanding Specific Learning Difficulties* (Hove: Psychology Press, 1996) provides a useful handbook for clinicians, teachers, and parents.

Chapter 10

HEALTH CARE PROBLEMS OF CHILDHOOD

See Eiser (1990) for further reading on the topic of this chapter.

It may be a statement of the obvious to say that good health enhances the possibility of success at school. It is more than that of course; it engenders a sense of well-being and enjoyment of life. But a large number of children miss out on these benefits. The fact is that we face a daunting health care and educational problem: the total prevalence of children with chronic illness of one kind or another is estimated to be as high as 10% (Pless and Douglas, 1971). Good health is the prerequisite for the stamina required by long hours of concentration in the classroom. Regular attendance at school depends upon it, and effective learning, in turn, depends upon a reasonably consistent presence at lessons. But even regular attenders may not be able to learn efficiently if they are tired, apathetic or if their physical systems are impaired in some way. Physical problems are not only responsible for undermining scholastic endeavours; they may also lead to low perceived self-efficacy, and perhaps emotional disturbance.

HEALTH CARE PSYCHOLOGY

Health care psychology for children has a longer history than its adult counterpart. Clinical child psychologists have found a niche for their skills in primary care (general practice), paediatric departments, child development and assessment centres and intensive care units. Psychologists are able to respond to a variety of illness-related problems (Lask and Fosson; 1989) e.g. encopresis, failure-to-thrive, anorexia nervosa, allergic conditions, meningitis and other diseases with behavioural sequelae. Obesity, physical or psychogenic pain, orthopaedic complications, and a whole array of previously baffling disorders are now being treated with a high degree of success. The move into this area marks a shift in emphasis from the secondary and tertiary preventative health care which is characteristic of the clinical child psychologist's more traditional concern with psychopathology (e.g. neurotic and psychotic conditions), to the *primary* prevention which engages much of the attention of general practitioners, community doctors and paediatricians (Caplan, 1964). Primary prevention aims at reducing the *incidence* or the number of new cases or disorders in a population. Secondary prevention or treatment has as its goal the reduction of the *prevalence* (the number of existing cases) of disorders or dysfunctions. Tertiary prevention focuses on reducing the sequelae resulting from established disorders or dysfunctions.

Pain in children has received a considerable amount of attention in recent years (McGrath, 1987; McGrath and Unrah, 1987; Ross and Ross, 1988). The area has been extensively reviewed by several authors (Anderson and Masur, 1983; Bush, 1987; Eland and Anderson, 1977; Jay, 1988; Zeltzer and LeBaron, 1986). Since Eland and Anderson's (1977) review of the medical literature on pain which highlighted the relatively cursory attention paid to childhood pain in contrast to adult pain, there has been increased research into the problem of pain in children, in terms of both its psychological assessment and management. Much progress has been made regarding procedural pain in children, associated with invasive medical procedures. These involve penetration of tissue or body orifices for diagnostic or treatment purposes (Anderson and Masur, 1983). Such invasive procedures constitute a significant threat for many children, particularly for children with chronic illness who have to undergo invasive procedures on a regular basis. These procedures often evoke anxiety and fear, which may compound the child's perception of pain. It is not uncommon for children to also develop conditioned generalized anxiety to acute medical situations. Interventions which have been helpful in reducing children's distress include types of preparation, cognitive–behavioural interventions and hypnosis. Methods such as these have been empirically validated by Ioannou (1991).

Much work remains to be done in developing more sophisticated reliable and valid assessment methods. Controlled outcome studies are required to evaluate the effectiveness of different interventions, and to assess which interventions are most appropriate for which type of children, and under what conditions. Issues of treatment maintenance and generalization also need to be addressed in future. Fielding (1985) draws attention to the importance of developmental factors in children's concept of illness, and the corollary that an understanding of the child patient's level of cognitive development underpins effective communication with him or her. She presents Table 13 as an aid to assessment.

Clinical child psychologists in community settings, in primary care settings and general hospitals are likely to find themselves involved in the following activities:

Table 13 Developmental stages of children's concepts of illness. (Source: Fielding, 1985, reproduced by permission of the British Psychological Society.)

Approximate age range (years)	Cognitive level	Concept of illness	Examples
	0 Incomprehension	0 No answer or response unrelated to question	
		1 Don't know	
	1 Phenomenism ⌐	2 Circular, magical or global response	'How do people get colds?' 'From the sun.' 'How does the sun give you a cold?' 'It just does.'
	PRELOGICAL	3 Concrete rules: concrete rigid response with parrot-like quality — little comprehension by children	'How do people get colds?' 'By going out without a coat in cold weather.' 'By eating junk food.'
4–7	2 Contagion ⌐		
	3 Contamination ⌐		
	CONCRETE	4 Internalization and relativity; increased generalization with some indication of child's contribution to response — quality of invariant causation remains	'What is a cold?' You sneeze a lot, you talk funny and your nose gets clogged up.' 'How do people get colds?' In winter they breathe in too much air into their noses and it blocks up the nose.' 'How does this cause colds?' The bacteria gets in by breathing. Then the lungs get too soft (child exhales), and it goes to the nose.'
7–11	LOGICAL 4 Internalization ⌐		
		5 Generalized principles Beginning use of underlying principles — greater delineation of causal agents or illnesses	'How does it get better?' 'Hot fresh air, it gets in the nose and pushes the cold air back.'
11	5 Physiologic ⏤ FORMAL LOGICAL	6 Physiologic processes and mechanisms	'What is a cold?' 'It's when you get all stuffed up inside, your sinuses get filled up with mucus. Sometimes your lungs do, too, and you get a cough.'
	6 Psychophysiologic ⌐		'How do people get colds?' 'They come from viruses, I guess. Other people have the virus and it gets into your blood-stream and it makes you ill.'

- The preparation of children for hospitalization and surgery (Vernon *et al.*, 1965; Zabin and Melamed, [1980) and for dentistry (Melamed, 1979).
- Encouraging compliance with treatment regimes (Henneborn and Cogan, 1975; Varni, 1983).
- Symptomatic control (Creer, Renne and Chai, 1982; Rose *et al.*, 1983; Steinhausen, 1984).
- Preventative work on coping with stress (Ayalon, 1988; Meichenbaum, 1977; Prinz, 1994).
- Treating (directly or indirectly) specific illnesses: e.g., recurrent abdominal pain (Apley, 1975), cancer (Dolgin and Jay, 1989), headaches (Williamson, Davis and Kelley, 1987), atopic dermatitis.
- Helping children to cope with the ramifications of accidents and illness (pain injections, nausea, epileptic fits, burns) (e.g. Elliott and Olson, 1983).
- Facilitating effective communication with children and their families (Ley, 1977).
- Counselling families facing terminal illness or experiencing bereavement (Lansdown and Goldman, 1988; Parkes, 1973); helping families to come to terms with chronic illness (Lask and Fosson, 1989; Douglas, 1993).

Family Needs

With regard to the last item, there are few reports on the impact of illness on the family, and the value of those that have been published tends to be reduced because of methodological inadequacies such as the absence of control groups. Family therapists point out the importance of two characteristics when dealing with families and illness: (a) family group life and its regulatory mechanisms, and (b) family growth and development. Chronic illnesses have the capacity to alter both of these profoundly. A process often unfolds in which family life becomes increasingly organized around illness-generated needs and demands, to the detriment of the development of individual members and the family as a group. The ultimate consequence of this can be the suppression of those family priorities which are not related to illness, and a neglect of matters that are part of a normal family's development. During the crisis phase of an illness life plans are frequently put on 'hold' by the family in order to accommodate its adaptation to the illness; in the transition to the chronic phase a renegotiation takes place during which a clinical psychologist can help them to ensure that important individual and family interests are not unnecessarily sacrificed.

PSYCHOPHYSIOLOGICAL ILLNESS

Psychosomatic (psychophysiological) medicine was the first medical discipline to acknowledge wholeheartedly the influence of psychological processes in disease. Its approach encompasses research into relationships between biological, psychological and psychosocial factors in health and disease, a holistic approach to patient care, and the use of methods developed at the interface between medicine and the behavioural sciences. Psychophysiological illnesses consist of bodily (somatic) symptoms—such as bronchial asthma, hayfever, skin complaints (eczema), ulcerative colitis, migraine and others—which are associated in some children with psychological complications. These bodily disturbances are not limited to any particular age or phase of development. But they do occur frequently in school-age children. Next to acute respiratory illnesses they are the commonest cause of repeated absence from school.

It has been found that in many of these conditions, particular attacks or phases of the illness can be precipitated or prolonged by psychological stresses, such as conflict, anxiety and anger, as well as physical stresses (e.g. dietary factors, allergies, infections, etc). Treatment of the symptoms by physical means alone is often ineffective. The advance brought about by a psychophysiological perspective in medicine is due to the reinstatement of the person into the consideration of his or her illness. There is space for *one* example only: bronchial asthma. However it does illustrate the range of work being carried out by clinical psychologists these days.

Bronchial Asthma (see Creer, 1982)

This is one of the most common childhood ailments; it can be serious in its implications, sometimes leading to death. Bronchial asthma illustrates general principles which are (or have been) thought to apply to psychophysiological conditions in general.

The emphasis on the personality of the sick individual (in systematic clinical studies) was very much a post-second-world-war phenomenon. The revolutionary advances made in the early part of this century in medical technology, particularly in physical methods of diagnosis and treatment and the uncovering of hitherto unseen physical agents (microorganisms) which cause certain illnesses, tended to reinforce a one-sided organic approach to disease. For a long time, in keeping with the prevailing medical bias, asthma was considered almost solely as a physical (an allergic and infective) illness, and physical desensitization and the use of drugs became the main methods of treatment. However, an analysis of the literature of the 1940s and 1950s, in particular, reveals a considerable shift in orientation.

Crucial to this approach was the assumption that some illnesses represent, in certain circumstances, an individual's specific reaction to his or her life-situation—almost what one might call a mode of behaviour. Patients were no longer regarded simply as collections of separate bodily organ systems, each of which is subject to breakdown, but rather as unique individuals living in certain types of environment, subject to a variety of physical and psychological stresses to which they react as *whole* persons. Thus, in disease, causation is sought both in the nature of the individual and in his or her environment; it is the child who has a particular illness; not just a disease that 'has' the child.

The context—the 'body language' and meanings associated with physiological functioning—are considered in a psychological assessment. The effects of emotion upon physical states, have long been implicit in language and folklore and confirmed in laboratories (Wolff and Goodell, 1968). Our language contains numerous metaphorical expressions for the effects of emotions upon respiratory functioning: sighing in sadness and in grief and fear; the rapid breathing of excitement and anticipation; the 'breath-taking' quality of wonder and amazement: the expansion of the chest in joy and in the choking of anxiety. Speech and crying which are closely related to respiratory functioning are also complex expressive phenomena.

An important consideration in the relationship of emotion to asthma may be the profound significance of attitudes related to breathing. For example, there is the fundamental anxiety caused by the asthma attack. Asthma involves a frightening disturbance of the normal breathing pattern, and the reasons for the anxiety—not least in a parent—are deep seated and probably have to do with the fact that breathing is the first and last act of life.

Some researchers—particularly those with a psychodynamic background—have tried to check on the popular notion that there is a very specific asthmatic 'personality type'. They have attempted experimentally to correlate personality profiles with specific psychosomatic illnesses. The present author and other investigators have been unable to substantiate the claims that there is a personality structure characteristic of asthmatics only (Herbert, 1965). Neuhaus (1958) found that the members of his group of asthmatic children were significantly more maladjusted or neurotic than were the children of a normal control group. They were characterized by traits of anxiety, insecurity and dependency. But he also found that a control group of children with cardiac disease exceeded normals in degree of neuroticism and dependency feelings. Neuhaus concluded that the lack of significant differences in test results between the asthmatic and cardiac patients indicates that the personality picture of the asthmatic child cannot wholly be described to the nature of the asthmatic disorder. He is of the opinion that not only do the data clearly refute the concept of differential personality patterns for asthmatic and cardiac children, but, on the contrary, the presence of personality traits common to both illnesses are possibly common to protracted illnesses in general. Rees (1963), too, was unable to find any evidence of specificity of personality type in a large-scale study of 388 asthmatic children and a control group of accident cases. However, the incidence of factors such as maternal overprotection, insecurity and emotional tension in this group of asthmatics was found to be substantial.

What makes asthma so interesting from the aspect of learned behaviour is the fact that breathing, while largely an involuntary activity, is also subject to voluntary control. This implies that specific attacks of asthma might be conceptualized in classical conditioning and/or operant learning terms.

Intervention

Creer, Renne and Chai (1982) describe a successful five-component treatment package which contains these elements:

- The first stage consists in detecting the onset of the attack by reporting shortness of breath and wheezing.
- If these symptoms have been a reliable predictor of an asthmatic attack, the child then has to restrict his or her physical activity, especially if that is normally a trigger, as is reported in about 80% of children.
- Practising relaxation can counteract feelings of panic. Progressive muscular relaxation can be practised beforehand together with imaginary rehearsal of the experience of the onset of the attack. Children as young as 5 may be able to make use of relaxation (see Herbert, 1987b).
- The next step consists of drinking warm liquid, a full cup every 15 minutes.
- The use of a bronchodilator is the next procedure. Some children have difficulty in reporting the warning symptoms, so it may be appropriate to give them some practice in reporting what they experience when peak expiratory rates are low. This is done by frequent daily measurement of peak expiratory rates. Sampling of respiratory performance in this way may indicate which flow rates are critical for the onset of an attack.

A careful assessment (see p. 42) may uncover the presence of reinforcement from various sources, such as avoidance of social activities which are feared, or unpleasant school activities. Unacceptable behaviours (e.g. temper tantrums) may become reinforced by parents who are afraid of provoking an asthmatic episode. Single-case experimental investigation is a valuable aid in elucidating possible causal relationships (Morley, 1989).

School refusal can be reinforced in a similar manner by parents. Frequent absences from school are likely to undermine a child's attainment there: this may lead to further reluctance to go to school.

Anorexia Nervosa

The term *anorexia nervosa* (literal translation: nervous loss of appetite) was coined in the late 1880s by the English physician William Gull, but was vividly depicted under the name nervosa phthisis by Richard Morton in 1694 as follows:

> I do not remember that I did ever in all my practice see one, that was conversant with the living, as much wasted with the greatest degree of a consumption (like a skeleton only clad with skin); yet there was no fever but on the contrary a coldness of the whole body ... only her appetite was diminished, and her digestion uneasy.

This girl was 18 years old; she appears to have suffered an eating disturbance that occurs primarily in adolescent females. The term anorexia nervosa is a misnomer in the sense that all the evidence suggests that loss of appetite in anorexic individuals is uncommon; they *do* suffer from pangs of hunger (Garfinkel, 1974), and these can be intense. Leon and Dinklage (1989) state that the consistent feature of this condition is 'the relentless pursuit of thinness, that is the phenomenon of continual dieting or food restriction to the point of self-starvation and sometimes death'. Anorexic individuals commonly *deny* that they experience hunger, even when emaciated. More specifically they seem driven by an obsession to avoid being fat, although few have a history of being overweight. This results in a sharp reduction in food intake, and is often accompanied by an almost frantic, indeed *compulsive* regime of exercising. Despite striking resemblances among anorexic patients, there is convincing evidence that anorexia nervosa is a heterogeneous syndrome.

There appear to be three subtypes among the feeding disorders with regard to the patterns of food consumption and elimination:

(1) *Restricters* who are characterized by a dieting pattern in which there is a consistently extreme limitation on the amount of food ingested. They exclusively starve themselves and indulge in excessive exercise.
(2) *Purgers* are those who starve and purge but do not binge.
(3) *Bingers* are notable for a severe dieting regime which is interspersed with episodes of bingeing followed by vomiting or other means of purgation. (In bulimia nervosa—the bingeing subgroup—the premorbid weight level is generally higher than is the case in anorexia nervosa).

Psychological Correlates

A distinctive set of psychological correlates of anorexia has been reported by various investigators (e.g. Bemis, 1987; Crisp *et al.*, 1980; Garfinkel and Garner, 1982). The anorexic person is often described as:

- withdrawn;
- isolated;
- introverted;
- stubborn;
- selfish;
- manipulative;
- perfectionistic;
- hyperactive;
- controlling.

Differential Diagnosis between Anorexia and Bulimia

There is a case for dealing with these problems separately because of differences in:

- clinical symptoms;
- their pattern of age at onset;
- heritability (high in anorexia; low in bulimia).

Steinhausen (1994) makes the point that anorexia nervosa is typically associated with the transition from childhood to adolescence and, in most cases, bulimia nervosa reflects the transition from adolescence to young adulthood. The former peaks in onset at 14 years of age, the latter at about 18 or 19 years.

Diagnosis of Anorexia Nervosa

There is a large area of agreement between the ICD-10 and DSM-IV diagnostic criteria for anorexia nervosa, with regard to:

- criteria of weight loss (15% below that expected for age and height);
- body-image distortion;
- weight phobia (self-induced loss of weight/fear of becoming obese);
- amenorrhoea (absence of at least three consecutive menstrual cycles when otherwise expected to occur, DSM-III-R, p. 67)

Whether the distinctions between anorexia nervosa and bulimia and the typologies mentioned earlier (restricters, purgers and bingers) simply represent different indices of severity or are valid clinical entities, remains unresolved. However, it is the opinion of many clinicians that they have pragmatic value as the bulimic features of anorexia nervosa require different management. In the final analysis, what constitutes the consistent feature in persons suffering from this disorder, irrespective of subtype, is a *phobia of gaining weight and of taking food*.

Prevalence

Epidemiological reports estimating the prevalence of anorexia nervosa are fraught with methodological problems, inconsistent diagnostic criteria and inadequate archival records. Certainly we can say that the presence of anorexia nervosa before the age of 14 or before the menarche is rare. When it does occur before puberty its features are, in essence, similar to the later onset disorder (Gowers *et al.*, 1991; Lask and Bryant-Waugh, 1992); the process of puberty tends to be arrested.

The prevalence rates of anorexia nervosa in males are low although it may not always be recognized/diagnosed. Estimates of the prevalence rates for females tend to vary but the figure of below 1% for the *adolescent population* may be close to being accurate. When taking the entire *anorexic population* into consideration, it appears that males account for between 5 and 15% of the total.

There are consistent findings to suggest that anorexia nervosa is probably becoming more frequent. Whether the rise in numbers is a true increase or due to better identification, remains a moot point (see Lucas *et al.*, 1991).

Social classes I and II (i.e. the highest socioeconomic strata) appear (although the evidence is meagre) to manifest more cases of anorexia nervosa than other sections of society (Crisp, Palmer and Kalucy, 1976; Kendall *et al.*, 1973). This selectivity is paralleled in the higher socio-economic status of countries. Severe eating disorders, particularly food restriction, appear to be a mark of an affluent society. In those parts of the world where food is scarce, most persons do not have the luxury of gaining attention through refusing to eat or of getting fat because of having too much to eat. In countries such as India and Sri Lanka, obesity has traditionally been valued as a sign of wealth, but there, for many, food is scarce, extremely low rates of anorexia nervosa are found.

The epidemiology of childhood-onset anorexia nervosa and related eating disorders is as yet relatively unexplored (see Lask and Bryant-Waugh, 1992).

Clinical Features

Behavioural characteristics

- Phobic fear of being fat/drive for thinness

The outward and physical signs of this dread are the person's obsessive dieting and a conviction that her/his body (whatever the objective indications to the contrary) is too large.

The typical progression is:

- Dieting is introduced (as by many other adolescents)—sometimes as a result of teasing about being fat.
- An increasing range of items is reduced or cut out; also an increasing expertise is acquired re calorie content of foods.
- Loss of control of dieting. (It may be months before the thinness and/or the severity/abnormality of the dieting is noticed.)
- There is sometimes a distortion of body image (e.g. emaciation is not seen as thinness or as being repellent).
- Parents feel helpless in the face of the single-mindedness and drivenness of their adolescent.
- There may be rigorous exercising and abuse of laxatives/diuretics and self-induced vomiting.
- There is a powerful need to be *in control* of all aspects of food intake.
- For some young people there are episodes of bingeing (followed by fasting or purging). Bulimic features within the spectrum of anorexia nervosa tend to be infrequent in adolescence.
- Extreme hyperactivity of a highly ritualized nature is common, e.g. complex daily rituals of rigorous exercise.
- A restriction of interests (e.g. preoccupation with topics such as diet and food) takes place.
- Social contacts are lost.
- Sexual interest is reduced.
- Mood swings/irritability/insomnia/depression occur.
- Self-esteem is lowered.
- Obsessional behaviour (e.g. peculiar eating rituals) appears.

Physical characteristics might involve:

- emaciation;
- anaemia;
- autonomic nervous system down-regulation (e.g. hypotension, hypothermia, bradycardia);
- complications that can affect almost every organ system;
- primary or secondary amenorrhoea (see Bemis, 1978);
- in males, a significant decrease in plasma testosterone levels at maximum weight loss, with an increase during weight restoration.

There are medical illnesses to be checked out (e.g. acquired immune deficiency disease, inflammatory bowel disease, diabetes mellitus) as they can cause weight loss.

Assessment (see Williamson, 1990)

Clinical interviews. Outlines of detailed interviews are available (e.g. Garner and Garfinkel, 1985; Harris *et al.* 1983). In addition to eliciting information about eating patterns and weight-control behaviour, interviews should collect information about the following:

- history of the disorder: onset, development of symptoms;
- evidence of psychopathology;
- family background;
- food intake, eating behaviours (e.g. keep a food diary);
- thoughts and attitudes towards weight issues;
- thoughts and attitudes towards food and eating;
- functional analysis (ABC) of contingencies surrounding food refusal/ binges, etc.;
- events preceding food refusal/binge–purge episodes;
- events following food refusal/binge–purge episodes;
- attempts to alter the eating disorder (help from others/self-help);
- special relationships with family and peers;
- academic performance;
- drug and alcohol use;
- motivation to change;
- medical checks including routine laboratory investigations.

Available aids to assessment

- Binge Scale (Hawkins and Clement, 1980);
- Eating Disorder Examinations (Cooper and Fairburn, 1987);
- Clinical Eating Disorder Rating Instrument (Palmer *et al.* 1987);
- Structural Interview for Anorexia and Bulimia Nervosa (Fichter *et al.* 1990);
- Eating Attitude Test (Garner and Garfinkel, 1979).

Aetiology

The causes of eating disorders remain far from clear. What can be said is that the search for a single all-embracing cause has rightly been abandoned by most theorists. Causation is multifactorial, as one would expect with problems as complex and many-sided as anorexia and bulimia nervosa. The causal factors include individual, family, sociocultural and biological influences, invariably functioning in an interactive fashion.

(1) *Individual influences*

(a) *Psychoanalytic theories.* It is hardly surprising that anorexia nervosa, with its strong age-related (pubertal) association, should be explained in terms of extreme sexual conflicts entailing symbolism of fear of pregnancy, incestuous impregnation, the denial of femininity. These highly speculative notions have failed to gain empirical support. Nevertheless, the hypothesized intense fear of the anorexic youth of becoming physically and emotionally mature has proved a popular formulation by developmental theorists from differing theoretical orientations (see Crisp, 1980).

Hilde Bruch, who is widely known for her book *The Golden Cage: The Enigma of Anorexia Nervosa* (1978) was of the opinion that anorexia is the result of a very early and profound disturbance in mother–child interactions. (One has to say that there is a lack of specificity in such theorizing in the sense that a similar psychodynamic script has been written for autism, schizophrenia and bronchial asthma—to mention but a few problems of childhood.) According to Bruch the young person's ego development is deficient, manifesting itself by a disturbance in body identity that includes a lack of a sense of owning one's body. The refusal to eat gives many anorexic patients a sense of specialness and superiority and a feeling of being a better person, more worth while, through the self-control of losing weight in such a disciplined manner.

The anorexic male or female, in Bruch's view, is continually fearful of not being fully acknowledged and loved within the family; also—as a consequence of pubertal changes in their bodies—anxious about expectations that they assume more independence. There is a sense of life-events removing their control over life, forcing them to be autonomous. The anorexic individual's desire for specialness becomes confused with the pursuit of thinness. The implication of this notion for treatment is to help him or her to develop a sense of competence in areas of activity in which they feel inadequate. Duker and Slade (1988) make the point that how a practitioner believes anorexia works is of great practical importance as the understanding of the disorder determines the kind of help that is provided to the patient.

> The helper whose theoretical view takes into account the psychological effects of starvation will see anorexia nervosa as a gradually intensifying state of incapacity in which different processes are at work at different stages. This is ... provided the helper has a set of ideas concerning the sufferer that are flexible and differentiated enough to meet her exactly where she happens to be as, in the long course of the illness, her weight, her behaviour and her subjective experiences change.

The approach Duker and Slade caution, which ignores the inevitable psychological consequences of starvation, is likely to be too fixed. An example of aetiological 'tunnel vision' is those explanations that ignore the psychological consequences of restricting food intake. They rest instead on the idea that the refusal to eat is something he or she may be carrying on in pursuit of a particular purpose or for some symbolic or figurative meaning. These explanations 'carry the assumption that, if the meaning or purpose that lies behind the behaviour is discovered, then the whole self-starvation episode will be understood'.

(b) *Behavioural theories*. In the case of behavioural and social learning theories, there has been less concern with formulating all-embracing causal theories of anorexia nervosa and its development (as occurs in psychodynamic aetiologies) than with tackling specific aspects of the problem with behavioural techniques. One such aspect—food refusal—is considered a manifestation of avoidance behaviour. A functional analysis would be considered vital in understanding the development of the eating disturbance for the particular individual (e.g. Blinder *et al.*, 1970; Leitenberg *et al.*, 1968; Slade, 1982).

Leon (1979) proposed that, in anorexia nervosa, a learned association develops between negative thoughts and images about weight gain and eating. Gradually this learning process becomes strengthened and generalizes to an association between thoughts or images of food and feelings of revulsion. This aversive affect then also occurs in association with the actual eating of food. A conditioned aversion to food intake becomes established, and a judgement is made that eating will lead to weight gain. The reinforcer maintaining this sequence is the anxiety reduction associated with the affirmation of self-control and control over one's life through food restriction.

(c) *The need to be in control*. Those persons suffering from anorexia nervosa may not be manifesting a severe perceptual distortion as much as an evaluation that they would like to be thinner—thinness serving as an affirmation of control over life in general. A confirmation of this hypothesis was found in the work of Leon, Bemis and Lucas (1980) with 18 newly hospitalized anorexic patients who indicated that dieting and weight loss resulted in a feeling of self-control and willpower, and in a generally greater feeling of control over their lives. Anorexic individuals indicated that food that they had found pleasant-tasting in the past and that they had previously enjoyed eating was not aversive—support for the hypothesis above.

(d) *Sexual trauma*. Several studies have indicated a correlation between the experience of sexual abuse and eating disorders (see Lask and Bryant-Waugh, 1992). The pathway from childhood sexual trauma to an eating disorder is unclear and a reminder to us of the fact that anorexia nervosa is a *heterogeneous* condition.

(e) *Premorbid personality profile.* A common premorbid pattern described in the literature is of a compliance, perfectionism and dependence in the child. There is little hard evidence of psychosexual problems as complicating factors in the causation of eating disorders (Scott, 1987).

(2) *Familial factors.* In studying the family process in anorexia nervosa, it is worth remembering Yager's caution (1988) against developing stereotypes about anorexic families. Families (in general) undergoing intensive treatment may be different on a number of factors from families not involved in therapy. Further, wide differences between families of anorexic patients may also be evident. Hypotheses (e.g. Minuchin, Rosman and Baker, 1978) about a typical family interactional style, constellation or dynamic for anorexic individuals have found no empirical support.

Reports do, however, suggest a raised incidence of emotional and weight problems and disturbed interactions and communications. Humphrey (1986) found that anorexic and bulimic individuals of normal weight viewed their parents as more blaming, rejecting, and neglectful toward them than did normal controls. Crisp *et al.* (1980) extensively evaluated the parents during the period of the anorexic's weight restoration and found that they became significantly more anxious and depressed as the anorexic youngster improved. In particular, severe anxiety in mothers and significant depression in fathers were commonly noted. Further, these changes in the psychological status of the parents concurrent with the improvement in their child were associated with long-standing, severely impaired marital relationships. The parents of anorexic patients have indicated marked degrees of unhappiness about their sexual relationship. These negative feelings are expressed in a manner suggesting dissatisfaction with the functioning of the family as a whole. The adolescent within the family may be seen as attempting to cope with the family psychopathology by modifying her shape.

(3) *Biological factors.* Various biological influences—hormonal and endocrine factors, malfunctioning of the hypothalamus—have been considered as causal in anorexia nervosa. The physical consequences of undernutrition must be a priority consideration.

(a) *Severe restriction of food intake.* Duker and Slade (1988) point out that increasing undernutrition and low weight can create or contribute to:

• dependence;
• restlessness and hyperactivity;
• a preoccupation with food;
• personality change;

- disturbances of thinking (reduction of complex thought, extremeness, lowered capacity for abstract thinking, reduced coping strategies, poor concentration, deteriorating memory);
- clumsiness;
- disorientation;
- diminished sexuality;
- attenuation of mood and feeling (leading to detachment);
- euphoria/elation.

Starvation and rigorous exercise produce a 'cocktail' of chemicals in the anorexic person's body. Duker and Slade put it this way:

> This is how an individual can come to derive a particular pleasure, or sense of wellbeing, from strenuous exercise. It is also how, by further stimulating the body's production of endomorphins, hyperactivity itself acts as its own spur in the anorexic, as it does in any person who is excessively dedicated to running, gymnastics or other activity. It is thus that chronic low-weight anorexia nervosa can be viewed as an addiction to starvation. Occasionally anorexics refer to themselves as starvation junkies, and some psychiatrists have now come to see the low-weight anorexic as being dependent on the biological states that result from starvation, as 'hooked' on recurrent fixes of internally generated brain chemicals.

(4) *Genetic factors* (see Garfinkel and Garner, 1982). There is a genetic influence at work. A review of twin studies suggests that 44–50% of monozygotic twins are concordant for anorexia nervosa (Scott, 1987). Holland *et al.* (1988) found 56% of monozygotic twins to be concordant for the disorder and only 5% concordant in the case of dizygotic twins. It would seem that a genetic predisposition for anorexia and adverse environmental influences interact to bring about the condition (Scott, 1987).

(5) *Premorbid obesity*. Many patients who become anorexic have had problems with regulating their food intake before the development of this self-starvation regime. Crisp *et al.* (1977) found a high proportion of premorbid obesity, including massive obesity, in the anorexic patients they treated. Halmi (1974) reported that 31% of the 94 cases of anorexia nervosa that she reviewed had a history of being overweight before the age of 12.

(6) *Food regulation*. Outcome studies indicate food regulation problems. Hsu (1980) noted that bulimia was present at follow-up evaluation in 14–50% of patients in the studies he reviewed, and that 10–28 per cent reported vomiting after food intake. It is clear that a normalization of eating patterns does not necessarily parallel a normalization of weight. At follow-up, many patients continue to express an inordinate concern with food and eating.

The issue of self-control, particularly in relation to food intake, continues to be a concern of many anorexic individuals, including those whose weight has been restored to a normal or near-normal level.

(7) *An overview.* Hsu (1990) suggests that adolescent dieting provides the entree into an eating disorder if such dieting is intensified 'by adolescent turmoil, low self and body concept, and poor identity formation'. In his opinion the dangers are further exacerbated if there is a family history of affective or eating disorders or alcohol or substance abuse. There could be other risk factors to do with personality and psychological attributes described earlier.

Biological factors have also been implicated (e.g. a hypothalmic disorder) by Russell (1985). Biological and psychological factors become inextricably intertwined (see Duker and Slade, 1988) and the question of what comes first, or what is primary, remains a chicken-and-egg conundrum.

Treatment (see Garfinkel 1985)

There are several approaches to intervention with this potentially life-threatening feeding disorder; however, there is a paucity of rigorous comparative studies indicating which (if any) methods are most effective. The major hurdle for any therapeutic approach is the one of overcoming the marked resistance to treatment displayed by many anorexic individuals.

In-patient vs out-patient treatment. The former may be preferable if:

- there is extreme emaciation (less than 70% of the average weight);
- serious conflict within the family sufficient to hinder out-patient treatment.

Goals of Treatment

- Weight restoration: a gradual but steady gain is usually aimed at (viz. 0.2 kg/day), brought about by more frequent (4–6) meals of small portions. The plan is to start at about 1500 calories per day and slowly move up to 2000/3000. (A dietician's help is invaluable.)
- Regular monitoring and feedback to the patient is crucial.
- Having someone to support/encourage the patient during meals is an advantage.
- So is the provision of a benign therapeutic milieu.

Duker and Slade (1988) in describing the 'helper's' dilemma make some important points. They preface their remarks by saying that:

In recognizing the potential hazards of a simple authoritarian response to the anorexic's food restriction, helpers themselves meanwhile come face to face with the dilemma that seems to lie at the heart of any attempt to assist or care for the anorexic who is low weight.

- The physical and psychological constraints of starvation (they continue) have to be reckoned with. This necessarily involves acknowledging the fact that much intellectual potential is temporarily unavailable, in proportion to the amount of weight lost. It also involves being aware that emotional development has slowed down, or stopped.
- There is an equal and opposite need to be aware that the anorexic is someone who, in being self-controlled, has discovered a way of feeling positive about herself that is profoundly relieving. It replaces a deep sense of failure and confusion. Food control is not only central to her sense of self; it is all she has to maintain it. If her control goes, she no longer has a self to be.

Duker and Slade (1988) formulate the dilemma as follows:

The helper would like to lift the constraints and dangers of the effects of starvation by refeeding the low-weight anorexic. To do this without attending to the way she feels is to risk annihilating her sense of self which is already very fragile. On the other hand, while the helper would like to respect the sufferer as a person, since the anorexic's sense of who she is resides in her successful food control, to adopt this course can lead to the helper's allowing her to persist with a lifestyle that can eventually lead to a degree of emaciation that is lethal. Parents, friends and inexperienced helpers who have not been aware of the nature of the anorexic's 'self' not infrequently find themselves confronted with the consequences of their having taken this latter option. Thus occasionally anorexics can die in the bosom of a caring family.

Meanwhile, to look at the dilemma in another way, the authors say that forcing her weight up risks moving the moderately low-weight anorexic to a position that can be medically more hazardous because of the complications of bingeing and vomiting, and where, because of the nature of her experiences when she is using these strategies, the chance of her dying can be doubled. Allowing her to continue to be her 'controlling self' is safer temporarily. But because of the whirlpool that starvation creates, the natural progression is further emaciation. The authors caution that all too often the cost of solving one problem is to make the other problem worse.

Thus those who are looking on from the outside can feel as trapped by the condition as the sufferer is on the inside. Yet there is no reason why those concerned to help should respond solely to the problem of weight and exclude any consideration of the sufferer's sense of self, or why they should respond solely to her anorexic 'self' and exclude any consideration of weight. It is possible to nurture a new sense of self whilst at the same time enabling the slow relaxation of dependence on food control. It is possible for an informed and sympathetic helper to encourage gradual weight gain in a way that is not a total assault on her person.

Behavioural therapy. There has been a continuing interest in the implementation of behavioural methods in the treatment of anorexia nervosa.

A wide range of behavioural interventions has been used:

- operant conditioning;
- systematic desensitization;
- social skills training;
- response prevention/exposure.

(a) *Operant methods.* A plethora of investigations has evaluated the application of operant conditioning procedures aimed at rapid weight restoration. They have provided some of the most careful treatment–outcome studies on large numbers of persons suffering from anorexia nervosa. The marked success seen in the first patient treated with operant conditioning procedures (Bachrach, Erwin and Mohr, 1965) has been documented by pictures in numerous abnormal-psychology textbooks. The patient weighed 47 pounds on hospital admission and 85 pounds two years later. However, a 16-year follow-up pointed to a markedly less favourable long-term outcome. Mrs A's weight at follow-up had declined to 55 pounds, only eight pounds higher than her pretreatment weight 16 years previously. It was reported, however, that there had been an enhancement in her social activities, and the ability to care for herself and her mother was considered her greatest sustained advance.

Leon (1979) and Bemis (1987) have provided reviews of the efficacy of a range of treatment methods used with anorexics. The behaviour therapy outcome studies initially seemed quite promising. The primary focus of these particular programmes was on the modification of anorexic eating patterns and on the reinforcement of eating larger quantities of food (e.g. Bhanji and Thompson, 1974; Halmi, Powers and Cunningham, 1975). Typically, a patient would be given material rewards or social privileges such as time out of his/her room, access to television, or visitors, based on daily weight or food consumption. However, the relative effectiveness of these particular procedures is blurred because other interventions, such as psychoactive medication in the former study and family involvement during the maintenance period in the latter study, were added to the behavioural programme. Several researchers (see review by Harris and Phelps, 1987) suggest that behavioural interventions aimed solely at weight restoration are not particularly effective in the longer term. (The caveats of Duker and Slade on p. 274 are particularly pertinent here!)

A further blow to the claim of the greater efficacy of behavioural pro-grammes is the result of a collaborative multicentre treatment study in which 40 anorexic patients completing a 35-day behaviour-modification therapy regimen were compared with 40 patients receiving milieu ther-apy (Eckert *et al.*, 1979). There were no significant differences in weight gain between the two groups at the end of treatment. No follow-up data were presented so it is not possible to evaluate the treatment effect at a later time.

The issue of choice of target behaviours has been critically reviewed by Bemis (1987) and Garfinkel (1985). Most contemporary operant programmes emphasize positive reinforcers and incentives rather than negative sanctions. Short-term gains may be made more durable by inter-ventions that address issues such as interpersonal problem-solving and concepts/dynamics of self-esteem (e.g. cognitive-restructuring; conversa-tional therapy).

Despite the criticism by Bruch (1978) and others of the dangers of using strict behaviour modification with anorexics, Garfinkel and Garner 1982) reported that patients treated with behaviour modification procedures did not show negative effects at follow-up, in comparison with patients treated with somatic or other types of treatment.

(b) *Systematic desensitization.* Systematic desensitization has been used to mitigate the anorexic individual's extreme fear of obesity (e.g. Ollendick, 1979b). Ollendick combines systematic desensitization with cognitive restructuring. This is our cue to look at the cognitive element in behav-ioural work.

(c) *Cognitive–Behavioural methods.* Cognitive behaviour therapy is con-ducted within the context of a trusting therapeutic relationship that also includes efforts at nutritional rehabilitation and education about eating disorders. Hospitalization may also be required, depending on the anorexic person's weight. Garner (1986) described a cognitive–behav-ioural treatment model focused on modifying faulty thinking patterns about body weight, food, and eating and its effects. The methods advo-cated by Garner and Bemis (1985) emphasize teaching the patient to examine the validity of his or her beliefs on a here-and-now basis; looking at such distortion of thinking as selective abstraction, over-generalization, magnification, dichotomous thinking, personalization and superstitious beliefs. A variety of cognitive–behavioural techniques are used to remedy cognitive distortions and also to enhance self-esteem.

(d) *Social skills.* Pillay and Crisp (1981) attempted to improve inter-personal competence in eating-disordered individuals; the results were disappointing.

Outcome and Prognosis

- Weight is restored in approximately 60% of anorexic patients (studies display a wide range in such figures).
- Normal eating behaviour is restored in about 44% of cases.
- Normal menstruation returns, on average, in about 55% of cases.

The issue of favourable/unfavourable prognostic predictors remains controversial and uncertain.

Summary

Except for operant conditioning programmes and some drug studies, very few outcome data exist that allow one to evaluate and compare the relative efficacy of different treatment procedures. There is a significant need for controlled trial outcome studies that systematically evaluate various individual treatment programmes or combinations of treatment programmes. Further, it is important to study carefully both short-term and long-term treatment effects through the use of a range of outcome criteria. The long-term maintenance of weight change is crucial to the ultimate success of any treatment programme.

It certainly seems the case that a broad-based (e.g. cognitive–behavioural) approach to treatment of anorexia is more likely to produce positive outcomes than a 'single-intervention' strategy.

Bulimia Nervosa

This term was introduced by Russell in 1979 to describe a variant of anorexia nervosa. This syndrome has been referred to variously as bulimarexia, binge–purge syndrome and dietary chaos syndrome. It is characterized by:

- frequent episodes of uncontrolled binge eating;
- self-induced vomiting and/or purging by means of laxatives and/or by fasting, and/or the use of appetite suppressant drugs following the binges;
- a marked fear of becoming fat (a determination to keep weight below a self-imposed threshold).

During eating binges, a person may ingest huge quantities of food in a very short time (between 1500 and 15 000 calories in a single binge according to Barrios and Pennebaker, 1983). The frequency varies from several times a day to once a week.

Similarities common to both conditions are:

- an extreme concern with body weight;
- a fear of becoming obese.

Differences are as follows:

- Bulimic individuals display a considerable fluctuation between gaining and losing weight; anorexic patients are characterized only by extreme, life-threatening weight loss.
- They tend to be heavier (the majority are of normal weight for their height); more sexually active, and more likely to have a continuation of menstruation, although irregularities are quite common.
- They exhibit more drug and alcohol dependency, suicidal ideation, affective reactivity, lability, impulsiveness, anxiety, depression.
- They display more social and sexual sophistication.

Assessment

Because the weight of most bulimic individuals is within normal levels there is *no* direct clinical sign of the disorder. A large number of sufferers remain undetected. Medical complications brought about by frequent purging may lead to the discovery of the eating disorder. (Physical examinations are critical when the condition comes to light!)

Prevalence

It is not surprising, in the light of what has just been said, that it is very difficult to determine accurately the prevalence of bulimia nervosa. Sufferers tend to be very secretive and social eating tends to be carefully controlled and appropriate. The prevalence rate among adolescents and young adult women is estimated to be about 1% (Fairburn and Beglin, 1990) but this could be an underestimate. One estimate was as high as 13%. It is more common than anorexia nervosa in the general (non-clinical) population. It is somewhat rare in males. The peak onset of the disorder is around 19 years of age; it rarely occurs after 30 years of age. The highest prevalence estimates have been found in samples of college students.

Causation

The causes of bulimia nervosa are still unclear. It shares, however, many aspects of the models of aetiology applied to anorexia nervosa and described earlier: viz. individual, familial, sociocultural and biological influences. The behavioural formulation is a negative reinforcement paradigm:

- Urges to eat result in a fear of gaining weight.
- They produce concurrent feelings of anxiety.
- Food refusal and/or purging are strengthened because
  — they decrease the likelihood of weight gain;
  — they minimize subjective feelings of anxiety.
- As this pattern continues, maladaptive eating behaviours generalize and are used to alleviate anxiety arising from sources other than a fear of weight gain.
- The problematic eating patterns are further reinforced by secondary gains (e.g. attention, ability to control/manipulate others).

Steinhausen (1994) describes the main features as follows.

> The vicious cycle in bulimic patients is perhaps even more pronounced than in patients with anorexia nervosa. Due to their low self-esteem and affective instability, the bulimic behaviour of these patients serves to secure emotional stability and conformity with external standards for weight and shape. However, the resulting psychological changes—which include fatigue, irritability and depression—and the physical effects in terms of malnutrition lead again to binge-eating behaviour, which in turn induces active instability.

Treatment

Treatment approaches to bulimia have included group therapy (eg. Boskind-Lodahl and White, 1978; White and Boskind-Lodahl, 1981) and behaviour therapy interventions (Fairburn, 1980, 1981; Linden, 1980; Turner *et al.*, 1979). Each of these approaches to treatment included differing elements and results indicated that they were effective, although the effectiveness was based to varying degrees on individual patient differences. Those bulimic individuals exhibiting the most severe symptoms over a longer period of time are the most difficult to treat.

The vast majority of studies have been of cognitive–behavioural treatments which have been shown to be effective with little relapse after improvement (see review by Mizes, 1995). In general, patients reduce their frequency of bingeing and purging by 75–80%, with 30–40% ceasing to binge and purge altogether. Sadly, there is a high attrition rate, with some 25–30% dropping out of treatment.

Two examples of interventions are:

Linden (1980) who used a multifaceted intervention including response delay, stimulus control and assertiveness training and produced a marked improvement in a bulimic patient's eating behaviour. Rosen and Leitenberg (1982) also produced improvements in eating behaviour, self-esteem, depression and mood lability by using exposure plus response prevention. These behavioural methods are described and reviewed by Steinhausen (1994).

The Seriously Ill Child

Every year approximately 15 000 deaths of children and young people under 20 years of age occur. Davis (1993) describes how parents are profoundly affected by illness in their children, with as many as 33% of parents of children with cancer, even in remission, having such severe depression and anxiety that they require professional help. In a study conducted by Davis and one of his students, 31% of mothers of children with diabetes were found to have stress levels that would have benefited from a professional mental health intervention.

Communication and relationship problems are reflected in increased marital distress, sometimes ending in divorce. There is evidence of increased disturbance in siblings, including irritability, social withdrawal, jealousy and guilt, academic under-achievement, behaviour problems, anxiety and low self-esteem. A major problem is the disturbance of the other children's social relationships, especially with their parents. They tend to feel neglected in comparison with the sick child.

It is plain to see that the social context—'the family unit'—cannot be overlooked in one's rightful concern about, and priority-giving to, the ill or dying child.

The parents

A diagnosis of serious (perhaps terminal) illness requires a huge adjustment in parents' thinking about their child, and this is a process which arouses fear and anxiety. Uncertainty prevails; parents cannot anticipate what will happen. The days, months and years that were taken for granted can no longer be counted on. Children also have to adapt to the disease, cope with the dawning awareness of death, and somehow come to terms with it.

Parents will need to overcome their own difficulties to nurture and communicate openly with the child. Davis believes that the skills of doing this are essentially similar to those used by professionals to communicate with parents so it becomes appropriate that professionals should explicitly share these skills with parents where necessary.

In order to be able to talk to children about death and to answer their questions, health professionals should be aware of how much the child understands about the concept of death itself.

DEVELOPMENT OF THE CONCEPT OF DEATH

The way in which children make sense of (or fail to comprehend) death and grief is related to their cognitive, emotional and physical stages of development. The information below is based on empirical studies; remember that it is based upon generalizations to which there are exceptions, especially with regard to differences in life-experience and individual differences in the rate of development.

Children under Four Years of Age

Cognitive factors

(a) The 'preconceptual stage' of cognitive development lasts from about two to four years of age (Piaget, 1954). At this stage children's concepts are not fully formed. They do not, for example, understand the permanence of death. A source of worry to the child is the misinterpretation of causality. The immature kind of thinking called 'psychological causality' refers to the tendency in young children to attribute a *psychological motive* as the cause of events. For example, children may think that a parent has gone to hospital because he or she is angry with them, rather than due to illness.

Children Aged Five to Ten Years of Age

Cognitive factors

- The *intuitive* stage of thinking (4–7 years) moves children on from the preconceptual stage (2–4) mentioned earlier, and they develop the ability to classify, order and quantify things, but they are still unaware of the principles which underlie these abilities. It is only in the next stage of *concrete operations* (7 plus) that these principles become more explicit, so that children can explain their logical reasoning in a satisfactory way.
- Before six or seven, children often attribute life to inanimate objects.
- It is between the age of seven and nine that there appears to be a nodal point in children's development of concepts about life and death. By about seven most children have a fairly clear idea of 'life' and a more or less complete concept of 'death'. It shouldn't be forgotten that many 5-year-olds have a fairly full concept.
- When children are about eight or nine they realize that dying can apply to themselves.

Kane (1979) describes the child's understanding of death between the ages of five and ten in terms of the components he or she is cognitively capable of comprehending, as follows:

- *Separation* (understood by most five-year-olds). Young children can be very aware that death means separation from their parents, friends or brothers and sisters. This may be the main concept they focus on, and they may be concerned that they will feel lonely or that their parents will be lonely without them.
- *Immobility* (understood by most five-year-olds). The awareness that dead people cannot move can concern some children who are not also aware that dead people cannot feel, see or hear.
- *Irrevocability* (understood by most six-year-olds). The fact that once people die they cannot come back to life again is essential in understanding death. Many children younger than five or six may not realise the finality of the process. Children play games at being shot and dying, but then leap to life the next minute. 'Pretend' death and 'real' death need to be made clear, so that the child realizes that 'real' death means never living again.
- *Causality* (understood by most six-year-olds). There is always a physical cause of death. Young children, however, often have unusual or 'magical' ideas about what causes death. For example, a nasty wish, saying something horrible or being naughty can sometimes be perceived as having caused illness or death. Children need to understand that it is not such imagined events that cause death, but that something is wrong with the body which is causing people to die.

DAWNING AWARENESS OF DEATH

Stages in the concept of illness that contribute to an awareness of death have been outlined as follows (see Clunies-Ross and Lansdown, 1988).

- Stage 1: I am very ill.
- Stage 2: I have an illness that can kill people.
- Stage 3: I have an illness that can kill children.
- Stage 4: I may not get better.
- Stage 5: I am dying.

The difficulty with assessing children's knowledge of the concept of death is the dependence on verbal expression. Children are not 'blind' to non-verbal signals, tones of voice, and 'special' expressions from staff and family. They notice their parents showing extreme worry and sadness, hear their ambiguous, guarded, stilted conversations, and they wish to know what is happening. Children often choose a particular person whom they want to talk to about death and dying. Although some children may not ask questions, it does not necessarily mean they are not preoccupied with concerns about death. After all, they may see the deaths of other children on the ward, or they may know of other children with the same illness where it proved to be fatal.

Whose rights should be given priority—the parents' or the child's? The parents may be unable to face the reality that their child is dying and so will not talk about it, even though the nearness of the end is clearcut. The generally held view at present is that parents' wishes should be respected as to whether the child should be told that he or she is dying. Health care professionals are likely to seek permission from parents who are reluctant to talk about these issues, or try to encourage them to talk with the child themselves; it is an emotionally fraught situation for everyone concerned when parents refuse to talk openly with their dying child, especially when he or she is asking for information or reassurance.

Points to Raise with Parents

- *The role of parents as models.* Parents are important as role models in determining the child's response to illness and death. If they can cope with courage and outer calmness, the child is likely to be better able to cope. For some children their particular concern is how their illness and death will affect their parents.
- *Resilience in the face of bad news.* A dying child is often far better able to cope with the information of their death than their parents are. Many children are resilient in the face of stress of all kinds.
- *Children have rights.* The question of whether they need to know the truth (that is, whether it is in their best interests) should be considered very carefully. Advocacy for the child is one of the professional's functions.

Impending Death (see Douglas, 1993)

Once hospital staff and family have accepted that the end is near, preparations and decisions can be made about how to best care for the child and family. If treatment has come to an end and the issue of death has not yet been raised by the child, it will be necessary to discuss with the parents how to raise it. Some children may not have even thought of it, while others may be fully aware. As death draws nearer, the child and the parents need to have the opportunity to say goodbye and to complete any final tasks. The child may want to return home for a last time to say goodbye to their house and pets, or they may request that certain toys and possessions be brought to the hospital. The extended family may want to say goodbye. The child may wish to write a letter or draw a special picture for friends or classmates to be remembered by, or to remember them by. It is important to ask the child if there is anything they feel they still need to do, and whether they have any special requests or need any special help.

When the child dies, health professionals should check with the parents whether they prefer company or privacy while with their child. Parents might be encouraged to touch the dead child and cuddle the body if they want to. It is essential at this stage for parents to feel that they have time with their child, without being rushed or feeling that they are inconveniencing staff. Families need to be told that siblings might wish to see the dead child, as sometimes their feelings are overlooked. It can help the process of grieving if everyone has a chance to say goodbye, and to say what they wish, to the dead child. Younger children may like to draw a goodbye card for their brother or sister.

Once arrangements have been made for the transfer of the child's body to the funeral directors, the parents go home, very much alone with their loss. This is often their last visit to the hospital, where they may have spent many months during the child's illness. Ward staff have been involved in the care of the child, and it is important to the families that nurses show concern after death as well as before it. The loss of contact with ward staff and the hospital itself can be an additional loss for the parents whose lives may have been totally occupied with visiting their ill child. Some hospitals have ward–home liaison teams which provide continued care in the community, supporting the family and community health care staff.

Siblings are sometimes overlooked when there is a bereavement in the family. Children are at risk of what I call a 'double jeopardy': the loss, not only of a sibling, but a temporary 'loss' of their grieving, preoccupied caregiver(s). They may feel rejected and abandoned, and grandparents' care and solidity at such times (and, indeed, that of older siblings and other relatives) may be crucial, and therefore should not be forgotten in your work with bereaved parents. Given the vital importance of children's emotional attachments to the family, the loss of a sibling is a particularly poignant experience.

BEREAVEMENT

We need a good knowledge base about the nature and development of children's grief if we are to be effective in counselling bereaved children and their parents (these matters are dealt with in Davis (1993) and Douglas (1993).

To help families come to terms with the death you need to help them:

- to accept the loss;
- to express their feelings/emotions;
- to accept their feelings as normal;
- to live without the loved one;
- to deal with 'tasks' that families have to get on with in life;
- to clarify distortions and misconceptions;
- to cope with family changes;

You will also need to: help the sibling to cope and understand the surviving parents' grief; help the parents to cope and understand the child's grief; and encourage 'healing family tasks'. This implies:

- a shared knowledge of the reality of death and shared experience of loss; and,
- reorganization of the family system and reinvestment in other relationships and life pursuits.

Encourage the parents and surviving children to communicate with each other. Explore, using conversation, play, drawing, genograms and stories, how siblings who are bereaved are thinking, feeling and coping. This will tell you the 'coping tasks' they are working on. We need to look sensitively at the 'stories' they are telling themselves about why their brother or sister died.

Most bereaved persons are feeling somewhat 'better' at the end of the first year following the loss, but the child's grieving process generally takes approximately two years in all, as for adults. Of course, this does not preclude the return of the pain of sadness and yearning, especially at anniversary and holiday times, nor the wide range of individual differences in the expression of grief.

Part IV ANTISOCIAL DISRUPTIVE BEHAVIOUR DISORDERS

There is a mounting tide of public concern about violence and disruptive behaviour in homes, classrooms and on the streets. Accounts in the media of violence at school (bullying and blackmail of peers, attacks on teachers), the flouting (or lack) of authority at home, not to forget vandalism and hooliganism on the streets, sound a note of hysteria and moral panic. A glance through old newspaper archives may reassure us that there is nothing new about such phenomena, but will not appease the apocalyptic school of thought which detects a feral quality in the sheer mindlessness of much contemporary antisocial behaviour.

A representative of this pessimistic viewpoint is Patricia Morgan (Morgan, 1975) who paints a sombre picture of growing numbers of poorly socialized individuals who have scarcely acquired the rudiments of human culture. As she puts it:

> The most alarming aspect is probably the sharp increase in crime, violence and aimless destruction of all kinds, with larger proportionate increases as one goes down the age scale. Also much crime, often of a highly dangerous and serious nature, is committed by those well under the age of criminal responsibility . . . Actually, to use the expression 'crime' for much modern anti-social behaviour is rather misleading, since it has no end beyond the most transitory titillation. The delinquent is frequently far too unsocialized to control his pursuit of instant excitement for rational gain.

The prevalence of disruptive behavioural disorders is increasing, creating a need for services that far exceeds available resources and personnel (Hobbs, 1982; Knitzer, 1982). Worse still, children with less serious difficulties are more likely to receive the scarce resources of therapy than those with the more extreme disorders (Herbert, 1994a; Kazdin, 1988). The consequences of a mismatch between the need for help for children with the more serious disorders and the available provision are serious enough in the short term: one thinks of the distress that goes unalleviated for so many young people. But there is another concern: the possibility (especially for the subcategory of conduct disorders with their grave prognosis) of blighted futures over the longer term; these 'aggressive', antisocial children are at increased risk of being rejected by their peers. They are also at risk of developing problems later in life such as truancy, alcoholism, drug abuse, juvenile delinquency, adult crime and interpersonal problems (see Robins, 1981; Robins and Price, 1991). In the absence of early treatment the long-term outlook for children with conduct disorders is particularly grave, thus a large percentage remain circulating through the revolving door of the social services, mental health agencies and criminal justice systems. Their scholastic underachievement and failure have debilitating short-term and long-term consequences—notably (in the latter case) in high rates of unemployment and dependency on state support (Sturge, 1982). Parents (particularly mothers) are quite likely to manifest stress-related disorders such as anxiety states, depression and psychophysiological disorders (Brody & Forehand, 1986; Webster-Stratton & Hammond, 1988).

Clearly, there is an urgent need to develop and evaluate standardized programmes which can be widely available for purposes of remediation and prevention (see Taylor and Biglan, 1998).

Disruptive behaviour disorder in the DSM-III-R is something of a diagnostic ragbag; it includes the following:

(a) oppositional defiant behaviour;
(b) conduct disorder;
(c) attention-deficit hyperactivity disorder (ADHD).

Between one-half and two-thirds of all children and adolescents referred to mental health services are assessed as having *disruptive behaviour disorders* (Herbert, 1987a; Kazdin, 1987a,b). Their management thus constitutes an important part of the psychologist's therapeutic armamentarium—the subject matter of Chapters 11 and 12.

Chapter 11

CONDUCT DISORDERS

The terms 'oppositional behaviour' and 'conduct disorder' can be distinguished: the former is characterized primarily by obstreperous disobedience, while the latter is characterized by physical aggression and serious flouting of conventions and social norms. In practice, a younger child is more likely to be referred to as oppositional, though this problem can occur in late childhood and adolescence as well (American Psychiatric Association, 1980). Oppositional problems were dealt with in a developmental context in Chapter 5.

Conduct disorders of childhood and adolescence entail far too many diverse problems, not to mention a long and eventful developmental timespan, for any one chapter to cover fully (see Kazdin, 1987a, b). In the USA a majority of all young children who are referred to mental health agencies are eventually classified as antisocial, oppositional, or conduct disordered. These problems (as we have seen) are on the increase and demand for help outstrips available personnel and resources (President's Commission on Mental Health 1978).

ASSESSMENT

As with the generic term 'disruptive behaviour' any definition of conduct disorder must involve a consideration of the social and subjective judgements that lead to a child being assessed in this way. This is an important caveat given the attempts that have been made to treat the label as a precise diagnostic category.

In the tenth edition of the 'International Classification of Disease' (ICD-10) (World Health Organization, 1988) conduct disorders are defined as 'repetitive and persistent patterns of antisocial, aggressive or defiant conduct. Such behaviour, when at its most extreme for the individual, should amount to major violations of age-appropriate social expectation, and is therefore more severe than ordinary child's mischief or adolescent rebelliousness' (p. 163). In DSM-III-R (code 312xx) conduct disorders are characterized as a 'persistent pattern of conduct in which the basic rights of others and major age-appropriate social norms or rules are violated. The behaviour pattern typically is present in the home, at school, with peers, and in the community.'

There is an impressive consensus among studies of childhood problem behaviours using multivariate statistical methods (Collins, Maxwell, and Cameron, 1962) about the reality of the constellation of problems involving physical and verbal aggressiveness, disruptiveness, irresponsibility, non-compliance, and poor interpersonal relationships. This behaviour pattern has been referred to by many names other than conduct disorders. Some of the synonyms in use are 'acting-out', 'externalizing', 'anti-social aggressive', 'unsocialized aggressive reaction', and 'outward' behaviour problems. They all point to a directional and dichotomous concept of maladaptive responses—those directed towards or (in the case of personality problems) away from the child's environment. What is impressive is that the behaviour clusters suggesting a bipolar dimension of excess approach behaviour (aggression) and excess avoidance behaviour (inhibition/withdrawal) have emerged in several empirical studies carried out in different countries on children in a variety of schools, child guidance clinics, and residential institutions (Collins, Maxwell and Cameron, 1962; Dreger, 1982; Quay, 1985; Herbert, 1987b, 1989a; Webster-Stratton and Herbert, 1993, 1994).

Certainly, parents with children manifesting conduct disorders often state that professionals simply do not understand their predicament. A major gap in the literature (and our knowledge base) is what it feels like from the parents' point of view to cope with a child's conduct disorder, and to manage the stresses within the family system and their relationships with outside individuals and agencies.

THE CHILD'S PROFILE

An extensive qualitative analysis by Webster-Stratton of what parents say about these matters (see Webster-Stratton and Herbert, 1994) has begun to address this issue. When asked to name the dominant characteristics of their child's misbehaviour parents specified *aggression* towards various victims (parents, animals, other children, siblings). The overall impression conveyed by parents was one of the child being a tyrant in the family, also a 'Jekyll and Hyde': at times highly destructive and defiant, and at other times loving, to parents. Parents often recounted incidents in which their children had been destructive to the house or household objects. It was the unpredictability and volatility of the negative behaviours—and their tendency to escalate—that caused parents so much distress. They had to be unceasingly vigilant as behaviour problems might occur at any time, in any place or in any situation.

Such repeated episodes of verbal and physical aggression towards other children led to their rejection and ridicule by others—adults and children. This was a key element in the tension between parents of children with conduct disorders and parents of 'normal' children, contributing to their own feelings of humiliation, rejection and isolation. Children's invariable refusal to comply with parental requests compounded the misery; they seemed to control not only the parents but the entire family by virtue of the power they commanded through their wilful resistance. Many of the parents described their children as overactive, easily 'wound up', excitable, loud, wild and out-of-control—characteristics that tended to show up early on in life. Moreover, their children had trouble listening and concentrating even for brief periods of time. The children's activity level could be so frenetic at times as to make their safety and their survival a major parenting issue. Parents expressed concern about their child's inability to learn from experience. They would see their child suffer the negative consequences of a particular action, yet repeat the same self-defeating behaviours within a short time.

It is evident from the parents' descriptions that their children are not only unreinforcing towards their child-rearing efforts but actually physically and emotionally punishing (Webster-Stratton and Herbert, 1994). Of course, trying to disentangle coercive interactions in families gives rise to the age-old chicken/egg conundrum. Whatever the origins of the conduct disorders (and they are many sided), Grusec and Mammone (1995) make the point that, by and large, the attempts to predict parenting behaviour and child outcomes from parents' general attitudes about child rearing, have been disappointing.

The most common complaints from parents and teachers about the children who present as conduct problems tend to be as follows: 'He acts first and thinks (if he ever thinks) afterwards'. 'He doesn't seem to know right from wrong', 'He never listens', 'He is so selfish: he never thinks of anyone but himself'. The theme that underlies these complaints about lack of self-control, dishonesty, disobedience, and self-centredness is, first of all, uncompromisingly non-compliant behaviour, and beyond that a defiance (or lack of appreciation) of rules. These children, in the short and/or long term do not obey adult requests, commands, and prohibitions. This is what makes conduct-disordered children so disturbing to parents and teachers and others who have to care for them. Obedience of rules—whether they are prescribed by convention, codified in laws, or internalized in what we call our consciences—is a prerequisite for social living.

Lefkowitz *et al.* (1977) followed a group of New York children from the age of 8 to age 19 years, the study having a particular focus on the persistence of aggression. Aggression was much less common in girls than in boys but in both sexes children who were highly aggressive at age 8 years tended also to be unduly aggressive at 19 years (correlations of 0.38 for boys and 0.47 for girls). In West and Farrington's study of London boys, substantial continuity was again evident (West and Farrington, 1973). Of the youths rated most aggressive at 8 to 10 years, 50% were in the most aggressive group at 12 to 14 years (compared with 19% of the remaining boys) and 40% were so at 16 to 18 years (compared with 27% of the remainder). The boys who were severely aggressive at 8 to 10 years were especially likely to become violent delinquents (14% vs 4.5%).

The same study demonstrated the very considerable extent to which troublesome, difficult and aggressive behaviour in young boys was associated with later juvenile delinquency. Both the measure at age 8 to 10 years of 'combined conduct disorder', which was based on combined ratings of teachers and social workers, and that of 'troublesomeness' at the same age, which was a combined rating of peers and teachers, proved to be powerful predictors of delinquency. This was especially so with respect to severe and persistent delinquency going on into adult life. Some half of such individuals showed deviant ratings on these measures compared with only one-in-six of non-delinquent boys.

CAUSATION: A SOCIAL LEARNING PERSPECTIVE

The Coercion Hypothesis

This hypothesis formulated and tested, notably, by Patterson (1982) illuminates the manner in which children's noxious, antisocial behaviours can serve as punishment or negative reinforcement for the behaviour of other family members. The essential idea is that an aversive stimulus such as hitting, teasing or crying is applied contingently and repeatedly to increase or decrease certain behaviours displayed by the other member of a parent–child, sibling–sibling dyad. The impact of these aversive behaviours is reflected in changes in the ongoing behaviours of both members of the dyad involved in the coercive interchanges. Probably it is the immediate shift in the ongoing behaviour of one individual that is reinforcing for the other. Wahler and Dumas (1986), asking how coercive mother–child interactions are maintained and escalate, formulate two hypotheses to explain how some parent–child dyads ratchet up their aversive exchanges into progressively more 'painful', coercive interactions: the compliance hypothesis, and the predictability hypothesis. The compliance hypothesis proposes that the mother's caving in to her child's aversive behaviour acts as a positive reinforcer and therefore is a major influence for the maintenance of his kind of behaviour. She complies—gives in, gives way—to 'turn off' her child's temper tantrum, hitting, screaming, or whatever. The payoff—relief from painful stimuli, with its escape and avoidance implications—makes further compliance more and more likely (negative reinforcement). The predictability hypothesis suggests that aversive behaviour of conduct disordered children may be maintained by mother's consistent aversive reactions to it. Children know where they stand because reactions to their deviant behaviour is always punitive, whereas the response to their positive behaviour is extremely unpredictable; they never know what to expect—indifference, praise or punishment. For some youngsters, the predictable response seems preferable to the unpredictable.

Observations suggest that mothers and siblings are the most affected in these coercive spirals because their rates of noxious behaviour are significantly higher than those manifested by their counterparts in non-problem families (Patterson, 1982). He suggests that inspection of observational data suggests that such behaviours tend to come in bursts. For example, given the occurrence of one response, there tends to be a significant increase in the probability that the same response will recur or persist. Children who are described as highly aggressive are characterized by a longer duration of such behavioural bursts and also by shorter time intervals between these behavioural bursts. Comparing non-problem boys with socially aggressive children, the latter are more likely to come up with a second noxious response, having just presented one perhaps only a few seconds ago. To summarize: noxious behaviours tend to be exhibited by socially aggressive boys not only more frequently and with greater intensity than non-problem children, but such behaviours are likely to be emitted with fairly high probability in extended 'runs' of aversive behaviours.

Patterson (1982) lists the following possible reasons for children's failure to substitute more adaptive, more mature behaviours for their infantile and primitive coercive repertoire:

(i) The parents may neglect to condition pro-social skills (e.g. seldom reinforcing the use of language or other self-help skills).
(ii) They may provide rich schedules of positive reinforcement for coercive behaviours.
(iii) They may allow siblings to increase the frequency of aversive stimuli which are terminated when the target child uses coercive behaviours.

(iv) They may use punishment inconsistently for coercive behaviours, and/or

(v) They may use weak-conditioned punishers as consequences for coercion.

Previous Learning Experience

There is a confidently expressed consensus that aggressive behaviour in children can be related to broader (long-term) attitudes and child-rearing practices. To summarize the findings (see Herbert, 1987a,b,c), lax discipline (especially with regard to the offsprings' acts of aggression) combined with hostile attitudes in the parents produces very aggressive and poorly controlled behaviour in the offspring. Parents with hostile attitudes are mainly unaccepting and disapproving of children: they fail to give affection, understanding or explanations to children, and tend to use a lot of physical punishment, but not give reasons when they do exert their authority—something applied erratically and arbitrarily.

Punishment

The position taken by Patterson (1982)—and he qualifies it carefully—is that the control of antisocial behaviour requires the contingent use of some kind of punishment. This claim seems, on the surface at least, to run counter to the many studies from developmental psychology that investigated parental reports about their punitive practices. They consistently show a positive correlation with antisocial child behaviour (Feshbach, 1970). Parents of problem children report that they use punishment *more frequently* than parents of normal children; also their punitive practices are more likely to be extreme. As we have seen in this chapter, the parents of socially aggressive children do punish more often in reaction to sibling and problem child aggressive behaviour.

The *modelling–frustration hypothesis* is formulated by Bandura (1973). He maintains that in exercising punitive control, prohibitive agents model aggressive styles of behaviour not unlike those they wish to discourage in others. Recipients may, on later occasions, adopt similar aggressive solutions in coping with the problems confronting them. He adds that although the direction of causal relationships cannot be unequivocally established from correlational data, it is clear from controlled studies that aggressive modelling breeds aggression. Here then is the seedcorn for intergenerational violence, but why does aggressive behaviour that is punished not diminish or disappear, as would be predicted from learning theory?

Berkowitz (1993) emphasizes the likelihood that it is the *kind of punishment* used by parents of aggressive children that may be ineffective. He makes a case for the necessity of punishing aggressive child behaviours, but in the context of being a warm, loving parent, who uses reasoning or explanations in conjunction with *non-violent punishment*, such as time out. This view reflects the Patterson team's conclusion from a decade of intervention studies with families of aggressive children. Time out and analogous consequences (such as work details or loss of privileges) are definitely aversive; however, they are *not* violent. Patterson vouches for their relative effectiveness—a matter we return to.

Modifying self-perceptions/reinforcers

Given the low self-esteem and underachievement commonly found in aggressive, conduct disordered youngsters, it is worth bearing in mind as potent sources of reinforcement for aggressive behaviour—the aggressors themselves. To some extent, children regulate their actions by self-produced consequences. They tend to repeat behaviour which has given them feelings of satisfaction and worth. Conversely, they tend to refrain from behaviour that produces self-criticism or other forms of self-devaluation. Irrational beliefs about oneself may be acquired through the remarks and teaching of other people.

INTERVENTIONS

There have been many attempts over more than 30 years to mitigate conduct problems using different approaches in a variety of settings: in clinics (e.g. individual and group psychotherapy); within institutions (places of incarceration); in community social programmes (e.g. group homes); in home settings; in prevention projects (e.g. community diversion programmes). Sadly, much of this work has met with limited success in reducing adolescent conduct problems (e.g. Graziano and Mooney, 1984; Trojanowicz and Morash, 1992); many promising-looking results are compromised by research designs which were inadequate for evaluating treatment-specific outcomes. At the offender end of the conduct disorders there is a bewildering contrast of views as to whether rehabilitation is possible. Views range from the pessimistic 'nothing works' (Martinson, 1974) to the optimistic 'treatment can be successful' (Gendreau and Ross, 1987; Ross and Gendreau, 1980).

A growing number of practitioners acknowledge the significance of the cognitive representation of events and experiences in the development of the conduct disorders and other antisocial manifestations (e.g. delinquent activities) of children and adolescents. The view taken by cognitive theorists of their uncontrolled, rebellious and aggressive behaviour is that they are characterized by a range of social–cognitive distortions and ineffectual problem-solving skills (e.g. Bright and Robin, 1981; Hollin, 1990; Kazdin, 1987a, b, 1994; Kendall, 1993; Kendall and Hollon, 1994; Lochman et al., 1984; Powell and Oei, 1991). Adolescents with conduct disorders tend to:

- have difficulty anticipating consequences of their behaviour;
- recall high rates of hostile cues present in social stimuli;
- attend to fear cues when interpreting the meaning of others' behaviour;
- attribute others' behaviour in ambiguous situations to their hostile intentions;
- under-perceive their own level of aggressiveness;
- under-perceive their responsibility for early stages of dyadic conflict;
- generate few verbal assertion solutions to social problems;
- generate impulsively more action-oriented and aggressive solutions without stopping to think of non-aggressive solutions.

They appear to be hypervigilant in scanning their social environment for hostile cues which encourage them to respond in a non-verbal, action-orientated manner. An aggressive adolescent is likely to believe that aggression will enhance his or her self-esteem, create a positive image, but not cause suffering to the victims (Slaby and Guerra, 1988). Lochman (1992) has shown how adolescent boys' aggressive solutions to problems involve little or no bargaining.

Therapeutic Goals

As aggression and poor control are among their foremost problems, the focus might be:

- attributional processes (e.g. misinterpreting others' intentions);
- cognitive distortions (e.g. their aggression does not have injurious consequences);
- negotiating conflict situations;
- labelling affect appropriately;
- social skills deficits;
- general problem-solving strategies.

Given the nature of the problems and the intimate relationship of cognitive–behavioural therapy and social learning theory, there is a strong focus on social influence, social cognitions and relationships (Bandura, 1977; Herbert, 1987b, 1998c; Webster-Stratton and Herbert, 1994).

INDIVIDUAL PROGRAMMES

Self-instruction Training

'Self-statements', or 'self-talk' are perceived by the individual as plausible and logically related to the situation at hand. For example, a child exhibiting intense aversion to social evaluation might think, 'If I make a mistake, the teacher and the other kids might think I'm stupid, everyone says so anyway.' These self-statements underpin cognitive functions such as self-instruction, self-control, self-evaluation and self-reinforcement. The modification of self-statements to achieve *self-control* through self-instruction training has been attempted successfully with hyperactive aggressive boys (also using modelling) by Goodwin and Mahoney (1975) and with aggressive young offenders by Snyder and White (1979).

Role- and Perspective-Taking

Chandler (1973) described a programme designed to encourage male young offenders to see themselves from the perspective of other people and so to develop their own role-taking abilities. The study was a clear clinical success, enhancing the young offenders role-taking skills in a manner that enhanced pro-social behaviour. A similarly successful programme in social perspective-taking skills, carried out with female delinquents, has been reported by Chalmers and Townsend (1990).

Problem-Solving Skill Training (PSST)

Problem-solving training with children and adolescents suffering from conduct problems has been implemented in schools, clinics, day treatment and in-patient hospital settings (see Kendall and Braswell, 1993). Deficits in cognitive problem-solving processing abilities which mediate social interaction may reduce a young person's interpersonal effectiveness. Research has indicated that when presented with interpersonal problem situations, rejected children, those with conduct disorders, find it difficult to consider alternative courses of action.

Social Skills Training (SST)

Social skills training has had a number of aims: to encourage related problem-solving skills, to reduce delinquent behaviour, to improve specific skills such as interview skills, and to increase the effectiveness of penal staff–delinquent interaction.

There is a fairly considerable literature on social skills training (SST) with young offenders and pre-delinquent youths (Herbert, 1986; Hollin, 1990; Spence and Marzillier, 1981). Henderson and Hollin (1983) critically reviewed 15 studies on social skills training with young offenders and concluded that both practitioners and administrators need to recognize the limitations of the technique; it cannot cure the 'causes of crime' and it is naive to assume it can. SST techniques may have a role to play for some aspects of young offenders' development, but considerable experimental investigation is required before any unqualified faith in, or firm commitments for, the intervention can be made.

MULTIMODAL (COMBINED TREATMENT) PROGRAMMES

The rationale of multimodal programmes is the inclusion of several therapeutic strategies to address the many-sided problems that are manifested in adolescents with conduct problems. These include:

(1) dysfunctional parent–child relationships;
(2) verbal abuse;
(3) parenting skills deficits;
(4) intra-familial communications;
(5) negative self-talk;
(6) academic difficulties;
(7) coercive interactions of family members.

The Kendall and Braswell (1993) approach is a fairly typical multimodal programme which includes problem-solving, instructional training, behavioural contingencies, modelling, role-play, and training in the identification of feelings about oneself and others.

One of the most widely cited programmes in the literature is the Preparation through Responsive Education Programme (PREP) described in several publications in the late 1970s (see Burchard and Lane, 1982, for a review). Based in Maryland, USA, PREP was designed for pupils recommended to the programme because of academic, social and offending problems. PREP consisted of academic tutoring, social skills training and some family work. The outcome data, from over 600 pupils, showed that the programme had a significant impact on school discipline and academic performance. However, there was little indication that the programme had an effect on offending.

RESIDENTIAL TREATMENT

Not infrequently, children and adolescents with conduct/delinquent dis-orders are removed from their homes and are ostensibly exposed to treat-ment or rehabilitation programmes in a variety of residential settings. The success rates of what used to be called 'approved schools' in England dif-fer considerably one from the other: nevertheless, overall rates of success in the UK—based on a three-year period free from reconviction—reach no higher than 30–35% (Her Majesty's Stationery Office, 1972). One explanation for the failure of institutional programmes is a model of human deviance that places the main source of behavioural variance within the individual. The primary thrust of therapy is in changing the individual; the hope is that a change in behaviour in the institutional set-ting represents a fundamental change (e.g. in character formation, matu-rity, or self-discipline) which will therefore remain with the individual upon return to the community—no matter what its temptations, frustra-tions or other disadvantages. A more productive form of residential treat-ment—achievement place—is described in Herbert (1998b).

PARENT TRAINING

See Webster–Stratton (1991) for further reading on this topic.

As a reaction, in part, to the large numbers of conduct disordered chil-dren and the shortfall of professional personnel, agencies have looked increasingly to parent training. In a sense all parents are informal behav-iour modifiers; certainly all are in the business of changing behaviour by using homespun applications of 'learning theory'. They use various methods—rewarding, punishing, ignoring, time out and fines—familiar to behaviour modifiers to train, influence, and change the children in their care. The systematic investigation of parents and other caregivers as more formal, primary mediators of behavioural change began in the 1960s (e.g. Patterson, 1965; Wahler, 1969). Many of the studies of the fea-sibility and efficacy of using parents—particularly for conduct prob-lems—have appeared in the last ten years. Reviews (e.g., Herbert, 1994a; Dumas, 1989; Moreland et al., 1982) suggest that behavioural parent training is an effective intervention for conduct disordered children. A variety of methods have been used, either individually or in combina-tion, to teach parents contingency management and contracting, conflict resolution skills, parent–child interaction, and household organization. The methods include oral and written instructions, live and videotape modelling.

Today, there is less emphasis on the contingency management of specific target behaviours, and more on broad principles of child management, the interpersonal interactions of members of the family, the marital relationships (which are often poor in the parents of problematic children— e.g. Webster-Stratton, 1989)—and the perceived efficacy of parents—e.g. Bandura, 1987. What we are talking about is a *multimodal* treatment/training package. Examples of the use of these methods appear in Herbert and Wookey (1997) and Webster-Stratton and Herbert (1994).

Many of the problems dealt with in families with conduct disordered children are eminently capable of modification, even if the task is a difficult one (Moreland *et al.*, 1982). Parents of deviant children display a significantly greater proportion of commands and criticisms and high rates of threats, anger, nagging and negative consequences than parents of non-referred children (Delfini, Bernal and Rosen, 1976; Lobitz and Johnson, 1975). There is frequently a lack of contingent consequences among the distressed family members. The probability of receiving a positive, neutral or aversive consequence for coercive behaviour seems to be independent of the behaviour—a gross inconsistency. Indeed, there may be positive consequences for deviant behaviour and punishment for those rare prosocial actions (Patterson, 1977; Snyder and Brown, 1983). Patterson and Fleischman (1979) hypothesize that the disturbed social interactions among the members of the family induce powerful feelings of frustration, anger and helplessness (see Figure 13 for the coercive sequence).

Parent training programmes therefore emphasize methods designed to reduce confrontations and antagonistic interactions among the family members, to increase the effectiveness of positive interactions and moderate the intensity of parental punishment.

The need to train parents of non-compliant children to give clear instructions has been well documented in the literature (e.g. Roberts *et al.*, 1978). The focus has been on the content of what is said; and also the non-verbal aspects of instruction giving. In a study by Hudson and Blane (1985) eight clinic and eight non-clinic mother–child pairs were observed. The non-verbal elements of (i) distance from child, (ii) body orientation of mother, (iii) eye contact between mother and child, (iv) tone of voice, and (v) mother's orientation towards objects involved in the instruction, were all related to the rate of child compliance.

Patterson and his colleagues at the Oregon Research Institute have been a prolific source of ideas and data on the subject (*inter alia*) of children's conduct disorders, notably aggression and stealing. They have developed a treatment package that involves training parents (and teachers) in child management skills (Patterson *et al.*, 1975); also methods for addressing the

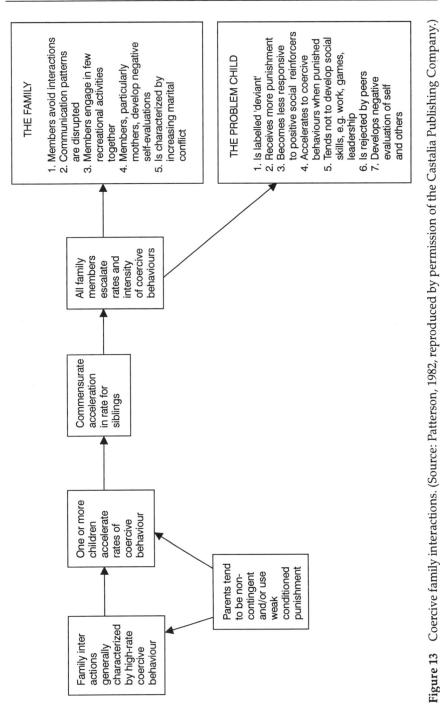

Figure 13   Coercive family interactions. (Source: Patterson, 1982, reproduced by permission of the Castalia Publishing Company.)

marital problems of parents. It is difficult to summarize such an extensive contribution, but it is worth reporting the team's results with 27 conduct disordered boys referred to them and accepted for treatment from January 1968 to June 1972. Training the families took an average of 31.5 hours of professional time. The treatment programme (parents read a semi-programmed text followed by a multiple choice test; staff teach parents to pinpoint problem areas and learn appropriate change techniques: home visits occur where necessary) lasted on average from three to four months. Most parents opted to work on reducing their children's non-compliance to requests, but overall a further 13 behaviours in the conduct disorder syndrome were also pinpointed for treatment.

With regard to criterion measures such as the targeted deviant behaviours of the boys, an average 60% reduction from baseline level to termination was achieved. In 75% of cases, reductions exceeded 30% from baseline levels. In six cases the rate of problematic behaviour deteriorated. On another criterion—total deviant scores—the 27 boys showed a reduction from higher than normal overall rates (scores computed for normal boys over 14 'problem areas') to within normal limits. According to parental daily reports there was a significant drop in the level of reported problems during follow-up (data were obtained here on 14 families only). About two-thirds of the families reported marked reductions in the problems for which they were originally referred. Follow-up data were obtained monthly for the first six months after termination of treatment, and every two months after that until a year after termination. Booster treatment programmes during follow-up took an average of 1.9 hours of professional time.

It was soon discovered that improvements at home did not generalize to school, so a separate but parallel package was prepared for use in classroom settings (Patterson, Cobb and Ray, 1972). Patterson (1975) found, as we have using the Child-Wise Parenting Skills Training Programme (Herbert and Wookey, 1997), that a substantial proportion of families (approximately one-third in his sample) requires much more in the way of intervention than child management skills: the parents need help with social problems, negotiation skills, depression, and resolving marital conflict. Despite the attractiveness (in earlier years) of a clinical intervention, which was clearly underpinned by assessments and formulations drawn from the learning theory canon, and the move towards working in the triadic model in which parents were trained to be 'therapists' for their own children, it soon became obvious that teaching behavioural principles to parents was not always sufficient to improve child behaviour. The narrower behavioural model which attributed child conduct problems solely to deficient parenting skills in the parents ignored other aspects of parents' functioning such as parental attitudes to child rearing, parental attributions and psychopathology, and also interpersonal (marital and sibling) relationships. Failures in treatment began to be associated with difficulties in these and other areas; social and cognitive factors were identified as moderating variables influencing the outcome of behavioural parent training. Consequently, conduct problems in children could no longer be conceptualized in such relatively simple terms as the child's response to maladaptive environmental contingencies. Rather, conduct problems needed to be viewed in a much wider systemic context in which many other aspects of family functioning have to be assessed.

In recent years the work of Carolyn Webster-Stratton (among others) has helped to identify active change-inducing ingredients of parent training programmes. For example Webster-Stratton, Kolpacoff and Hollinsworth (1989) carried out a programme based on therapist-led group discussion and videotape modelling (GDVM). They randomly assigned families with conduct-problem children to one of four conditions: an individually self-administered videotape modelling treatment (IVM), a group discussion videotape modelling treatment (GDVM), a group discussion treatment (GD), and a waiting-list control group (CON). Results immediately post-treatment suggested that all three treatment programmes resulted in significant parent–report and parent–child behavioural improvements compared with waiting-list control families. There were relatively few differences between the three treatment conditions, although the differences found consistently favoured the combined GDVM treatment. The results relative to the IVM treatment also suggested the potential power of parents to learn how to change their own behaviours, as well as their children's behaviours, from self-administered videotape programmes. However, it was unclear whether the IVM treatment programme that did not have skilled therapist feedback or group support would be able to sustain its effectiveness, whether the GDVM programme would be able to sustain its effectiveness or whether the GDVM programme would be able to maintain its superiority over the other two treatment approaches over time. In a further development Kolpacoff and Hollinsworth (1989) evaluated the long-term effectiveness of the three cost-effective parent training programmes for conduct-problem children. One year post-treatment, 93.1% of families (94 mothers and 60 fathers) were assessed on the basis of teacher and parent reports and home observations. Results indicated that all the significant improvements reported immediately post-treatment were maintained one year later. Moreover, approximately two thirds of the entire sample showed 'clinically significant' improvements. There were few differences between the three treatment conditions except for the 'consumer satisfaction' measure indicating that the treatment combining group discussion and videotape modelling was superior to treatments without both components.

While the *content* of such programmes is widely known and well researched, it is our contention (Webster-Stratton and Herbert, 1994) that it is not sufficient to bring about success with a substantial proportion of cases (see Schmaling and Jacobson, 1987). We have therefore attempted (Webster-Stratton and Herbert, 1994) to categorize the operations defining the therapeutic *processes* that arise from adopting a collaborative style with clients. These operations or strategies are classified by us in terms of knowledge, skills and values, and detailed later in Table 14.

Collaboration implies a non-blaming, supportive, reciprocal relationship based on using the therapists' knowledge and the parents' unique strengths and perspectives; it implies respect for each person's contribution. The Rogerian influence here is clear (Rogers, 1957); more recently collaboration in cognitive behavioural work has been emphasized by theorists such as Kendall (1993). In a collaborative relationship, the therapist works with the parents by actively soliciting their ideas and feelings, involving them in the joint process of setting goals, sharing their experiences, discussing and debating ideas, and problem solving together. The role, as therapeutic partner or collaborator, is to understand the parents' perspectives, to clarify issues, to summarize important ideas and themes raised by the parents, to help them see that their child is trying to solve developmental/life problems just as they are, to teach (coach) and interpret in a way that is culturally sensitive, and finally, to suggest possible alternative approaches or choices when parents request assistance and when misunderstandings occur.

Parents are encouraged to explore different solutions to a problem situation, rather than settling for 'quick fixes' or the first solution that comes to mind. The therapist studiously avoids giving any pat answers, keeping the focus of the discussion on the parents' insights. When parents seek professional help for their problems, they usually have experienced, or are experiencing, thoughts and feelings of powerlessness and mounting frustration with their children due to a history of unsuccessful attempts to discipline them. This powerlessness is often expressed in terms of feeling victimized by their children: the 'Why me?' question. The feeling of helplessness typically is accompanied by intense anger and a fear of losing control of themselves when trying to discipline their children. Attention is paid to the 'self-talk' of parents and attempts are encouraged to modify cognitions that are negative, distorted or illogical. We teach parents actively to formulate positive statements about themselves, e.g. 'I was able to stay in control, I stayed calm, I am doing well.'

Parents are encouraged to look at their strengths and think about how effectively they handled a difficult situation. We ask them to express their

Table 14 Sources of increased self-empowerment

	Content	Process
Knowledge		
Child development	Developmental norms and	Discussion
Behaviour management	tasks	Books/pamphlets to read
Individual and	Behavioural (learning)	Modelling (videotape,
temperamental	principles	live role play, role
differences	Child management	reversal, rehearsal)
	(disciplinary strategies)	Metaphors/analogies
	Relationships (feelings)	Homework tasks
	Self-awareness (self-talk,	Networking
	schema, attributions)	Developmental counselling
	Interactions (awareness of	Videotape viewing and
	contingencies,	discussion
	communications)	Self-observation/recording
	Resources (support, sources	at home
	of assistance)	Discussing records of
	Appropriate expectations	parents' own data
	Parent involvement with	Teaching, persuading
	children	
Skills		
Communication	Self-restraint/anger	Self-reinforcement
Problem-solving	management	Group and therapist
including problem	Self-talk (depressive	reinforcement
analysis)	thoughts)	
Tactical thinking (use of	Attend–ignore	Self-observations of
techniques/methods)	Play–praise–encourage	interactions at home
Building social	Contracts	Rehearsal
relationships		
Enhancing children's	Consistent consequences	Participant modelling
academic skills		Homework tasks and practice
	Sanction effectively (time	Video modelling and
	out, loss of privileges,	feedback
	natural consequences)	Self-disclosure
	Monitoring	Therapist use of
		humour/optimism
	Social/relationship skills	Relaxation training
	Problem-solving skills	Stress management
	Fostering good learning	Self-instruction
	habits	Visual cues at home
	Self-assertion/confidence	
	Empathy for child's	
	perspective	
	Ways to give and get support	
Values		
Strategic thinking	Treatment/life goals	Discussion/debate
(working out goals,	Objectives (targeted child	Sharing
philosophy of child	behaviours)	Listening
rearing, beliefs)	Ideologies	Respecting/accepting
	Rules	Negotiating
	Roles	Demystifying
	Relationships	Explaining/interpreting
	Emotional barriers	Reframing
	Attributions	Resolving conflict
	Prejudices	Clarifying
	Past history	Supporting
		Adapting

Source: Reproduced with permission from Webster-Stratton and Herbert (1994)

positive feelings about their relationship with their child and to remember good times. The therapist also helps the parent (or the parent and partner) to define ways in which they can support each other when feeling discouraged, tired, or unable to cope with a problem (see DeKlyen, Speltz and Greenberg (1998) on positive and negative fathering, and father–son attachment).

Chapter 12

ATTENTION-DEFICIT HYPERACTIVITY DISORDER (ADHD)

Hyperactivity and disruption tend to go together in formidable tandem. The first written record of the disruptive qualities of a hyperactive child is quite likely to be the one in a poem about 'fidgety Phil who wouldn't sit still', written in 1854 by a German physician named Hoffman (see Opie and Opie, 1973). And the first representation on film of this kind of child could well be one who drives Charlie Chaplin to distraction in one of his early silent movies. Hyperactive children had to wait until the early 1960s to be studied systematically. This scholarly concern was long overdue as hyperactive children are notorious for their knack of generating very special learning and management problems at home and in the classroom.

> ADHD is the most recent diagnostic label for children presenting with significant problems with attention, impulse control, and overactivity. Children with ADHD are a heterogeneous population who display considerable variation in the degree of their symptoms, the pervasiveness across situations of these problems, and the extent to which other disorders occur in association with it. The disorder represents one of the most common reasons why children are referred to mental health practitioners.

It has been said that attempting to define ADHD is like entering a semantic jungle. Hyperactive children are like the proverbial elephant: difficult to define, but, by golly, we know one when we see one—or live with one. Their nomadic wilful style in the sitting room or the classroom is their hallmark. Behaviour can be so disruptive and frenetic that they may be referred to a GP and thence to a psychologist, psychiatrist, or paediatrician, by parents or teachers who, not infrequently, feel demoralized by their inability to manage their children and pupils. The hyperactive child is the cause of significant and frequent complaints at school.

There has been a proliferation of terms (some 40 or so) put forward to describe the hyperactive child, among them labels that imply causation (e.g. post-encephalitic behaviour, minimal brain damage, brain damage syndrome, and organic drivenness); those without a clearly hypothesized aetiological basis (e.g. minimal brain dysfunction and cerebral dysfunction); and descriptive labels which avoid implications about pathology (e.g. hyperkinetic impulsive disorder and hyperactive child syndrome).

The latest version of the *Diagnostic Statistical Manual* (4th Edition, American Psychiatric Association, 1994) codes and classifies three subgroups of conditions under the umbrella term of 'attention-deficit hyperactivity disorder':

314.00   *Attention-deficit/hyperactivity disorder, predominantly inattentive type.* The patient has recently met the criteria for inattention but not for hyperactivity–impulsivity. (This is the so-called attention deficit disorder of the earlier version of DSM.)

314.01   *Attention-deficit/hyperactivity disorder, predominantly hyperactive–impulsive type.* The patient has recently met the criteria for hyperactivity–impulsivity but not for inattention.

314.01   *Attention-deficit/hyperactivity disorder, combined type.* The patient has recently met the criteria for both inattention *and* hyperactivity–impulsivity. (Most ADHD children have symptoms of the combined type.)

DIAGNOSIS

Observation, usually by the clinician, aided by information from parents and the classroom teacher, is the initial tool in effectively documenting the child's level of activity, attention and distractibility. Observations should occur in a variety of settings, including the following:

- during solitary, parallel, and group play;
- at home with parents, siblings, and other significant people;
- at school: classroom/playground;
- in new environments such as the clinic playroom, the psychologists' consulting room, or the supermarket.

The goals of the observation are:

- to describe the child's general behaviour and how it relates to the criteria set out in the DMS-IV or ICD-10 (see below);
- to observe skills in a variety of areas to determine whether developmental delays are present;
- to note any atypical behaviours that warrant more formal testing; for example, weak visual-motor skills noted in copying a design, motor incoordination (clumsiness), or cognitive difficulties.

DSM-IV Criteria for Attention-deficit Hyperactivity Disorder

The patient has *either inattention* or *hyperactivity–impulsivity* (or both), per-sisting for at least six months to a degree that is maladaptive and imma-ture, as shown by the following:

- *Inattention.* At least six of the following *often* apply:
    — Fails to pay close attention to details or makes careless errors in schoolwork, work, or other activities.
    — Has trouble keeping attention on tasks or play.
    — Doesn't appear to listen when being told something.
    — Neither follows through on instructions nor completes chores, schoolwork, or jobs (*not* because of oppositional behaviour or failure to understand).
    — Has trouble organizing activities and tasks.
    — Dislikes or avoids tasks that involve sustained mental effort (home-work, schoolwork).
    — Loses materials needed for activities (assignments, books, pencils, tools, toys).
    — Is easily distracted by external stimuli.
    — Is forgetful.
- *Hyperactivity–impulsivity.* At least six of the following *often* apply:
    — *Hyperactivity*:
        — squirms in seat or fidgets;
        — inappropriately leaves seat;
        — inappropriately runs or climbs (in adolescents or adults, this may be only a subjective feeling of restlessness);
        — has trouble quietly playing or engaging in leisure activity;
        — appears driven or 'on the go';
        — talks excessively.
    — *Inpulsivity*:
        — answers questions before they have been completely asked;
        — has trouble awaiting turn;
        — interrupts or intrudes on others.

The following criteria are also applied:

- Some of the symptoms above began before age seven.
- Symptoms are present in at least two types of situations, such as school, work, home.
- The disorder impairs school, social, or occupational functioning.
- The symptoms do not occur solely during a pervasive developmental disorder or any psychotic disorder, including schizophrenia.
- The symptoms are not explained better by a mood, anxiety, dissocia-tive, or personality disorder.

Barkley (1994) cautions us never to view these criteria as infallible; they are simply guidelines or suggestions for identifying the possible presence of ADHD. He is of the opinion that the criteria have the following problems:

- DSM-IV criteria make no adjustments for age. Since children are less likely to show the listed behaviours as they mature, using one cut-off score for all ages means too many young children and too few older children will be diagnosed as ADHD.
- The guidelines make no adjustment for gender, despite the fact that we know young girls show the listed behaviours less than young boys. So little girls will have to have more severe behaviour problems compared to other girls to be diagnosed as ADHD than boys compared to other boys will.
- DSM-IV requires that the behaviour problems show up in two of the three settings of home, school, and work. In practice this means that parents and teachers must agree that the child has ADHD before the child can be given that diagnosis—and experience shows that parent–teacher disagreement is quite common.
- The DSM criteria do not tell us just how deviant from normal a child's 'developmentally inappropriate' behaviour must be, which makes diagnosis difficult in borderline or mild cases.
- DSM-IV categorizes ADD or those with only attention deficits as just another type of ADHD, whereas the differences are probably significant enough to classify the two as separate disorders.

The World Health Organizations's ICD-10 (International Classification of Diseases) refers to hyperkinetic disorders rather than ADHD.

PREVALENCE

Lambert, Sandoval and Sassone (1978) indicate how prevalence figures appear to differ significantly as a function of how many people must reach a consensus about the diagnostic label. Parents, teachers and physicians of 5000 elementary school children were asked to identify children they considered to be hyperactive. Approximately 5% of these children were defined as hyperactive when the opinion of only one of these caregivers (parent, teacher, physician) was required—a prevalence figure very close to that found both by Szatmari, Offord and Boyle (1989) in their Canadian survey and by Du Paul and Barkley (1990) in the United States. However, this prevalence figure dropped to about 1% when agreement among all three was required.

Given these problems of definition it is not surprising that prevalence rates in the literature range from 1 to 20%. The occurrence of ADHD fluctuates to a minor degree across cultures and socioeconomic status, urban and rural areas (see Barkley, 1990), but to a significant extent as a function of gender. Boys are more often diagnosed as ADHD than girls on a 4 to 1 basis.

In the case of attention deficits, 10–20% of the school-age population (in a 1991 survey of more than 2000 third and fourth graders in Arizona by Shaywitz and Shaywitz) were identified as sufferers.

The Course of the Problem

The onset of ADHD is placed no later than 7 years of age for more than half of those diagnosed as such, the disorder often being recognized later in life for girls than boys—before ages eight and 12 respectively. The high degree of activity when present in early childhood tends to peak at around five or six and then undergo a low downward trend by adolescence. Symptoms of overactivity and associated behaviour problems may persist for 50–65% of children into adulthood.

The Attentional Component

The ability to apply persistent concentration over a period of time depends upon intact cortical and subcortical brain function. In the 1970s, the focusing on attentional deficits went into the ascendance as researchers and clinicians became disenchanted with the earlier emphasis on hyperactivity as the *sine qua non* of the disorder. The disorder was even renamed attention deficit disorder (ADD) in the 1980 DSM-III giving predominance (for several years) to attentional problems over symptoms of extreme activity levels.

It is all very well to talk about attention deficits but what constitutes a deficit, a disabling deviation from the norm? Many factors will affect how well a child attends: the type of ongoing activity, what has preceded the activity throughout the child's day, and the child's level of interest in the task.

Call (1985) estimates that a developmentally appropriate length of attention for a sustained attention activity, such as viewing television, is as follows:

- 2 years old: 7 minutes
- 3 years old: 9 minutes
- 4 years old: 13 minutes
- 5 years old: 15 minutes
- 6 to 7 years old: 60 minutes

These times are presented as guidelines only; all children vary greatly in their attention spans. However, children with attention disorders will find it challenging to maintain attention on a structured task for these lengths of time.

Cooke and Williams (1987) outlined six levels of normal development of attention control, based on Jean Reynell's research. These levels may be used to assess the child's development of attention skills.

- *Level 1* (birth to 1 year). Level 1 is characterized by extreme distractibility, in which the child's attention shifts from one object, person, or event to another. Any new event (such as someone walking by) will immediately distract the child.
- *Level 2* (1 to 2 years). Children in level 2 can concentrate on a concrete task of their own choosing but will not tolerate any verbal or visual intervention from an adult. These children may appear obstinate or wilful but, in fact, their attention is single-channelled, and they must ignore all extraneous stimuli in order to concentrate upon the task at hand.
- *Level 3* (2 to 3 years). Children's attention is still single-channelled in level 3. They cannot attend to competing auditory and visual stimuli from different sources. For example, they cannot listen to an adult's directions while playing but, with the adult's help, they can shift their full attention to the speaker and then back to the game.
- *Level 4* (3 to 4 years). The child in level 4 must still alternate full attention (visual and auditory) between the speaker and the task, but now does this spontaneously without an adult needing to focus that attention.
- *Level 5* (4 to 5 years). By level 5, attention is two-channelled; that is, the child understands verbal instructions related to the task without interrupting the activity to look at the speaker. The child's concentration span may still be short, but group instruction is possible.
- *Level 6* (5 to 6 years). In the final stage, auditory, visual, and manipulatory channels are fully integrated, and the child's attention is well established and sustained.

For school-based observations Claire Jones (1994) provides observational questions/criteria for the teacher as follows:

- Does the child impulsively answer questions (or select answers in forced-choice formats) without appearing to think about alternatives?
- Does the child fidget even when appearing interested in the task?
- Does the child's conversation appear random or sound like a 'free flight of ideas'?
- Does the child look away from the task in response to noises or visual distractions? Does the child comment on external noises or objects in the room that are unrelated to the task at hand?

- Does the child frequently ask questions such as, 'When will this be over?' 'What's next?' or 'What other things can we do?'
- Does the child yawn after activities requiring sustained attention?
- Does the child doodle in class or draw on hands, sneakers, and other things?
- Does the child stare off into space or appear to be 'glass-eyed'?
- Does the child lose papers, assignments, books, and the like?
- Are the student's desk and backpack messy and disorganized?
- Is the child able to stay alert during tasks requiring sustained attention?
- Does the student appear to lack persistence?

AETIOLOGY

In the ICD-10 it is said that constitutional abnormalities play a crucial role in the genesis of these disorders, but knowledge on specific aetiology is lacking at present. In recent years the use of the diagnostic term 'attention deficit disorder' for these syndromes was promoted. It has not been used in the ICD-10 because it implies a knowledge of psychological processes that is not yet available. It also suggests the inclusion of anxious, preoccupied, or 'dreamy' apathetic children whose problems are probably different. However, it is clear that, from the point of view of dysfunctional behaviour, problems of inattention constitute a central feature of these hyperkinetic syndromes.

Although research on the causes of ADHD remains inconclusive, there is compelling evidence linking the disorder to genetic, prenatal, environmental or physical factors.

Genetic Factors

Twin studies have indicated a genetic component in ADHD. Full siblings of hyperactive children are more likely than half-siblings to be hyperactive themselves (see Barkley, 1994). Temperamental differences can arise from the production of particular chemicals in the body. Shaywitz (1987) states that evidence from several investigations supports the view that such genetic biological factors are related to abnormalities in neurological function, in particular to disturbance of brain neurochemistry.

Brain Neurochemistry

There is now impressive evidence for the hypothesis that the disorder results from the brain's inability to regulate itself appropriately via the neurotransmitters dopamine and norepinephrine. There appears to be a chemical inbalance or shortage of certain neurotransmitters in the brain. Furthermore, a study carried out in the US showed differences in brain activity between ADHD and non-ADHD adults, with significantly lower activity in the brains of ADHD sufferers. Paradoxically, this seems to cause physical over-activity. The activity is particularly low in the area of the brain responsible for attention, motor control and inhibiting responses.

Allen Zametkin and his research team at the National Institute of Mental Health (e.g. Zametkin and Rapoport, 1986), using the PET SCAN (Positron Emission Tomography) machine, they were able to show that the rate at which the brain uses glucose—its main energy source—was lower in subjects with hyperactivity of childhood onset as compared with normals. In the PET SCAN procedure, radioactive substances that emit positrons are used to label glucose, which is then introduced into the body by injection so that it may be traced in the brain. Using the PET SCAN, the glucose can be tracked as it is absorbed by the brain and used as fuel. The most active parts of the brain use the largest amounts of glucose.

Zametkin and his researchers have determined that the frontal lobes of the brain are involved in regulating attention, emotional responses, and activity level. In addition, the frontal lobes play a role in planning, an area in which children with attention disorders typically have great difficulty. Children or young adults who have had some type of damage in the frontal lobe area seem to have great difficulty controlling impulsive actions. Although they are able to function in a perfectly normal intelligence range, their ability to plan and to abide by rules seems to be impaired. Hence, Zametkin's research demonstrates that neurotransmitters play a role in behaviour, concentration, and impulsivity.

Dietary Factors

Although there is some evidence that diet may be a factor in ADHD for some people, recent UK research shows that only a small proportion of children may respond to dietary help. Studies by the US government have never replicated test results asserted by Ben Feingold, who originally put forward the dietary link in the US (see Barkley, 1990).

Overview

Barkley's (1994) conclusions, following a comprehensive review of the literature on the aetiology of ADHD, are that studies endorse a biological predisposition, as is the case with severe mental handicap. In both heterogenous conditions a variety of causal influences (e.g. pregnancy and birth complications, acquired brain damage, toxins, infections, and heredity) can play their part, through some fault in a final common pathway in the nervous system.

In the case of ADHD, it would seem that hereditary factors play the largest role in the occurrence of these symptoms in children. It may be that what is transmitted genetically is a tendency towards dopamine depletion in, or at least underactivity of, the prefrontal-striatal-limbic regions and their rich interconnections. Neurological studies are converging on the conclusion that a dysfunction in the orbital-limbic pathways of the frontal area (and particularly the striatum) is the probable impairment that gives rise to the primary features of ADHD, particularly its behavioural disinhibition and diminished sensitivity to behavioural consequences or incentive learning.

It is these behavioural and learning implications that require—whatever the medical intervention—a psychological input. ADHD can be exacerbated by pregnancy complications, exposure to toxins, or neurological disease but also by social factors (such as environmental and family adversity, dysfunctional child rearing and management, or educational environment).

It seems that ADHD can occur without a genetic predisposition to the disorder, provided the child is exposed to significant disruption or neurological injury to this final common neurological pathway; however, this would seem to account for a small minority of ADHD cases.

TREATMENT

Research suggests that the most effective form of intervention in ADHD is a multimodal/multilevel intervention. Clare Jones (1994) maintains that if we respect that each child is unique, then the treatment plan for each child should be unique. The following strategies are frequently effective:

- *family understanding of attention disorder*: Parent training, counselling, and support.
- *behaviour therapy*: Consistent behaviour intervention based on positive reinforcement and the use of *response cost*–that is, losing tokens for undesirable behaviour.
- A *healthy sense of self-esteem*: Experiences of success in which peer and family response to the child is positive and immediate.
- *Medical interventions*: Drug therapy as a short-term treatment.

- *Educational interventions*: Appropriate educational accommodation provided by knowledgeable teachers.
- *Counselling*: Training in social skills, coping skills, and goal-directed strategies.

Planning an Intervention

The planning of a programme of treatment for a hyperactive child can only be discussed realistically with regard to individual circumstances (see Herbert, 1987b, 1995). However, it is possible to make a few generalizations. The following considerations (most of which are current influences) are likely to enter into most assessments:

(1) High level of arousal and excess motor activity.
(2) Poor performance (socialization) at home and performance (scholastic attainment) at school.
(3) Distractibility and poor attention span.
(4) Concomitant behaviour problems such as non-compliant, attention-seeking and commanding behaviour (surplus behaviours such as excessive crying, tantrums, and whining may also be a feature).
(5) Reinforcement history, which is likely to be unusual in its ratio of punishments to rewards. The hyperactive child's behaviour is so below the norm in so many aspects that he or she has a remarkable experience of failure.
(6) Great need of attention and success. So great may be this need that the child may actively seek any attention even if it looks to other people like punishment (e.g. naggings and smackings).
(7) Social isolation, being rejected by peers. This may be a result of his or her inappropriateness, oddity and aggression.
(8) Mother and father are likely to have lost confidence in their effectiveness as parents; they may feel that the child is beyond their control and is manipulating them. They are also likely to be exhausted (hyperactive children tend to have sleeping problems), despairing, and guilty about their feelings of rejection and violence towards the child.
(9) Disappointing/unrewarding quality for his/her parents: they don't enjoy the child (and, sometimes, the reverse may be true).

In designing a treatment strategy for the problems of hyperactive children, their hyperactive behaviours can be conceived of as operants. Several behaviour therapists have successfully employed operant techniques to reduce the high rates of behaviour associated with the syndrome. Of course, it is quite possible that hyperactive behaviours are a final common

pathway for the expression of various disorders. Thus high levels of cortical arousal (due to brain dysfunction) may influence the probability of the
maladaptive behaviours being emitted. Pharmacotherapy is successful, in
some cases, in reducing the emission of such behaviours. Indeed, a combined somatic and behavioural approach may be indicated in some clients.
We look at these choices in turn, beginning with what is the most common
approach: medication.

Medication

Werry and Sprague (1970) make the point that excess motor activity is
characteristic of inefficiently functioning organisms—e.g. developmentally immature organisms. It is not surprising, therefore, that treatment of
ADHD has traditionally fallen into the remit of medicine, which means,
essentially medication (see Table 15).

Table 15 Commonly prescribed medications for ADD/ADHD

Drug class	Common name	Technical name	Possible effects

Stimulants	Ritalin
	Dexedrine
	Cylert
		Methylphenidate
		  hydrochloride
		Dextroamphetamine
		
		Pemoline
			+ Increases attention
			+ Controls impulsiveness
			+ Reduces task-irrelevant
			  activity
			+ May increase compliance
			+ May improve writing
			– May reduce appetite
			– May restrict range of
			  emotional responses
			– May result in mild insomnia
			– May cause tics to occur
			– Licking of lips, finger
			  picking

Tricyclic
Anti-
depressant
	Tofranil
	
	Norpramin
	
	Wellbutrin
	
	Elavil
		Imipramine
		
		Desipramine
		  hydrochloride
		Bupropion
		
		Amitriptyline
			+ Increases attending
			  behaviour
			+ Increases verbal/gestural
			  communication
			+ Decreases depression/
			  anxiety
			+ Decreases disruptive
			  behaviour
			– Some effects on
			  cardiovascular system
			– Dry mouth, constipation

Despite its popularity, there is little evidence as to the most appropriate way in which to evaluate the effectiveness of pharmacological treatment or the optimum dosage for individual-children. Subjective impressions of parents, carers and teachers are often used to judge the efficacy of the treatment and gauge dosage. Due to the idiosyncratic way in which children respond to the medication and the strong placebo effect demonstrated by a number of researchers (see Fischer and Newby, 1991), this method of evaluation is far from satisfactory.

One of the major difficulties is the question of how to monitor change. First, should it be behaviour, academic performance, learning or some other activity which should be rated? Second, should this attribute be rated in a variety of settings such as home and school? Third, it may be difficult for individuals who are close to the child to provide reliable, objective assessments. Barkley (1977) reviewed a large number of studies of the effects of drug treatment (predominately Ritalin). His review suggests an average of 75.5% of children displaying some 'improvement' once drug treatment had commenced. Eight placebo studies revealed an average of 39% demonstrating an improvement (Barkley, 1982).

In 1993, James Swanson, Project Director of the Child Development Centre at the University of California, Irvine, showed that some 60 to 90% of children diagnosed with ADHD received stimulant therapy for prolonged periods during their schooling. Over the short-term students receiving pharmacological treatment demonstrated more self-control, better concentration, less hostility, fewer behaviour problems, more cooperation, and more academic productivity. However, educators cannot expect large changes in academic skills or higher-order processes. Stimulant medications apparently do not boost academic achievement or relieve antisocial behaviour or depression. Swanson equated the expectation that medication will cure attention deficit disorder to giving a child glasses to improve vision, then expecting the child to spontaneously begin reading. 'You still have to teach them to read', he observed.

Side Effects (see Table 15)

The major side effect of stimulants is mild insomnia, which occurs in about 70% of cases (Conners, 1989). Another side effect is appetite reduction. The child will typically pick at lunch and not appear hungry. For some children, this may result in temporary growth suppression, but the effect appears to be quite minor. Sometimes adjusting the child's mealtimes or providing an after-school snack may eliminate this difficulty.

In the 1–2% of children with ADHD who exhibit a tic disorder—such as a gesture, twitch, or uncontrolled laugh—the condition may be exacerbated by medication. Sometimes the physician will experiment with a lower dosage to see if the condition abates; if not, the medication may have to be eliminated.

Behavioural Methods

These methods which, in individual or group-training mode, are so effective are described in a form parents can use, in Webster-Stratton and Herbert (1994) and—in manual form—in Herbert and Wookey (1997).

EDUCATIONAL IMPLICATIONS

The child is generally placed in a regular classroom under the management of the classroom teacher, possibly with additional support services, if the child qualifies for special education (i.e. is 'statemented' as having special needs).

Teachers can employ methods that help students succeed in the classroom. They include the following: preferential seating, activities which offer brevity, variety, and structure, avoidance of unnecessary detail, less intense detail, and smaller chunks of required work. Hyperactive children require strategies to help them complete their work, slow down and control their movements, and remember information.

Here are some guidelines for evaluating when a hyperactive (or any other) child requires special attention:

- if his or her social behaviour interferes significantly with academic work;
- if he or she interferes with the other children's academic work or social behaviour;
- if he or she interferes with the teacher's ability to function effectively.

Teachers typically complain about the following:

- getting out of seat too frequently;
- deviating from what the rest of the class is supposed to be doing;
- talking out of turn or calling out;
- losing and forgetting equipment;
- Handing in incomplete or sloppy work.

Given this catalogue of *negatives* it is (or should be) plain to see that the basic need of hyperactive children is for *success*—success in something in which adults and adult society genuinely believe. All children have this need, but unlike most children, hyperactive youngsters seldom enjoy even a modicum of success. Unfortunately, such children are likely to have experienced a sort of 'built-in' failure. Their unacceptable behaviour increasingly excludes them from the circle of acceptance in the family, the neighbourhood, the school and the community at large. They tend to be strangers to the usual range of social reinforcers which regulate appropriate behaviour, for example, encouragement and esteem.

Planning more effective classroom management of hyperactive children requires careful 'target assessment'. First, it is vital for the teacher to find a *level* of social or academic performance at which the child has already experienced success. This provides a realistic basis on which to begin whatever educational programme is planned; this programme must directly reflect the *problems* which the child is presenting. The programme is presented to the child within a setting and *time span* which permit learning to take place. Finally, the educational programme is highly *structured* in terms of the methods used and the environment created for the child.

Although there are a great many difficulties faced by parents, teachers and professionals, there are a number of characteristics of ADHD children which are deemed to be socially desirable. These characteristics reflect creativity and awareness and have been linked with gifts and special talents, not always present in so-called 'normal' children. More positive characteristics include spontaneity, enthusiasm and curiosity. Taylor (1994), suggests that ADHD children:

> ... have rich imaginations and can quickly generate new and different ideas. They have an acute awareness of nuances and sensations that others miss and can combine unrelated ideas in novel ways so that their art productions and written work show special creativity.

The point has been made by people like Hartmann (1991) that parents and teachers can think of the characteristics of children with ADHD in positive or negative ways. For example, the 'debit' list presented above could be set out with these 'asset' items:

(1) eager/enthusiastic;
(2) independent/inquisitive;
(3) keen to contribute;
(4) thoughtful/absorbed in own ideas;
(5) signs of effort in spite of difficulties

They represent two different ways of thinking about ADHD characteristics (Hartmann, 1991). We can think of these characteristics on the one hand, in terms of deficits that render pupils incapable of sustaining attention, following instructions, organizing themselves or being patient. On the other hand we can see them as representing cognitive and in some cases physical vitality that is blunted by classroom settings and tasks that do not focus on their positive qualities. Teachers and others need to behave towards the pupil with ADHD in ways that are positive and geared to enhancing his or her self-esteem.

Mnemonic for Listening Skills

A strategy that may be helpful for children with attention deficit is the use of a mnemonic during a large-group activity. Bauwens and Hourcode (1989) developed a technique called 'The listening strategy'. The word LISTEN is a device to help students with attention deficits remember strategies to improve their listening skills. The teacher instructed each student to listen, and then wrote on the board the key words:

L = Look
I = Idle your motor
S = Sit up straight
T = Turn to me
E = Engage your brain
N = Now

Visual reinforcement was provided by listing the six listening instructions on a card on each student's desk, as well as on a poster at the front of the room. Initially, the teacher paused after saying each step out loud, but as the students gained familiarity with the procedure, these pauses were minimized and ultimately eliminated.

After giving students the complete list of instructions on several occasions, the teacher reduced the amount of assistance by saying 'listen', and then pointing to the six steps. These verbal prompts were then reduced further, with the teacher saying only 'listen' and quietly pointing to the acronym on the card or poster. Eventually the teacher was able to simply say 'listen', and the students reviewed the acronym quickly, silently, and independently. The results of this technique in a classroom situation showed that all students consistently attended more effectively to oral instructions, decreasing the number of times the teacher had to repeat information, and also reducing student frustration over mistakes caused by misunderstanding instructions.

Part V ANXIETY DISORDERS OF CHILDHOOD (FEARS, PHOBIAS, OBSESSIONS AND POST-TRAUMATIC DISORDERS)

INTERNALIZING (EMOTIONAL) PROBLEMS

Studies of the internalizing or emotional problems of childhood indicate that some of them are so common that it might be said to be 'normal' for children to be fearful, worried or shy about one thing or another at different stages in their development. Many investigators (e.g. Lapouse and Monk, 1985) found that it was commonplace for a majority of their samples of non-clinic-attending children to report having one or more fears. Obviously, if a degree of fearfulness is widespread during childhood we have to judge the seriousness of a particular child's anxieties by the consequences they have in his or her day-to-day life.

CHILDREN'S ANXIETY DISORDERS

The DSM-III-R classifies three anxiety disorders of childhood or adolescence: separation anxiety disorder, avoidant disorder, and overanxious disorder.

- *Separation anxiety disorder* is characterized by 'excessive anxiety concerning separation from those to whom the child is attached' (American Psychiatric Association, 1987, p. 60). A child with separation anxiety disorder may be reluctant to go to school in order to stay near his or her mother or with some other important attachment figure. Headaches and stomach aches and other physical symptoms are also common. To warrant a diagnosis, the separation anxiety must go well beyond that manifested as part of normal development and also extend for a period of at least two weeks.

- *Avoidant disorder* is characterized by 'excessive shrinking from contact with unfamiliar people that is of sufficient severity to interfere with social functioning in peer relationships' (American Psychiatric Association, 1987, p. 61). A child with this disorder is likely to appear shy, socially withdrawn, embarrassed and timid when in the company of peers and adults. Of course, these behaviours may be appropriate at specific stages of development. For this reason the DSM-III-R diagnosis is not applied until the child is at least two-and-a-half-years of age; in addition the avoidant reaction must be extended in duration for at least six months.
- *Overanxious disorder* is characterized by 'excessive or unrealistic anxiety or worry' (American Psychiatric Association, 1987, p. 63). An overanxious child tends to worry excessively about school work and future events, and usually appears nervous or tense. The child has an incessant need for reassurance or comfort. Further, he or she complains of a variety of physical complaints (e.g. nausea and dizziness), and shows frequent self-consciousness. The problem, to be defined as such, must be relatively long-lived (i.e. at least six months in duration). Developmental guidelines are not indicated, however, since pervasive anxiety is not expected to be typical of any age group.

In addition to these three primary types of disorder, the DSM-III-R recognizes the presence of phobic disorders in children that are not subsumed under the categories mentioned above. Simple or 'specific' phobias are defined as persistent fears involving circumscribed stimuli such as animals, blood, closed spaces, heights, and air travel.

In addition to these phobic disorders, there are other anxiety diagnoses included in the DSM-III-R that may be applied to children and adults. For example, obsessive–compulsive disorder is characterized by recurrent obsessions (persistent thoughts and impulses) or compulsions (repetitive behaviours performed according to certain rules or in a stereotyped fashion). These obsessions or compulsions are 'sufficiently severe to cause marked distress, be time-consuming, or significantly interfering with the person's normal routine, occupational functioning, or usual social activities or relationships with others' (American Psychiatric Association, 1987, p. 245). Other anxiety disorders include agoraphobia, panic disorder, and post traumatic stress disorder.

POST-TRAUMATIC STRESS DISORDER IN CHILDREN

Many children experience several distressing reactions including anxiety, fear and depression following major emotional/physical upheavals (disasters, accidents). It is now appreciated that they may be suffering from symptoms of post-traumatic stress disorder (PTSD), and that without treatment their disorder can persist over long periods of time. Such children may be troubled by some or all of the following symptoms, the key criteria being:

(1) The existence of a recognizable stressor that would evoke significant symptoms of distress in almost everyone.
(2) Re-experiencing the trauma as evidenced by at least *one* of the following:
  —recurrent intrusive recollections of the event;
  —recurrent dreams of the event;
  —suddenly acting or feeling as if the traumatic event were recurring, because of an association with an environmental stimulus or mental reminder.
(3) Numbing of responsiveness to, or reduced involvement with, the external world, beginning some time after the trauma, and shown by at least *one* of the following:
  —markedly diminished interest in one or more significant activities;
  —feelings of detachment or estrangement from others;
  —constricted affect (that is, inability to experience feelings).
(4) At least *two* of the following symptoms that were not present before the trauma:
  —hyperalertness or exaggerated startle response;
  —sleep disturbance;
  —guilt about surviving when others have not, or about behaviours which were required for survival;
  —memory impairment or trouble concentrating;
  —avoidance of activities which arouse recollection of the traumatic event;
  —intensification of symptoms by exposure to events that symbolize or resemble the traumatic event.

If a person meets some, but not all of the major criteria, then it would be more correct to say that they have a post-traumatic stress *reaction*, rather than the disorder.

The diagnosis of PTSD rests not only on the individual having a specific set of symptoms, but also on the nature of the stressor which has been seen to precipitate the symptoms. It is the combination of the trauma and the distressing psychological reaction that is necessary for the diagnosis of PTSD. Until recently, the definition of PTSD, notably in the DSM-III-R (APA, 1987), specified that the stressor should be 'outside the range of usual human experience'.

The difficulty that arises with the notion that PTSD is a normal reaction to an abnormal situation is that we are unable to adequately operationalize the criteria for specifying which stressors are outside the range of usual/normal human experience. To take one example, epidemiological studies of the prevalence of child sexual abuse indicate that as many as 54% of females have experienced some form of sexual abuse by the time they are eighteen years old. Given this, it could be argued that according to the DSM-III-R criteria sexual abuse is not outside the range of usual experience for a large majority of girls and young women and therefore cannot be a precipitator of PTSD. Possibly as a response to such controversy, the DSM-IV (APA, 1994) has revised the terminology to there being evidence that: 'the person experienced, witnessed or was confronted with an event or events that involved actual or threatened death or injury, or a threat to the physical integrity of self or others' (Criterion 1A, p. 427, DSM-IV, APA 1994). In other words, the traumata which give rise to PTSD seem to be those which violate the individual's safety assumptions more than events leading to other forms of anxiety. In addition, there is far more re-experiencing of the traumatic event.

Yule (1994) has drawn attention to the fact that the range of symptoms presented by children fail to replicate some of the 'adult symptoms', vary widely with developmental age, and cast uncertainty on the extent to which the ICD and DSM categories accurately reflect the symptoms presented by the children. The damaging effects of traumatic events on children manifest themselves in a variety of symptoms. Frequently documented symptoms have included adverse changes in interpersonal relations, mood, memory, learning, impulse control, school performance, sleep, state of arousal and intensifications of symptoms that symbolize or resemble the traumatic event. Psychic numbing has been found to be less evident in children than in adults. The onset of new fears, or the re-occurrence of old ones, somatic complaints, reckless behaviour and feelings of guilt have been found to be associated with a diagnosis of PTSD in children and adolescents and therefore warrant further consideration in the inclusion of PTSD criteria.

The extent of the reactions appear to be determined in the first instance by the severity of the life threat. Beyond that, the nature of the post-traumatic reaction is likely to be determined partly by the developmental age of the child, partly by the parental and family responses, and partly by the child's gender. We return to this, and other anxiety conditions, in Chapter 13.

Chapter 13

FEARS AND PHOBIAS

Children's fears show a clear pattern as they grow up—each age would seem to have its own set of 'adjustment' crises or anxieties. Until about six or seven months, a baby will probably show no concern about being with strangers, but from then on it is quite common for this to change. Babies gradually learn to discriminate between familiar people, like mother, and the other—unknown—people in the world. In many infants, the first fear of separation from mother is quickly followed by a fear of people who are strange or new to them. This fear may generalize, becoming a temporary but widespread fear of the unfamiliar and unknown.

Later, the situations that the pre-school child fears are still mainly those linked to his sense of security and his apprehensions over strangeness and suddenness. Things beyond control—like darkness, large barking dogs, noises, storms, the ocean, the doctor or strange people—are typically feared by youngsters. As the child gets older, fears change from the tangible to the intangible. There is an increase in the number of fears of the occult, the dark, being alone, accidents and injuries, bad people, the loss or death of relatives, medical treatment, high places, ridicule and personal failure, and dying or ill health. These are 'outgrown' in the natural way that the youngster outgrows toys and childish enthusiasms.

PHOBIAS

The parameters that separate behaviours defined as phobic from the anxieties, avoidance, fears, indecisiveness, and obsessions shown by all children at one time or another are, as we have seen, their rate and intensity, the persistence (duration) with which they are manifested and their pervasiveness. Their *implications* for the individual's well-being and 'effective' functioning provide a diagnostic guidelight for the therapist (see point 7 in Figure 3). The meaning of the problems for the child—the sense made of them, the payoff they provide—and indeed for his or her family, also constitutes a vital element of the overall assessment. In behavioural work, in the author's opinion, explanations in terms of a functional analysis can operate at two levels. At its simplest, behaviour is a function of certain contingent stimuli, originating in the person's internal and external environment. Here, the important questions are 'What triggers (elicits) the phobia?' or 'What reinforcement does the child get for behaving in this way?' At a more interpretive level, the child's behaviour may have the function of solving (or attempting to solve) a developmental or life problem. To make sense of it, one might ask (*inter alia*): 'What immediate "solutions" (even if self-defeating in the longer term) do the child's actions provide for himself or herself?' Also: 'What purpose does the child's behaviour serve in terms of his or her family life and its psychological and social dynamics?'

ASSESSMENT

A useful strategy is to begin with broad-based assessment of the child and his or her environment (e.g. family, school, peers) and then to obtain information regarding specific stimulus features, response modes, antecedents and consequences, severity, duration, and pervasiveness of the particular phobias. The assessment begins with a behavioural interview and utilizes a multimethod, problem-solving approach to obtain as complete a picture of the child and his or her family as is possible (Mash and Terdal, 1988; Ollendick and Hersen, 1984).

Behavioural Interviews

The behavioural interview is the initial step in the assessment process. The purposes of the interview are to establish rapport with the child and family, obtain information as to the nature of the anxiety condition as well as its antecedents and consequences, assess the child's developmental level, determine the broader sociocultural context in which the phobic behaviour occurs, and formulate treatment plans (Bierman and Schwartz, 1986; Ollendick and Cerny, 1981).

Interviewing a phobic child and his or her family requires an understanding that such a child may be timid, shy, fearful, anxious, and relatively unresponsive to interview questions. It also demands an appreciation of the child's developmental level and how his or her cognitive development places constraints on the types of questions that can be asked and how they should be phrased. It is frequently necessary to phrase questions in specific, direct terms so that the child will understand them and to provide the child with additional support and encouragement to respond.

With interviews, as well as other assessment procedures, there are psychometric concerns. Often, children and parents are inconsistent and unreliable reporters of behaviour, particularly past behaviour. That is, parents and children may not agree on the occurrence of behaviours, particularly anxious or phobic behaviours, and whether such behaviours are a significant problem. One way to maximize the reliability of reporting is to assess current behaviours and the conditions under which they occur (e.g. Ollendick and Cerny, 1981). Thus the focus of the interview should be on the phobic behaviour and its antecedents and consequences in the here and now.

Anxiety, as we have seen, is thought of as abnormal when it occurs to a much greater degree than is usual for most people—when it occurs more often and with greater severity than the stimulus (circumstance) warrants. It is not only high levels of anxiety that are dysfunctional; low levels, such as those postulated in the sociopathic individual that are thought to adversely affect socialization (notably social cognition and moral development), can also be maladaptive.

The behaviours and beliefs that make for an anxiety disorder are likely to vary in intensity and frequency depending on setting events relating to persons, places, times, and situations (see point 1 in Figure 3). This raises the issue of specificity, this time with regard (broadly) to response systems rather than stimulus conditions.

One of the difficulties in assessing anxiety, not least in children, stems from its generic nature—notably, the range of phenomena that the term is used to cover. Four broad components can be distinguished: physiological arousal, cognitive factors, behavioural components, and subjective (experiential) aspects. With regard to the first three—the 'three systems' model of anxiety—it is suggested that the components may be only loosely coupled. They may vary together (synchrony) or they may not (desynchrony) (Hodgson and Rachman, 1974). Certainly, it is inappropriate to reify anxiety into an entity or single system. This model has provided new understanding of the determinants of anxiety, but it too requires further refinement (Hugdahl, 1981).

Questions for Parents/Older Children re Circumstances Related to the Disorder

- In what ways is the anxiety affecting his or her personal life?
- Has the child had any special experiences which she or he may not have discussed with anyone else before, e.g. sexual abuse or other unpleasant sexual experiences?
- Has the child been the victim of a physical assault or verbal attack at any time, e.g. bullying, mugging, racial harassment, name-calling?

- Does the child feel he or she has experienced a traumatic or overwhelming stress at any time, even one he or she feels others would not see as traumatic; has he or she experienced major loss or bereavement(s) during his or her life?
- Was he or she able to grieve about these losses?

Obtaining Baseline Data

This involves:

- keeping records of daily levels of anxiety
- pinpointing *precise* triggers of anxiety:
  —a situation;
  —a person;
  —a thought;
  —a memory;
  —a 'flashback' (a vivid, unexpected memory of a distressing event);
- diary—teaching the person (child or parent) to keep a diary of events and how he or she dealt with them.

Parent and Teacher Measures

A variety of parent- and teacher-rating scales and checklists have been used in the assessment of fears and anxieties in children. Among the more frequently used are Achenbach's Child Behaviour Checklist and Quay and Peterson's Behaviour Problem Checklist. Both of these rating forms have been developed and standardized for use with children between 4 and 16 years of age.

The Child Behaviour Checklist (CBCL; Achenbach, 1978; Achenbach and Edelbrock, 1979) has been used extensively in factor-analytic studies by Achenbach and his colleagues. Parents or teachers are asked to fill out this 138-item scale that taps both behaviour problems and social competence. Social competency items assess the child's participation in social organizations, activities, and school. The behaviour problem items are rated on a three-point scale as to how well each describes the child. The inclusion of social competency and behaviour problem items allows for a comprehensive assessment of the child's strengths and weaknesses. In addition, the scale allows for identification of children who display a variety of behaviours including withdrawal, depression and somatic complaints. Specific anxiety items include 'clings to adults', 'school fears', and 'shy, timid'. This scale has been found to be reliable and valid and provides important normative data for boys and girls of varying ages (see Achenbach 1985 for additional detail regarding the use of the CBCL with anxious and fearful children).

The Revised Behaviour Problem Checklist (Quay and Peterson, 1983) consists of 89 problem behaviours that are also rated on a three-point scale ranging from 'not a problem' to 'mild problem' to 'severe problem'. Factor analysis of the scale yields the following six dimensions; conduct problem, socialized aggression attention problem–immaturity, anxiety–withdrawal, psychotic behaviour, and motor excess. The Problem Behaviour Checklist is a reliable and valid way in which to assess significant-other reports of children's anxiety behaviour and its relationship to other deviant or pathological behaviour.

Self-report Instruments

A wide variety of self-report instruments are available to supplement information obtained from the interview. In general, they consist of fear survey schedules that provide lists of fear-evoking stimuli and anxiety measures that provide the child with a set of responses with which to describe subjective experiences felt in the fear-producing situations.

- *Fear survey schedules.* The revision of the Fear Survey Schedule for Children (FSSC-R; Ollendick, 1983) is a useful tool for determining specific fear stimuli related to children's phobias. School-aged children are instructed to rate their fear of the 80 items on a three-point scale ranging from being frightened by the item 'none', 'some', or 'a lot'. Normative data for children between 7 and 16 years of age are available. Further, the instrument has been used in cross-cultural studies in Australia, England, and the United States.
- *Anxiety measures.* In contrast to fear survey schedules, measures of anxiety have been used to determine the subjectively experienced effects of being in phobic or anxiety-producing situations. The Children's Manifest Anxiety Scale (CMAS: Casteneda, McCandless and Palmero, 1956), a scaled-down version of the Manifest Anxiety Scale for Adults (Taylor, 1951), consists of 42 anxiety items and 11 lie items that assess a child's report of pervasive anxiety. Reynolds and Richmond (1978) developed a revised version of the CMAS titled 'What I Think and Feel' (CMAS-R). The purpose of this 37-item revision was to clarify the wording of items, decrease administration time, and lower the reading level of the items. The CMAS-R is suitable for children and adolescents between 6 and 18 years of age.

FORMULATION: IDENTIFYING CONTROLLING VARIABLES

In identifying controlling variables, two categories are generally considered: current environmental variables (antecedent and consequent events (see points 5 and 6 in Figure 3) and organismic variables (see point 4). The contemporary causes of phobic behaviour may exist in the client's environment or in his or her own thoughts, feelings, or bodily processes (organismic variables), and they may exert their influence in several ways: as eliciting or discriminative antecedent stimuli or as outcomes (consequences) of a reinforcing kind.

Proximal antecedents. Proximal (current) influences (point 5b) are direct in their effects and close in time to the actions they influence. They are functionally related to behaviour and can thus be tested in therapy—as hypotheses about causation—using single-case experimental designs. The formulation is directed toward the precise identification of the antecedent outcome and symbolic conditions that control the problematic behaviour or beliefs.

An early statement of stimulus-contingent and response-contingent aspects of anxiety is that of Mowrer (1960) in his two-process theory of fear and anxiety. Fear and avoidance are established by two processes, the first of which is classic conditioning of fear to stimuli associated with a painful event. The second process is the reinforcement by fear reduction of any responses that remove the individual from the fear-eliciting stimuli. This escape behaviour will eventually become avoidance and may lead to well-established dysfunctional patterns of behaviour of the type frequently faced by clinicians.

Antecedents/Precursors of Anxiety

Anxiety may be learned or elicited by the following processes:

- *The appraisal of threat*—e.g. separation in young children, distressing life events, conditions of living or work, family relationships especially during childhood, and physical illnesses manifesting themselves with an anxiety component.
- *Classical conditioning*—the pairing of a previously neutral stimulus with a situation of pain or fear.
- *Modelling*—the person perceives others whom he or she perceives as being like him- or herself behaving in an anxious way. This person acts as a model for the acquisition of anxiety.
- *Traumatic learning*—an experience of intense fear or pain can lead to acute anxiety being experienced in similar subsequent situations, e.g. following a road accident.

- *Generalization* of learned anxiety to other settings—e.g. a person who suffered humiliation at school may experience acute anxiety in any situation involving being tested or judged, e.g. at a driving test.
- *Vicarious learning*—a person may become fearful through seeing someone else undergoing a fearful event.
- *Cognitive processes*—the highly individual way in which people perceive situations is crucial in understanding anxiety. Some people typically see danger in situations which are simply stimulating or routine to others, e.g. having an argument or travelling by aeroplane.

The human being's appraisals of threat are essentially personal. He or she responds to perceived danger or threat by:

- fighting—an aggressive response, to deal by combat with potential threat;
- fleeing—a retreat designed to avoid potential threat;
- freezing—an alert, but immobile, response, in the hope of escaping the attention of the potential threat.

The fact that in modern times it is more often than not the symbols of danger rather than real life-endangering threat, to which the body's emergency system reacts, means that the physical reactions are inhibited and are not resolved in active, vigorous physical activity. If the stress is repetitive and the physical reactions thus 'chronic', we could get a situation in which previously adaptive reactions become dysfunctional and contribute to psychosomatic illness (e.g. hypertension, ulcers, asthma).

The theories of Lazarus (1982, 1984), for one, and Schachter (1971), for another, have been important in illuminating the role of cognitive appraisal and attributions in the subjective appraisal of stress. These authors both believe that cognitive processes are indispensable elements in any causal theory of emotion. For Lazarus, emotional activity results from the child's appraisal of the situation—whether it is dangerous (primary appraisal)—and the evaluation of the coping processes he or she has available (secondary appraisal). One of the determining factors—*dispositional* conditions—refers to the individual's psychological structure (e.g. beliefs, attitudes (see point I, in Figure 3, where the B stands for *belief* as well as *behaviour*).

Zimrin (1986) relates her findings on the cognitive functioning of abused children to this work: she found evidence that abused children who managed to survive the trauma of their childhood and whom she described as well adjusted on a series of clinical measures were distinguishable from a matched group of abused children with high degrees of psychopathology on various measures of cognitive skill and cognitive attainment.

The theories of Ellis (1970) and Beck (1976) also build on the existence of cognitive structures or schemas such that abused children suffer severely dysfunctional thinking processes. The characteristics of the dysfunctional thoughts that lead to anxiety are that they repetitively construe events as harmful or dangerous, that they cannot be 'reasoned away', and that they become readily attached to a wide range of stimuli that can elicit them. Jehu (1992) has demonstrated clearly how important negative schemata are in the long-term sequelae of sexual abuse, explaining why some young females develop severe anxiety disorders that persist into adulthood, while others remain relatively unscathed.

When analysing childhood anxiety and coping strategies, it is vital to remember that children mature cognitively in a manner that changes the way they construe the world they live in and the interpretation they put on people and events. Several authors, noting the developing of statistically 'normal' fears in childhood, have demonstrated how they arise from increasingly sophisticated cognitive structures in the maturing child (e.g. Bauer, 1976; Ferrari, 1986). Infants and very young children show fear in response to events that occur in their immediate environment (e.g. separation from parents, approach of strangers). The more advanced cognitive development of preschool children allows them to show fear to more imaginary, global stimuli (e.g. the dark, monsters). Older children demonstrate more specific, realistic fears as they become capable of differentiating internal representations from objective reality (see Bauer, 1976).

Age

We have already seen the considerable attention given to the developmental features of anxiety in childhood. There is undoubtedly a patterning in the type of fears present at various ages (see Campbell, 1985). Simple phobias seem to date back to early childhood, whereas social phobias tend to have their onset in adolescence or later. Separation anxiety occurs at about 8 months of age and is related to attachment developments. It may also contribute to the raised incidence of school phobias at age 11. One can only speculate about the reasons for these age-related patterns: the notion of developmental and life tasks and the crises to which they give rise may throw some light on this conundrum. Certainly cognitive factors are significant.

Sex

The findings regarding sex are not consistent, although some investigations suggest that girls are somewhat more fearful than boys and are more vulnerable to neurotic disorder (Herbert, 1974). Whether this is a true organismic variable or a social artifact of willingness to admit to fears on the part of girls is a moot point.

Genetic Variables

The background to the question of a genetic etiology in anxiety conditions, in particular, and emotional disorders, in general, is that in no example of a psychological condition that has been investigated is the heritability of psychological attributes so high that there is no room for environmental effects (Rutter, 1985). In fact, this statement can be reversed in the case of emotional disorders to a question: Is there any room for a genetic component?

Family resemblances provide an important datum: that is to say, the extent to which influences operate *within* or *between* families may be significant. Emotional disorders commonly affect just one child in the family, whereas conduct disorders usually affect several (Rutter, 1985). In examining the nature–nurture issue from another angle (familial concordance in anxious children), studies of parents of anxious children (e.g. Gittelman–Klein, 1975) and studies of the children of adults with anxiety disorders (e.g. Berg, 1976) produce some ambiguous findings, but on balance indicate a familial predisposition. These findings are not of the order that allows one to be precise about the relative contribution of inherited influences as compared with environmental influences, except to say that the former have a minor role.

Life Structure

Brown and Harris (1989) use the term 'life structure' to tackle the interface of the *internal* and *external* worlds of the individual and to reflect the fact that despite great complexity at any particular time, there is some structure to life—some regularity. The term refers to the current psychosocial totality of the child and to the transition and change in his or her family life, and according to Sloan (1987) 'encompasses not only behaviour but also unexpressed longings, moods, regrets and attitudes about one's life as well as all referents to these activities and feelings'. This significant aspect of the child's life moves the assessment on from a consideration of current antecedent influences to an inquiry into distal (historical) antecedents (see point 5a in Figure 3).

Very early environmental influences, even those going back to the child's uterine environment, are thought by some to sensitize the child to overreact to stimuli (see Joffe, 1968). It has been suggested that if the mother is under considerable stress during pregnancy, the child may be more reactive and highly strung than he or she would otherwise be. Many postnatal life events have been studied for their adverse consequences on children's psychological well-being: separation from parents (hospitalization, reception into care, divorce, bereavement), trauma (disaster, abuse), and family violence.

There is a range of separation anxieties shown by children—from the normal protest they make when parents go out to the morbidly fearful preoccupation at all times with mother's whereabouts. The sort of child who fits into the latter category is often referred to as 'clinging' or 'overdependent'. Theorists (see Belsky and Nezworski, 1988; Sluckin, Herbert and Sluckin, 1983) have long been interested in the development of bonds or attachments (secure vs. insecure) between children and their parents (notably mothers). They have also studied the weakening of these bonds—the period of psychological weaning from the parents—whereby children become persons in their own right. Another area of research concerns the fear of separation that, when it persists, is thought to be central to neurotic anxiety conditions. From the clinical point of view, the evidence (Rutter, 1971) suggests that psychological distress, of a kind commonly termed neurotic results (at least in part) from the early *disruption* of bonds.

TREATMENT

In this section, we will review behavioural strategies that are frequently used in the treatment of fears and phobias in children. Conceptually, these strategies are derived from principles of classical, vicarious, and operant conditioning, as well as recent advances in information processing theory. Although strategies based on each of these principles and theories will be presented separately, it should be understood from the outset that the more effective and durable treatments draw on all of these principles and theories in a complex interactive fashion. The use of such integrated approaches recognizes that fears and phobias, from the behavioural perspective, are acquired and maintained through an interactive combination of conditioning and mediational processes.

Systematic Desensitization

In its most basic form, systematic desensitization consists of three components: (a) induction of relaxation, (b) development of a fear-producing stimulus hierarchy, and (c) the systematic, graduated pairing of items in the hierarchy with relaxation. Generally, the fear-producing stimuli are presented imaginally (in order of least to most fear-producing) while the child is relaxed. This aspect of treatment is the desensitization proper and is thought to lead to the direct inhibition of the fear response. As noted by Wolpe (1973), it is imperative that the counterconditioning response (i.e. relaxation) be sufficient to inhibit fear at each step of the hierarchy.

Although studies have questioned the active mechanisms and the necessary ingredients of systematic desensitization (see review of Hatzenbuehler and Schroeder, 1978) there is little doubt that it is frequently used to good effect with children and adolescents.

Systematic desensitization has typically involved imaginal representation of the fear-producing stimuli and has employed muscular relaxation as the competing, inhibiting response. Although these procedures appear to work reasonably well with adolescents and older children (e.g. Ollendick, 1979b; Van Hasselt *et al.*, 1979), younger children appear to have difficulty in acquiring the muscular relaxation response and in being able to image clearly the fear-producing stimuli (Kissel, 1972; Rosenstiel and Scott, 1977). As a result, *in vivo* desensitization (as originally used by Jones, 1924) and emotive imagery (as suggested by Lazarus and Abramowitz, 1962) have become increasingly popular, at least with younger children (Hatzenbuehler and Schroeder, 1978; Ollendick, 1979a).

There is good evidence that behaviourally based interventions involving modelling can be very effective in helping people with anxiety disorders. It is often beneficial if the person sees the therapist carrying out the feared activity. This has of course to be performed in a way that is perceived as supportive of the child or adolescent—not in a way which makes them feel even more inadequate.

Cognitive approaches

Children can be taught to check self-defeating 'automatic' thinking such as 'I'll never manage' or 'I am getting tense ...' by coping self-statements, e.g. 'I can deal with this situation ...', 'Take it calmly; you're doing well.' People often do not recognize anxiety for what it is, and may misinterpret the physiological changes they are experiencing—pounding heart, headaches, changes in breathing—as evidence of an awful illness. This can set up a vicious spiral of increasing anxiety, so that children become 'afraid of being afraid—a common basis for panic attacks (see Ollendick, Matts and King, 1994).

A useful strategy is to teach self-talk (e.g. the mnemonic) below:

C: catch youself getting anxious
A: assert 'I can cope with this!'
L: long, deep breathing
M: muscular relaxation

In helping children to arrive at some understanding of why their problems have occurred, the following ideas could be explored with them:

- the nature of the anxiety or stress response—racing heart, sweating, churning stomach and anxiety-laden thoughts;
- the fact that these are normal, not abnormal, responses of the body to threatening experience and that he or she is not in danger of becoming insane;
- the possible link between the person's present experiences and earlier events, e.g. what he or she was taught to fear, life events, traumatic stress;
- the fact that the anxious child already in treatment is almost certain to experience some lapses in therapeutic progress.

Zatz and Chassin (1983) have documented the cognitions of test-anxious children. Anxious children not only endorse more debilitating statements (e.g. 'I'm doing poorly; I don't do well on tests like this; everyone usually does better than I'), they also ascribe to fewer facilitative, coping statements (e.g. 'I am bright enough to do this: I am doing the best that I can; I do well on tests like this'). Stefanek *et al.* (1987) have affirmed a similar pattern of self-statements in fearful, socially withdrawn children.

Probably the most frequently used cognitive approach with anxious and fearful children is verbal self-instruction training (Graziano and Mooney, 1980, 1982; Graziano *et al.*, 1979, Kanfer, Karoly and Newman, 1975).

Graziano and his colleagues conducted a series of studies with clinically phobic children (Graziano and Mooney, 1980; Graziano *et al.*, 1979), including a two- to three-year follow-up (Graziano and Mooney, 1982). Forty children between 6 and 13 years of age were treated. The children were severely night-time fearful, displaying panic behaviours (e.g. frequent crying and frightened calling out to the parents) that had disrupted the families nearly every night for a mean of five years. Children were randomly assigned to the treatment and waiting-list control group. The treatment rationale illustrative of the cognitive approach, was as follows:

> All of you have told us you are afraid of the dark or of being alone. As you know, some kids are afraid in the dark and others are not. The main difference between you and those other kids who are not afraid is that those other kids know how to *make* themselves not be afraid. In this class, we are going to teach you how to make yourselves less afraid. We are going to teach you how to relax, *think pleasant thoughts*, and *say special words*, all of which will help you become braver. (p. 209, italics added)

Results clearly attested to the efficacy of this approach. Significant changes were noted for the treatment group on a host of variables including number of minutes to get in bed and time to fall asleep, self-reported willingness to go to sleep, and proportion of days that delay tactics (e.g. ask for water, light on) were used. Following treatment the waiting-list group was also treated in total, 39 of the 40 children showed significant change in behaviour as judged against a single criterion: ten consecutive nights of fearless night-time behaviour. Long-term follow-up information was obtained two to three years after treatment from 34 of the 40 families using a mail questionnaire and extensive telephone contacts. Maintenance of improvement was noted for 31 of the 34 children.

Post-trauma Treatment (see Meichenbaum, 1997)

Sadly, relatively little (although not too little to leave health professionals pessimistic or helpless) is known about treating child survivors of a traumatic event. In the immediate aftermath of a trauma, children usually need to be reunited with their parents and family. Teenagers as well as younger survivors may wish to sleep in their parents' bed. The professional's first task is to help parents to understand the nature of PTSD and thus mobilize their tolerance, patience and reassurance. All may be needed. We do know that parental involvement in treatment is a vital component of success.

The other core component in virtually all formal treatment strategies has been some form of *re-exposure* to the traumatic cues, conducted in a structured and supportive manner. Activities such as semi-structured art activities, writing, storytelling, music, and puppetry are all thought to be useful, particularly with younger children, as activities which facilitate the process of re-exposure.

Such activities can occur spontaneously in children's play and may well form the basis of developmentally appropriate styles of coping, especially when they take place in the context of a supportive family.

The technique called *Critical Incident Stress Debriefing* has been adapted for use with children (see Yule, 1994). As he describes it:

Soon after an incident (within a few days) the survivors are brought together in a group with an outside facilitator/leader who formulates the rules for the introductory meeting. The goals are to share feelings and help each other in a context of privacy and confidentiality. No one is required to talk, although all are encouraged to participate.

Next, there is a clarification of the facts concerning what actually occurred during the traumatic events; this helps to reduce the rumours that surround such incidents. Group members are asked what they thought when they realized something was wrong. This moves the discussion on to how the children felt at the time and to their current emotional reactions. Children can thus share the variety of feelings they have experienced and learn, and often get comfort, from the similarity of the emotions and reactions experienced by their fellow survivors. The leader labels their reactions as normal and understandable responses to an abnormal situation, and the children often feel relief that their strange feelings (for example, symptoms of PTSD) are not signs of madness. The leader summarizes the information that emerges from the group discussion and educates the children with regard to simple strategies (such as deep, slow breathing, muscular and mental relaxation, thought stopping and distraction) they can adopt in order to control some of the reactions. Yule (1994) cautions that given the few evaluative studies of debriefing, and the assumption that individuals will adapt to crises at different rates, care must be exercised before offering debriefing as a panacea to all survivors.

Chapter 14

OBSESSIVE–COMPULSIVE DISORDER (OCD)

What is OCD?

Obsessive–compulsive disorder is one of the more intractable anxiety disorders—a potentially disabling condition that can persist throughout a person's life. The child or adult who suffers from OCD becomes embedded in a pattern of repetitive thoughts and actions that are senseless and distressing, but extremely difficult to control or banish.

The disorder occurs over a *spectrum*, from mild to severe. If it remains untreated, and is severe, it can impair (indeed destroy), an individual's capacity to function satisfactorily at work, at school, or even at home.

The general misery caused to children with the disorder, their parents and others who teach and care for them, makes an understanding of the condition, and an early intervention, a matter of urgent concern. The ramifications for adult sufferers and their families are also likely to be distressing in various ways that reduce the quality of their lives.

The Course of OCD

OCD often begins in childhood or adolescence—some 50% of cases according to the Epidemiological Catchment Area (ECA) study (Karno and Golding, 1990). The average age of onset is around 10 years, boys tending to develop OCD earlier than girls. The everyday, isolated obsessions and rituals so common in child development are discontinuous with OCD, and are not predictive of the acquisition of the condition.

There may be long intervals when the symptoms are mild, but for many individuals when once established, the symptoms of OCD (untreated) continue throughout life. The reasons for these fluctuations in severity in this condition are not understood. Remission, even after years of illness, occurs in something like a third of patients (Karno and Golding, 1990).

Fortunately, fairly recent discoveries in the areas of pharmacological and behaviour therapy have made what was once considered an irretrievably chronic condition, a *somewhat* less formidable clinical problem. Nevertheless, about 10% of patients suffer a continuous deteriorating course.

ASSESSMENT

See Rapoport (1989a–e) for the topic of this section.

Diagnosis

Obsessive–compulsive disorder (OCD) is a psychological (psychiatric) disorder, specifically an anxiety disorder. The ICD-10 and DSM-IV state that the diagnosis of OCD requires that the child, adolescent or adult has *obsessions* (repetitive intrusive thoughts) and/or *compulsions* (unwanted rituals) that cause distress and interfere with his/her social or role functioning.

(*Note*: By no means all sufferers have both conditions.)

- *Obsessions* are recurrent and persistent ideas, thoughts, impulses, or images that are experienced at least initially as intrusive and senseless.

  (Most obsessive thoughts focus on contamination, orderliness, aggression and sexual and religious themes).
- *Compulsions* are repetitive, purposeful, and intentional behaviours that are performed in response to an obsession, or according to certain rules, or in a stereotyped fashion. The behaviour is designed to neutralize or prevent discomfort or some dreaded event or situation. However, either the activity is not connected in a realistic way with what it is designed to neutralize or prevent, or it is clearly excessive.

  (The most common compulsions are checking and cleaning to prevent a catastrophe.)

  Younger children may not realize—unlike most adults—that the behaviour is unreasonable. However, the person with OCD generally realizes that his/her concerns and actions are senseless or excessive, indeed 'ego alien'.

Phenomenology of OCD

Baer (1991) points out that most people with OCD have both obsessions and compulsions. They often feel trapped in a 'loop' between the two. A frightening thought enters their mind, like 'I'm contaminated' or 'I injured someone'. As a result, they feel compelled to clean, check or perform some other ritual to reduce such thoughts and feelings. But since these rituals don't satisfy them, they become trapped into a loop of ever-increasing obsessions and compulsions that can last for hours. Judith Rapoport describes this loop in *The Boy Who Couldn't Stop Washing* as an 'obsessive–compulsive attack' that distorts the individual's view of reality (1989e, p. 21).

Baer provides examples of the various ways in which patients describe being trapped in this loop:

> One stares at a light switch for an hour, and although he sees that it is off, the longer he stares at it, the less certain he is that it really is off. And so he switches it on and off repeatedly, searching for that satisfying feeling of certainty that eludes him. Another fears that she has cut herself while handling scissors. She stares at her skin and sees no wound, but after an hour she still cannot be certain that she is not injured. A trip to the emergency room and reassurance don't satisfy her, and her checking continues long into the night.

Other people, he states, get trapped in another kind of OCD loop. Although they may have a few compulsions, like continually asking for reassurance, they get caught in a loop between their obsessions and *avoiding* situations. They therefore avoid situations that provoke their obsessions. The longer they stay away from them, the stronger their thoughts become. When they do venture into the situation, the thoughts are overwhelming, and they immediately return to avoiding it. And so the obsession–avoidance loop persists!

People who don't suffer from OCD find it difficult to understand the power of these loops. For a person who has OCD it isn't easy to 'just stop doing it!' as these patients are often advised or instructed. The OCD sufferer usually knows that his/her thoughts and rituals are senseless but not when he or she is trapped in the middle of the OCD loop. Then it seems that peace of mind, even their survival, depends on performing these rituals. They feel out of control!

Prevalence

OCD is the fourth most common psychiatric disorder with a prevalence rate of 1.9% cent in adults. Surveys suggest that OCD affects about 1 in every 100 children. Estimates indicate that less than 10% of OCD sufferers are receiving treatment.

Individuals are frequently reluctant—because of the shaming or macabre nature of their symptoms as they perceive them—to disclose their problems.

Co-morbidity

Only about 26% of children have OCD as a single diagnosis. The disorders most commonly associated with (sometimes predating) OCD are depression and anxiety. Other related disorders include phobias, panic attacks, alcohol abuse, trichotilomania (hair-pulling) tic disorders such as Gilles de la Tourette's syndrome (GTS) (with which OCD may be genetically linked), eating disorders, attention deficit disorder (ADD), conduct/oppositional disorder, body dysmorphic disorder (preoccupation with exaggerated defects in appearance) and hypochondriasis.

CAUSAL INFLUENCES

Widely different views have been put forward to explain OCD throughout the ages. Possession by the devil, who forced sufferers to perform their strange rituals, was an early theory. OCD was thought later to be the result of insanity. This view was held until the mid-19th century. The 20th century gave us Freudian theories (S. Freud, 1913; A. Freud, 1965). However, psychoanalytic speculations about intrapsychic causes, or life-events of a traumatic nature causing OCD, have not stood the test of time, and have not generated a therapy that works.

Derek Bolton, (1996) author of an invaluable paper on developmental issues in OCD, has this to say.

> One of the fascinations of obsessive–compulsive disorder (OCD) is its apparent similarity to phenomena which, from the point of view of psychopathology, are quite distinct. On one hand, there are apparent similarities to normal behaviour, and on the other to symptoms associated with known or suspected cerebral disorder. These distinct connections suggest quite different types of aetiology, and this is reflected in current research programmes. They focus either on what is normal or continuous with the normal in OCD, or on signs of central nervous dysfunction. Generally speaking, the former are in the tradition of viewing OCD as an anxiety disorder, while the latter take it to be fundamentally a neurological disorder, a view that currently has something of the status of a new orthodoxy. (Bolton, 1996, p. 131)

Neurobiological Factors (see Rapoport, Swedo and Leonard, 1994).

Certainly, with regard to that last remark, neurobiological influences—genetic (twin studies) biochemical, pharmacological successes, structural and functional brain imaging studies (by positron emission tomography and magnetic resonance imagery) give support to the view that there is neurobiological deficit in OCD. It has long been recognized that there is an association between obsessive–compulsive symptomatology and cerebral diseases such as encephalitis lethargica (von Economo, 1931) and Sydenham's chorea (Swedo et al., 1989). Symptomatology sometimes follows a head injury (McKeon, McGuffin and Robinson, 1984)—these are also associated with tics—and other signs of cerebral disorder.

There are soft neurological signs at above normal frequency in OCD. Performance on psychoneurological tasks tends to be below normal (see Cox, Fedio and Rapoport, 1989).

Basal Ganglia Dysfunction

A number of basal ganglia disorders (e.g. Sydenham's chorea, Parkinson's disease, Tourette's disorder) are associated with OCD. The aetiological role of the frontal lobe–basal ganglia circuits, in OCD, is a current area of research producing much excitement and optimism.

Researchers at UCLA, Harvard, and the National Institute of Mental Health have published several PET scanning studies that indicate that when OCD patients improve with medication, or even with behaviour therapy without medication, a certain region of the basal ganglia (an important switching centre in the middle of the brain called the caudate nucleus) changes proportional to the OCD treatment response. These findings are very different after treating unipolar major depression with the same medication. The basal ganglia, in association with other brain regions, is important in all animals for learning and breaking habits.

Serotonergic Theory

With current therapies serotonin in the basal ganglia is a mediator of brain mechanisms that somehow compensate for the abnormalities leading to OCD.

The serotonergic hypotheses of OCD is derived from the *selective efficacy* in the treatment of OCD of drugs that have specific serotonergic activity (Insel and Winslow, 1990). A widely accepted theory is that OCD may be mediated by biochemical abnormalities in the basal ganglia. Additionally, OCD symptoms may be exacerbated by a metachlorophenyl-piperazine (mCPP), a serotonergic agonist (Pigott *et al.*, 1991). (For a discussion of the standing of these theories see Rapoport, Swedo and Leonard, 1994; Murphy *et al.*, 1989).

Bolton (1996) concludes from his review of the evidence that:

> Neurological deficit models of psychopathology are complex and hard to assemble. Such a model has to include specification of the lesion, structural and/or biochemical; its immediate effects on information processing, which may be above or below the level of consciousness, and linked to motor outputs or not, specification of the ways in which the system as a whole adapts to the information-processing deficit, and of how this adaptation is expressed in intentional action and phenomenology. To all of those problem areas may be added further major complications including genetics, if genetic predisposition or vulnerability is part of the story, and developmental themes, which determine presentation at different ages and stages. Typically parts of the picture have to be attended to separately *with work* then to piece them together, to sketch something like a whole. Paradigm examples of these multi-faceted, multi-layered research programmes are in schizophrenia (Ancill, Holliday & Higenbottam, 1994), and autism (Dawson, 1989). In the case of OCD crucial pieces of the jigsaw puzzle or the connection between them remain particularly unclear.

Neuroethological Models

There is a view that at least some obsessive–compulsive behaviours are *displacement behaviours*. These are fixed action patterns carried out in the absence of a normal releasing stimulus in circumstances of frustration or drive conflict. Fixed action patterns are innate and adaptive motor actions or sequences normally elicited by a releasing stimulus (e.g. grooming, pecking).

The ethological view of OCD posits at least some compulsive symptomatology as being like displacement behaviour (Bolton, 1996). Bolton states that this view may be combined with the hypotheses that in OCD the behaviours are caused by a structural and/or biochemical neurological lesion. A neurological model along the lines implicating specifically the basal ganglia as well as the regulatory role of serotonin is put forward by Wise and Rapoport (1989).

Psychological Influences

- *Learning*. The undoubted efficacy of behaviour therapy in OCD (see below) is suggestive of some role for learning in the evolution and/or maintenance of the problem, although treatment effectiveness *per se* does not necessarily offer proof of the hypothesized aetiology.

There are various ways of constructing psychological models of the genesis of irrational fears. The conditioning paradigm positing an over-generalization from or association with traumatic experience is the simplest mechanism. A more sophisticated approach has become possible with the cognitive therapy paradigm, which deals more with thoughts, and particularly with thoughts about thoughts. The cognitive–behavioural model links OCD to normal psychological functioning.

Salkovskis (1985) applies the cognitive–behavioural therapy paradigm to OCD as follows:

> Everyone has normal, unwanted, intrusive thoughts. Patients with OCD place special significance on these, perhaps because they have an exaggerated sense of responsibility. This leads to feeling responsible for producing the thought, to feeling that they are a bad person, and to guilt. It also prompts the feeling that they themselves must act to prevent a disaster. The 'neutralizing' action results in recurrence of the thought. Thus there arises a vicious circle involving unwanted, intrusive thoughts, feelings of responsibility and guilt, attempts to neutralize the thoughts, and hence their recurrence. Feelings of responsibility and guilt might be exacerbated particularly in the absence of a clear distinction between having a negative thought, and carrying out the negative action itself, a blurring which has been called 'thought–action fusion'.

Behaviour therapy (as we shall see) exposes the patient to the source of the obsessional thought followed by prevention of the compulsion. This is regarded as fundamentally an extinction procedure. In this formulation, the compulsions make sense—they are viewed as methods of reducing anxiety prompted by obsessional thoughts. The obsessions do not make sense; they typically remain just 'irrational' fears.

Magical Thinking. Bolton states that it is critical to living beings to experience control over what matters to them, the alternatives being anxiety and helplessness, with consequent inertia (Bandura, 1977, Seligman, 1975). He argues that superstitious belief and action can be used when rational belief and action fail to secure or avert a highly salient positive or negative outcome. Such a strategy may have no effect on reality, but its intrapsychic reinforcement effect is high. It reduces or removes the anxiety, sense of helplessness, and despair that goes with perceived lack of control over what really is of concern. This function of pre-rational thought and its potential relevance to OCD has been frequently recognized (S. Freud, 1913, Rachman & Hodgson, 1980; Pitman *et al.*, 1987). Anna Freud noted that obsessions and compulsions have some features in common with childhood superstitions and rituals (A. Freud, 1965).

The major differences are that obsessive–compulsive symptoms, compared with normal childhood superstitions and rituals, are longer in duration, are experienced as distressing, and interfere with normal activities (Leonard, 1989). All the above considerations seem to point to a developmental cognitive model of OCD. The search for causes of OCD is far from complete. Today the focus is on the interaction of neurobiological factors and environmental influence, and additionally, cognitive processes (information processing).

TREATMENT

Lee Baer, Director of Research at the OCD Clinic at Massachusetts General Hospital and Professor of Psychology at the Harvard Medical School, is of the opinion that the question 'Can we treat OCD successfully' would have been answered 'Probably not' when posed in the 1960s. The picture is a much more optimistic one today because of advances in *behaviour therapy* on the psychological side of the OCD equation and discoveries about pharmacological therapy on the medical side.

Baer makes the important point that any evaluation of OCD therapies must take into account the fluctuation of untreated OCD symptoms (see Rasmussen and Tsuang, 1985). Periods of remission (rarely 100% of the duration time or totally free of symptoms) may involve improvements over fairly long periods of time.

Baer's team have set themselves the following criteria for evaluating effective treatments:

- treatments that have been demonstrated to help more than 50% of patients;
- treatments that accomplish this in a short time;
- treatments that result in lasting improvement.

Traditional Psychotherapy

Traditional ('talking') therapies (including psychoanalysis) designed to help the patient develop insight into his or her problem, have not been demonstrated to be effective with OCD if we go by the criteria described above. The attempts to find 'hidden' symbolic meanings for the symptoms, unconscious conflicts about forbidden impulses, or early dynamics within the family which underly the manifest symptomatology, have not borne fruit in the reduction of the obsessions and compulsions which beset the sufferer (see Esman, 1989).

Nor has symptomatic treatment (as opposed to intrapsychic, depth explorations) led to the symptom substitution or other 'side effects' despite the warnings of psychoanalysts who insist that the symptoms are only the outward and visible sign of the real causes—which reside in the unconscious and the early history of the patient.

This is not to discount the value, indeed importance, of a comprehensive and sensitive clinical assessment and history, as patients with OCD often have other difficulties, related or unrelated to the OCD.

Behaviour Therapy

This approach focuses particularly on the methods of exposure and response-prevention. In adults it is established as a major therapeutic tool for dealing with OCD. Despite less systematic research in children and adolescents the available evidence (e.g. Wolff and Rapoport, 1988; Berg *et al.*, 1989) confirms that the method is highly appropriate and similar for them.

The essence of the method is that it

- *confronts* the things the child/adolescent fears as often as possible;
- *resists* avoidance (if they feel like avoiding something they must resist the urge);
- *resists* the urge to carry out a compulsive action (if they feel they have to perform a ritual to feel better they must resist the feeling);
- *continues* these three steps as long as possible.

To summarize: the patient deliberately and voluntarily confronts the feared object or idea, either directly or by imagination. At the same time the patient is strongly encouraged to refrain from ritualizing, with support and structure provided by the therapist, and possibly by others whom the patient recruits for assistance. For example, a compulsive hand washer may be encouraged to touch an object believed to be contaminated, and then urged to avoid washing for several hours until the anxiety provoked has greatly decreased. Treatment then proceeds on a step-by-step basis, guided by the patient's ability to tolerate the anxiety and control the rituals. As treatment progresses, most patients gradually experience less anxiety from the obsessive thoughts and are able to resist the compulsive urges.

Of course, this is a great deal harder to achieve than it sounds. The work involved must be done systematically, with the aid of detailed planning, record forms, and most vitally help—an experienced professional (or self-help guide) and/or a human support-giver and helper. For children this means parents or other caregivers. Particular care and delicacy are required in planning treatment for children. Parental agreement and support (and detailed explanations of the method for them and the child) are crucial.

Strange to say, the French Neurologist, Pierre Janet, at the turn of the century, described in remarkably similar terms (while using the word 'exposure') what we now call exposure therapy.

Sadly, psychoanalysis—founded by his contemporary, Sigmund Freud—swept into oblivion these ideas—until the 1960s when psychologists (among them notably Vic Meyer in London) put their behavioural methods to work on OCD.

Evaluation

Studies of behaviour therapy for OCD have found it to be a successful treatment for the majority of adult patients who complete it. For the treatment to be successful, it is important that the therapist be fully trained to provide this specific form of therapy. It is also helpful for the patient to be highly motivated and have a positive, determined attitude.

The positive effects of behaviour therapy tend to endure once treatment has ended in the case of adults. A recent compilation of outcome studies indicated that, of more than 300 OCD patients who were treated by exposure and response prevention, an average of 76 per cent still showed clinically significant relief from 3 months to 6 years after treatment (Foa and Kozak, 1996). Another study has found that incorporating relapse-prevention components in the treatment programme, including follow-up sessions after the intensive therapy, contribute to the maintenance of improvement (Hiss, Foa, and Kozak, 1994).

Relatively few publications on the use of behavioural treatment of OCD in children are available (see Apter *et al.*, 1984; Bolton, Collins and Steinberg, 1983; Zikis, 1983). However the results have been encouraging. Involvement of the family is critical.

The cognitive behavioural approach focuses on making explicit real and imagined threat, and on teaching/modelling more rationally-based coping strategies, along the lines of clinical management for child anxiety disorders generally (Kendall *et al.*, 1991; Bolton, 1994). Cognitive-behavioural therapy—a variant of behaviour therapy—emphasizes changing the OCD sufferer's beliefs and thinking patterns. It follows from the theories put forward by Salkovskis (1984) and Rachman (1997) that 'the most direct and satisfactory treatment of obsessions is to assist patients in the modification of the putatively causal catastrophic misinterpretations of the significance of the intrusive thoughts' (Rachman, 1997, p. 799). Additional studies are required before the promise of cognitive-behavioural therapy for children can be adequately evaluated. The hypothesis that OCD is basically a neurological disorder is just beginning to generate treatment rationales and protocols (including specifically for children, references to compulsions as 'hiccoughs of the brain' or 'brain short circuits', March, Mulle and Herbel, 1994; Wever and Phillips, 1994).

Physical Treatments

Psychosurgery

Surgical lesions that result in the disconnection of the basal ganglia from the frontal cortex are used—usually as a method of last resort—the preferred methods for OCD being capsulotomy and cingulectomy (see Chiocca & Martzuzza, 1990; Mindus, 1991).

ECT

This is not an effective treatment for OCD.

Pharmacology

Almost every antidepressant, antianxiety and antipsychotic drug in the pharmacology armamentarium has been tried, over the years, on OCD—but to little or no effect. The breakthrough for this approach arrived in the early 1970s with research on Clomipramine (Anafranil)—a drug very similar to other tricyclic antidepressants.

Since then three medications have received the official approval of the American authorities (Food and Drug Administration) having survived multiple double-blind trials, showing superiority over placebo in dual treatment of OCD. These are as follows (although others are on the horizon):

(1) Clomipramine (Anafranil)
(2) Fluoxetine (Prozac)
(3) Fluvoxamine (Luvox)

Most drugs that are effective in reducing symptoms of OCD are thought to have effects on serotonin. Clomipramine (Anafranil), fluoxetine (Prozac) and fluvoxamine (Luvox) keep more serotonin available in the synapses between nerve cells. Normally, serotonin is quickly reabsorbed by the transmitting nerve cell (reuptake). The drugs delay this uptake so the serotonin remains in the synapse longer and brain signals can be transmitted. As a result, these drugs are referred to as *serotonin reuptake inhibitors*.

Prescribing dosage. This is a matter for a psychiatrist with pharmacological knowledge, and experience with OCD Patients.

Effectiveness. All these drugs take about 2–3 months to work on OCD. Typically 'response' is a 30–50% reduction in symptoms as measured on the Yale–Brown Obsessive–Compulsive Scale. Many practitioners advise that, with few exceptions, patients who have obsessive–compulsive disorder should *also* have behaviour therapy. Currently 80–90% eventually received *significant relief* if treated with vigour.

A compelling reason for a combined approach is the fact that the symptoms rarely go away *completely*. They do tend to 'fade' rather than 'vanish' dramatically. Medications are of help in controlling the symptoms of OCD, but often, if the medication is discontinued, relapse will follow. Indeed, even after symptoms have subsided, most people will need to continue with medication indefinitely, perhaps with a lowered dosage. Behaviour therapy provides a method which reduces patients' sense of learned helpless, increases their perceived self-efficacy, and thus their sense that they have the wherewithal to enjoy rather than endure life.

Augmenters. Some medications which are of little value when used *alone* for OCD (e.g. methylphenidate (Ritalin), haloperidol (Haldol) or pimozide (Orap), augment/enhance the effect of the anticompulsive medication like clomipramine or fluoxitine.

As with all medication, but particularly when using augmenters, it is *critical* for patients to be precisely and well informed about the administration of the medication and the short- and long-term side-effects

PLANNING A BEHAVIOUR THERAPY PROGRAMME

Lee Baer gives an example of behavioural treatment of patients suffering from compulsive hand washing and showering due to fears of being contaminated by cancer 'germs'. Exposure would consist of gradually bringing them into contact with objects they believe to be contaminated such as a magazine or chair in the waiting area of a cancer clinic. They would then be encouraged to stay in contact with the 'contaminated' object for as long as possible (*exposure*) and then to keep from washing their hands or showering for one to two hours afterwards (*response prevention*).

Baer describes habituation as the key to exposure and response prevention and the control of OCD symptoms giving the following day-to-day examples of its working (1991, p. 35):

Have you ever visited friends who live near an airport or train station? You've probably wondered how in the world they can stand the noise. But your friends seem hardly to notice it. Or have you ever squeezed into a painfully tight pair of shoes in the morning, only to find that by evening you've forgotten you have them on? If you've had either of these experiences, you've witnessed your body's process of habituation firsthand. 'Habituation', which comes from the Latin word *habitus*, for 'habit', means 'to accustom; to make familiar by frequent use or practice'. In other words, after long familiarity with a situation that at first produces a strong emotional reaction, our bodies learn to get used to or ignore that situation.

Another key element in self-control is the reframing or cognitive restructuring of the patient's self-talk about his or her OCD. The distinction between claims that *one cannot* resist a compulsion and stating that one is *unwilling* to put up with the discomfort/anxiety that accompanies the resistance, is a critical one.

Baer has this to say:

Just learning this principle is sometimes a revelation for my patients. At first they say things like 'I have to check the lock' or 'I have to wash my hands'. I immediately correct them and have them be more precise: 'I *feel* like I have to check the lock' and 'I *feel* like I have to wash my hands'. Once patients recognize this distinction, they realize that they can always control their behaviours, provided they put in the effort and, if they need it, get assistance.

A fair trial of behaviour therapy requires a total of at least 20 hours of exposure and response prevention—with periods of 1–2 hours per session of exposure and response prevention. The main requirements are patience, persistence and optimism!

Baer encourages OCD patients to copy onto an index card—as reminders during practice assignments—the following (reassuring) elements of a basic behavioural principle:

- You cannot always control your thoughts.
- You cannot always control your feelings.
- But you *can* always control your behaviour.
- As you change your behaviour, your thoughts and feelings will also change.

Steps in Behavioural Treatment

(1) Describe the main symptoms clearly.
(2) Conduct a functional analysis.
(3) Write down the long-term goals.

(4) Write down the patient's practice goals (breaking them down into small achievable steps).

(5) Use SUDS ratings to guide the patient's practice goals (see Figure 14). How does the patient know when to stop working on a practice goal and move on to a new one? A SUDS rating will tell him/her when they have become habituated to a practice goal:

  (a) Make a SUDS rating when you begin working on a practice goal.

  (b) Next, after 30 minutes or so of practice, note your SUDS rating again.

  (c) When the SUDS rating, decreases to 30 or lower for two practice sessions in a row, it's time to move on to another, more difficult practice goal.

  (d) The therapist and patient will have to decide on the rating you will aim for before switching to another practice goal—but it should be a rating at which the patient feels comfortable.

(6) Persist despite setbacks.

(7) Make a note of small gains/achievements.

(8) Keep long-term goals in mind.

(9) Make use of thought stopping.

(10) Maintain correct and rigorous standards in exposure and response prevention. Parents are essential in helping children with their programmes; it is important to record them when they succeed in their practice. (Reinforcers in the form of treats should help.)

(11) Monitor and evaluate change. Feelings, thoughts and behaviour do not usually change simultaneously. Behaviours usually change first, followed by feelings and then by thoughts.

The rating scale is 1–10				
1	25	50	75	100
Not anxious/ distressed	Mild	Moderate	Severe	Extreme anxiety

Figure 14 The Subjective Units of Distress (SUDS) rating scale (developed by Dr Joseph Wolpe).

Thought-stopping

Baer (1991) describes one method he used:

First, I stretched a rubber band around his wrist and told him to close his eyes and, as soon as he began thinking the obsessive thought, to snap the rubber band and shout 'Stop!' out loud. After he practised this a few times, I taught him to shout 'Stop!' under his breath, so that no one could hear it and he could use thought stopping in private. Finally, I asked him to put all the pieces together: picture a bright red stop sign, silently shout the word 'stop' to himself, and snap the rubber band the first instant he was aware of thinking the obsessive thought. This man was able to learn the entire thought-stopping procedure in only fifteen minutes.

EPILOGUE

Living and working, as we do, in a multi-ethnic society, it is of critical importance that psychologists should be sensitive, not only to the norms, sensibilities and sensitivities of people from different cultures but also the stressful life experiences they endure in a sadly racist society. Racism extends, far too often, into service delivery.

It is not only in matters of race, nationality and creed where prejudice has its corrosive influence; it affects women and female children in many subtle and unsubtle ways. In many senses of the word they are 'disabled' in our society and demeaned in the way that those of our clients to whom we attach the label 'disabled' are patronized and robbed of their self-fulfilment.

I am conscious at the end of this book of a paradox for the reader, be he or she a student or an experienced practitioner. These pages contain so much about families, parents, children and their problems . . . and, yet, so little. The subject is so vast that we have only scratched the surface. This is not simply a matter of the limited space available in one volume; it is intrinsic to the topic. We have so much to learn, so much research to initiate. Fortunately, there is no reason for an attitude of pessimism or helplessness. We know enough to be of service to those whose family life is floundering, whose children are in distress, and who, consequently, are calling for help.

REFERENCES

Abramson, L.Y., Seligman, M.E.P. and Teasdale, J.D. (1978). Learned helplessness in humans: Critique and reformulation. *Journal of Abnormal Psychology*, **87**, 49–74.

Achenbach, T.M. (1974). *Developmental psychopathology*. New York: Ronald Press.

Achenbach, T.M. (1978). The child behavior profile: I. Boys aged 6–11. *Journal of Consulting and Clinical Psychology*, **46**, 478–488.

Achenbach, T.M. (1982). *Developmental psychopathology* (2nd edn). New York: Wiley.

Achenbach, T.M. (1985). Assessment of anxiety in children. In A.H. Tuma and J. Maser (eds), *Anxiety and the anxiety disorders*. Hillsdale, NJ: Lawrence Erlbaum.

Achenbach, T.M. and Edelbrock, C.S. (1979). The child behavior profile: II. Boys aged 12–16 and girls aged 6–11 and 12–16. *Journal of Consulting and Clinical Pyschology*, **47**, 223–233.

Achenbach, T.M. and Edelbrock, C.S. (1983). Taxonomic issues in child psychology. In T. Ollendick and M. Hersen (eds), *Handbook of child psychopathology*. New York: Plenum.

Achenbach, T.M. and Edelbrock, C.S. (1989). Diagnostic taxonomic, and assessment issues. In T.H. Ollendick and M. Hersen (eds), *Handbook of child psychopathology* (2nd ed). New York: Plenum.

Achenbach, T.M., McConaughy, S.H. and Howell, C.T. (1987). Child/adolescent behaviors and emotional problems: Implications of cross-informant correlations for situational specificity. *Psychological Bulletin*, **101**, 213–232.

Ager, A. (1985). Alternatives to speech for the mentally handicapped. In F.N. Watts (ed.). *New developments in clinical psychology*. Leicester: British Psychological Society/Wiley.

Agras, W.S., Chapin, H.H. and Oliveau, D. (1972). The natural history of phobias: Course and prognosis. *Archives of General Psychiatry*, **26**, 315–317.

Agras, W.S., Sylvester, D. and Oliveau, D. (1969). The epidemiology of common fears and phobias. *Comprehensive Psychiatry*, **10**, 151–156.

Ainsworth, M.D.S., Behar, M.C., Walters, E. and Wall, S. (1978). *Patterns of attachment: A psychological study of the strange situation*. Hillsdale, NJ: Erlbaum.

Akiskal, H.S. and McKinney, W.T. (1975). Overview of recent research in depression. *Archives of General Psychiatry*, **32**, 285–305.

Alexander, J.F. and Parsons B.V. (1982). *Functional family therapy*. Monterey: Brooks/Cole

Alexander, R.N., Corbett, T.F. and Smigel, J. (1976). The effects of individual group consequences on school attendance and curfew violations with predelinquent adolescents. *Journal of Applied Behavior Analysis*, **9**, 221–6.

Allen, D.A. and Affleck, G. (1985). Are we stereotyping parents? A postscript to Blacher. *Mental Retardation* **23**, 200–202.

American Psychiatric Association (1980). *Diagnostic and statistical manual of mental disorders (DSM-III)* 3rd edn. Washington, DC: APA.

American Psychiatric Association. (1987). *Diagnostic and statistical manual of mental disorders* (3rd edn revised). Washington, DC: APA.

American Psychiatric Association (1994). *Diagnostic and statistical manual of mental disorders.* (4th edn) (DSM-IV). Washington DC: APA.

Anastasi, A. (1982). *Psychological testing.* New York: Collier Macmillan.

Ancill R.J., Holliday, S. and Higenbottam J. (eds) (1994). *Schizophrenia: exploring the spectrum of psychosis.* Chichester: Wiley.

Anderson H. and Goolishian H. (1988). Human systems as linguistic systems: preliminary and evolving ideas about the implications for clinical theory. *Family Process*, **27**, 371–393.

Anderson, K.O. and Masur, F.T. (1983). Psychological preparation for invasive medical and dental procedures. *Journal of Behavioural Medicine*, **6**,(1), 1–37.

Andrews, G. and Harris, M. (1964). *The syndrome of stuttering. Clinics in developmental medicine*, vol. 17, London: Heinemann Medical Books.

Angold, A. (1994). Clinical interviewing with children and adolescents. In: M. Rutter, E. Taylor, and L. Hersov (eds) *Child and adolescent psychiatry: modern approaches* (3rd edn). Oxford: Blackwell Scientific Applications.

Angold, A., Weissman, M., Merikangas, J.K., Prusoff, B., Wickramaratne, P., Gammon, G. and Warner, B. (1987). Parent and child reports of depressive symptoms in children at low and high risk of depression. *Journal of Child Psychology and Psychiatry*, **28**, 901–915.

Anthony, E.J. (1957). An experimental approach to the psychopathology of childhood: Encopresis. *British Journal of Medical Psychology*, **30**, 146–175.

Apley, J. (1975). *The child with abdominal pain.* Oxford: Blackwell Scientific.

Apter A. *et al.* (1984). Severe obsessive-compulsive disorder in adolescence: a report of eight cases. *Journal of Adolescence* **1**, 349–358.

Aries, P. (1973). *Centuries of childhood: A social history of family life.* Harmondsworth: Penguin.

Asperger, H. (1944). Die 'Autischen Psychopathen' im Kindesalter. *Archiv, fur Psychiatrie und Nervenkrankheiten*, **117**, 76–136. (Translation 'Autistic Psychopathy in childhood.' In: Frith, 1994, pp. 37–92.

August, G.J., Stewart, M.A. and Holmes, C.S. (1983). A four-year follow-up of hyperactive boys with and without conduct disorder. *British Journal of Psychiatry*, **143**, 192–198.

Austin, J. (1811). *Sense and sensibility.* London: Collins Clear Type Press.

Ausubel, D.P., Balthazar, E.E., Rosenthal, I., Blackman, L.S. Schpoont, S.H. and Welkowitz, J. (1954). Received parental attitudes as determinants of children's ego structure. *Child Development*, **25**, 173–183.

Axline, V.M. (1947). *Play therapy.* Boston: Houghton-Mifflin.

Ayalon, O. (1988). *Rescue! Community oriented preventive education for coping with stress.* Haifa: Nord Publications.

Ayllon, T., Smith, D. and Rogers. M. (1970). Behavioral management of school phobia. *Journal of Behavior Therapy and Experimental Psychiatry*, **1**, 125–138.

Bachrach, A.J., Erwin, W.J. and Mohr, J.P. (1965). The control of eating behaviour in an anorexic by operant conditioning techniques. In L.P. Ullmann and L. Krasner (eds). *Case studies in behaviour modification.* New York: Holt, Rinehart & Winston.

Baer L. (1991). *Getting control: Overcoming your obsessions and compulsions*. Boston: Little, Brown.

Baer, D.M., Wolf, M.M. and Risley, T.R. (1968). Some current dimensions of applied behaviour analysis, *Journal of Applied Behavior Analysis*, **1**, 91–97.

Bailey, V., Graham, P. and Boniface, D. (1978). How much child psychiatry does a general practioner do? *Journal of the Royal College of General Practitioners*, **28**, 621–626.

Bailey *et al.* (1993). Prevalence of the fragile-X anomaly amongst autistic twins and singletons. *Journal of Child Psychology and Psychiatry*, **34**, 673–688.

Baldwin, S. (1985). No silence please. *Times Educational Supplement*, **679**, (8th November), p. 25.

Baller, V.R. (1975). *Bedwetting: Origins and treatment*. New York: Pergamon.

Bancroft, J.H. (1970). Homosexuality in the male. *British Journal of Hospital Medicine*, **3**, 168–181.

Bandura, A. (1968). Modeling approaches to the modification of phobic disorders. In R. Porter (ed.), *Ciba Foundation Symposium: The role of learning in psychotherapy*. London: Churchill.

Bandura, A. (1969). *Principles of behavior modification*. New York: Holt, Rinehart & Winston.

Bandura, A. (1973). *Aggression: A social learning analysis*. Englewood Cliffs, NJ: Prentice-Hall.

Bandura, A. (1977). *Social learning theory*. Englewood Cliffs, NJ: Prentice-Hall.

Bandura, A. (1986). *Social foundations of thought and action: A social cognitive theory*. Englewood Cliffs. NJ: Prentice-Hall.

Bandura, A. and Walters, R.H. (1963). *Social learning and personality development*. New York: Holt, Rinehart & Winston.

Barkley, R.A. (1977). A review of stimulant drug research with hyperactive children. *Journal of Child Psychology and Psychiatry*, **18**, 137–165.

Barkley, R.A. (1982). *Hyperactive children: A handbook for diagnosis and management*. New York: Guilford Press.

Barkley, R.A. (1990). *Attention-deficit hyperactivity disorder: A handbook for diagnosis and treatment*. New York: Guilford Press.

Barkley, R.A. (1994). *Taking charge of ADHD*. New York: Guilford Press.

Baron-Cohen, S. and Howlin, P. (1993). The theory of mind deficit in autism: some questions for teaching and diagnosis. In S. Baron-Cohen, H. Tager-Flusberg and D.J. Cohen (eds), *Understanding Other Minds: Perspectives from Autism*. London: Oxford University Press, 466–479.

Baron-Cohen, S., Leslie, A. and Frith, U. (1985). Does the autistic child have a theory of mind? *Cognition*, **21**, 37–46.

Barrios B.A. and Pennebaker J.W. (1983). A note in the early detection of bulimia nervosa. *Behavior Therapist*, **6**, 18–19.

Barrish, A.H., Saunders, M. and Wolf, M.M. (1969). Good behavior game. *Journal of Applied Behavior Analysis*, **2**, 119–124.

Bates, J.E. and Bayles, K. (1984). Objective and subjective components in mothers' perceptions of their children from age 6 months to 3 years. *Merrill-Palmer Quarterly*, **30**, 111–130.

Bateson, G., Jackson, D.D., Haley, J. and Weakland, J. (1956). Toward a theory of schizophrenia. *Behavioral Science*, **1**, 251–264.

Bauer, D.H. (1976). An exploratory study of developmental changes in children's fears. *Journal of Child Psychology and Psychiatry*, **17**, 69–74.

Baumrind, D. (1966). Effects of authoritative parental control on child behaviour. *Child Development*, **37** (4), 887–907.

Baumrind, D. (1971). Current patterns of parental authority. *Developmental Psychology Monograph*, **4** (1), Pt. 2, 1–103.

Bauwens, J. and Hourcore, J.J. (1989). Hey, would you just listen. *Teaching the Exceptional Child*, **21** (Spring), 22–61.

Beck, A.T. (1976). *Cognitive therapy and the emotional disorders*. New York: Meridian.

Beidel, D.C., Neal, and Lederec (1991). The feasibility and validity of a daily diary for the assessment of anxiety in children. *Behavior Therapy*, **22**, 505–517.

Bell, R.A. (1971). Stimulus control of parent or caretaker behaviour by offspring. *Developmental Psychology*, **4**, 63–72.

Belsky, J. (1984). The determinants of parenting: A process model. *Child Development*, **55**, 83–96.

Belsky, J. and Nezworski, T. (eds) (1988). *Clinical implications of attachment*. Hillsdale, NJ: Lawrence Erlbaum.

Bemis, K.M. (1987). The present status of operant conditioning treatment of anorexia nervosa. *Behaviour Modification*, **11**, 432–463.

Bennun, I. (1986). Evaluating family therapy: a comparison of the Milan and problem-solving approaches. *Journal of Family Therapy*, **8**, 225–242.

Beresford, B.A. (1994). Resources and strategies: How parents cope with the care of a disabled child. *Journal of Child Psychology and Psychiatry*, **35**, 171–209.

Berg, C.Z. *et al.* (1989). Childhood obsessive–compulsive disorder: a two-year prospective follow-up of a community sample. *Journal of the American Academy of Child and Adolescent Psychiatry*, **28**, 528–533.

Berg, I. (1976). School phobia in the children of agoraphobic women. *British Journal of Psychiatry*, **128**, 86–89.

Berger, M.M. (1978). Video feedback confrontation review. In M.M. Berger (ed.), *Videotape Techniques in Psychiatric Training and Treatment*. New York: Brunner/Mozel.

Berger, M. (1986). Toward an educated use of IQ tests: A reappraisal of intelligence testing. In B.B. Lahey and A.E. Kazdin (eds). *Advances in clinical child psychology*, Vol. 9, New York: Plenum.

Berger, M. (1996). Outcomes and effectiveness in clinical psychology practice. Division of Clinical Psychology Occasional Paper, No. 1. British Psychological Society.

Berger, M., Yule, W. and Rutter, M. (1975). Attainment and adjustment in two geographical areas. II: The prevalence of specific reading retardation. *British Journal of Psychiatry*, **126**, 510–519.

Bergin, A.E. and Lambert, M.J. (1978). The evaluation of therapeutic outcomes. In: S.L. Garfield and A.E. Bergin (eds) *Handbook of psychotherapy and behaviour change*. New York: Wiley.

Berkowitz (1978). Experiments on the reactions of juvenile delinquents to filmed violence. In L.A. Hersov and M. Berger (eds), *Aggression and antisocial behaviour in childhood and adolescence*. Oxford: Pergamon.

Berman, L. (1942). Obsessive–compulsive neurosis in children. *Journal of Nervous and Mental Disease*, **95**, 26–39.

Bernstein, G.A. and Garfinkel, B.D. (1986). School phobia: The overlap of affective and anxiety disorders. *Journal of the American Academy of Child and Adolescent Psychiatry*, **25**, 235–241.

Bertalanffy, L. (1968). *General system theory*. Harmondsworth: Penguin.

Bettelheim, B. (1967). *The Empty Fortress–Infantile Autism and the Birth of the Self*. New York: The Free Press.

Bhanji, S. and Thompson, J. (1974). Operant conditioning in the treatment of anorexia nervosa. *British Journal of Psychiatry*, **124**, 166–172.

Bidder, T.R., Bryant, G. and Gray, O.P. (1975). Benefits to Down's syndrome children through training their mothers. *Archives of Disease in Childhood*, **50**, 383–386.

Bierman, K.L. and Schwartz, L.A. (1986). Clinical child interviews: Approaches and developmental considerations. *Journal of Child and Adolescent Psychotherapy*, **3**, 267–278.

Bijun, P., Golding, J., Haslum, M. and Kurzon, M. (1988). Behavioural predictors of injury in school-age children. *American Journal of Diseases in Children*, **142**, 1307–1312.

Bishop, D.V.M. (1989). Semantic pragmatic disorders and the autistic continuum. *British Journal of Disorders of Communication*, **24**, 115–122.

Bishop, D.V.M. and Adams, C. (1989). Conversational characteristics of children with semantic–pragmatic disorders. *British Journal of Disorder of Communication*, **24**, 241–263.

Blacher, J. (1984). Sequential stages of parental adjustment to the birth of a child with handicaps: Fact or artifact? *Mental Retardation*, **22**, 55–68.

Blagg, N. (1987). *School phobia and its treatment*. London: Croom Helm.

Blinder, B.J. *et al.* (1970). Behavior therapy of anorexia nervosa: effectiveness of activity as a reinforcer of weight gain. *American Journal of Psychiatry*, **126**, 72–82.

Bolton, D. (1994). Family systems interventions. In T.H. Ollendick, N.J. King, W. Yule (eds). *International handbook of phobic and anxiety disorders in children and adolescents*. New York: Plenum.

Bolton, D. (1996). Developmental issues in Obsessive–Compulsive Disorders. *Journal of Child Psychology and Psychiatry*, **37**, 131–137.

Bolton, D., Collins, S. and Steinberg, D. (1983). The treatment of obsessive–compulsive disorder in adolescence: a report of 15 cases. *British Journal of Psychiatry*, **142**, 456–464.

Bornstein, P.H. and Kazdin, A.E. (eds). (1985). *Handbook of clinical behaviour therapy with children*. Homewood, IL: Dorsey Press.

Boskind-Lodahl, M. and White, W.C. (1978). The definition and treatment of bulimarinia in college women—a pilot study. *Journal of American College Health Association*, **27**, 84–97.

Boucheau, L.D. and Jeffrey, C.D. (1973). Stuttering treated by desensitization. *Journal of Behaviour Therapy and Experimental Psychiatry*, **4**, 209–212.

Bowlby, J. (1981). *Attachment and loss: Attachment*. New York: Basic Books.

Braswell, L. (1995). Cognitive–behavioural approaches in the classroom. In S. Goldstein (ed.) *Understanding and managing children's classroom behaviour*. New York: Wiley.

Bremner, J.G. (1988). *Infancy*. Oxford: Basil Blackwell.

Brewin, C.R. (1988). *Cognitive foundations of clinical psychology*. London: Lawrence Erlbaum.

Bright, P.D. and Robin, A.L. (1981). Ameliorating parent–adolescent conflict and problem-solving communication training. *Journal of Behavior Therapy and Experimental Psychiatry*, **12**, 275–280.

Brody, G.H. and Forehand, R. (1986). Maternal perceptions of child maladjustment as a function of child behaviour and maternal depression. *Journal of Consulting and Clinical Psychology*, **54**, 237–240.

Bromley, D. (1986). *The case-study method in psychology and related disciplines*. Chichester: Wiley.

Brown, B.J. and Lloyd, H. (1975). A controlled study of children not speaking at school. *Journal of the Association of Workers for Maladjusted Children*, **3**, 49–63.

Brown, G.W. and Harris, T.O. (eds). (1989). *Life events and illness*. London: Unwin Hyman

Brown, G. and Harris, T. (1978). *Social origins of depression: a study of psychiatric disorder in women*. London: Tavistock.

Brown, W. (1979). What is a good school for this child? In *Collected Papers 'Asperger's syndrome'*. London: The Inge Warehurst Trust

Browne, K. and Herbert, M. (1997). *Preventing family violence*. Chichester: Wiley.

Brownell, K.D. and Foreyt, J.P. (eds) (1986). *Handbook of eating disorders*. New York: Basic Books.

Bruch, H. (1978). *The golden cage: The enigma of anorexia nervosa*. Cambridge: Harvard University Press.

Burchard, J.D. and Lane, T.W. (1982). Crime and deliquency. In A.S. Bellack, M. Hersen and A.E. Kazdin (eds.) *International handbook of behavior modification and therapy*. New York: Plenum.

Burns, D. and Brady, J.P. (1980). The treatment of stuttering. In: A. Goldstein and E.B. Foa (Eds). *Handbook of behavioural interventions*. New York: Wiley.

Butler, N. and Golding, M. (1986). *From birth to five: A study of the health and behaviour of British five year olds*. Oxford: Pergamon Press.

Call, J.D. (1985). *Practice of pediatrics*. Philadelphia, CA: Harper & Row.

Cameron, J.R. (1978). Parental treatment, children's temperament, and risk of childhood behavior problems. *American Journal of Orthopsychiatry*, **48**, 140–147.

Campbell, M., Cohen, I.L., Perry, R. and Small, M. (1989). *Psychopharmocological treatment*. In T.H. Ollendick and M. Hersen (eds), *Handbook of child psychopathology*. New York: Plenum.

Campbell, S.B. (1985). Developmental issues in childhood anxiety. In R. Gittelman (ed.). *Anxiety disorders of childhood*. New York: Guilford Press.

Campbell, S. (1989). Developmental perspectives. In T.H. Ollendick and M. Hersen (eds), *Handbook of child psychopathology*. New York: Plenum.

Campbell, S.B. (1995). Behavior problems in prescribed children: A review of recent research. *Journal of Child Psychology and Psychiatry*, **36**, 113–149.

Cantwell, D.P., and Baker, L. (1985). Speech and language: Development and disorders. In M. Rutter and L. Hersov (eds), *Child psychiatry: Modern approaches* (2nd ed.). Oxford: Blackwell.

Cantwell, D.P., and Carlson, G.A. (eds). (1983). *Affective disorders in children and adolescence: An update*. New York: Spectrum.

Caplan, G. (1964). *Principles of preventive psychiatry*. New York: Basic Books.

Capps, L., Sigman M. and Mundy P. (1994). Attachment security in children with autism. *Development and Psychopathology*, **6**(2), 249–261.

Caron, C. and Rutter, M. (1991). Comorbidity in child psychopathology: Concepts, issues and research strategies; *Journal of Child Psychology and Psychiatry*, **32**, 1063–1080.

Carr, E.G. and Durand, V.M. (1985). Reducing behaviour problems through functional communication training. *Journal of Applied Behavior Analysis*, **18**, 111–126.

Carter, B. and McGoldrick, M. (1988). *The changing family life cycle: a framework for therapy* (2nd ed.) New York: Gardner.

Case, H.W. (1960). Therapeutic methods in stuttering and speech blocking. In H.J. Eysenck (ed.), *Behaviour therapy and neuroses*. pp. 207–220. Oxford: Pergamon Press.

Casteneda, A., McCandless, B.R. and Palmero, D.S. (1956). The children's form of the Manifest Anxiety Scale. *Child Development*, **16**, 317–320.

Cawthorn, P., James, A., Dell, J. and Seagroatt, V. (1994). Adolescent onset psychosis: A clinical and outcome study. *Journal of Child Psychology and Psychiatry*, **35**, 1321–1332.

Chalmers, J.B. and Townsend, M.A.R. (1990). The effects of training in social perspective taking on socially maladjusted girls. *Child Development*, **61**, 178–190.

Charlop, M.H. and Walsh, M.E. (1986). Increasing autistic children's spontaneous verbalisations of affection: An assessment of time delay and peer modelling procedures. *Journal of Applied Behavior Analysis*, **19**, 307–314.

Chandler, M.J. (1973). Egocentrism and anti-social behavior: The assessment and training of social perspective-taking skills. *Development Psychology*, **9**, 326–332.

Chazan, M. and Jackson, S. (1974). Behaviour problems in the infant school: Changes over two years. *Journal of Child Psychology and Psychiatry*, **15**, 33–46.

Cherry, C. and Sayers, B. Mc. A. (1956). Experiments upon the total inhibition of stammering by external control and some clinical results. *Journal of Psychosomatic Research*, **1**, 233–246.

Chiocca, A.E. and Martzuzza, R.L. (1990). Neurosurgical therapy of obsessive–compulsive disorder. In M.A. Jenike, L. Baer and W.E. Minichiello. (eds), *Obsessive compulsive disorders: theory and management* Chicago: Yearbook Medical Publishers.

Cicchetti, D. (1984a). The emergence of developmental psychopathology. *Child Development*, **55**, 1–7.

Cicchetti, D. (1984b). *Developmental psychopathology*. Chicago: University of Chicago Press.

Cicchetti, D., Toth, S. and Bush, M. (1988). Developmental psychopathology and incompetence in childhood: Suggestions for intervention. In B.B. Lahey and A.E. Kazdin (eds). *Advances in Clinical Child Psychology* (Vol. II), New York: Plenum.

Clark, P. and Rutter, M. (1981). Autistic children's responses to structure and to interpersonal demands. *Journal of Autism and Developmental Disorders*, **11**, 201–217.

Clark, R.G.V. (1977). Psychology and crime. *Bulletin of the British Psychological Society*, **30**, 280–283.

Clayden, G.S. (1988). Is constipation in childhood a neurodevelopmental abnormality? In P.J. Milla (ed.), *Disorders of gastrointestinal motility in childhood*. Chichester: Wiley.

Clayden, G.S. and Agnarsson, U. (1991). *Constipation in childhood*. Oxford: Oxford University Press.

Clements, J.C., Bidder, R.T., Gardner, S., Bryant, G. and Gray, O.P. (1979). A home advisory service for pre-school children with developmental delays. *Child Care, Health and Development*, **6**, 25–33.

Clunies-Ross, C. and Landsdown, R. (1988). Concepts of death, illness and isolation found in children with leukaemia. *Child Care, Health and Development*, **14**, 373–386.

Cohen, P., Cohen, J., *et al.* (1993). An epidemiological study of disorders in late childhood and adolescence, I. Age- and gender-specific prevalence. *Journal of Child Psychology and Psychiatry*, **34**, 851–867.

Cohn, J.F. and Tranick, E.L. (1983). Three-month-old infant's reactions to simulated maternal depression. *Child Development*, **54**, 185–193.

Coleman, J., Wolkind, S. and Ashley, L. (1977). Symptoms of behaviour disturbance and adjustment to school. *Journal of Child Psychology and Psychiatry*, **18**, 201–210.

Collins, L.F., Maxwell, A.E. and Cameron, C. (1962). A factor analysis of some child psychiatric clinic data. *Journal of Mental Science*, **108**, 274–285.

Conners, C.K. (1970) Symptom patterns in hyperkinetic, neurotic and normal children. *Child Development*, **41**, 667–682.

Conners, C.K. (1989). *Conners' teacher and parent rating scales*. Toronto: Multi-Health Systems.

Cooke, J. and Williams, D. (1987). *Working with children's language*. Tucson, AZ: Communication Skill Builders.

Cooper, P. (1993) *Effective schools for disaffected pupils*. London: Routledge.

Cooper, Z. and Fairburn, C. (1987). The eating disorder examination: a semi-structured interview. *International Journal of Eating Disorders*, **6**, 1–8.

Coopersmith, S. (1967). *The antecedents of self-esteem*. San Francisco: W.H. Freeman.

Cox, A.D. (1994). Interviews with parents. In M. Rutter, E. Taylor and L. Hersov (eds.) *Child and adolescent psychiatry: modern approaches* (3rd edn) Oxford: Blackwell.

Cox C., Fedio, P. and Rapoport J. (1989). Neurospychological testing of obsessive-compulsive adolescents. In J.L. Rapoport (ed.), *Obsessive–compulsive disorder in children and adolescents* (pp. 73–85). Washington: American Psychiatric Press.

Craighead, W.E., Meyers, A., Wilcoxon-Craighead, L. and MacHale, S.M. (1983). Issues in cognitive–behaviour therapy with children. In M. Rosenbaum, G.M. Franks and Y. Joffe (eds), *Perspectives on behavior therapy in the eighties*. New York: Springer-Verlag.

Crandall, V.J. and Bellugi, U. (1954). Some relationships of interpersonal and intrapersonal conceptualizations to personal-social adjustment. *Journal of Personality*, **23**, 224–232.

Creak, E.M. (1961). Schizophrenic syndrome in childhood: Progress report of a working party. (April 1961). *Cerebral Palsy Bulletin*, **3**, 501–504.

Creak, E.M. (1964). Schizophrenic syndrome in childhood: further progress report at a working party. *Developmental Medicine and Child Neurology*, **6**, 530–535.

Creer, T.L. (1982). Asthma. *Journal of Consulting and Clinical Psychology*, **50**, 912–921.

Creer, T.L., Renne, C.M. and Chai, H. (1982). The application of behavioural techniques to childhood asthma. In D.C. Russo and J.W. Varni (eds), *Behavioural pediatrics: Research and practice*. New York: Plenum.

Crisp A.H. (1980). *Anorexia nervosa: Let me be*. London: Academic Press.

Crisp A.H., Palmer R.L. and Kalucy, R.S. (1976). How common is anorexia? A prevalence study. *British Journal of Psychiatry*, **128**, 549–554.

Crisp A.H. *et al.* (1977). The long-term prognosis in anorexia nervosa: some factors predictive of outcome. In R.A. Vigersky (ed.) *Anorexia Nervosa*. New York: Raven Press.

Crisp A.H. *et al.* (1980). Clinical features of anorexia nervosa. *Journal of Psychosomatic Research*, **24**, 179–191.

Crowell, J.A. and Feldman, S.S. (1988). Mothers' internal models of relationships and children's behavioral and developmental status: A study of mother–child interaction. *Child Development*, **59**, 1273–1285.

Cunningham, C.E., Cataldo, M.F., Mallion, C. and Keyes, J.B. (1983). A review and controlled single case evaluation of behavioral approaches to the management of elective mutism. *Child and Family Behavior Therapy*, **5**, 25–49.

Dadds, M.R. (1995) *Families, children and the development of dysfunction*. Thousand Oaks, CA: Sage.

Dadds, M.R., Rapee, R.M. and Barrett, P.M. (1994). Behavioural observation. In T.H. Ollendick, N.J. King and W. Yule (eds.) *International handbook of phobic and anxiety disorders in children and adolescents*. New York: Plenum.

Dalali, I.D. and Sheehan, J.G. (1974). Stuttering and assertion training. *Journal of Communication Disorders*. **7**, 97–111.

Daley, B., Addington, J., Kertoot, S. and Sigston, A. (1985). *Portage: The importance of parents*. Windsor: NFER/Nelson.

Damon, W. (1989). *The Social World of the Child*. San Francisco: Jossey-Bass.

Danziger, K. (1971). *Socialization*. Hardmondsworth: Penguin.

Dare, C. (1985). Family therapy. In: M. Rutter and L. Hersov (eds), *Child and adolescent psychiatry* (2nd ed.). Oxford: Blackwell Scientific Publications.

Davis, H. (1993) *Counselling parents of children with chronic illness and disability*. Leicester: BPS Books.

Dawson, G. (ed.) (1989). *Autism: nature, diagnosis and treatment*. New York: Guilford

DeKlyen, M., Speltz, M.L. and Greenberg, M.T. (1998). Fathering and early onset conduct problems: Positive and negative parenting, father–son attachment, and the marital context. *Clinical Child and Family Psychology Review*. **1**.

Delfini, L., Bernal, M. and Rosen, P. (1976). Comparison of deviant and normal boys in home settings. In E. Marsh, L. Hamerlynck and L. Handy (eds), *Behaviour Modification and Families*. New York: Brunner/Mazel.

DES (1989) *Discipline in Schools* (The Elton Report). London: HMSO.

de Shazer, S. (1985). *Keys to solution in brief therapy*. New York: Newton.

Devlin, J.B. and O'Cathain, C. (1990) Predicting treatment outcome in nocturnal enuresis. *Archives of Disease in Childhood*, **65**, 1158–1161.

Deykin, E.Y. and MacMahon, B. (1979). The incidence of seizures among children with autistic symptoms. *American Journal of Psychiatry*, **136**, 1310–1312.

Di Lorenzo, T.M., and Matson, J.L. (1981). Stuttering. In M. Hersen and V.B. Van Hasselt (eds). *Behaviour Therapy with Children and Adolescents*. Chichester: Wiley.

Docking, J.W. (1987) *Control and discipline in schools: perspectives and approaches*. New York: Harper & Row.

Doleys, D.M. (1977). Behavioral treatments for nocturnal enuresis in children: A Review of the recent literature. *Psychological Bulletin*, **8**, 30–54.

Dolgin, M.J., and Jay, S.M. (1989). Childhood cancer. In T.H. Ollendick and M. Hersen (eds). *Handbook of Child Psychopathology* (2nd ed). New York: Plenum.

Dollard, J. and Miller, N.E. (1950). *Personality and psychotherapy.* New York: MacGraw-Hill.

Douglas, J.W.B., Ross, J.M., and Simpson, H.R. (1968). *All our future.* London: Peter Davies.

Douglas, J. (1993). *Psychology and nursing children.* Leicester: BPS Books (The British Psychological Society).

Douglas, J. and Richman, N. (1984). *My Child Won't Sleep.* Harmondsworth: Penguin.

Dreger, R.M. (1982). The classification of children and their emotional problems: An overview. *Clinical Psychology Review,* 2, 239–386.

Duker, M. and Slade R. (1988). *Anorexia nervosa: how to help.* Milton Keynes: Open University Press.

Dumas, J.E. (1989). Treating anti-social behavior in children: Child and family approaches. *Clinical Psychology Review,* 9, 197–222.

Du Paul, G.J. and Barkley, R.A. (1990) Medication therapy. In R.A. Barkley, (1990). *Attention deficit hyperactivity disorder: A handbook for diagnosis and treatment.* New York: Guilford Press.

Durkin, K. (1995). *Developmental social psychology: From infancy to old age.* Cambridge, Mass.: Blackwell.

Durlak, J.A. (1979). Comparative effectiveness of paraprofessional and professional helpers. *Psychological Bulletin,* 86, 80–92.

D'Zurilla, T.J. and Goldfried, M.R. (1971). Cognitive processes, problem-solving and effective behaviour. In M.R. Goldfried and M. Merbaum (eds). *Behaviour change through self-control.* New York: Holt, Rinehart & Winston.

Earls, F. (1980). Prevalence of behavior problems in 3-year-old children: A cross maternal replication. *Archives of General Psychiatry,* 37, 1153–1157.

Earls, F. (1981). Temperamental characteristics and behavior problems in three-year-old children. *The Journal of Nervous and Mental Disease,* 169, 367–374.

Earls, F. and Richman, N. (1980a). The prevalence of behavior problems in three year old children of West Indian-born parents. *Journal of Child Psychology and Psychiatry,* 21, 99–106.

Earls, F. and Richman, N. (1980b). Behavior problems in preschool children of West Indian parents: A re-examination of family and social factors. *Journal of Child Psychology and Psychiatry,* 21, 107–117.

Eckert, E.D., Goldberg, S.C., Halmi, K.A., Casper, R.C. and Davis, J.M. (1979). Behaviour therapy in anorexia nervosa. *British Journal of Psychiatry,* 134, 55–59.

Edelstein, J. (1998). *Psycho-social consequences of divorce: A group counselling programme of prevention.* Unpublished Ph.D., University of Leicester.

Egan, G. (1975). *The Skilled Helper: A Model for Systematic Helping and Interpersonal Relating.* Monterey, CA: Brooks Cole.

Ehrhardt, A. and Money, J. (1967). Progestin-induced hermaphroditism: IQ and psychosexual identity in a study of ten girls. *Journal of Sex Research,* 3, 83–100.

Eisenberg, L. and Kanner, L. (1956). Early infantile autism. *American Journal of Orthopsychiatry,* 26, 556–566.

Eiser, C. (1990). Psychological effects of chronic disease. *Journal of Child Psychology and Psychiatry,* 31, 85–98.

Eland, J.M. and Anderson, J.E. (1977). The experience of pain in children. In A. Jacox (ed.), *Pain: a source book for nurses and other health professionals*. Boston, MA: Little, Brown.

Elkind, D. (1967). Egocentrism in adolescence. *Child Development*, **38**, 1034–1044.

Elliott, C.H. and Olson, R.A. (1983). The management of children's distress in response to painful medical treatment for burn injuries. *Behaviour Research and Therapy*, **21**, (6), 675–683.

Ellis, A. (1970). *The essence of rational psychotherapy.* New York: Institute for Rational Living.

Elmhorn, K. (1965). Study in self-reported delinquency among school children. In *Scandinavian Studies in Criminology*. London: Tavistock.

Epstein, M.H., Singh, N.N., Luebke, J. and Stout, C.E. (1991). Psycho-pharmaco-logical intervention II: Teacher perceptions of psychotropic medication for students with learning disabilities. *Journal of Learning Disabilities*, **24**, 477–483.

Erikson, E. (1965). *Childhood and society*, (rev. edn). Harmondsworth: Penguin.

Erikson, E. (1968). *Identity, youth and crisis*, New York: Norton.

Erken, N. and Henderson, H. (1976). *Practice Skills Mastery Program*. Logan U.T: Mastery Programs.

Eron, L.D., Walder, L.O., Toigo, R. and Lefrowitz, M.M. (1963). Social class, parental punishment for aggression, and child aggression. *Child Development*, **34**, 849–867.

Erwin, E. (1979). *Behaviour Therapy: scientific, philosophical and moral foundations.* Cambridge: Cambridge University Press.

Esman, A. (1989). Psychoanalysis and general psychiatry: obsessive–compulsive disorder as a paradigm. *Journal of the American and Psychoanalytic Association*, **37**, 319–336.

Esser, G., Schmidt, M.I. and Woerner, W. (1990). Epidemiology and course of psychiatric disorders in school-age children. *Journal of Child Psychology and Psychiatry*, **31**, 243–263.

Esveldt-Dawson K. *et al.* (1982). Treatment of phobias in a hospitalized child. *Journal of Behavior Therapy and Experimental Psychiatry*, **13**, 77–83.

Evans, I.M. (1989). A multi-dimensional model for conceptualizing the design of child behavior therapy. *Behavioural Psychotherapy*, **17**, 237–251.

Evans, I.M. and Meyer, L.H. (1985). *An educative approach to behavior problems: A practical decision model for intervention with severely handicapped learners*. Baltimore: Paul H. Brookes.

Fairburn C.G. (1980). Self-induced vomiting. *Journal of Psychosomatic Research*, **24**, 193–197.

Fairburn C.G. (1981). A cognitive behavioral approach to the treatment of bulimia. *Psychological Medicine*, **11**, 707–711.

Fairburn, C.G. and Beglin, S.J. (1990) Studies of the epidemiology of bulimia nervosa. *American Journal of Psychiatry*, **147**, 401–408.

Farnes, J. and Wallace C. (1987). Pilot study for a sleep clinic. *Health Visitor*, **60**, 41–43.

Farrell, B.A. (1970). Psychoanalysis: The method. In S.G. Lee and M. Herbert (eds). *Freud and psychology*. Harmondsworth: Penguin.

Farrell, P.T. (1982). An evaluation of an EDY course in behaviour modification: techniques for teachers and care staff in an ESN(S) school. *Special Education: Forward Trends*, **9**, 21–25.

Farrington, D.P. (1995). The development of offending and antisocial behaviour from childhood: Key findings from the Cambridge Study in Delinquent Development. *Journal of Child Psychology and Psychiatry*, **36**, 929–964.

Feindler, E.L. and Ecton, R.B. (1986). *Adolescent anger control: Cognitive-behavioral techniques*. Elmsford, NY: Pergamon Press.

Ferber, R. (1985). *Solve your child's sleep problems*. New York: Simon & Schuster.

Fergusson, D.M., and Horwood, L.J. (1987). The trait and method components of ratings of conduct disorder. Part 1. Maternal and teacher evaluations of conduct disorder in young children. *Journal of Child Psychology and Psychiatry*, **28**, 249–260. Part 2. Factors related to the trait component of conduct disorder scores. *Journal of Child Psychology and Psychiatry*, **28**, 261–272.

Fergusson, D.M., Horwood, L.J. and Shannon F.T. (1986). Factors related to the age of attainment of nocturnal bladder control: an 8-year longitudinal study. *Pediatrics*, **78**, 884–890.

Ferrari, M. (1986). Fears and phobias in childhood: some clinical and developmental considerations. *Child Psychiatry and Human Development*, **17**, 75–87.

Ferster, C. (1961). Positive reinforcement and behavioral deficits of autistic children. *Child Development*, **32**, 437–456.

Feshbach, S. (1970). Aggression. In S. Feshbach and P.H. Massen (eds.) *Carmichael's Manual of Child Psychology*. Chichester: Wiley.

Fichter, M.M. *et al.* (1990) The structured interview for anorexia and bulimia nervosa (SIAB). In M.M. Fichter (ed.) *Bulimia nervosa: basic research, diagnosis and therapy*. Chichester: Wiley.

Fielding, D. (1983). Adolescent services. In A. Liddell (ed.), *The practice of clinical psychology in Great Britain*. Chichester: Wiley.

Fielding, D. (1985). Chronic illness in children. In F. Watts (ed.), *New developments in clinical psychology*, Leicester: British Psychological Society/Wiley.

Finch, A.J. and Politano, P.M. (1994). Projective techniques. In T.H. Ollendick, N.J. King and W. Yule. *International handbook of phobic and anxiety disorders in children and adolescents*. New York: Plenum.

Fine S., Forth, A., Gilbert, M. and Haley, G. (1991). Group therapy for adolescent depressive disorder: a comparison of social skills and therapeutic support. *Journal of the American Academy of Child and Adolescent Psychiatry*, **30**, 79–85.

Fischer, M. and Newby, R.F. (1991). Assessment of stimulant response in ADHD children using a refined multimethod clinical protocol. *Journal of Clinical Child Psychology*, **20** *(3)*, 232–244.

Fischer, M., Rolf, J.E., Hasazi, J.E. and Cummings, L. (1984). Follow-up of a preschool epidemiological sample: Cross-age continuities and predictions of later adjustment with internalizing and externalizing dimensions of behavior. *Child Development*, **55**, 137–150.

Flanagan, B., Goldiamond, I. and Azrin, N. (1958). Operant stuttering: The control of stuttering behavior through response-contingent consequences. *Journal of Experimental Analysis of Behavior*, **1**, 173–178.

Foa E.B. and Kozak M.J. (1996). Obsessive–compulsive disorder: long-term outcome of psychological treatment. In Mavissakalian and Prien (eds), *Long-term treatments of anxiety disorders*. Washington, DC: American Psychiatric Press, pp. 285–309.

Folstein S. and Rutter M. (1977). Infantile autism: a genetic study of 21 twin pairs. *Journal of Child Psychology and Psychiatry*, **18**, 297–231.

Fontana, D. (1984) (ed.) *Behaviourism and learning theory in education*. Edinburgh: Scottish Academic Press (for the British Journal of Educational Psychology).

Fontana, D. (1986) *Teaching and personality*. Oxford: Blackwell.

Fontana, D. (1986). *Classroom control*. Leicester: British Psychological Society/ Methuen.

Forehand, R. and MacMahon, R.J. (1981). *Helping the noncompliant child: A clinician's guide to effective parent training*. New York: Guilford.

Frame, C., Matson, J.L., Sonis, W.A., Fialkov, M.J. and Kazdin, A.E. (1982). Behavioral treatment of depression in a prepubertal child. *Journal of Behavior Therapy and Experimental Psychiatry*, **3**, 239–243.

Francis, G. and Ollendick, T.H. (1986). Anxiety disorders. In C.L. Frame and J.L. Matson (eds.) *Handbook of assessment in child psychopathology*. New York: Plenum.

Frank, J. (1973). *Persuasion and healing*. Baltimore, MD: The Johns Hopkins University Press.

Freud, A. (1958). *Adolescence: Psychoanalytic study of the child*. New York: International Universities Press.

Freud, A. (1965). *Normality and pathology in childhood*. New York: International Universities Press.

Freud, S. (1913). Obsessions and phobias. In J. Strachey (ed.) *The complete works of Sigmund Freud*, Vol. 1, London: Hogarth Press.

Freud, S. (1917). Mourning and melancholia. In J. Strachey, (ed.) *The standard edition of Sigmund Freud's works* (Vol. 14), London: Hogarth Press.

Frith, U. (1989). *Autism: explaining the enigma*. Oxford: Basil Blackwell.

Frith, U. (ed.) (1994). *Autism and Asperger syndrome*. Cambridge: Cambridge University Press.

Fryers, T. (1984). *The epidemiology of intellectual impairment*. London: Academic Press.

Gambrill, E. (1990). *Critical thinking in clinical practice*. San Francisco: Jossey-Bass.

Gardner, F. (1997). Observational methods for recording parent–child interaction: How generalisable are the findings? *Child Psychology and Psychiatry Review*, **2**, 70–74.

Garfinkel, B.G., Wender, P.H., Sloman, L. and O'Neill, L. (1983). Tricyclic anti-depressant and methylphenidate treatment of attention deficit disorder in children. *Journal of American Academy of Child and Adolescent Psychiatry*, **22**, 343–348.

Garfinkel, P.E. (1974). Perception of hunger and satiety in anorexia nervosa. *Psychological Medicine*, **4**, 309–315.

Garfinkel, P.E. (1985). Review: The treatment of anorexia nervosa in Toronto. *Journal of Psychiatric Research*, **19**, 405–412.

Garfinkel, P.E. and Garner, D.M. (1982). *Anorexia nervosa: A multidimensional perspective*. New York: Brunner/Mazel.

Garner, D. (1986). Cognitive therapy for anorexia. In K.D. Brownell and J.P. Foreyt (eds). *Handbook of eating disorders*. New York: Basic Books.

Garner, D.M. and Bemis, K.M. (1985). Cognitive therapy for anorexia nervosa. In Garner and Garfinkel (1985).

Garner, D. and Garfinkel, P.E. (1979). The eating attitudes test. *Psychological Medicine*, **9**, 273–279.

Garner, D. and Garfinkel, P.E. (1985). *Handbook of psychotherapy for anorexia nervosa and bulimia* (2nd edn) London: Guilford Press.

Gath, A. (1972). The mental health of siblings of congenitally abnormal children. *Journal of Child Psychology and Psychiatry*, **13**, 211–218.

Gelfand, D.M., Jenson, W.R. and Drew, C.J. (1988). *Understanding child behavior disorders* (2nd ed). New York: Holt, Rinehart & Winston.

Gelfand, D.M., Jensen, W.R. and Drew, C.J. (1985). *Understanding child behavior disorders*. New York: Holt, Rinehart & Winston.

Gendrau, P. and Ross, R.R. (1987). Revivification of rehabilitation: evidence from the 1980s. *Justice Quarterly*, **4**, 349–407.

Gil, D.G. (1970). *Violence against children: Physical child abuse in the United States*. Cambridge, MA: Harvard University Press.

Gillespie, W.H. (1968). The psychoanalytic theory of child development. In E. Miller (ed.), *Foundations of child psychiatry*. Oxford: Pergamon.

Gittelman-Klein, R. (1975). Psychiatric characteristics of the relatives of school phobic children. In D.V. S. Sankar (ed). Mental health in children, Vol. I. Westbury, N.Y.: PJD Publications.

Goldenberg I. and Goldenberg H. (1985). *Family therapy: An overview* (2nd edn). Monterey, CA: Brooks/Cole.

Goldfarb, W. (1961). *Childhood schizophrenia*. Cambridge, MA: Harvard University Press.

Goldstein, A.P., Heller, H. and Sechrest, L.B. (1966). *Psychotherapy and the psychology of behavior change*. New York: Wiley.

Goldstein, S. (1995). *Understanding and managing children's classroom behavior*. New York: Wiley.

Goodnow, J.J. (1988). Parents' ideas, actions and feelings: Models and methods for developmental and social psychology. *Child Development*, **59**, 286–320.

Goodwin, S.E. and Mahoney, M.J. (1975). Modification of aggression through modelling: an experimental probe. *Journal of Behavior Therapy and Experimental Psychiatry*, **6**, 200–202.

Gould, M.S., Wunsch-Hitzig, R. and Dohrenwend, B.P. (1980). Formulation of hypotheses about the prevalence, treatment and prognostic significance of psychiatric disorders in children in the United States. In B.P. Dohrenwend, B.S. Dohrenwend, M.S. Gould, B. Link, P.R. Neugebaur and R. Wunsch-Hitzig (eds), *Mental illness in the United States: Epidemiological estimates*. New York: Praeger.

Gowers, S.G. *et al.* (1991). Premenarcheal anorexia nervosa. *Journal of Child Psychology and Psychiatry*, **32**, 515–524.

Graham, D.T., Rutter, M. and George, S. (1973). Temperamental characteristics as predictors of behaviour disorders in children. *American Journal of Orthopsychiatry*, **43** (3), 328–339.

Graham, P. (1980). Epidemiological studies. In H.C. Quay and J.C. Werry (eds). *Psychopathological disorders of childhood* (2nd edn). New York: Wiley.

Graham, P. and Rutter, M. (1973). Psychiatric disorders in the young adolescent: A follow-up study. *Proceedings of the Royal Society of Medicine*, **66**, 1226–1229.

Graziano, A.M. and Mooney, K.C. (1980). Family self-control instruction for children's night-time fear reduction. *Journal of Consulting and Clinical Psychology*, **48**, 206–213.

Graziano, A.M. and Mooney, K.C. (1982). Behavioral treatment of 'night-fears' in children: Maintenance of improvement at 2- to 3-year follow-up. *Journal of Consulting and Clinical Psychology*, **50**, 598–599.

Graziano, A.M. and Mooney, K.C. (1984). *Children and behavior therapy*. New York: Aldine Publishing.

Graziano, A.M., Mooney, K.C., Huber, C. and Ignaziak, D. (1979). Self-control instruction for children's fear reductions. *Journal of Behavior Therapy and Experimental Psychiatry*, **10**, 221–227.

Greenwood, C., Hops, H., Dolquadri, J. and Walker, H.M. (1977). *PASS Consultant Manual*. Eugene, Ore: Center at Oregon for Research in the Behavioral Education of the Handicapped.

Groden, G. and Baron, M.G. (eds) (1988). *Autism: Strategies for change: A comprehensive approach to the education and treatment of children with autism and related disorders*. New York: Gardner Press.

Grusec, J.E. and Mammone, N. (1995). Features and sources of parents' attributions about themselves and their children. In N. Eisenberg (eds) *Social development*. London: Sage.

Gurman, A.S., Kniskern D.P. and Pinsof W.M. (1986). Research on the process and outcome of marital and family therapy. In: S.L. Garfield and A.E. Bergin (3rd edn) *Handbook of psychotherapy and behaviour change*. New York: Wiley.

Haley, J. (1976). *Problem solving therapy*. San Francisco: Jossey-Bass.

Hall, S. (1904). *Adolescence: Its psychology and its relation to physiology, anthropology, sociology, sex, crime, religion, and education* (Vols. I and II). New York: D. Appleton.

Halmi, K.A. (1974). Anorexia nervosa: demographic and clinical features of 94 cases. *Psychosomatic Medicine*, **36**, 18–25.

Halmi, K.A., Powers, P. and Cunningham, S. (1975). Treatment of anorexia nervosa with behavior modification. *Archives of General Psychiatry*, **32**, 93–95.

Hampson, J.L. and Hampson, J.G. (1961). The ontogenesis of sexual behavior in man. In W.C. Young and G.W. Corner (eds). *Sex and internal secretion*, Vol 2. (3rd edn). Baltimore, MD: Williams & Wilkins.

Harrington, R. Bredenkamp, D., Groothues, M. Rutter, M. Fudge, H. and Pickles, A. (1994). Adult outcomes of childhood and adolescent depression. III Links with suicidal behaviour. *Journal of Child Psychology and Psychiatry*, **35**, 1309–1320.

Harris, F.C. and Phelps, C.F. (1987). Anorexia and bulimia. In M. Hersen and V.B. Van Hasselt (eds) *Behavior therapy with children and adolescents: A clinical approach*. New York: Wiley–Interscience.

Harris, F.C. et al. (1983). Problems in adolescence: assessment of treatment of bulimia nervosa. In M. Hersen (ed.) *Outpatient behavior therapy: A clinical guide*. New York: Grune & Stratton.

Harris, P. (1989). *Children and emotion*. New York: Basil Blackwell.

Harris, S.L. et al. (1990). Changes in language development among autistic and peer children in segregated and integrated preschool settings. *Journal of Autism and Developmental Disorders*, **20**, 23–31.

Hartmann, D.P. (ed.) (1982) *Using observers to study behavior*. San Francisco, CA: Jossey-Bass.

Hartmann, L. (1991) cited in Jones (1994).

Hartup, W.W. (1974). Aggression in childhood: Developmental perspectives. *American Psychologist*, **29**, 336–341.

Hatzenbuehler, L.C. and Schroeder, R. (1978). Desensitization procedures in the treatment of childhood disorders. *Psychological Bulletin*, **85**, 831–844.

Hawkins, R.C. and Clement P.F. (1980). Development and construct validation of a self-report measure of binge eating tendencies. *Addictive behaviors*, **5**, 219–226.

Hawkins, R.P. (1972). It's time we taught the young how to be good parents (and don't you wish we'd started a long time ago?). *Psychology Today*, November, 28–32.

Hawton, K. (1982). Motivation aspects of deliberate self-poisoning in adolescents. *British Journal of Psychiatry*, **141**, 286–291.

Hay, D.F. (1994). Prosocial development. *Journal of Child Psychology and Psychiatry*, **35**, 29–72.

Haynes, S.N. (1978). *Principles of behavioral assessment*. New York: Gardner Press.

Haynes, S.N. and O'Brien, W.H. (1990). Functional analysis in behavior therapy. *Clinical Psychology Review*, **10**, 649–668.

Henderson, M. and Hollin, C.R. (1983). A critical review of social skills training with young offenders. *Criminal Justice and Behaviour*, **10**, 316–341.

Henneborn, W.J. and Cogan, R. (1975). The effect of husband participation in reported pain and the probability of medication during labor and birth. *Journal of Psychosomatic Research*, **19**, 215–222.

Hepworth, D. and Larsen, J. (1990). *Direct social practice: theory and skills* (3rd edn). Belmont, CA: Wadsworth.

Her Majesty's Stationery Office. (1972). *Statistics relating to approved schools, remand homes and attendance centres in England and Wales for the year 1970*. London: HMSO.

Herbert, M. (1964). The concept and testing of brain-damage in children: A review. *Journal of Child Psychology and Psychiatry*, **5**, 197–216.

Herbert, M. (1965). Personality factors and bronchial asthma. *Journal of Psychosomatic Research*, **8**, 353–356.

Herbert, M. (1974). *Emotional problems of development in children*. London: Academic Press.

Herbert, M. (1985a). Triadic work with children. In F. Watts (ed.), *Recent developments in clinical psychology*. Chichester: Wiley.

Herbert, M. (1985b). *Caring for your children: A practical guide*. Oxford: Basil Blackwell.

Herbert, M. (1986). Social skills training with children. In C.R. Hollin and P. Trower (eds), *Handbook of social skills training. Vol. 1: Applications across the life-span*. Oxford: Pergamon Press.

Herbert, M. (1987a). *Conduct disorders of childhood and adolescence: a social learning perspective*. (2nd edn) Chichester: Wiley.

Herbert, M. (1987b). *Behavioral treatment of children with problems*. London: Academic Press.

Herbert (1987c) *Living with teenagers*. Oxford: Basil Blackwell.

Herbert, M. (1989a). Aggressive and violent children. In K. Howells and C.R. Hollin (eds), *Clinical approaches to violence*, Chichester: Wiley.

Herbert, M. (1989b) *Discipline*. Oxford: Basil Blackwell.

Herbert, M. (1990) *Planning a research project*. London: Cassell.

Herbert, M. (1991). *Child care and their family: resource pack*. Windsor: National Foundation of Educational Research/Nelson.

Herbert, M. (1993). *Working with children and the Children Act.* Leicester: BPS/ Routledge.

Herbert, M. (1994a). Etiological considerations. In T.H. Ollendick, N.J. King, and W. Yule (eds), *International handbook of phobic and anxiety disorders in children and adolescents.* New York: Plenum Press.

Herbert, M. (1994b). Behavioral methods. In M. Rutter, E. Taylor and L. Hersov (eds). *Child and adolescent psychiatry* (3rd edn). Oxford: Blackwell Scientific.

Herbert, M. (1995). A collaborative model of training for parents of children with disruptive behavior disorders. *British Journal of Clinical Psychology*, **34**, 325–342.

Herbert, M. (1996). Supporting bereaved and dying children and their parents. Leicester: BPS Books, (British Psychological Society).

Herbert, M. (1998a) Clinical formulation. Chapter in T.H. Ollendick (ed.), *Children and adolescents: clinical formulation* (in the Comprehensive Clinical Psychology Series (II volumes) edited by A.S. Bellak and M. Hersen). New York: Elsevier.

Herbert, M. (1998b) *Cognitive-behavior therapy of adolescents with conduct disorders.* In P. Graham (ed.), *Therapy for Children and Families*, Cambridge: Cambridge University Press.

Herbert, M. (1998c). Family treatment. In T.H. Ollendick and M. Hersen (eds), *Handbook of child psychopathology* (3rd edn). New York: Plenum.

Herbert, M. and Iwaniec, D. (1981). Behavioural psychotherapy in natural home-settings: An empirical study applied to conduct disordered and incontinent children. *Behavioural Psychotherapy*, **9**, 53–76.

Herbert, M. and Sluckin, A. (1985). A realistic look at mother–infant bonding. In M.L. Chiswick (ed.), *Recent advances in perinatal medicine*, No. 2. Edinburgh: Churchill Livingstone.

Herbert, M., Sluckin, W. and Sluckin, A. (1982). Mother-to-infant bonding. *Journal of Child Psychology and Psychiatry*, **23**, 205–221.

Herbert, M. and Wookey, J.A. (1997). *Child-wise parenting skills manual.* Exeter: Impact Publications, PO Box No. 342, Exeter EX6 7ZD.

Hermelin, B. and O'Connor, N. (1970). *Psychological experiments with autistic children.* Oxford: Pergamon Press.

Hermelin, B. and O'Connor, N. (1985). Logico-affective states and non-verbal language. In: E. Schoplier and G. Mesibov (eds) *Communication problems in autism.* New York: Plenum Press.

Hersen, M. and Van Hasselt, V. B. (1987). *Children and adolescents.* New York: Wiley.

Hersov, L.A. (1960). Refusal to go to school. *Journal of Child Psychology and Psychiatry*, **1**, 137–145.

Hewett, S. (1970). *The family and the handicapped child.* London: Allen & Unwin.

Hewstone, M. (1989). *Causal attribution.* Oxford: Blackwell.

Hill, R., and Aldous, J. (1969). Socialization for marriage and parenthood. In D.A. Goslin (ed.), *Handbook of socialization.* New York: Plenum.

Hinde, R.A. (1979). *Towards understanding relationships.* London: Academic Press.

Hiss, H., Foa, E.B. and Kozak M.J. (1994). Relapse prevention program for treatment of obsessive–compulsive disorder. *Journal of Consulting and Clinical Psychology*, **62**, 210–217.

Hobbs, N. (1982). *The troubled and the troubling child.* San Francisco: Jossey-Bass.

Hobson, R.P. (1990a) On the origins of self and the case of autism. *Development and Psychopathology*, **2**, 163–182.

Hobson, R.P. (1990b). Concerning knowledge of mental states. *British Journal of Medical Psychology*, **63**, 199–213.

Hobson, R.P. (1990c). On acquiring knowledge about people and the capacity to pretend: response to Leslie (1987). *Psychological Review*, **97**, 114–121.

Hobson, R.P. (1991). Against the theory of 'theory of mind'. *British Journal of Developmental Psychology*, **9**, 33–51.

Hobson, R.P. (1993a). *Autism and the development of mind*. Hove/Hillsdale: Lawrence Erlbaum Association.

Hobson, R.P. (1993b). Through feeling and sight to self and symbol. In: U. Neisser (ed.) *The perceived self ecological and interpersonal sources of self-knowledge*. New York: Cambridge University Press.

Hodgson, R. and Rachman, S. (1974). Desynchrony in measures of fear. *Behaviour Research and Therapy*, **12**, 219–230.

Hoffman, L. (1995). Foreword: In S. Reimers and A. Treacher. *Introducing user-friendly family therapy*. London: Routledge.

Hoffman, M.L. (1970). Moral development. In: P.H. Mussen (ed.) *Carmichael's manual of child psychology*. Chichester: Wiley.

Hogg, J. (1991). Developments in further education for adults with profound intellectual and multiple disabilities. In J. Watson (ed.) *Innovatory practice and severe learning difficulties (Meeting educational special needs: a scottish perspective*, Vol. 1, series editors G. Lloyd and J. Watson). Edinburgh: Moray House Publications.

Holland, A.J., Hall, A., Murray, R., Russell, G.F.M. and Crisp, A.H. (1984). Anorexia nervosa: A study of 34 twin pairs and one set of triplets. *British Journal of Psychiatry*, **145**, 414–419.

Hollin, C.R. (1990). *Cognitive-behavioral interventions with young offenders*. Elmsford, NY: Pergamon Press.

Hollin, C.R., Wilkie, J and Herbert, M. (1987). Behavioural social work: Training and application. *Practice*, **1**, 297–304.

Hollon, S.D. and Beck, A.T. (1994). Cognitive and cognitive behavioural therapies. In A.E. Bergin and S.L. Garfield (eds), *Handbook of psychotherapy and behavior change* (4th edn). New York: Wiley, pp. 428–466.

Holmes, F. (1935). An experimental study of fear in young children. In A. Jersild and F. Holmes, *Children's fear*. Child Development Monographs, No. 20.

Howells, K. (1989). Anger-management methods in relation to the prevention of violent behaviour. In J. Archer and K. Browne (eds), *Human aggression: Naturalistic approaches*. London: Routledge.

Howlin, P. (1984). Parents as therapists: A critical review. In D. Muller (ed.), *Remediating children's language: Behavioural and naturalist approaches*. London: Croom Helm.

Howlin, P. (1994). Special educational attainment. In M. Rutter, E. Taylor and L. Hersov (eds) (3rd edn). *Child psychology and psychiatry: Modern approaches*. Oxford: Blackwell Scientific Publication.

Howlin, P., Rutter, M., Berger, M., Hemsley, R., Hersov, L. and Yule, W. (1987). *Treatment of autistic children*. Chichester: Wiley.

Hsu, L.K.G. (1980). The etiology of anorexia nervosa. *Psychological Medicine*, **13**, 231–238.

Hudson, A. (1982). Training parents of developmentally handicapped children: A component analysis. *Behavior Therapy*, **13**, 325–333.

Hudson, A. and Blane, M. (1985). The importance of non-verbal behaviour in giving instructions to children. *Child and Family Behaviour Therapy*, **7**, 1–10.

Hugdahl, K. (1981). The three-systems-model of fear and emotion—a critical examination. *Behaviour Research and Therapy*, **19**, 75–85.

Humphrey, L.L. (1986). Structural analyses of parent–child relationships in eating disorders. *Journal of Abnormal Psychology*, **95**, 395–402.

Hutt, C. and Ounsted, C. (1966). The biological significance of gaze aversion with particular reference to the syndrome of infantile autism. *Behavioural Science*, **11**, 346–356.

Hutter, A. (1938). Endegene ein Functionelle Psychosen bei Kindern in den Pubertatsjahren. *A Kinder Psychiatry*, **5**, 97–112.

Hsu, L.K.G. (1980). Outcome of anorexia nervosa. *Archives of general psychiatry*, **37**, 1041–1046.

Inheldler, B., and Piaget, J. (1964). *The early growth of logic in the child*. London: Routledge & Kegan Paul.

Insel T.R. and Winslow J.T. (1990) Neurobiology of obsessive–compulsive disorder. In M.A. Jenike, L. Baer and W.E. Minichiello (eds) *Obsessive compulsive disorders: theory and management*. Chicago: Yearbook Medical Publishers, pp. 118–131.

Iwaniec, D. (1995). *Emotional abuse and neglect*. Chichester: Wiley.

Iwaniec, D., Herbert, M., and MacNeish, S. (1985). Social work with failure-to-thrive children and their families. Part I: Psychosocial factors. Part II: Behavioural casework. *British Journal of Social Work*, **15**(3), 243–260; **15**(4), 281–291.

Iwaniec, D., Herbert, M., and Sluckin, A. (1988). Helping emotionally abused children who fail to thrive. In K. Browne, C. Davies and P. Stratton (eds), *Early prediction and prevention of child abuse*. Chichester: Wiley.

Jackson, D. (1957). The question of family homeostasis. *Psychiatric Quarterly Supplement*, **31**, 79–80.

Jay, S.M. (1988). Invasive medical procedures: Psychological intervention and assessment. In D.K. Routh (ed.), *Handbook of pediatric psychology*. New York: Guilford Press.

Jeffree, D.M., MacConkey, R., and Hewson, S. (1977). A parental involvement project. In P. Mittler (ed.), *Research to practice in mental retardation, Vol. 1. Care and Intervention*. Baltimore: University Park Press.

Jehu, D. (1992). Personality problems among adults molested as children. *Sexual and marital therapy*, **7**, 231–250.

Joffe, J.M. (1968). *Prenatal determinants of behaviour*. Oxford: Pergamon.

Johansson, S., Johnson, S. M., Wahl, G. and Martin, S. (undated). *Compliance and noncompliance in young children: A behavioral analysis*. University of Oregon paper, Eugene, Oregon.

Johnson, J.H. and Goldman, J. (1993). Approaches to developmental assessment. In T.H. Ollendick and R.J. Prinz. (eds). *Advances in clinical child psychology*. New York: Plenum Press.

Jones, C. (1994). *Attention deficit disorder: strategies for school-age children*. Tucson: Ari: Communication Skill Builders.

Jones, M.C. (1924). The elimination of children's fears. *Journal of Experimental Psychology*, **7**, 382–390.

Jordan, R. (1993). The nature of linguistic and communication difficulties of children with autism. In D.J. Messer and G.J. Turner (eds) *Critical influences on child language acquisition and development*. New York: St Martin's Press.

Kagan, J. (1958a). The concept of identification. *Psychological Review*, **65**, 296–305.

Kagan, J. (1958b). Acquisition and significance of sex-typing and sex-role identity. In M.L. Hoffman and L.W. Hoffman (eds). *Review of Child Development Research*, Vol. 1. New York: Russell Sage Foundation.

Kagan, J. and Moss, H.A. (1962). *Birth to maturity: a study in psychological development*. New York: Wiley.

Kane, B. (1979) Children's concepts of death. *Journal of Genetic Psychology* **134**, 141–145.

Kanfer, F.H., Karoly, P. and Newman, A. (1975). Reduction of children's fear of the dark by competence-related and situational threat-related verbal cues. *Journal of Consulting and Clinical Psychology*, **43**, 251–258.

Kanner, L. (1943). Autistic disturbances of affective contact. *Nervous Child*, **2**, 217–250.

Kanner, L., (1953). *Child Psychiatry*. Springfield, IL: Thomas.

Karno, M. and Golding, J. (1990). Obsessive compulsive disorder. In L. Robins and D.A. Regrer, (eds) *Psychiatric disorders in America: The epidemiologic catchment area study*. New York: The Free Press.

Kaslow, N.J. and Rehm, L.P. (1982). Childhood depression. In R.J. Morris and T.R. Kratochwill (eds). *The practice of child therapy*. New York: Pergamon Press, pp. 27–51.

Kaye, K. (1982). *The mental and social life of babies: how parents create persons*. London: Methuen.

Kazdin, A.E. (1975). *Behavior modification in applied settings*. Homewood, IL: Dorsey Press.

Kazdin, A.E. (1977). Assessing the clinical or applied significance of behaviour change through social validation. *Behaviour Modification*, **1**, 427–552.

Kazdin, A.E. (1978). *History of Behavior Modification: Experimental Foundations of Contemporary Research*, Baltimore: University Park Press.

Kazdin, A.E. (1987). *Conduct Disorders in Childhood and Adolescence*. Newbury Park, CA: Sage.

Kazdin, A.E. (1987b). Treatment of antisocial behaviour in children: current status and future directions. *Psychological Bulletin*, **102**, 187–203.

Kazdin, A.E. (1988). *Child psychotherapy: developing and identifying effective treatments*. Oxford: Pergamon.

Kazdin, A.E. (1990). Childhood depression. *Journal of Child Psychology & Psychiatry*, **31**, 121–160.

Kazdin, A.E. (1994). Psychotherapy for children and adolescents. In A.E. Bergin and S.L. Garfield (eds), *Handbook of psychotherapy and behavior change* (4th edn). New York: Wiley, pp. 543–594.

Kazdin, A.E. (1997). Annotation. *Journal of Child Psychology and Psychiatry*, **39**, 7–17.

Kazdin, A.E., Esveldt-Dawson, K., French, N.H. and Unis, A.S. (1987). Problem solving skills training and relationship therapy in the treatment of antisocial child behavior. *Journal of Consulting and Clinical Psychology*, **55**, 76–85.

Kelly, G.A. (1955). *The psychology of personal constructs*. New York: Norton.

Kendall, P. (1984). Cognitive-behavioural self-control therapy for children. *Journal of Child Psychology & Psychiatry*, **25**, 173–179.

Kendall, P.C. (1993). Cognitive–behavioural therapies with youth: Guiding theory, current status, and emerging developments. *Journal of Consulting and Clinical Psychology*, **61**, 235–247.

Kendall, P.C. and Braswell, L. (1985). *Cognitive–behavioral therapy for impulsive children*. New York: Guilford Press.

Kendall, P. and Braswell, L. (1993). *Cognitive–behavioural therapy for impulsive children* (2nd edn). New York: Guilford Press.

Kendall, P.C. and Lochman, J. (1994). *Cognitive–behavioral therapies*. In M. Rutter, E. Taylor and L. Hersov (eds) *Child and adolescent psychiatry*. (3rd edn) Oxford: Blackwell Scientific.

Kendall, P.C., Chansky, T.E., Friedman, M., Kim, R., Kortlander, E., Sessa, F.M. and Siqueland, L. (1991). Treating anxiety disorders in children and adolescents. In: P.C. Kendall (ed.) *Child and adolescent therapy: cognitive-behavioural procedures* (pp. 131–164). New York: Guilford Press.

Kendall, P.C. and Hollon, S.D. (eds) (1994). *Cognitive–behavioural interventions: theory, research and procedures*. New York: Academic Press.

Kendell, R.E. *et al.* (1973). The epidemiology of anorexia nervosa. *Psychological Medicine*, **3**, 200–203.

Kiernan, C.C. (1983). The exploration of sign and symbol effects. In J. Hogg and P.J. Mittler (eds). *Advances in mental handicap research, Vol. 2. Aspects of competence in mentally handicapped people*. Chichester: Wiley.

Kifer, R.E., Lewis, M.A., Green, D.R. and Phillips, E.L. (1974). Training predelinquent youths and their parents to negotiate conflict situations. *Journal of Applied Behavior Analysis*, **7**, 357–364.

King, N.J., Hamilton, D.I. and Ollendick, T.H. (1988). *Children's phobias: A behavioural perspective*. London: Academic Press.

King, N.J. and Ollendick, T.H. (1997). Treatment of childhood phobias. *Journal of Child Psychology and Psyche*, **38**, 389–404.

King, N.J., Ollendick, T.H. and Tonge, B. (1995). *School Refusal: Assessment and Treatment*. Boston: Allyn & Bacon.

King, N.J., Ollier, K., Iacuone, R., Schuster, S., Bays, K., Gullone, E. and Ollendick, T.H. (1989). Fears of children and adolescent: cross-sectional Australian study using the Revised Fear Survey Schedule for Children. *Journal of Child Psychology and Psychiatry*, **30**, 775–784.

Kirschenbaum, D.S. and Flanery, R.C. (1983). Behavioural contracting: outcomes and elements. *Progress in Behavior Modification*, **15**, 217–275.

Kissel, S. (1972). Systematic desensitization therapy with children: A case study and some suggested modifications. *Professional Psychology*, **3**, 164–169.

Klaus, M. H. and Kennell, J.H. (1976). *Maternal-infant bonding*. St Louis, C.V.: Mosby.

Knapp, M.R.J. and Robertson, E. (1989). The costs of child care services. In B. Kahan (ed.)., *Child Care Research, Policy and Practice*. Milton Keynes: Open University Press.

Knitzer, J. (1982). *Unclaimed Children: The failure of public responsibility to children and adolescents in need of mental health services*. Children's Defense Fund: Washington, D.C.

Koegel, R. and Covert, A. (1972). The relationship of self-stimulation to learning in autistic children. *Journal of Applied Behavior Analysis*, **6**, 1–14.

Kohlberg, L. (1978). Revisions in the theory and practice of moral development. In W. Damson (ed.). *New directions in child development: Moral development*. San Francisco, CA: Jossey-Bass.

Kolvin, I., and Fundudis, T. (1981). Elective mute children: Psychological development and background factors'. *Journal of Child Psychology and Psychiatry*, **22**, 219–233.

Kolvin, I., Garside, R.F., Nicol, A.R., MacMillan, A., Wolstenholme, F. and Leitch, I.M. (1981). *Help Starts Here: the Maladjusted Child in the Ordinary School*. London: Tavistock.

Kovacs, M. (1980). Rating scales to assess depression in school-aged children. *Acta Paedopsychiatrica*, **46**, 305–313.

Kratochwil, T. (1981). Selective mutism: Implications for research and treatment. Hillsdale, NJ: Lawrence Erlbaum Associates.

Krug D.A., Arick J. and Almond P. (1980). Behaviour checklist for identifying severely handicapped individuals with high levels of autistic behaviour. *Journal of Child Psychology and Psychiatry*, **21**, 221–229.

Labbe, E.E. and Williamson, D.A. (1984). Behavioral treatment of elective mutism: A review of the literature. *Clinical Psychology Review*, **4**, 273–292.

LaGreca, A. (1981). Social behaviour and social perception in learning-disabled children: A review with implications for social skills training. *Journal of Pediatric Psychology*, **6**, 385–416.

Lambert, N.M., Sandoval, J. and Sassone, D. (1978). Prevalence of hyperactivity in elementary school children as a function of social system definers. *American Journal of Orthopsychiatry*, **48**, 446–463.

Lansdown, R. and Goldman, A. (1988). Annotation: The psychological care of children with malignant disease. *Journal of Child Psychology and Psychiatry*, **29**, 555–567.

Lapouse, R. and Monk, M.A. (1958). An epidemiologic study of behaviour characteristics in children. *American Journal of Public Health*, **48**, 1134–1144.

Lask, B. (1987). Family therapy. *British Medical Journal*, **294**, 203–204.

Lask, B. and Bryant-Waugh, R. (1992). Early onset anorexia nervosa and related eating disorders. *Journal of Child Psychology and Psychiatry*, **33**, 281–300.

Lask, B. and Fosson, A. (1989). *Childhood illness: The psychosomatic approach*. Chichester: Wiley.

Last, C.G., Francis, G., Hersen, M. *et al.* (1987). Separation anxiety and school phobia: a comparison using DSM-III criteria. *American Journal of Psychiatry*, **144**, 653–657.

Lazarus, A.A. and Abranovitz, A. (1962). The use of emotive imagery in the treatment of children's phobias. *Journal of Mental Science*, **108**, 191–195.

Lazarus, R.S. (1982). Thoughts on the relation between emotion and cognition. *American Psychologist*, **37**, 1019–1026.

Lazarus, R.S. (1984). On the primacy of cognition. *American Psychologist*, **39**, 124–129.

Le Couteur, A. *et al.* (1996). A broader phenotype of autism: the clinical spectrum in twins. *Journal of Child Psychology and Psychiatry*, **37**, 785–802.

Lee, S.G. and Herbert, M. (1970). *Freud and psychology*. Harmondsworth: Penguin.

Lefkowitz, M.M., Eron, L.D., Walder, L.O. and Heussmann, L.R. (1977). *Growing up to be violent: A longitudinal study of aggression*. Oxford: Pergamon.

Leitenberg *et al.* (1968). Sequential analyses of the effect of selective positive reinforcement in modifying anorexia nervosa. *Behaviour Research and Therapy*, **6**, 211–28.

Leon, G. (1979). Cognitive–behavior therapy for eating disturbances. In P. Kendall and S. Hollon (eds), *Cognitive behavioural interventions: Theory, research and procedures*. New York: Academic Press.

Leon G.R. and Dinklage D. (1989). Obesity and anorexia nervosa. In T.H. Ollendick and M. Hersen (eds) *Handbook of Child Psychopathology* (2nd edn) New York: Plenum.

Leon G.R., Bemis K.M. and Lucas A.R. (1980). Family interactions, control and other interpersonal factors as issues in the treatment of anorexia nervosa. Paper read at *World Congress on Behavior Therapy*, Jerusalem, Israel.

Leonard H.L. (1989). Childhood rituals and superstitions: developmental and cultural perspective. In J.L. Rapoport (ed.). *Obsessive–compulsive disorder in children and adolescents*. Washington: American Psychiatric Press, pp. 289–309.

Leslie A.M. (1987). Pretense and representation. The origins of 'Theory of Mind'. *Psychological Review*, **94**, 412–426.

Lewinsohn P.M. (1974). *Behavioral study and treatment of depression*. In M. Hersen, R.M. Eisler and P.M. Miller (eds) *Progress in behavior modification*. New York: Academic Press.

Ley, P. (1977). Psychological studies of doctor–patient communication. In S. Rachman (ed.), *Contributions to medical psychology*, Vol. 1. Oxford: Pergamon.

Liddiard, M. (1928). *The mothercraft manual*. London: Churchill.

Lidz, T. (1968). *The person*. New York: Basic Books.

Linden W. (1980). Multi-component behavior therapy in a case of compulsive binge-eating followed by vomiting. *Journal of Behavior Therapy and Experimental Psychiatry*, **11**, 297–300.

Lobitz, G.K. and Johnson, S.M. (1975). Normal versus deviant children: a multi method comparison. *Journal of Abnormal Child Psychology*, **3**, 353–374.

Lochman, J.E. (1992). Cognitive–behavioral intervention with aggressive boys: three-year follow-up and preventive effects. *Journal of Consulting and Clinical Psychology*, **60**, 426–432.

Lochman, J.E., Burch, P.P., Curry, J.F. and Lampron, L.B. (1984). Treatment and generalization effects of cognitive–behavioural and goal-setting interventions with aggressive boys. *Journal of Consulting and Clinical Psychology*, **52**, 915–916.

Lochman, J.E., Lampron, L., Gemmer, R.C., Harris, S. and Wycroff, G. (1989). Teacher consultation and cognitive–behavioral interventions with aggressive boys. *Psychology in the Schools*, **26**, 179–188.

Lockyer, L. and Rutter, M. (1970). A five to fifteen-year follow-up study of infantile psychosis: IV. Patterns of cognitive ability. *British Journal of Social and Clinical Psychology*, **9**, 152–163.

Lockyer, L. and Rutter, M. (1969). A five to fifteen year follow-up study of infantile psychoses: II Psychological Characteristics. *British Journal of Psychiatry*, **115**, 865–882.

Long, C.G. and Hollin, C.R. (1997). The scientist–practitioner model in clinical psychology: A critique. *Clinical Psychology and Psychotherapy*, **4**, 75–83.

Lord, C. and Rutter, M. (1994). Autism and pervasive developmental disorder. In M. Rutter, E. Taylor and L. Hersov. (eds) *Child and adolescent psychiatry: Modern approaches*. Oxford: Blackwell Scientific Publications.

Lord, C. *et al.* (1989). Autism diagnostic observation schedule. *Journal of Autism and Developmental Disorders*, **19**, 185–212.

Lorenz, K. (1966). *On Aggression*. New York: Harcourt, Brace & World.

Lotter, V. (1978). Follow-up studies. In Rutter, M. and Schopler, Z. (eds) *Autism: A reappraisal of concepts and treatment*. New York: Plenum Press.

Lovaas, O.I. (1973). *The autistic child: language development through behaviour modification*. New York: Wiley.

Lucas, E.V. (1980). *Semantic and pragmatic language disorders: Assessment and remediation*. Rockville: Aspen.

Lucas, A.R., Beard, C.M., O'Fallon, W.M. and Kurland, L.T. (1991) Fifty-year trends in the incidence of anorexia nervosa in Rochester. Minnesota: a population-based study. *American Journal of Psychiatry*, **148**, 917–922.

Lukeman, D. and Melvin, D. (1993). *Journal of Child Psychology and Psychiatry*, **34**, 837–850.

Lumsden-Walker, W. (1980). Intentional self-injury in school age children: A study of 50 cases. *Journal of Adolescence*, **3**, 217–228.

Luria, A.R. (1961). *The role of speech in the regulation of normal and abnormal behavior*. New York: Liveright.

Maccoby, E.E. (1984). Socialization and developmental change. *Child Development*, **55**, 317–328.

Maccoby, F.E. and Martin, J.P. (1983). Socialization in the context of the family: Parent–child interaction. In P. Mussen (ed.). *Handbook of child psychology* (Vol. 4). New York: Wiley.

MacClelland, D. (1961). *The achieving society*. Princeton: Van Nostrand.

MacDougall, C., Barnett, R.M., Ashurst, B. and Willis, B. (1987). Cognitive control of anger. In B.J. MacGurk, D.M. Thornton and M. Williams (eds), *Applying Psychology to Imprisonment: Theory and Practice*. London: HMSO.

McEachin, J.J., Smith, T. and Lovaas, O.I. (1993). Long-term outcome for children with autism who received early intensive behavioural treatment. *American Journal of Mental Retardation*, **97**, 359–372.

Macfarlane, J.W. *et al.* (1954). *A developmental study of the behavior problems of normal children*. Berkeley: University of California Press.

McGrath, P.A. (1987). *Pain in children: The perception, assessment and control of childhood pain*. New York: Guilford Press.

McGrath, P.A. and Unrah A.M. (1987). *Pain in children and adolescents*. Amsterdam: Elsevier.

MacKinnon, O.E. and Arbuckle, B.S. (1989). The relation between mother–son attributions and the coerciveness of their interactions. Paper read at Society for Research in Child Development (April meeting). Kansas City, Miss.

MacNeil, T.F. and Kaij, L. (1977). Prenatal, perinatal and post-partum factors in primary prevention of psychopathology. In G.W. Albee and J.M. Joffe (eds), *Primary prevention of psychopathology*: Vol. 1. *The issues*. Hanover, New Hampshire: University of New England Press.

Malewska, H.E. and Muszynski, H. (1970). Children's attitudes to theft. In K. Danziger (ed.), *Readings in child socialization*. Oxford: Pergamon.

Maratos, O. (1996). Psychoanalysis and the management of pervasive developmental disorders, including autism. In Trevarthen *et al.* (1996).

March, J.S., Mulle, K. and Herbel, B. (1994). Behavioural psychotherapy for children and adolescents with obsessive–compulsive disorder: an open trial of a new protocol-driven treatment package. *Journal of The American Academy of Child and Adolescent Psychiatry*, **33**, 333–341.

Martinson, R. (1974). What works? Questions and answers about prison reform. *The Public Interest*, **35**, 22–54.

M.A.S. Review (1989). Sharing skills and care. (Summary of the major findings by B. Kat). *The Psychologist*, October, 434–438.

Mash, E.J. and Terdal, L.G. (1988). *Behavioral assessment of childhood disorder*. New York: Guilford Press.

Masters, J.C., Burish, T.G., Hollon, S.D. and Rimm, D.C. (1987). *Behavior therapy: Technique and empirical findings* (3rd edn). New York: Harcourt Brace Jovanovich.

Mayer-Gross, W., Slater, L. and Roth, M. (1955). *Clinical psychiatry*. London: Cassell.

Meehl, P.E. (1960). The cognitive activity of the clinician *American Psychologist*, **15**, 19–27.

Meichenbaum, D.H. (1976). A self-instructional approach to stress management: A proposal for stress inoculation training. In *Stress and anxiety in modern life*. New York: Winston & Sons.

Meichenbaum, D. (1977). *Treating post-traumatic stress disorder*. Chichester: Wiley.

Meichenbaum, D.H., Bream, L.A. and Cohen, J.S. (1985). A cognitive–behavioural perspective of child psychopathology: Implications for assessment and training. In R.J. MacMahon and R. Dev. Peters (eds), *Childhood disorders: behavioural developmental approaches*. New York: Bruner/Mazel.

Meichenbaum, D.H. and Goodman, J. (1971). Training impulsive children to talk to themselves: A means for developing self-control. *Journal of Abnormal Psychology*, **77**, 115–126.

Melamed, B.G. (1979). Behavioural approaches to fear in dental settings. In M. Hersen, R.M. Eisler and P.M. Miller (eds), *Progress in behaviour modification*. New York: Academic Press.

Miller, L.C., Barrett, C.L. and Hampe, E. (1974). Phobias in children in a pre-scientific era. In A. Davids (ed.), *Child personality and psychopathology: Current topics*, Vol. 1. New York: Wiley.

Miller, S.A. (1986). Parents' beliefs about their children's cognitive abilities. *Developmental Psychology*, **22**, 276–284.

Mindus, P. (1991) *Capsulotomy in anxiety disorders: A multidisciplinary study*. Karolinska Institute Press, Stockholm.

Minuchin, S. (1974). *Family and family therapy*. Cambridge, MA: Harvard University Press.

Minuchin S., Rosman B.L. and Baker L. (1978). *Psychosomatic families*. Cambridge: Harvard University Press.

Mischel, W. (1970). Sex-typing and socialization. In P.H. Mussen (ed.), *Carmichael's manual of child psychology* (3rd edn). New York: Wiley.

Mitchell, S. and Shepherd, M. (1966). A comparative study of children's behaviour problems at home and at school. *British Journal of Educational Psychology*, **36**, 248–254.

Mizes, J.S. (1995). Eating disorders. In: M. Hersen and R.T. Ammerman (eds) *Advanced abnormal child psychology*. Hillsdale, New Jersey: Lawrence Erlbaum.

Money, J. (1965). Psychosexual differentiation. In J. Money (ed.), *Sex research: New developments*. London: Holt, Rinehart & Winston.

Money, J., and Ehrhardt, A. (1972). *Man and woman: Boy and girl*. Baltimore: Johns Hopkins University Press.

Moore, C., Bobblitt, W. and Wildman, R. (1968). Psychiatric impressions of psychological reports. *Journal of Clinical Psychology*, **24**, 373–376.

Moreland, S.R., Schwebel, A.L., Beck, S. and Wells, K.C. (1982). Parents as therapists: a review of the behaviour therapy parent training literature 1975 to 1981. *Behavior Modification*, **6**, 250–276.

Morgan, P. (1975). *Child care: Sense and fable*. London: Templesmith.

Morgan, R.T.T. (1984). *Behavioural treatments with children*. London: Heinemann Medical Books.

Morgan, R.T.T., and Young, G.C. (1972). The conditioning treatment of childhood enuresis. *British Journal of Social Work*, **2**, 503–509.

Morley, S.V. (1989). Single case methodology in behaviour therapy. In S.J.E. Lindsay and G.E. Powell (eds), *An introduction to clinical child psychology*. Aldershot: Gower.

Morris, E.K., and Braukmann, C.J. (eds). (1987). *Behavioral approaches to crime and delinquency: A handbook of application, research and methods*. New York: Plenum Press.

Morris, R.J., and Kratochwill, T.R. (1983). *Treating children's fears and phobias: A behavioural approach*. New York: Pergamon Press.

Mowrer, O.H. (1960). *Learning theory and behaviour*. New York: Wiley.

Murphy D. *et al.* (1989). Obsessive–compulsive disorder as subsystem behavioural disorder. *British Journal of Psychiatry*, **155**, 15–24.

Mussen, P.H., Conger, J.J. and Kagan, J. (1984). *Child development and personality* (6th edn). London: Harper & Row.

Neuhaus, E.C. (1958). A personality study of asthmatics and cardiac children. *Psychosomatic Medicine*, **20**, 181–183.

Nietzel, M.T. (1979). *Crime and its modification: A social learning perspective*. Elmsford, NY: Pergamon Press.

Novaco, R.W. (1975). *Anger control: The development and evaluation of an experimental treatment*. Lexington, MA: Heath.

Novaco, R.W. (1979). The cognitive regulation of anger and stress. In P. Kendall and S. Hollon (eds), *Cognitive-behavioral interventions: Theory, research and procedures*. New York: Academic Press.

Novaco, R.W. (1985). Anger and its therapeutic regulation. In M.A. Chesney and R.H. Rosenman (eds), *Anger and hostility in cardiovascular and behavioral disorders*. New York: Hemisphere.

O'Donnell, C.R., and Worell, L. (1973). Motor and cognitive relaxation in the desensitization of anger. *Behaviour Research and Therapy*, **11**, 473–481.

Oliver, C. (1995). Self-injurious behaviour in children with learning disabilities: recent advances in assessment and intervention. *Journal of Child Psychology and Psychiatry*, **36**, 909–928.

Ollendick, D.G. and Matson, J.L. (1983). Stereotypic behaviors, stuttering, and elective mutism. In T.H. Ollendick and M. Hersen (eds), *Handbook of child psychopathology*. New York: Plenum Press.

Ollendick, T.H. (1979a). Fear reduction techniques with children. In M. Hersen, R.M. Eisler and P.M. Miller (eds), *Progress in behaviour modification*, New York: Academic Press.

Ollendick, T.H. (1979b). Behavioral treatment of anorexia nervosa: a five-year study. *Behavior Modification*, 3, 124–135.

Ollendick, T.H. (1983). Reliability and validity of the Revised Fear Survey Schedule for Children (FSSC-R). *Behaviour Research and Therapy*, 21, 685–692.

Ollendick, T.H. (1986). Behavior therapy with children and adolescents. In S.L. Garfield and A.E. Bergen (eds), *Handbook of psychotherapy and behaviour change* (3rd edn). New York: Wiley.

Ollendick, T.H. and Cerny, J.A. (1981). *Clinical behavior therapy with children*. New York: Plenum Press.

Ollendick, T.H. and Francis, G. (1988). Behavioral assessment and treatment of childhood phobias. *Behavior Modification*, 12, 165–204.

Ollendick, T.H. and Hersen, M. (1984). *Child behavior assessment: Principles and procedures*. New York: Pergamon Press.

Ollendick, T.H., King, N.J. and Frary, R.B. (1989). Fears in children and adolescents: Reliability and generalizability across gender, age, and nationality. *Behaviour Research and Therapy*, 27, 19–26.

Ollendick, T.H., Mattis, S.G. and King, N.J. (1994). Panic in children and adolescents: A review. *Journal of Child Psychology and Psychiatry*, 35, 113–134.

Olweus, D. (1994). Bullying at school: basic facts and effects of a school based intervention program. *Journal of Child Psychology & Psychiatry*, 35, 1171–1190.

Opie, I. and Opie, P. (eds). (1973). *The Oxford Book of Children's Verse* contains the story of Fidgety

Orford, J. (1992). *Community Psychology: theory and practice*. Chichester: Wiley.

Palmer R. *et al.* (1987). The clinical eating disorder rating instrument (CEDRI): a preliminary description. *International Journal of Eating Disorders*, 6, 9–16.

Parkes, C.M. (1973). *Bereavement*. London: Tavistock.

Pasamanick, B. and Knoblock, H. (1961). Epidemiologic studies on the complications of pregnancy and the birth process. In G. Caplan (ed.), *Prevention of mental disorders in childhood*. New York: Basic Books.

Patterson, G.R. (1965). Responsiveness to social stimuli. In L. Krasner and L.P. Ullmann (eds), *Research in behavior modification*. New York: Holt, Rinehart & Winston.

Patterson, G.R. (1975). *A social learning approach to family intervention*. Vol. I. *Families with aggressive children*. Eugene, Oregon: Castalia.

Patterson, G.R. (1977). Accelerating 'stimuli' for two classes of coercive behaviors. *Journal of Abnormal Child Psychology*, 5, 334–350.

Patterson, G.R. (1982). *Coercive family process*. Eugene, Oregon: Castalia.

Patterson, G.R. and Chamberlain, P. (1988). Treatment process: a problem at three levels. In L.C. Wynne (ed.). *The state of the art of family therapy research*. New York: Family Process Press.

Patterson, G.R., Cobb, J.A. and Ray, R.S. (1972). Direct intervention in the classroom: A set of procedures for the aggressive child. In F. Clark, D. Evans and L. Hamerlynck (eds), *Implementing behavioral programs for schools and clinics*. Champaign, IL: Research Press.

Patterson, G.R. and Fleischman, M.J. (1979). Maintenance of treatment effects: Some considerations concerning family systems and follow-up data. *Behavior Therapy*, **10**, 168–185.

Patterson, G.R., Reid, J.B., Jones, J.J. and Conger, R.E. (1975). *A social learning approach to family intervention. Vol. I. Families with aggressive children.* Eugene, Oregon: Castalia.

Paul, G.L. (1967). Outcome research in psychotherapy. *Journal of Consulting Psychology*, **31**, 109–118.

Penfield, W. and Roberts, L. (1959). *Speech and brain mechanisms.* New Jersey: Princeton University Press.

Peter, B.M. and Spreen, O. (1979). Behavior rating and personal adjustment scales of neurologically and learning handicapped children during adolescence and early adulthood. Results of a follow-up study. *Journal of Clinical Neuropsychology*, **1**, 75–92.

Piacentini, J.C. (1987). Language dysfunction and childhood behavior disorders. In B.B. Lahey and A.E. Kazdin (eds), *Advances in clinical child psychology* Vol. 10. New York: Plenum.

Piaget, J. (1953). *Origins of intelligence in the child.* London: Routledge & Kegan Paul.

Piaget, J. (1954). *The construction of reality in the child.* New York: Basic Books.

Piercy, F.P., Sprenkle, D. *et al.* (1986). *Family therapy sourcebook.* New York: Guilford Press.

Pigott, M. *et al.* (1991). *Biological Psychiatry*, **29**, 418–426.

Pillay, M. and Crisp, A.H. (1981). The impact of social skills training within an established in-patient treatment program for anorexia nervosa. *British Journal of Psychiatry*, **139**, 533–539.

Pitman, R.K., Green, R.C., Jenike, M.A. and Mesulam, M.M. (1987). Clinical comparison of Tourette's disorder and obsessive compulsive disorder. *American Journal of Psychiatry*, **144**, 1166–1171.

Pless, I.B. and Douglas, S.W.B. (1971). Chronic illness in childhood: Part 1. Epidemiological and clinical characteristics. *Pediatrics*, **47**, 405–414.

Plomin, R. (1995). Genetics and children's experiences in the family. *Journal of Child Psychology and Psychiatry*, **36**, 33–68.

Powell, M.B. and Oei, T.P.S. (1991). Cognitive processes underlying the behaviour change in cognitive behaviour therapy with childhood disorders: a review of experimental evidence. *Behavioural Psychotherapy*, **19**, 247–265.

Power, M.J. (1991). Cognitive science and behavioral psychotherapy: where behavior was there shall cognition be. *Behavioral Psychotherapy*, **19**, 20–41.

President's Commission on Mental Health (1978). *Report to the President*, Vols. 1–4, Washington, DC: US Government Printing Office.

Prior, M.R. and Cummins, R. (1992). Questions about facilitated communication and autism. *Journal of Autism and Developmental Disorders*, **22**, 331–337.

Proven, L. (1990). Personal communication.

Puig-Antich, J., Lukens, E., Davies, M., Goetz, D., Brennan-Quattrock, J. and Todak, L. (1985). Psychosocial functioning in prepubertal major depressive disorders. *Archives of General Psychiatry*, **42**, I Interpersonal relationships during the depressive episode, pp. 500–507, II Interpersonal relationships after sustained recovery from affective episode, pp. 511–517.

Quay, H.C. (1984). A critical analysis of DSM-III as a taxonomy of psychopathology in childhood and adolescence. Unpublished manuscript, University of Miami.

Quay, H.C. (1985). Classification. In H.C. Quay and J.S. Werry (eds) *Psychopathological disorders of childhood* (3rd edn) (pp. 1–34). New York: Wiley.

Quay, H.C. and Peterson, D.R. (1983). Manual for the Revised Behavioral Problem Checklist (unpublished manuscript).

Rachman, S. (1962). Learning theory and child psychology: Therapeutic possibilities. *Journal of Child Psychology and Psychiatry*, 3, 149–163.

Rachman, S.J. (1997). A cognitive theory of obsessions. *Behaviour Research and Therapy*, 35, 793–802.

Rachman, S. and Hodgson, R. (1980). *Obsessions and compulsions*. Englewood Cliffs, NJ: Prentice-Hall.

Randall, J. (1970). Transvestism and trans-sexualism. *British Journal of Hospital Medicine*, 3, 211–213.

Rapin, I. and Allen, A. (1983). Developmental language disorders: nosological considerations. In U. Kirk (ed.) *Neuropsychology of language, reading and spelling*. London: Academic Press. Reber, S.A.

Rapoport, J.L. (ed.) (1989a). *Obsessive compulsive disorder in children and adolescents*. American Psychiatric Press, New York.

Rapoport, J.L. (1989b). The neurobiology of obsessive compulsive disorder. *Journal of the American Medical Association*, 260, 2888–2890.

Rapoport, J.L. (1989c). The new biology of obsessive compulsive disorder. *Scientific American*, 260, 82–89.

Rapoport, J.L. (1989d). Childhood obsessive compulsive disorder. *Journal of Child Psychology and Psychiatry*, 27, 289–295.

Rapoport, J.L. (1989e). *The boy who couldn't stop washing*. E.P. Dutton, New York.

Rapoport, J.L. (1991). Recent advances in obsessive compulsive disorder *Neuropsychopharmacology*, 5, 1–9.

Rapoport, J.L. Swedo, S. and Leonard, H. (1994). Obsessive–compulsive disorder. In M. Rutter, E. Taylor and L. Hersov (eds) *Child and adolescent psychiatry: modern approaches* (3rd edn). Oxford: Blackwell Scientific Publications.

Rasmussen, S.A. and Tsuang, M.T. (1985). The epidemiology of obsessive–compulsive disorder. *Journal of Clinical Psychiatry*, 45, 450–454.

Reed, G.F. (1963). Elective mutism in children. A reappraisal. *Journal of Child Psychology and Psychiatry*, 4, 99–107.

Rees, L. (1963). The significance of parental attitudes in childhood asthma. *Journal of Psychosomatic Research*, 7, 181–185.

Reid, M.K. and Borkowski, J.G. (1987). Causal attributions of hyperactive children: implications for teaching strategies and self-control. *Journal of Educational Psychology*, 79, 296–307.

Reimers, S. and Treacher, A. (1995). *Introducing user-friendly family therapy*. London: Routledge.

Reiss D. (1988). Theoretical versus tactical inferences: Or how to do family therapy research without dying of boredom. In L.C. Wynne (ed.) *The state of the art in family therapy research*. New York: Family Process Press.

Revill, S. and Blunden, R. (1979). A home training service for pre-school developmentally handicapped children. *Behaviour Research and Therapy*, 17, 207–214.

Reynolds, C.R. and Richmond, B.O. (1978). 'What I think and feel': A revised measure of children's manifest anxiety. *Journal of Abnormal Child Psychology*, **6**, 271–280.

Reynolds, M.M. (1982). Negativism of preschool children: An observational and experimental study. *Contributions to Education*, No. 228. Bureau of Publications, Teachers College, Columbia University, New York.

Reynolds, W.M. (1984). Depression in children and adolescents: Phenomenology, evaluation and treatment. *School Psychology Review*, **13**, 171–182.

Reynolds, W.M. and Coats, K.I. (1986). A comparison of cognitive-behavioral therapy and relaxation training for the treatment of depression in adolescents. *Journal of Consulting and Clinical Psychology*, **54**, 653–660.

Richman, N. (1981). A community survey of characteristics of one- to two-year-olds with sleep disruptions. *Journal of the American Academy of Child and Adolescent Psychiatry*, **20**, 280–291.

Richman, N., Stevenson, J. and Graham, P. (1975). Prevalence and patterns of psychological disturbance in children of primary age. *Journal of Child and Adolescent Psychology and Psychiatry*, **16**, 101–103.

Richman, N., Stevenson, J. and Graham, P. (1982). *Preschool to school: A behavioural study*. London: Academic Press.

Richman, N., Douglas, J., Hunt, H., Lansdown, R. and Levere, R. (1985). Behavioural methods in the treatment of sleep disorders—a pilot study. *Journal of Child Psychology and Psychiatry*, **26**, 581–590.

Ritvo, E.R., Mason-Brothers, A., Freeman, P.B., Pingree, C., Jenson, W.R., MacMahon, W.M., Peterson, P.B., Jorde, L.B., Mo, A. and Ritvo, A. (1990). The UCLA-University of Utah epidemiologic survey of autism—the etiologic of rare diseases. *American Journal of Psychiatry*, **147**, 1614–1621.

Roberts, M.U., MacMahon, R.J., Forehand, R. and Humphreys, L. (1978). The effects of parental instruction-giving on child compliance. *Behavior Therapy*, **9**, 793–798.

Robins, L.N. (1966). *Deviant children grown up*. Baltimore: Williams & Wilkins.

Robins, L.N. (1981). Epidemiological approaches to natural history research: Antisocial disorders in children. *Journal of the American Academy of Child and Adolescent Psychiatry*, **20**, 566–580.

Robins, L.N. and Price, R.K. (1991). Adult disorders predicted by childhood conduct problems: The NIMH ECA project. *Psychiatry*, **54**, 116–132.

Robson, K.M. and Powell, E. (1982). Early maternal attachment. In I.F. Brockington and R. Kumar (eds), *Motherhood and mental illness*. London: Academic Press.

Rogers, C.R. (1957). *Client centered therapy*. Dallas: Houghton Mifflin.

Rose, M.I., Firestone, P., Heick, H.M.C. and Fraught, A.K. (1983). The effects of anxiety on the control of juvenile diabetes mellitus. *Journal of Behavioural Medicine*, **6**, 382–395.

Rosenstiel, S.K. and Scott, D.S. (1977). Four considerations in imagery techniques with children. *Journal of Behavior Therapy and Experimental Psychiatry*, **8**, 287–290.

Ross, R.R. and Gendreau, P. (1980). *Effective correctional treatment*. Toronto: Butterworths.

Ross, D.M. and Ross, S.A. (1988). *Childhood pain: Current issues, research and management*. Maryland: Urban & Schwarzenberg.

Russell, G.F.M. (1985). Premenarchal anorexia nervosa and its sequelae. *Journal of Psychiatric Research*, **19**, 363–369.

Rutter, M. (1970). Autistic children: infancy to adulthood. *Seminar in Psychiatry*, **2**, 435–450.

Rutter, M. (1971). Parent–child separation: psychological effects on the children. *Journal of Child Psychology and Psychiatry*, **12**, 233–260.

Rutter, M. (1977). Speech delay. In M. Rutter and L. Hersov (eds). *Handbook of child psychiatry: modern approaches*. Oxford: Blackwell Scientific.

Rutter, M. (1978). Diagnosis and definition of childhood autism. *Journal of Autism and Developmental Disorder*, **8**, 139–161.

Rutter, M. (1979a). Protective factors in children's responses to stress and disadvantage. In M.W. Kent and J.E. Rolfe (eds). *Primary prevention of psychopathology, Vol. 3: Social competence in children*, pp. 49–74. Hanover, NH: University Press of New England.

Rutter, M. (1979b). *Changing youth in a changing society*. The Nuffield Provincial Hospitals Trust.

Rutter, M. (1981a). *Maternal deprivation revisited*. Harmondsworth: Penguin.

Rutter, M. (1981b). Stress, coping and development: some issues and some questions. *Journal of Child Psychology and Psychiatry*, **22**, 323–356.

Rutter, M. (1981c). Social/emotional consequences of day care for pre-school children. *American Journal of Orthopsychiatry*, **51**, 4–28.

Rutter, M. (1983). Cognitive deficits in the pathogenesis of autism. *Journal of Child Psychology and Psychiatry*, **24**, 513–531.

Rutter, M. and Madge, N. (1976). *Cycles of disadvantage*. London: Heinemann.

Rutter, M. (1985). Family and school influences on behaviour development, *Journal of Child Psychology and Psychiatry*, **26**, 349–368.

Rutter, M. (1990). Psychological resilience and protective mechanisms. In J. Rolf *et al.*, *Risk and protective factors in the development of psychopathology*. New York: Cambridge University Press.

Rutter, P.L. and Schopler, F. (1992). Classification of pervasive developmental disorders: Some concepts and practical considerations. *Journal of Autism and Developmental Disorders*, **22**, 459–482.

Rutter, M., Taylor, E., Hersov (1994). *Child and Adolescent Psychiatry: Modern Approaches*, Oxford: Pergamon.

Rutter, M., Tizard, J. and Whitmore, K. (eds). (1970). *Education, health and behaviour*. London: Longmans (Reprinted, Krieger, New York, 1980).

Rutter, M., Maughan, B., Mortimore, P., Ouston, J. and Smith, A. (1979). *Fifteen thousand hours: Secondary schools and their effects on children*. Open Books, London: Harvard University Press.

Ryall, R. (1968). Delinquency: The problem for treatment. *Social Work Today*, **5**, 98–104.

Rycroft, C. (1970). Causes and meaning. In S.G. Lee and M. Herbert (eds), *Freud and psychology*. Harmondsworth: Penguin.

Salkovskis, P. (1985). Obsessional–compulsive problems: a cognitive–behavioural analysis. *Behaviour Research and Therapy*, **23**, 571–583.

Sanok, R.L. and Stiefel, S. (1979). Elective mutism: Generalization of verbal responding across people and settings. *Behavior Therapy*, **10**, 357–371.

Sarason, I.G. and Sarason, B.R. (1981). Teaching cognitive and social skills to high school students. *Journal of Consulting and Clinical Psychology*, **49**, 908–918.

Scaife, J.M. and Holland, A. (1987). An evaluation of the Leicestershire Portage training scheme. In R. Hedderley and K. Jennings (eds), *Extending and developing Portage*. Windsor: NFER-Nelson.

Schachter S. (1971). *Emotion, obesity and crime*. New York: Academic Press.

Schaffer, H.R. (1977). *Mothering*. London: Open University/Fontana.

Schaffer, H.R. (1996). *Social development*. Oxford: Blackwell.

Schaffer, R. and Collis, G. (1986). Social responsiveness and child behaviour. In W. Sluckin and M. Herbert (eds), *Parental behaviour*. Oxford: Basil Blackwell.

Schmaling, K.B. and Jacobson, N.S. (1987). The clinical significance of treatment resulting from parent training interventions for children with conduct problems: An analysis of outcome data. Paper presented at a meeting of the Association for the Advancement of Behaviour Therapy. Boston, MA, November.

Schneider, M. (1973). Turtle technique in the classroom. *Exceptional Children*, 42, 201.

Schofield, M. (1973). *The sexual behaviour of young adults*. London: Longman.

Schopler, E. and Reichler, R.J. (1979). *Individualized assessment and treatment of autistic and developmentality disabled children; psychoeducational profile* (vol. 1). Baltimore: University Park Press.

Schopler, E. Reichler, R.J. and Lansing M. (1980). *Individualized assessment and treatment of autistic and developmentally disabled children*, Vol. 2, *Teaching strategies for parents and professionals*. Dallas, Tx: Pro-Ed.

Schopler, E., Reichler, R.J. and Renner, B.R. (1986) *The childhood autism rating scale (CARS) for diagnostic screening and classification of autism*. New York: Irvington Publishers.

Schopler, E., Short, A. and Mesibov, G. (1989) Relation of behavioral treatment to normal functioning: comment on Lovaas. *Journal of Consulting and Clinical Psychology*, 57, 162–164.

Schopler, E. (1983). *New developments in the definition and diagnosis of autism*. In B.B. Lahey and A.E. Kazdin (eds.). *Advances in clinical psychology*. New York: Plenum Press.

Schopler, E., Reichler, R.J. and Renner, B.R. (1988). *A childhood autism rating scale*. Los Angeles, CA: Western Psychological Services.

Schopler, E., Reichler, R.J., DeVellis, R.F. and Kock, K. (1980). Toward objective classification of childhood autism: Childhood Autism Rating Scale (CARS). *Journal of Autism and Developmental Disorders*, 10, 91–103.

Schopler, E., Reichler, R.J., Bashford, A., Lansing, M.D. and Marcus, L.M. (1990) *Psychoeducational profile revised*. Austin, TX: Pro-Ed.

Scott, D.W. (1987). The involvement of psychosexual factors in the causality of eating disorders: time for a re-appraisal. *International Journal of Eating Disorders*, 6, 199–213.

Seligman, M.E.P. (1975). *Helplessness*. San Francisco: Freeman.

Selman, R.L. (1980). *The growth of interpersonal understanding: Developmental and clinical analyses*. New York: Academic Press.

Shaffer, D. (1974). Suicide in childhood and early adolescence. *Journal of Child Psychology and Psychiatry*, 15, 275–279.

Shaffer, D. (1994). Enuresis. In M. Rutter, E. Taylor and L. Hersov (eds) (3rd edn). *Child and adolescent psychiatry: modern approaches*. Oxford: Blackwell Scientific Publications.

Shaffer, D. and Piacentini, J. (1994). Suicide and attempted suicide. In M. Rutter, E. Taylor and L. Hersov (eds) (3rd edn). *Child and adolescent psychiatry: modern approaches*. Oxford: Blackwell Scientific Publications.

Shaywitz, B.A. (1987). *Yale children's inventory*. New Haven, CT: Yale University Medical School.

Shaywitz, S.E. and Shaywitz, B.A. (1991). Attention deficit disorder: current perspectives. In J.F. Kavanough and T.J. Truss (eds) *Learning Disabilities: Proceedings of the National Conference*. Parkton, MD: York Press.

Silverman, W.K. (1991). Diagnostic reliability of anxiety disorders in children using structured interviews. *Journal of Anxiety Disorder*, 5, 105–124.

Silverman, W.K. (1994). Structured diagnostic interviews. In T.H. Ollendick, N.J. King and W. Yule (eds). *International handbook of phobic and anxiety disorders in children and adolescents*. New York: Plenum Press.

Slaby, R.G. and Guerra, N.G. (1988). Cognitive mediators of aggression in adolescent offenders: 1. Assessment. *Developmental Psychology*, 24, 580–588.

Slade, P.D. (1982). Towards a functional analysis of anorexia nervosa and bulimia nervosa. *British Journal of Clinical Psychology*, 21, 167–179.

Sloan, T.S. (1987). *Deciding: self-deception in life*. New York: Methuen.

Sloman, L. (1991). Use of medication in pervasive developmental disorders. *Psychiatric Clinics of North America*, 14, 165–182.

Sluckin, A., Foreman, N. and Herbert M. (1990). Behavioural treatment programmes and selectivity of speaking at follow-up in a sample of 25 selective males. *Australian Psychologist*, 26, 132–137.

Sluckin, W., and Herbert, M. (eds). (1986). *Parental behaviour*. Oxford: Basil Blackwell.

Sluckin, W., Herbert, M. and Sluckin, A. (eds). (1983). *Maternal bonding*. Oxford: Basil Blackwell.

Smith, B.R. and Leinonen, E. (1992). *Clinical pragmatics: unravelling the complexities of communicative failure*. London: Chapman & Hall.

Smith, P.K. (1990). The silent nightmare: Bullying and victimization in school peer groups. Paper read to British Pychological Society London Conference.

Smith, P.S. and Smith, L.J. (1987). *Continence and incontinence*. London: Croom Helm.

Snyder, J. and Brown, K. (1983). Oppositional behaviour and noncompliance in pre-school children. Environmental correlates and skill deficits. *Behavioural Assessment*, 5, 333–348.

Snyder, J.J. and White, M.J. (1979). The use of cognitive self-instruction in the treatment of behaviorally disturbed adolescents. *Behavior Therapy*, 10, 227–235.

Sorensen, R.C. (1973). *Adolescent sexuality in contemporary America*. New York: World Publishing.

Sowder, B.J. (1975). *Assessment of child mental health needs* (Vols I-VIII). McLean, VA: General Research Corporation.

Speck R. and Attneave C. (1973). *Family networks*. New York: Vintage Books.

Spence, S.H. (1994) Practitioner Review: Cognitive therapy with children and adolescents: From theory to practice. *Journal of Child Psychology and Psychiatry*, 35, 1191–1228.

Spence, S.H. and Marzillier, J.S. (1981). Social skills training with adolescent male offenders: II. Short-term, long-term and generalized effects. *Behaviour Research and Therapy*, 19, 349–368.

Spitz, R.A. (1945). Hospitalism: An enquiry into the genesis of psychiatric conditions in early childhood. *Psychoanalytic Study of the Child*, 1, 53–74.

Spitz, R. (1946). Anaclitic depression. *Psychoanalytic Study of the Child*, 2, 313–342.

Spivack, G., Platt, J.J. and Shure, M.B. (1976). *The problem-solving approach to adjustment*. San Francisco: Jossey-Bass.

Sroufe, L.A. and Rutter, M. (1984). The domain of developmental psychopathology. *Child Development*, 55, 17–29.

Stayton, D., Hogan, R. and Ainsworth, M.D.S. (1971). Infant obedience and maternal behavior: The origins of socialization reconsidered. *Child Development*, 42, 1057–1069.

Stefanek, M.E., Ollendick, T.H., Baldock, W.P., Francis, G. and Yaeger, N.J. (1987). Self-statements in aggressive, withdrawn, and popular children. *Cognitive Behavior Therapy and Research*, 2, 229–239.

Stein, L. and Mason, S.E. (1968). Psychogenic and allied disorders of communication in childhood. In E. Miller, *Foundations of Child Psychiatry*. Oxford: Pergamon.

Steinhausen H.C. (1994). Anorexia and bulimia. In M. Rutter, E. Taylor, L. Hersov (eds) *Child and Adolescent psychiatry: modern approaches*. Oxford, Blackwell Scientific Publications.

Stevenson, J. (1984). Predictive value of speech and language screening. *Developmental Medicine and Child Neurology*, 26, 528–538.

Stumphauzer, J.S. (1986). *Helping delinquents change: A treatment manual of social learning approaches*. New York: Haworth Press.

Sturge, C. (1982). Reading retardation and antisocial behaviour. *Journal of Child Psychology and Psychiatry*, 23, 21–31.

Sturmey, P. (1990). *Functional analysis in clinical psychology*. Chichester: Wiley.

Sutton, C. and Herbert, M. (1992). *Mental health: a client support resource pack*. Windsor: NFER-Nelson.

Swedo, S.E., Rapoport J.L., Cheslow D.L., Leonard H.L., Ayoub E.M., Hosier D.M. and Wald E.R. (1989). High prevalence of obsessive–compulsive symptoms in patients with Sydenham's chorea. *American Journal of Psychiatry*, 146, 246–249.

Sylva, K. (1994). School influences on children's development. *Journal of Child Psychology and Psychiatry*, 35, 135–170.

Szatmari, P., Offord, D.R. and Boyle, M.H. (1989) Ontario child health study: prevalence of attention deficit disorder and hyperactivity. *Journal of Child Psychology and Psychiatry*, 30, 219–230.

Tanner, J.M. (1978). *Foetus into man: Physical growth from conception to maturity*. London: Open Books.

Taylor, E. (1994). Syndromes of attention deficit and overactivity. In M. Rutter, E. Taylor, L. Hersov (eds) *Child and adolescent psychiatry: modern approaches* (3rd edn) Oxford: Blackwell Scientific Publications.

Taylor, T.K. and Biglan, A. (1998). Behavioral family interventions for improving child-rearing: A review of the literature for clinicians and policy makers. *Clinical Child and Family Psychology Review*, 1, 41–60.

Thomas, A. and Chess, S. (1977). *Temperament and development*. New York: Brunner/Mazel.

Thomas, A., Chess, S. and Birch, H.G. (1968). *Temperament and behaviour disorders in children*. London: University of London Press.

Thornton, P., Walsh, J., Webster, J. and Harris, C. (1984). The sleep clinic. *Nursing Times*, 14 March, 40–43.

Tierney, A. (1973). Toilet training. *Nursing Times*, 20/27 December, 1740–1745. Warnock Report on Special Education Needs Cmnd. 7212, London: HMSO.

Tomm K. (1984). One perspective of the Milan systemic approach: Part 1: Overview of development, theory and practice. *Journal of Marital and Family Therapy*, **10**, 253–271.

Toolan, J.M. (1975). Suicide in children and adolescents. *American Journal of Psychotherapy*, **79**, 339–344.

Torgersen, A.M. and Kringlen, E. (1978). Genetic aspects of temperament differences in infants. *Journal of the American Academy of Child and Adolescent Psychiatry*, **17**, 433–444.

Torgesen, J. (1975). Problems and prospects in the study of learning disabilities. In E.M. Hetherington (ed.), *Review of Child Development Research*, Vol. 5. Chicago: University of Chicago Press.

Trevarthen, C. *et al.* (1996). *Children with autism*. London: Jessica Kingsley.

Trites, R. and Fidorowicz, C. (1976). Follow-up study of children with specific or primary reading disability. In R. Knights and D. Bakkar (eds), *The neuropsychology of reading disorders*. Baltimore: University Park Press.

Trojanowicz, R.C. and Morash, M. (1992). *Juvenile delinquency: concepts and control*. Englewood Cliffs, NJ: Prentice Hall.

Truax, C.F. and Carkhuff, H.R. (1967). *Toward effective counseling and psychotherapy*. Chicago: Aldine.

Tuma, J.M. (1989). Traditional therapies with children. In T.H. Ollendick and M. Hersen (eds), *Handbook of child psychopathology* (2nd edn). New York: Plenum.

Turner, R.K., Hersen, M., Bellak, A. and Wells, C. (1979). Behavioral treatment of obsessive–compulsive neuroses. *Behaviour Research and Therapy*, **17**, 95–106.

Van Eerdewegh, M., Clayton, P. and Van Eerdewegh, P. (1985). The bereaved child: variables influencing early psychopathology. *British Journal of Psychiatry*, **147**, 188–194.

Van Eerdevegh, M.M., Bieri, M.D., Parrilla, R.H. and Clayton, P.J. (1982). The bereaved child. *British Journal of Psychiatry*, **140**, 23–29.

Van Hasselt, V.B., Hersen, M., Bellack. A.S., Rosenbloom, N. and Lamparski, D. (1979). Tripartite assessment of the effects of systematic desensitization in a multiphobic child: An experimental analysis. *Journal of Behavior Therapy and Experimental Psychiatry*, **10**, 57–66.

Van Krevelen, D.A. (1971). Psychoses in adolescence. In J.G. Howells (ed.), *Modern perspectives in adolescent psychiatry*. Edinburgh: Oliver & Boyd.

Varni, J.W. (1983). *Clinical behavioural pediatrics*. New York: Pergamon.

Venter A. *et al.* (1992). A follow-up study of high-functioning autistic children. *Journal of Child Psychology and Psychiatry*, **33**, 489–507.

Vernon, D.T., Foley, J.M., Sipowicz, R.R and Schulman. J.L. (1965). *The psychological responses of children to hospitalization and illness*. Springfield: Charles C. Thomas.

Vetere, A. and Gale, A. (1987). *Ecological studies of family life*. Chichester: Wiley.

Volkmar, F.R. and Schwab-Stone, M. (1996). Childhood disorders in DSM-IV. *Journal of Child Psychology and Psychiatry*, **37**, 779–784.

von Economo C. (1931) *Encephalitis lethargica: its sequelae and treatment*. Oxford: Oxford University Press.

Wahler, R.G. (1969). Oppositional children: A quest for parental reinforcement control. *Journal of Applied Behavior Analysis*, **2**, 159–170.

Wahler, R.G. (1976). Deviant child behaviour within the family. Development speculations and behaviour change strategies. In H. Leitenberg (ed.), *Handbook of behaviour modification and behaviour therapy*. Englewood Cliffs, NJ: Prentice-Hall.

Wahler, R.G. and Dumas, J.E. (1986). Maintenance factors in coercive mother-child interactions: The compliance and practicability hypothesis. *Journal of Applied Behavior Analysis*, **19**, 3–22.

Walsh, F. (1982). Conceptualizations of normal family functioning. In F. Walsh (ed.), *Normal family processes*. New York: Guilford.

Warnock Report (1978) *Special educational needs*. Report of the Committee of Enquiry in the educational needs of children and young people. London: HMSO.

Watson, J.B. and Rayner, R. (1920). Conditioned emotional reactions. *Journal of Experimental Psychology*, **3**, 1–14.

Watts, F.N. (1990). *The efficacy of clinical applications of psychology: An overview of research*. Cardiff: Shadowfax Publishing.

Webster-Stratton, C. (1988). Mothers' and fathers' perceptions of child deviance: Roles of parent and child behaviors and parent adjustment. *Journal of Consulting and Clinical Psychology*, **56**, 909–915.

Webster-Stratton, C. (1989). The relationship of marital support, conflict, and divorce to parent perceptions, behaviours and child conduct problems. *Journal of Marriage and the Family*, **51**, 417–430.

Webster-Stratton, C. and Hammond, M. (1988). Maternal depression and its relationship to life stress, perceptions of child behaviour problems, parenting behaviours and child conduct problems. *Journal of Abnormal Child Psychology*, **16**, 299–315.

Webster-Stratton, C. and Herbert, M. (1993). What really happens in parent training? *Behavior Modification*, **17**, 407–456.

Webster-Stratton, C. and Herbert, M. (1994). *Troubled families, problem children: Working with parents—a collaborative approach*. Chichester: Wiley.

Webster-Stratton, C., Kolpacoff, M. and Hollinsworth, T. (1988). Self-administered videotape therapy for families with conduct problem children. Comparison with two cost-effective treatments and a control group. *Journal of Consulting and Clinical Psychology*, **56**, 558–566.

Webster-Stratton, C., Kolpacoff, M. and Hollinsworth, T. (1989). The long-term effectiveness and clinical significance of three cost-effective training programs for families with conduct-problem children. *Journal of Consulting and Clinical Psychology*, **57**(4), 550–553.

Weiner, I.B. (1970). Depression and suicide. In I.B. Weiner (ed.), *Psychological disturbance in adolescence*. New York: Wiley.

Weir, K. (1982). Night and day wetting among a population of three-year olds. *Developmental Medicine and Child Neurology*, **24**, 479–484.

Weisz, J.R., Weiss, B., Alicke, M.D. and Klotz, M.L. (1987). Effectiveness of psychotherapy with children and adolescents. A meta-analysis for clinicians. *Journal of Consulting and Clinical Psychology*, **55**, 542–549.

Welch, M.G. (1983). Retrieval from autism through mother–child holding therapy. In N. Tinbergen and E.A. Tinbergen (Eds.) *Autistic children: New hope for a cure.* London: Allen & Unwin.

Werner, E. and Smith, R.S. (1977). *Kauai's children come of age.* Honolulu: University Press of Hawaii.

Werner, E.E. and Smith, R.S. (1982). *Vulnerable, but invincible: A longitudinal study of resilient children and youth.* New York: McGraw-Hill.

Werry, J.S. and Aman, M.G. (eds) (1993). Practitioner's guide to psychoactive drugs for children and adolescents. New York: Plenum Press.

Werry, J.S. and Sprague, R.L. (1970) Hyperactivity. In C.G. Castello (ed.) *Symptoms of psychopathology handbook.* Chichester: Wiley.

West, D.J. (1980). The clinical approach to criminology. *Psychological Medicine.* **10**, 619–631.

West, D.J. and Farrington, D.P. (1973). *Who becomes delinquent?* London: Heinemann Educational.

Wever, C. and Phillips, N. (1994). *The secret problem.* Sydney: Shrink-Rap Press.

White, W.C. and Boskind-Lodahl M. (1981) An experiential–behavioral approach to the treatment of bulimiarexia. *Psychotherapy: Theory, Research and Practice,* **18**, 501–507.

Wiggins, J.S. (1973). *Personality and prediction: Principles of personality assessment.* Reading MA: Addison-Wesley.

Williams, M. (1997). *Cry of pain: Understanding suicide and self-harm.* Harmondsworth: Penguin.

Williamson, D. (1990). *Assessment of eating disorders: obesity, anorexia and bulimia nervosa.* New York: Pergamon Press.

Williamson, D.A., Davis, C.J. and Kelley, M.L. (1987). Headaches. In T.H. Ollendick and M. Hersen (eds), *Handbook of child psychopathology* (2nd edn). New York: Plenum.

Wing, L. (1971a). *Autistic children.* London: Constable.

Wing, L. (1971b). Perceptual and language development in autistic children: A comparative study. In M. Rutter (ed.), *Infantile autism: Concepts, characteristics and treatment.* Edinburgh: Churchill Livingston.

Wing, L. (1988). The continuum of autistic characteristics. In E. Schopler and G.B. Mesibov (eds) *Diagnostis and assessment in autism.* New York: Plenum.

Wing, L. and Gould, J. (1979). Severe impairments of social interaction and associated abnormalities in children: epidemiology and classification. *Journal of Autism and Childhood Schizophrenia,* **9**, 11–29.

Wise, S. and Rapoport, J. (1989). Obsessive–compulsive disorder: is it basal ganglia dysfunction? In J.L. Rapoport (ed.), *Obsessive–compulsive disorder in children and adolescents.* Washington: American Psychiatric Press, pp. 327–344.

Wolfe, D.A. (1987). *Child abuse: Implications for child development and psychopathology.* Newbury Park. LA: Sage.

Wolfensberger, W. (1980). The definition of normalization. In R.J. Flynn and K.E. Nitsch (eds). *Normalization, social integration and community service.* Baltimore: University Park Press.

Wolff R.A. and Rapoport J.L. (1988) Behavioral treatment on childhood compulsive disorder. *Behavior Modification,* **12**, 252–266.

Wolff, S. and Goodell, G. (eds) (1968). *Harold G. Wolff's stress and disease.* Springfield, IL: Charles C. Thomas.

Wolpe, J. (1973). *The practice of behaviour therapy.* Oxford: Pergamon.

Wong, B.Y.L., Harris, K. and Graham, S. (1991). Academic applications of cognitive–behavioural programs with learning disabled students. In P.C. Kendall (ed.) *Child and adolescent therapy: cognitive–behavioural procedures.* New York: Guilford Press.

Worden, J.W. (1996). *Children and grief: When a parent dies.* New York: Guilford Press.

World Health Organization (1988). *International Classification of Diseases* (10th edn). (ICD-10). Geneva: World Health Organization.

World Health Organization (1992). *International Classification of Impairments. Disabilities and Handicaps.* Geneva: World Health Organization.

World Health Organization (1992). *The ICD-10 classification of mental and behavioral disorders: clinical descriptions and diagnostic guidelines.* World Health Organization, Geneva.

Wright, D. (1971). *The psychology of moral behaviour.* Harmondsworth: Penguin.

Yager, J. (1988). The treating of eating disorders. *Journal of Clinical Psychiatry,* **49,** 18–25.

Yalom, I.D., Green, R. and Fisk, N. (1973). Prenatal exposure to female hormones: Effect on psychosexual development in boys. *Archives of General Psychiatry,* **28,** 554–561.

Yarrow, L.J. (1960). Interviewing children. In P. Mussen (ed.), *Handbook of research in child development.* New York: Wiley.

Yarrow, M.R., Campbell, J.D. and Burton, R.V. (1968). *Child rearing: an inquiry into research and methods.* San Francisco: Jossey-Bass.

Yule, W. (1981). The epidemiology of child psychopathology. In B.B. Lahey and A.E. Kazdin (eds), *Advances in clinical child psychology* (Vol. 4). New York: Plenum.

Yule, W. (1989). An introduction to investigation in clinical child psychology. In S.J.E. Lindsay and G.E. Powell (eds), *An introduction to clinical child psychology.* Aldershot: Gower.

Yule, W. and Rutter, M. (1985). Reading and other learning difficulties. In M. Rutter and L. Hersov (eds), *Child psychiatry: Modern approaches* (2nd edn). Oxford: Blackwell.

Zabin, M.A. and Melamed, B.G. (1980). Relationship between parental discipline and children's ability to cope with stress. *Journal of Behavioural Assessment,* **2,** 17–38.

Zametkin, A.J. and Rapoport, J.L. (1986). The pathophysiology of attention deficit disorder with hyperactivity: a review. In B.B. Lahey and A.E. Kazdin (eds) *Advances in clinical child psychology* (Vol. 9). New York: Plenum.

Zatz, S. and Chassin, L. (1985). Cognitions of test-anxious children under naturalistic test-taking conditions. *Journal of Consulting and Clinical Psychology,* **53,** 393–401.

Zeanah, C.H., Boris, N.W. and Scheeringa, M.S. (1997). Psychopathology in infancy. *Journal of Child Psychology and Psychiatry,* **38,** 81–99.

Zeltzer, L. and LeBaron, S. (1986). The hypnotic treatment of children in pain. *Advances in Developmental Paediatrics,* **7,** 197–234.

Zikis, P. (1983). Treatment of an 11 year old obsessive compulsive ritualizer tiqueur girl with *in vivo* exposure and response prevention. *Behavioural Psychotherapy,* **11,** 75–81.

Zimrin, H. (1986). A profile of survival. *Child abuse and neglect,* **10,** 339–349.

FURTHER READING

PART ONE: THE NATURE OF THE PROBLEM (ASSESSMENT, FORMULATION AND INTERVENTIONS)

Berger M. (1994). Psychological tests and assessment. In M. Rutter, E. Taylor and L. Hersov (eds) *Child and adolescent psychiatry: modern approaches*. Oxford: Blackwell Scientific.

British Psychological Society (1996). *Expert testimony: developing witness skills*. Leicester: BPS Books.

Bryant-Waugh, R. and Lask B. (1995). Annotation: Eating disorder in children. *Journal of Child Psychology and Psychiatry*, **36**, 191–202.

Clark L., Watson, D. and Reynolds, S. (1995). Diagnosis and classification of psychopathology: challenges to the current system and future direction. *Annual Review of Psychology*, **46**, 121–153.

Cohen P., Cohen, J., Kasen, S. *et al.* (1993). An epidemiological study of disorders in late childhood and adolescence. *Journal of Child Psychology and Psychiatry*, **34**, 851–867.

Cunningham, C., Bremner, R. and Boyle, M. (1995). Large group community based parenting programmes for families of preschoolers at risk for disruptive behaviour disorders: utilisation, cost effectiveness and outcome. *Journal of Child Psychology and Psychiatry*, **36**, 1141–1160.

Dadds, M. (1995). *Families, children and the development of dysfunction*. Thousand Oaks, CA: Sage.

Dunn J. and McGuire, S. (1992). Sibling and peer relationships in childhood. *Journal of Child Psychology and Psychiatry*, **33**, 67–105.

Falloon, I., Laporta, M., Fadden, G. and Graham-Hole, V. (1993). *Managing stress in families*. London: Routledge.

Garmezy, N. and Masten, A.S. (1994). Chronic adversities. M. Rutter, E. Taylor and L. Hersov (eds). *Child adolescent psychiatry: modern approaches*. Oxford: Blackwell Scientific.

Giles, T. (ed.). (1993). *Handbook of effective psychotherapy*. New York: Plenum.

Goodyer, I.M. (1990). *Life experiences, development and childhood psychopathology*. Chichester: Wiley.

Hibbs, E. and Jensen, P. (eds) (1996). *Psychosocial treatments for child and adolescent disorders: empirically based strategies for clinical practice*. Washington, D.C. APA.

Hodges, K. (1993). Structured interview for assessing children. *Journal of Child Psychology and Psychiatry*, **34**, 49–68.

Kagan, J., Reznick, L. and Gibbons, J. (1989). Inhibited and uninhibited types of children. *Child Development*, **60**, 838–845.

Kaufman A. (1995). *Intelligence testing and the WISC III*. New York: Wiley.

Lezak, M. (1995). *Neuropsychological assessment*. (3rd edn) New York: Oxford University Press.

Luthar, S. (1993). Annotation: Methodological and conceptual issues in research on childhood resilience. *Journal of Child Psychology and Psychiatry*, **34**, 441–453.

Mikesell, R., Lusterman, D. and MacDoniel, S. (eds) (1995). *Integrating family therapy: Handbook of family psychology and systems theory* Washington, D.C. APA.

O'Connor, K. (1991). *The play therapy primer*. New York: Wiley.

Robins, L.G. and Rutter, M. (eds) (1990) *Straight and devious pathways from childhood to adulthood*. Cambridge: Cambridge University Press.

Routh, D.K. (1990) Taxonomy in developmental psychopathology: consider the source. In Lewis, M. and Miller, S.M. (eds). *Handbook of developmental psychopathology*. New York: Plenum.

PART TWO: AGE-RELATED DIFFICULTIES (INFANCY TO EARLY ADOLESCENCE)

Asendorpf, J. (1993). Abnormal shyness in children. *Journal of Child Psychology and Psychiatry*, **34**, 1069–1081.

Buchanan, A. (1992). *Children who soil: assessment and treatment*. Chichester: Wiley.

Buckstein, O. (1995). *Adolescent substance abuse: assessment, prevention and treatment*. New York: Wiley.

Campo, J. and Fritsch, S. (1994). Somatization in children and adolescents. *Journal of the American Academy of Child and Adolescent Psychiatry*, **33**, 1223–1235.

Coleman, R. and Cassell, D. (1995). Parents who misuse drugs and alcohol. In P. Redo and C. Lucey (eds) *Assessment of parenting: psychiatric and psychological contributions*. London: Routledge.

Darling, N. and Steinberg, L. (1993). Parenting styles as context: an integrative model. *Psychological Bulletin*, **113**, 487–496.

Dowling, E. and Osborne, E. (1994). *The family and the school: a joint systems approach to problems with children* (2nd edn) London: Routledge.

Feindler, E. and Ecton, R. (1985). *Adolescent anger control: cognitive-behavioral techniques*. New York: Pergamon.

Feinman, S. (1992). *Social referencing and the social construction of reality in infancy*. New York: Plenum.

Fergusson, D. and Lynskey, M. (1996). Adolescent resilience to family adversity. *Journal of Child Psychology and Psychiatry*, **37**, 281–92.

Finch, A., Nelson, W. and Ott, E. (1993). *Cognitive behavioural procedures with children and adolescents: a practical guide*. Boston, MA: Allyn & Bacon.

Harrington, R. (1993). *Depressive disorder in childhood and adolescence*. Chichester: Wiley.

Hawkins, J., Castalano, R., and Miller, J. (1992). Risk and protective factors for alcohol and other drug problems in adolescence and early adulthood. Implications for substance use prevention. *Psychological Bulletin*, **112**, 64–105.

Kazdin, A.E., Colbus, D. and Rodgers, A. (1986). Assessment of depression and diagnosis of depressive disorder among psychiatrically disturbed children. *Journal of Abnormal Child Psychology*, **14**, 499–515.

Malik, N. and Furman, W. (1993). Practitioner review: problem in children's peer relations: what can the clinician do? *Journal of Child Psychology and Psychiatry*, **34**, 1303–1326.

Orbach, I. (1988). Children who don't want to live: *Understanding and treating the suicidal child*. San Francisco, CA, Jossey-Bass.

Ost G., and Caro, J. (1990). *Understanding and treating depressed adolescents and their families*. New York: Wiley.

Pagliaro, A. and Pagliaro, L. (1996). *Substance use among children and adolescents*. New York: Wiley.

Reynolds, H., and Johnson, F. (eds) (1994). *Handbook of depression in children and adolescents*. New York, Plenum Press.

Roll, J., Masten, A., Cichetti, D. *et al* (1990). *Risk and protective factors in the development of psychopathology*. New York: Cambridge University Press.

Rutter, M. and Casaer, P. (eds) *Biological risk factors for psychosocial disorders*. Cambridge: Cambridge University Press.

PART THREE: SPECIAL NEEDS (HANDICAP, ABUSE AND HEALTH PROBLEMS)

Anthony, E.J. (1987). Risk, vulnerability and resilience: an overview. In E.J. Anthony and B.J. Cohler (eds) *The invulnerable child*. New York: Guilford Press.

Bonner, M. and Finney J. (1996). A psychosocial model of children's health status. In T.H. Ollendick and R. Prinz (eds) *Advances in clinical child psychology*, Vol. 18. New York: Plenum Press.

Bradley, C. (1994). Contributions of psychology to diabetes management. *British Journal of Clinical Psychology*, **33**, 11–21.

Briere, J., Berliner, L., Bulkley, J., Jenny, C.. and Reid, T. (1996). *The APSAC handbook on child maltreatment*. Thousand Oaks, CA, Sage.

Browne, K. and Herbert, M. (1997) *Preventing family violence*. Chichester: Wiley.

Chang, P. (1991). Psychosocial needs of long term childhood cancer survivors: A review of the literature. *Paediatrician*, **18**, 20–24.

Clark, N., Gotsch, A. and Rosenstock, I. (1993). Patient, professional and public education on behavioural aspects of asthma: a review of strategies for change and needed research. *Journal of Asthma*, **30**, 241–255.

Cull, C. and Goldstein, L. (1997). *The clinical psychologist's handbook of epilepsy*. London: Routledge.

Frude, N. (1990). *Understanding family problems*. Chichester: Wiley.

Gardner, R. (1992). *Family evaluation in child custody litigation*. Cresskill, NJ, Creative Therapeutics.

Garralda, M.E. (1996). Somatization in children. *Journal of Child Psychology and Psychiatry*, **37**, 13–34.

Gelles, R. (1987). *The violent home* (Updated edn). Beverley Hills, CA: Sage.

Herbert, M. (1993). *Working with children and The Children Act*. Leicester: British Psychological Society (BPS Books).

Ioannou, C., (1991). Acute pain in children. In M. Herbert, *Clinical child psychology: social learning, development and behaviour*. Chichester: Wiley.

Jones, D. (1992). *Interviewing the sexually abused child* (4th edn). Oxford, Gaskell/ Royal College of Psychiatrists.

Kelly, C. (1996). Chronic constipation and soiling in children: A review of the psychological and family literature. *Child Psychology and Psychiatry Review*, 1, 59–66.

Klin, A. and Volkmar, F. (1997). Asperger's syndrome. In D. Cohen and F. Volkmar (eds) *Handbook of autism and pervasive developmental disorders* (2nd edn). New York: Wiley.

Lewis, C., Hitch, G. and Walker, P. (1994). The prevalence of specific arithmetic difficulties and specific reading difficulties in 9 to 10 years old boys and girls. *Journal of Child Psychology and Psychiatry*, 35, 283–292.

Maughan, B. (1995). Annotation: long term outcomes of developmental reading problems. *Journal of Child Psychology and Psychiatry*, 36, 357–371.

Prins, P. (1994). Anxiety in medical settings. In T.H. Ollendick, N. King and W. Yule (eds) *International handbook of phobia and anxiety disorders in children and adolescents* New York: Plenum.

Quin, V. and Macausian, A. (1988). *Dyslexia, what parents ought to know*. Harmondsworth, Penguin Books.

Robin, A. and Foster, S. (1989). *Negotiating parent–adolescent conflicts*. New York: Guilford Press.

Rolland J. (1994). *Families, illness and disability*. New York: Basic Books.

Stahl, H.P. (1994). *Conducting child custody evaluations: a comprehensive guide*. Thousand Oaks, CA, Sage.

Werner, E.E. and Smith, R.S. (1992). *Overcoming the odds: high risk children from birth to adulthood*. Ithaca, N.Y., Cornell University Press.

PART FOUR: ANTISOCIAL DISRUPTIVE BEHAVIOUR DISORDERS

Forehand, R. and Long, N. (1996). *Parenting the strong-willed child: the clinically proven five week program for parents of two to six year olds*. Chicago, Contemporary Books.

Gadow, K. (1992). Paediatric psychopharmacology: a review of recent research. *Journal of Child Psychology and Psychiatry*, 33, 153–195.

Kazdin, A.E. (1997). Psychosocial treatments for conduct disorder in children. *Journal of Child Psychology and Psychiatry*, 38, 161–178.

Olweus, D. (1993). *Bullying at school: what we know and what we can do*. Oxford: Blackwell.

Patterson, G.R., Reid, J.B. and Dishion, T. (1992). *Antisocial boys*. Eugene OR, Castalia.

Shure, M. (1992). *I can problem solve: an interpersonal cognitive problem solving program*. Champaign, IL, Research Press.

Taylor, E. (1994). Physical treatments. In M. Rutter, E. Taylor and L. Hersov (eds) *Child and adolescent psychiatry: modern approaches*. (3rd edn) Oxford: Blackwell Scientific.

Taylor, E., Schachar, R. *et al*. (1987). Which boys respond to stimulant medication?: A controlled trial of methylphenidate in boys with disruptive behaviour. *Psychological Medicine*, **17**, 121–143.

PART FIVE: ANXIETY DISORDERS OF CHILDHOOD

Francis, G. and Gragg, R. (1996). *Obsessive compulsive disorder*. Thousand Oaks, CA: Sage.

Kendall, P.C., Kane, M., Howard, B. and Siqueland, L. (1994). *Cognitive-behavioural therapy for anxious children: treatment manual*. Admore, PA: Workbook Publishing.

Klein, R.G. (1994). Anxiety disorders. In M. Rutter, E. Taylor and L. Hersov (eds) *Child and adolescent psychiatry: modern approaches*. Oxford: Blackwell Scientific.

March, J. (1994). Cognitive behaviour psychotherapy of children and adolescents with obsessive compulsive disorder. *Journal of the American Academy of Child and Adolescent Psychiatry*, **34**, 7–18.

Nelles, W. and Barlow, D. (1988). Do children panic? *Clinical Psychology Review*, **8**, 359–372.

INDEX

Index compiled by Sylvia Potter

The Wiley Series in

CLINICAL PSYCHOLOGY

Related titles of interest from Wiley...

Cognitive Developmental Therapy with Children
Tammie Ronen
Provides professionals with the knowledge, skills and application methods for the treatment of children using self-control therapy.
0-471-97006-9 202pp 1997 Hardback
0-471-97007-7 202pp 1997 Paperback

Culture and the Child
A Guide for Professionals in Child Care and Development
Daphne Keats
A handy practical guide for those professionals dealing with children whose cultural backgrounds differ from those of the mainstream of the society in which they live.
0-471-96625-8 160pp 1997 Paperback

Life-Span Developmental Psychology
Andreas Demetriou, Willem Doise and Cornelis F.M. van Leishout
Offers a broad coverage of all sub-fields of developmental psychology.
0-471-97078-6   528pp   1998   Paperback

Reference works...
Handbook of Child Psychology
Editor-in-Chief: William Damon
0-471-17893-4   4864pp   1997   4 Volume Set
(Individual volumes also available for purchase separately)

Handbook of Child and Adolescent Psychiatry
Editor-in-Chief: Joseph D. Noshpitz
0-471-19328-3 4488pp February 1998 7 Volume Set
(Individual volumes also available for purchase separately)